Bump Elliott, the
Michigan Wolverines and
Their 1964 Championship
Football Season

Bump Elliott, the Michigan Wolverines and Their 1964 Championship Football Season

E. BRUCE GEELHOED

McFarland & Company, Inc., Publishers
Jefferson, North Carolina

LIBRARY OF CONGRESS CATALOGUING-IN-PUBLICATION DATA

Geelhoed, E. Bruce, 1948–
　　Bump Elliott, the Michigan Wolverines and their 1964 championship football season / E. Bruce Geelhoed.
　　　p.　　cm.
　　Includes bibliographical references and index.

　　ISBN 978-0-7864-9605-1 (softcover : acid free paper) ∞
　　ISBN 978-1-4766-1767-1 (ebook)

　　1. University of Michigan—Football—History.　2. Michigan Wolverines (Football team)—History.　3. Elliott, Bump. I. Title.
GV958.U52863G44 2014
796.332'630977435—dc23　　　　　　　　2014031866

BRITISH LIBRARY CATALOGUING DATA ARE AVAILABLE

© 2014 E. Bruce Geelhoed. All rights reserved

No part of this book may be reproduced or transmitted in any form or by any means, electronic or mechanical, including photocopying or recording, or by any information storage and retrieval system, without permission in writing from the publisher.

On the cover: The 1964 University of Michigan football team at the Rose Bowl practice field (Bentley Historical Library, University of Michigan)

Printed in the United States of America

McFarland & Company, Inc., Publishers
　Box 611, Jefferson, North Carolina 28640
　　www.mcfarlandpub.com

Table of Contents

Acknowledgments		vii
Preface		1
Introduction: 1964, a Season of Breakthroughs		5
ONE	Quickness and Agility: Building the '64 Michigan Team	25
TWO	A Solid Start	43
THREE	One Step Forward, One Step Back	69
FOUR	Two Steps Up the Ladder	98
FIVE	Back in the Big Ten Race	115
SIX	"We gotta beat Ohio! We gotta beat Ohio!"	138
SEVEN	"We came to win and we did"	166
Afterword: Beyond Michigan Stadium		190
Appendix: The 1964 Michigan Wolverines Roster		203
Chapter Notes		207
Bibliography		229
Index		231

Acknowledgments

I wish to thank a number of helpful people who assisted in several aspects of this study. The staff of the Bentley Historical Library at the University of Michigan, The Ohio State University Archives, and the Archives of the National Collegiate Athletic Association were indispensable. I have noted their contributions, by name, in the footnotes to the various chapters and hope that they appreciate my gratitude. I truly owe them a debt of appreciation.

James Conley, the captain of the 1964 Michigan Wolverines, has lent me his assistance and encouragement at critical times during this project. No one knows the 1964 Michigan team better than Jim Conley and his insights into the season were invaluable. Chalmers W. ("Bump") Elliott gave me his memories of the 1964 season from his perspective as the head coach. Likewise, Don Dufek, one of Bump Elliott's assistant coaches in 1964, provided me with the benefit of his perspective on the season.

Several members of the Michigan team provided valuable interviews for the project. These individuals are listed in the bibliography but I wish to acknowledge, in particular, Jerry Mader and Brian Patchen, who, along with Jim Conley, read a draft of the original manuscript and enthusiastically made many helpful comments and suggestions. I also wish to acknowledge the interviews given by Tom Krzemienski, a member of Michigan State's team in 1964, and Randy Minniear and Rich Ruble, members of the 1964 Purdue team, who offered valuable information from the perspective of Michigan's opponents in 1964.

I also wish to thank my friend Thomas Raisor, attorney at law, who read the original manuscript and made some helpful suggestions for improvement. Tom was a member of Michigan's varsity basketball teams during the 1950s and he was able to offer some insights on my study from the perspective of a former Michigan athlete.

It would be unforgivable of me to overlook the contribution of Chris Coburn, who manages the Service Center in the Department of History at

Ball State University. Chris was indispensable in helping me with the myriad of technical details necessary to prepare the final manuscript for submission. I owe Chris an unbelievable debt of gratitude. I also wish to thank Jessie Smock, an outstanding student in the Honors College at Ball State University, for her help in the preparation of the index.

Finally, I wish to thank my family and dedicate this book to them: my wife Deborah, and our two sons, Marc and Steven (Michigan, LSA, 2012), who are always available to talk about Michigan football with me. The good humor, support, and encouragement of an author's family are always essential and I am blessed to have such a family. Thanks to each one.

Preface

On New Year's Day, 1965, the Michigan Wolverines defeated the Oregon State Beavers, 34–7, in the Rose Bowl game in Pasadena, California. Under the leadership of Bump Elliott, their head coach, the Wolverines dominated the game to such an extent that Tommy Prothro, Oregon State's coach, told reporters afterward that Michigan was the best college team that he had ever witnessed in his coaching career.

Michigan's triumph in the 1965 Rose Bowl was the exclamation point on its 1964 football season. In 1964, the Wolverines finished with an overall record of nine victories and one loss, a 21–20 heartbreaker to Purdue University on October 17 that deprived Elliott's team of an undefeated season and a possible national championship. Notwithstanding the disappointing loss to Purdue, however, Michigan's 1964 football team posted some truly remarkable achievements. It shut out 6th-ranked Navy, 20–0, on October 3, avenging a disheartening loss to the Midshipmen in 1963. Michigan also defeated its archrivals: Michigan State, Minnesota, and Ohio State, ending the winning streaks against the Wolverines by each of these three Big Ten opponents. Michigan won the undisputed Big Ten championship for the first time since 1950 and then preserved its undefeated record in the Rose Bowl. It finished 4th in the final college football rankings, according to the national polls. Bob Timberlake, Michigan's quarterback, and Bill Yearby, one of its defensive linemen, were consensus All-Americans, and Timberlake won the *Chicago Tribune*'s Silver Football award, given annually to the outstanding player in the Big Ten. Finally, with the exception of its 17–10 victory over Michigan State and its loss to Purdue, the 1964 team defeated all of its other opponents by double-digit margins.

Despite these achievements, Michigan's 1964 football team has received surprisingly little attention from observers of college football even though its record demonstrated that it was one of the premier Michigan teams of the post–World War II era. A review of the extensive literature written about the history of Michigan football reveals this relative lack of attention. Only Michigan broadcaster Tom Hemingway, in his fine book *Life Among the Wolverines: Inside U of M Sports* (1985), discusses Michigan's 1964 football season in considerable detail. Even so, Hemingway's treatment of the 1964 team occurs within the context of his longer exploration of his career as a broadcaster of Michigan's football games and basketball games.

Other studies tend to focus on more specific, narrower topics. For example, Greg Emmanuel, in his book *The 100-Yard War: Inside the 100-Year-Old Michigan–Ohio State Football Rivalry* (2004), and Michael Rosenberg, in *War as They Knew It: Woody Hayes, Bo Schembechler, and America in a Time of Unrest* (2008), give detailed accounts of the Michigan–Ohio State rivalry. John Kryk provides a fascinating glimpse into the Michigan–Notre Dame rivalry in his book *Natural Enemies: The Notre Dame–Michigan Football Feud* (1994). John U. Bacon has explored the coaching significance both of Bo Schembechler, in his collaboration with Schembechler, *Bo's Lasting Lessons: The Legendary Coach Teaches the Timeless Fundamentals of Leadership* (2007), and of Rich Rodriguez in *Three and Out: Rich Rodriguez and the Michigan Wolverines* (2011). In *Go Blue: Michigan's Greatest Football Stories* (2013), Steve Kornacki has provided a perspective on Michigan football based on the vantage point of former players and coaches.

Longer studies of Michigan football, such as Will Perry's *The Wolverines: A Story of Michigan Football* (1974) and Jerry Green's *Michigan Football Vault* (2008), discuss the exploits of the 1964 Michigan team, but only as part of their more general works. Autobiographical accounts written by former Michigan coaches, administrators, and players such as Schembechler, Don Canham, Jon Falk, Jim Brandstatter, Curt Stephenson, and Desmond Howard tend to concentrate on subjects within their realm of experience, experience that did not necessarily include the 1964 team.

Given this lack of attention, I believe that a book that covers Michigan's 1964 team is timely and fills a gap in the literature on the subject of Michigan's football history. The present study has two main purposes. First, I attempt to chronicle the exploits and accomplishments of the 1964 Michigan team. National observers of college football did not expect much from Michigan at the outset of the 1964 season, believing that the champion of the Big Ten would be either Illinois, the defending champion from 1963, or Ohio State. But Bump Elliott's Wolverines served notice early in the season that they were a team with championship potential, and even with the loss to Purdue, Michigan's players and coaches stayed focused on their goal of winning the Big Ten championship. This study, therefore, tells the detailed story of how the 1964 Wolverines succeeded in their championship ambitions and, more importantly, why their achievement matters in the long history of Michigan football.

Second, the study provides an analysis of Bump Elliott's coaching performance in 1964, another overlooked subject within the realm of the football literature. When Bump Elliott became Michigan's head coach in 1959, Michigan's football fortunes were clearly trending downward. In 1958, Michigan finished the season with a record of two wins, six losses, and a tie, its first losing season since 1951 and its worst single-season record since 1936. But Elliott was realistic; he knew that Michigan's future success depended on the establishment of an effective recruiting program. By 1964, Elliott and the members of his coaching staff had successfully recruited a roster of players that was able to compete with any football program in the Big Ten. Talented football players were coming to Michigan, primarily from the three Midwestern states of Michigan, Illinois, and Ohio, especially Ohio. Elliott had established the foundation for a championship-caliber team.

But, in addition to excelling at the hard slog of recruiting, Bump Elliott was the beneficiary of some unexpected good fortune in 1964. In January 1964, the National College Athletic Association's (NCAA) Football Rules Committee made a key change in the rules for substitution, opening up college football once again for a return to the two-platoon system. Bump Elliott and his coaching staff adapted to this re-emergence of two-platoon football better than any other coaching staff in the Big Ten. The new rules on substitution enabled Elliott to get more of his talented players into the game, thereby improving overall team morale, and perhaps just as important, escaping the debilitating effects of season-ending injuries to key players that had plagued Michigan football in previous years. Within this new environment, Elliott and his coaching staff prepared a team that not only played fundamentally sound football but one that also played with imagination and excitement. Simply put, in 1964, the Wolverines were fun to watch.

In conclusion, this study falls into the category of traditional, narrative history. For research, I relied on unpublished archival sources, primarily those at the Bentley Historical Library at the University of Michigan, as well as newspaper sources, published sources, oral histories, interviews with former players and coaches, including interviews with some former Michigan opponents, and some electronic correspondence with former players. Although these are traditional sources, I remain fairly confident that I am the first historian to conduct a thorough examination of several of them and, therefore, I hope that the reader will find that my conclusions are both fresh and original. Any errors of fact or interpretation are mine.

Introduction: 1964, a Season of Breakthroughs

On November 21, 1964, the Michigan Wolverines defeated the Ohio State Buckeyes, 10–0, on a bitterly cold day in Columbus, Ohio. Michigan's victory gave the Wolverines the undisputed Big Ten championship, their first outright title in fourteen years, extending back to 1950, when Michigan defeated Ohio State, 9–3, in the memorable "Snow Bowl" game in Columbus.

As the Big Ten champion in 1964, Michigan won the right to represent the conference in the Rose Bowl, played on New Year's Day, 1965, in Pasadena, California. The Wolverines defeated the 8th-ranked Oregon State Beavers, their Pacific Coast opponent, by a score of 34–7, keeping alive Michigan's unbeaten streak in the Rose Bowl that dated back to the early years of the twentieth century. Michigan ended the 1964 season—the regular season and the Rose Bowl—with a record of 9–1, for its best record since 1950 and a number 4 ranking in the final national football polls.

Michigan's victory over Ohio State in 1964 was the culmination of a season of breakthroughs for the Wolverine football program, coached by Chalmers ("Bump") Elliott, one of the "Mad Magicians" on Michigan's national championship team in 1947 and the team's head coach since 1959.[1] During the 1964 season, the Wolverines temporarily put to rest much of the frustration of the previous fourteen years as the proud Michigan program, while posting some strong teams with outstanding records during that period, failed to climb to the top of the Big Ten standings and win a coveted berth in the Rose Bowl. Michigan watched painfully from below as several of its arch-rivals—Ohio State, coached by Wes Fesler and Woody Hayes; Michigan State, coached by Biggie Munn and Duffy Daugherty; and Minnesota, coached by Murray Warmath—won multiple Big Ten championships and trips to Pasadena. Other Michigan opponents, including Iowa, coached by Forest Evashevski, a former Wolverine great from the Tom Harmon era; Wisconsin, coached by Milt

Bruhn; and Illinois, coached by Ray Eliot in 1951 and Pete Elliott (Bump's brother) in 1963, also won multiple Big Ten titles and made Rose Bowl appearances between 1951 and 1964.

In 1964, however, the Wolverines scored some historic triumphs, ending a pattern of big-game losses that extended, in some cases, back to the early 1950s. On October 3, Michigan shut out Navy, 21–0, led by Roger Staubach, the 1963 Heisman trophy winner. In Navy's game against Michigan in 1963, Staubach had turned in a magnificent performance, both passing and running, in leading the Midshipmen to a 26–13 victory. He gained 94 yards on the ground and completed 14 of 16 passes, including the first 10 in a row. Staubach's football wizardry in that game was so remarkable that Elliott later said that Staubach "was the finest quarterback he had ever seen." Some football observers even claimed that Staubach's performance in the Michigan game cemented his status as the front-runner for the Heisman award.[2] But the Wolverines' victory in 1964, over a Navy team then ranked 6th in the country, erased the bad memory of the 1963 defeat and gave the team a huge boost, both in morale and in confidence, as it began the Big Ten season.

The following week, on October 10, Michigan defeated 9th-ranked Michigan State, 17–10, before an all-time record crowd in Spartan Stadium of more than 78,000 in East Lansing. Among the spectators were the governor of Michigan, George Romney, and his wife Lenore, who followed the custom of observing the game from one side of the field for the first half and then moving to the other side of the field for the second half. Michigan's come-from-behind victory was its first defeat of the Spartans since 1955 (the teams played to tie games in 1958 and 1963) and its first win in East Lansing since 1948.[3] The Wolverines trailed for most of the game before closing to within 1 point, 10–9, midway through the fourth quarter and then scoring the winning touchdown with less than four minutes to play. On consecutive weeks, Michigan had defeated two rivals that were ranked in the top ten in the national polls.

Two weeks later in Ann Arbor, on October 24, Michigan defeated Minnesota, 19–12, in the process reclaiming the famed Little Brown Jug, "the most coveted piece of football crockery in the world," according to legendary Michigan radio broadcaster Bob Ufer.[4] Minnesota had presented some major problems recently for the Wolverines, defeating Michigan four successive times since 1960 and keeping the jug in Minneapolis. To make the situation even worse, Minnesota shut out Michigan in three of those four victories. Winning back the Little Brown Jug represented another milestone achievement for the Wolverines in 1964.

Finally, on November 21, the Wolverines defeated the Buckeyes in Columbus. Not only did the victory give the Wolverines the Big Ten title, it also marked the first Michigan win in Columbus since 1956 and only its fifth in the previous fifteen years against Ohio State. And, to a certain extent, it removed the pain of the bitter memory of the Michigan defeat against Ohio State in Ann Arbor in 1955, the last time that the two teams had played for the outright Big Ten title, when Ohio State won the game by a shutout, 17–0. The Buckeyes won the 1955 Big Ten title, but since they had gone to the Rose Bowl in 1954 and Big Ten rules prohibited a team from going to the Rose Bowl in consecutive years, the Big Ten's representative in Pasadena became Michigan State, the second-place team. Seeing their rival Spartans in the Rose Bowl, after losing to Ohio State, was a double dose of disappointment for the Maize and Blue faithful.

Coaching the '64 Michigan Team

Bump Elliott was 33 at the time of his appointment as Michigan's head coach in 1959. He also functioned as the team's offensive coordinator as well as the coach of the special teams. One of Michigan's most accomplished athletes, Elliott played three sports, football, basketball, and baseball, during his student years at Michigan between 1946 and 1948. A member of Michigan's national championship team in 1947, Elliott was a two-way player who excelled at right halfback in Coach Fritz Crisler's single wing attack. Crisler called Elliott the "greatest right halfback he ever saw," and in 1947, Elliott led the conference (then referred to as the Big Nine) in scoring with 54 points. Later described as the "perfect wingback: a blazing runner on the reverse, marvelous at going deep for the big pass, and capable of blocking any opponent either at the line or downfield," Elliott was voted the most valuable player on the 1947 team and was the recipient of the *Chicago Tribune*'s Silver Football Award given to the outstanding player in the conference.[5]

After graduating from Michigan, Elliott began his coaching career as an assistant coach under two former Wolverine greats, first for Kip Taylor at Oregon State from 1948 to 1952 and then under Forest Evashevski at Iowa from 1952 to 1956. Elliott coached the offensive backfield at Iowa and played a role in the Hawkeyes' championship season in 1956 and their Rose Bowl victory on New Year's Day, 1957. In 1957, Elliott returned to Michigan, where he became backfield coach under head coach Bennie Oosterbaan.[6]

Elliott's assistant coaches were also young men who, despite their youth, were nevertheless experienced football men. In fact, according to one observer, "the coaching staff looked like a young board of directors."[7] Several of the assistant coaches were former players at Michigan, including Henry ("Hank") Fonde, a former teammate of Elliott, who was the offensive backfield coach;

Bump Elliott, head football coach, University of Michigan, 1959–1968 (Bentley Historical Library, University of Michigan).

Bob Hollway, another of Elliott's former teammates, who coached the defensive line and was the *de facto* defensive coordinator; Don Dufek, the defensive backfield coach and the hero of Michigan's Rose Bowl victory in 1951; and Dennis Fitzgerald, the freshman coach.

Fonde joined Ellliott's coaching staff in 1959 after coaching football at Ann Arbor High School between 1949 and 1958. A native Tennessean, Fonde had come to Michigan in 1944 as a student in the Navy's wartime training program. Like Elliott, Fonde played in the offensive backfield, where he earned a reputation as "a fast, hard-running back." On the 1947 team, he scored three touchdowns and passed for another. After graduating from Michigan, Fonde entered the high school coaching ranks and, in the next decade, compiled a record of 69 victories against only 6 losses.[8]

Bob Hollway and Don Dufek were holdovers from the coaching staff of Bennie Oosterbaan, Elliott's predecessor as Michigan's head coach. Hollway handled the Michigan defense and, despite his relative youth, was widely respected for his ability to mold a fine defense. A standout defensive player on Michigan's teams of the late 1940s, Hollway coached briefly at Michigan before holding assistant coaching positions at the University of Maine and Eastern Michigan in the early 1950s. In 1954, he joined Bennie Oosterbaan's staff as an assistant coach.[9]

Don Dufek, from Evanston, Illinois, was a standout player for Michigan in the late 1940s and early 1950s. A hard-driving fullback, he scored both touchdowns in Michigan's 14–6 victory over California in the 1951 Rose Bowl. Dufek joined Bennie Oosterbaan's staff as an assistant coach in 1954 and coached the freshman team for the next three years. He also had the assignment of scouting Michigan's opponents, a task at which he excelled. In 1961, he took on the responsibility for the defensive secondary. Dennis Fitzgerald, the freshman coach, was one of Elliott's former players as a halfback between 1959 and 1960, and he coached the freshman team at a time when freshmen were ineligible for varsity competition.[10]

Joining Fonde, Hollway, Dufek, and Fitzgerald were Jack ("Jocko") Nelson, previously an assistant coach at Utah State and at Colorado who coached the offensive and defensive ends, as well as the linebackers; and Jack Fouts, formerly an assistant coach at Bowling Green in Ohio, who coached the offensive line. Fouts left Michigan after the 1963 season to become the head coach at Ohio Wesleyan University, his *alma mater*, where he remained until 1984. Replacing Fouts in the spring of 1964 was Tony Mason, formerly the head coach at McKinley High School in Niles, Ohio, and a man who had built what was arguably the most successful high school football program in Ohio during the 1960s.[11] Mason's ability to construct Michigan's offensive line in 1964 played a key role in the team's success.

The analogy made by the observer that Michigan's coaching staff resembled a young board of directors broke down when it came to a description of Mason. An intense, extroverted, and demonstrative man who was a veteran of the Korean War, Mason relished the opportunity to join the Michigan program and wasted no time in bringing his own unique signature to the coaching staff. During his military service, Mason had met several members of the Oklahoma National Guard who had played football at the University of Oklahoma under the legendary Bud Wilkinson. After the war, Mason, while still coaching in Ohio, made frequent visits to Oklahoma, where he learned about the innovative offensive system of the great Sooner teams. "I think Bump Elliott is a great coach and Michigan is a great university," Mason explained in early April 1964, as the rationale for his entry into the college coaching ranks. "They recruited five of my [high school] players, so it wasn't hard [for Michigan] to recruit me." Elliott offered him the position vacated by Fouts in mid–March 1964 and he "accepted immediately."[12]

On the practice field, Mason could be heard, encouraging his linemen and moving them energetically through their drills. Chewing a wad of tobacco and usually wearing a short-sleeved shirt, regardless of the weather, Mason brought a sense of energy and optimism to the coaching staff as it prepared for a new season.

Years later, Bump Elliott recalled the cohesion that existed on the Michigan coaching staff in 1964. "I really liked our coaching staff," Elliott remembered. "We were all about the same age and family-wise, we all had young children. [As a collection of personalities,] we fit just right."[13] The exception to Elliott's description, at the time, was Tony Mason, who came to Michigan as a bachelor.

The Maize and Blue Machine or the Scarlet and Gray Machine?

Michigan's 1964 football team displayed the attributes that characterized its successful teams of subsequent decades. These attributes included a strong, quick, and agile defense; a powerful running game that controlled the game's tempo as well as the time of possession; standout quarterbacking; effective play by the special teams, especially in the punting game; and forceful, determined leadership by the seniors on the team.[14]

First, Michigan boasted a strong defense in 1964. For the entire season, both in the regular season games and the Rose Bowl, Michigan's opponents scored only 83 points, an average of slightly more than 8 points per game. Even that statistic, though, impressive as it was, was misleading since 6 of the 83 points were scored on an interception return for a touchdown by Minnesota's Kraig Lofquist on a play when the defense was not on the field. So, in reality, the Michigan defense held its opponents to slightly more than 7 points per game and, perhaps just as importantly, the special teams gave up no points on punt returns or kickoff returns.

Bob Hollway, Michigan's defensive coordinator, coached the defense from a basic 6–2–3 alignment, with six defensive linemen, two linebackers, and three defensive backs. Hollway's defensive unit was a mixture of experi-

University of Michigan football coaching staff, 1964. Left to right: Henry Fonde, Don Dufek, Tony Mason, Jack Nelson, Bob Hollway, Dennis Fitzgerald, Bump Elliott, head coach (Bentley Historical Library, University of Michigan).

enced upperclass, returning lettermen, and talented incoming sophomores, who quickly made their mark as major contributors.

Michigan's defensive ends were Jim Conley (senior, Springdale, Pennsylvania) and Bill Laskey (senior, Milan, Michigan). The defensive tackles were Bill Yearby (junior, Detroit) and John Yanz (senior, Chicago). Yanz suffered a season-ending knee injury in the Illinois game and was replaced at that point by Jerry Mader (senior, Chicago).

The defensive guards were Arnie Simkus (senior, Detroit) and Rich Hahn (senior, Norton Village, Ohio). Hahn sustained a knee injury at mid-season against Purdue and was lost for the season. Replacing him in the defensive line was Bob Mielke (sophomore, Chicago). Bill Keating (junior, Chicago) also played extensively at the defensive guard position throughout the season.

Michigan's linebackers were Tom Cecchini (junior, Detroit) and Barry Dehlin (junior, Flushing, Michigan), who were both experienced returning lettermen from 1963. Dehlin, however, like Rich Hahn, suffered a season-ending knee injury in the Purdue game and was replaced by Frank Nunley (sophomore, Belleville, Michigan), who quickly emerged as one of the hardest-hitting members of the defensive unit.

The defensive secondary consisted of halfbacks Dick Rindfuss (senior, Niles, Ohio) and Rick Volk (sophomore, Wauseon, Ohio). The safety was Rick Sygar (sophomore, Niles, Ohio). Both Sygar and Rindfuss played for Tony Mason in high school before coming to Michigan. Volk, a converted quarterback, often received the assignment of covering the opposition's primary pass receiver. Rindfuss was hobbled intermittently by injury during the season, and Dick Wells (junior, Grand Rapids) often replaced him in the defensive lineup. Mike Bass (sophomore, Ypsilanti) also saw extensive playing time in the defensive secondary throughout the season, especially in situations that called for an extra defensive back.[15]

This stellar defensive unit posted some impressive achievements. First, the defenders shut out three opponents: Navy, 21–0; Northwestern, 35–0; and Ohio State, 10–0. A particularly strong aspect of the defense was its ability to stop the running attack of its opposition. For the season, the Michigan defense surrendered 88.1 yards per game on the ground, second in the Big Ten to Ohio State's 84.7 yards per game.[16]

As a result, Michigan's opponents faced the near-impossible task of controlling the football for an extended length of time. In fact, only five opponents—Air Force, Purdue, Minnesota, Iowa, and Oregon State—were able to mount a sustained offensive drive against Michigan in which they started a possession in their own territory and drove down the field for a touchdown. All of the other touchdowns scored against Michigan's defensive unit in 1964 came either by long passes or from drives that began deep in Michigan territory following a turnover by the offense or by a short punt. For example, when Michigan played Illinois, the defending Big Ten champion from 1963, the Illini scored on a 50-yard touchdown pass from quarterback Fred Custardo to end Bob Trumpy, but that score was Illinois' only penetration into Michigan territory until the final moments of the game.

Likewise, Michigan's secondary and defensive line proved to be troublesome obstacles for opposing quarterbacks. Facing some of the best passing quarterbacks in the country, such as Staubach, Custardo, Iowa's Gary Snook (the Big Ten's leading passer), Northwestern's Tommy Myers, and Michigan State's Steve Juday, the Michigan defense allowed the opposition a 44 percent completion percentage in conference action.[17]

Second, augmenting the strong defensive unit was the solid play of its special teams, especially in the punting game. Going into the 1964 season, the identity of Michigan's punter was unknown until sophomore end Stan Kemp (Greenville, Michigan) won the position. By the time of the Ohio State game, Kemp had punted 34 times for an average of 35.2 yards per punt, workmanlike numbers but not particularly outstanding. Nevertheless, Kemp proved to be one of Michigan's most valuable assets in 1964. As Tom Hemingway, the broadcaster of Michigan's football games on WUOM radio, later wrote, "Kemp could boom [punts] with the best of them when needed," and also had "a level of precision and accuracy that few could match."[18] As a result, Michigan's defense usually took the field without their opposition having its best field position.

Third, it was the Michigan offensive unit that turned the most heads in 1964. Elliott's offense operated out of a Winged-T formation, with the emphasis clearly on the running attack. Tony Mason, the newest addition to the coaching staff, fashioned the offensive line, the key to a strong ground game. Perhaps Michigan's biggest question mark going into 1964 was the personnel on the offensive line. Elliott admitted as much in the spring practice, saying, "We must rebuild our interior line and look for increased reserve strength as well as backfield speed."[19]

Whatever shortcomings Michigan may have had on the offensive line, either due to inexperience or lack of depth, did not bother Tony Mason, who brought a conceptual dimension to the Michigan offense that had hitherto been lacking. Emphasizing "desire and technique," and regarding the inexperience of the returning linemen as a "weakness on paper only," Mason preached that his job was to "eliminate all doubt," and his ability to simplify assignments resulted in outstanding performances by the offensive line. In the process, Mason assembled a potent offensive front that included Tom Mack (junior, Bucyrus, Ohio) and Charlie Kines (junior, Niles, Ohio) at the tackles, John Marcum (senior, Detroit) and Dave Butler (senior, Detroit) at the guards, and Brian Patchen (senior, Steubenville, Ohio) at center.[20] Patchen, Butler, and Marcum gained valuable playing time in 1963, but Kines and Mack were the most pleasant surprises among the linemen. Not recruited by Ohio State, Mack had received the Meyer Morton Award as the outstanding player in spring practice. Despite his size, Mack was one of the fastest players on the team and a crushing blocker. Mason had coached Kines in high school at Niles, Ohio, and made him "more mobile and just as big and strong" as a collegian.[21]

Joining the offensive interior linemen were two tight ends who alternated at the position throughout the season, Steve Smith (junior, Park Ridge, Illinois) and Ben Farabee (senior, Holland, Michigan). Both Smith and Farabee were strong blockers who also played effectively in the passing game. For the season, Smith had 8 pass receptions and Farabee had 9, a good level of production from the tight end position for that particular era in college football.

Brian Patchen, the team's starting center, referred to the Michigan offense in 1964 as the Maize and Blue Machine. Considering the preponderance of Ohioans on the offense (as well as the defense), especially at the so-called skilled positions, however, it may have been more accurate to describe it as the Scarlet and Gray Machine, in the words of Michigan's fullback Mel Anthony.[22]

A good place to begin when discussing Michigan's offensive prowess in 1964 was with the offensive backfield. In 1924, the legendary sportswriter Grantland Rice had given the enduring nickname of the Four Horsemen to Notre Dame's backfield of Elmer Layden, Harry Stuhldreher, Jim Crowley, and Don Miller, for their exploits in the Fighting Irish's 13–7 victory over Army in the Polo Grounds in New York. In the account written by Rice, the Notre Dame backfield combined speed, power, and versatility, truly a legendary unit.[23]

To its credit, Michigan also had its backfield version of the Four Horsemen 40 years later in 1964. Their names were Bob Timberlake (senior, Franklin, Ohio), Mel Anthony (senior, Cincinnati), Jim Detwiler (sophomore, Toledo), and Carl Ward (sophomore, Cincinnati). Timberlake's prowess as a runner led to an adjustment in Michigan's basic Winged-T attack as Elliott, Fonde, and Mason installed a quarterback option into the offensive system. At 6'4", 210, Timberlake was the largest member of the Michigan backfield and he quickly emerged as the team's primary ball carrier. In that respect, he introduced a feature into the Michigan offense, the quarterback as the lead running back, that distinguished the Michigan ground game from the others in the Big Ten. As Bob Pille, a reporter for the *Detroit Free Press* who covered Michigan football, wrote, Timberlake resembled "a fullback slamming for vital yardage rather than a quarterback trying light-footed sneaks."[24]

In previous years, the Michigan ground game was oriented more to speed and less to power. In 1964, with a backfield of Timberlake, Anthony, Detwiler, and Ward, the emphasis became one of power and then speed. Elliott remembered, "Basically, we were a team that was powerful on the left side with running [Detwiler and Anthony] and powerful on the right side with the option," meaning Timberlake could either keep the ball or pitch to Anthony or Ward, thereby introducing what was to become the famed Michigan quarterback option into the attack. In passing situations, "We didn't drop Timberlake straight back. We sprinted him to the right or the left. Timberlake was a threat to run and that forced the defense into some positions that [were] advantageous to [our] passing attack. We didn't use a lot of formations like they do now. This system fit our personnel."[25]

Assisted by its powerful offensive line, Michigan's backfield of four Ohioans (its first-ever all–Ohio backfield) established college football's strongest running attack, averaging 222.6 yards per game, easily leading the Big Ten in that particular offensive category, and in fact, making the Wolverines the only team in the Big Ten that rushed for more than 200 yards per game.[26] For the season, Timberlake rushed for 819 yards (4 yards-per-carry), Anthony for

717 yards (4.8 yards-per-carry), Ward for 515 yards (5.1 yards-per-carry) and Detwiler for 328 yards (4 yards-per-carry). "The statistics were pretty spread out that season," Jim Detwiler later remembered, "but no one was concerned about it. We had the right chemistry, and that was the strength of the team. The coaches felt that any one of the four backs could do well. A lot would depend on what was a good match-up for us."[27]

Timberlake, therefore, was clearly the leader of the group, the acknowledged field general of the offense and a player who combined size, strength, savvy, quick decision-making, and the capacity, in Bob Pille's words, "to keep a scoring drive moving."[28] Often overlooked about Timberlake, moreover, was his shiftiness and elusiveness, characteristics that made him even more valuable as an offensive weapon. In addition to being a running threat on the famed Michigan option, Timberlake passed for 884 yards in 1964. His favorite receiver, as in 1963, was split end John Henderson (senior, Dayton, Ohio) who led the team with 31 receptions during the 1964 season. But Timberlake also showed the ability to distribute his passes to other receivers including Detwiler (11 receptions), Smith (8 receptions), Farabee (9 receptions), and Craig Kirby (senior, Detroit, 7 receptions), who backed up Henderson at split end.

As if his running and passing were not enough, Timberlake also handled Michigan's place-kicking for extra points and field goals and, not surprisingly, the kickoff duties. Timberlake had emerged as Michigan's starting quarterback midway through the 1963 season after recovering from some early-season injuries. He picked up in 1964 where he had left off from the previous season and clearly became college football's most versatile quarterback, *a bona fide* triple-threat player, and one of the last of his kind.

Big Ten coaches were impressed by Timberlake, both in terms of his individual performances and his cool capacity to direct the Wolverine offense. As Timberlake later recalled, "Bump called almost all the plays with hand signals from the sidelines. 'Grabbing the tie' meant fullback up the middle. 'Hands to the right' meant for me to sweep," a rudimentary form of play-calling that seems laughingly simplistic today. While Elliott may have signaled the plays from the sideline, Timberlake ran the show on the field. Timberlake brought the team to the line and the Wolverines started the play on Timberlake's first sound. It was a no-nonsense attack. "We wanted the other team to know that we knew that they knew that we were going to snap it on the first sound and we were going to beat them anyway," Timberlake declared years later.[29]

Murray Warmath, Minnesota's head coach, suitably impressed by Timberlake's triple-threat qualities, believed that Timberlake was the Midwest's best pro prospect since Paul Hornung won the Heisman trophy for Notre Dame in 1956. Alex Agase, the Northwestern coach, praised Timberlake and the Michigan ground game effusively after the Wolverines ran for more than 300 yards against his team on October 31 in their 35–0 victory. Timberlake is "so big and strong," Agase said. "You can have him trapped for a loss and he'll get away for a 30- or 40-yard gain."[30]

If Timberlake was both a running and passing threat, Mel Anthony was the slashing runner who could get the tough yards inside or break off-tackle for a big gain. Anthony led the team in rushing in 1963 while going both ways as a linebacker on defense. In 1964, he shed (mostly) his linebacking duties to play almost exclusively on offense. Somewhat small for a fullback, Anthony nevertheless possessed outstanding speed and sure-handedness. Throughout the 1964 season, Anthony only lost 15 yards rushing while proving time and again his dependability in short-yardage situations.

Jim Detwiler was Michigan's left halfback. A hard-charging sophomore from Toledo, Detwiler began fall practice on the third offensive unit. Jack Clancy (junior, Detroit), a returning letterman from 1963, was originally slated to start at left halfback, and he was backed up by the fleet-footed John Rowser (junior, Detroit). But Clancy went to the sidelines with a back injury, and then Rowser suffered a season-ending knee injury, both before the first game of the season. Detwiler moved immediately into the starting lineup in the opening game against Air Force, and gained 72 yards in his first collegiate start. He followed that performance with 71 yards against Navy in the second game. After these first two games, Detwiler's rushing production fell off as the workload was progressively shared more by Timberlake, Anthony, and Carl Ward, another sophomore. But what should not be forgotten is that Detwiler was Michigan's best pass-catching option out of the backfield, with 11 receptions, second on the team. As matters developed, Detwiler's skills as a pass receiver became vitally important in the game against Ohio State.

Carl Ward was Michigan's right halfback. Like Mel Anthony, he was a highly recruited player from Cincinnati, who chose to attend Michigan because "I figured Michigan needed some help [since] they hadn't been winning much. I figured [that] I could step right in as a sophomore and help out." Ward provided Michigan with an outside threat to complement the power running of Timberlake, Anthony, and Detwiler. Unlike Detwiler, however, Ward was slated to move into Michigan's starting lineup as a sophomore. Ward had run the 100 yard dash in 9.7 seconds, and his speed made him an ever-present threat to break away for a long touchdown. Ward was also a devastating blocker who took as much pride in that facet of his game as in his rushing assignments. Little doubt remained in anyone's mind about Ward's importance to the Michigan offense. In the Navy game, Ward ran for 71 yards on 14 carries and scored two of Michigan's three touchdowns.[31]

Regardless of whether it was the Maize and Blue Machine or the Scarlet and Gray Machine, Michigan's powerful running game led to some time-consuming, clock-eating drives that kept the opposing team's offense on the bench while also giving the Wolverine defense time to rest. For the season, the lengths of Michigan's scoring drives were astonishing: one drive went for 94 yards; five drives went for 80 yards; and there were other scoring drives of 73, 72, 68, 65 (twice), 61 (twice), 56, 52, and 50 yards.[32] It was an awesome display of disciplined, well-executed offensive football.

The final attribute that characterized the strength of Michigan's 1964 team was the forceful, determined leadership of its seniors. For Michigan's seniors, the 1964 campaign was their last opportunity to make a mark in the Michigan tradition with a winning season, a long-sought Big Ten championship, and a trip to the Rose Bowl. The Michigan seniors of 1964 had suffered as sophomores through a distressing 2–7 season in 1962, Michigan's worst record in decades. In 1963, their record improved to 3–4–2, but the team's prospects received a serious jolt after the Navy game, the second game of the season: not only did Staubach turn in his masterful performance, but the team suffered so many injuries that it entered Big Ten competition seriously short of front-line performers. After watching Dehlin, Yearby, Hahn, Timberlake, and Rindfuss, as well as numerous other players, exit the Navy game, Bump Elliott commented that he "couldn't remember when Michigan had so many injuries at the end of a game."[33]

But, in 1964, the Wolverines seniors were determined to overcome the recent past. The seniors on offense—Timberlake, Anthony, Henderson, Farabee, Marcum, Butler, and Patchen—all played the best football of their college careers in 1964. The seniors on defense—Conley, Laskey, Simkus, Mader, Hahn, Yanz, and Rindfuss—executed Bob Hollway's defensive system with precision and confidence. Other seniors, such as Forest ("Frosty") Evashevski, Timberlake's backup and the designated holder on extra points and field goals, reserve linemen Bill Muir and Nick Frontczak, and reserve linebacker Michael Gorte, also contributed.

By the end of spring practice in April, Wolverine captain Jim Conley knew that the players were headed for a special season—and the seniors provided the leadership in voice and example to guarantee a maximum effort. In his role as team captain, Conley had the respect, and even admiration, of the coaching staff and the players. Both Bump Elliott and Don Dufek considered Conley as an outstanding captain and the players saw him as a "tough [leader] and he keeps us hopping." Conley's leadership galvanized the seniors on the team. "There was no doubt in anyone's mind that the seniors were in charge" of the team, Conley later observed.[34] It was a group of players, Michael Gorte later wrote, who arrived at Michigan "as teenage boys in the fall of 1961 [and] graduated as Champions of the West in the Spring of 1965."[35]

Team photograph, University of Michigan 1964 football team, 1964 Big Ten Champions and 1965 Rose Bowl Champions. Back row (left to right), Don Dufek, assistant coach, Jack "Jocko" Nelson, assistant coach, Bob Hollway, assistant coach, Mike Bass, Dave Fisher, Dick Wells, Carl Ward, Tony Mason, Henry "Hank" Fonde, assistant coach. Fourth Row (left to right), Dennis Fitzgerald, assistant coach, Louis Lee, Jeff Hoyne, Bill Keating, Frank Nunley, Craig Kirby, Charles Kines, Barry Dehlin, Don Bailey, Rick Sygar, student manager Bob Evans. Third Row (left to right), Bill Yearby, Tom Mack, Jim Detwiler, Clayton Wilhite, Arnold Simkus, Steve Smith, Rick Volk, Bob Mielke, Stan Kemp, Dave Butler. Second row (left to right) Mike Gorte, Forest "Frosty" Evashevkski, Jerry Mader, Ben Farabee, John Henderson, John Yanz, Dick Rindfuss, Bill Muir, Rich Hahn. Front Row (left to right), Bill Laskey, Bob Timberlake, H. O. "Fritz" Crisler, athletic director, captain Jim Conley, head coach Chalmers "Bump" Elliott, Tom Cecchini, Mel Anthony, Brian Patchen, John Marcum (Bentley Historical Library, University of Michigan).

The Unsung Victors: The Team That College Football Overlooked

Despite their success during the 1964 season, the Wolverines found themselves somewhat overlooked in terms of national recognition. Four factors accounted for this unusual circumstance: the tendency of the national media to overlook the Wolverines until the final weeks of the season; the season-long newspaper strike in Detroit that deprived the Wolverines of coverage among readers in southeastern Michigan and northern Ohio; the television schedule that neglected Michigan's important games; and the resurgence of Notre Dame's football fortunes in 1964 after several years of sub-par teams.

First, the national media showed a tendency to overlook the strength of the Michigan team until the final weeks of the season. A number of circumstances accounted for this factor. One must remember that Michigan had not finished near the top of the Big Ten for the better part of a decade, and sportswriters were generally disinclined to rank the Wolverines highly in their preseason forecasts. In fact, after the conclusion of Michigan's spring practice in 1964, one Detroit writer predicted that Michigan only possessed the talent level to finish with another .500 season.[36] Also, Roy Damer, the respected sportswriter for the *Chicago Tribune*, wrote that the leading contenders for the Big Ten championship were Illinois, the defending champion, and Ohio State. In Damer's opinion, Michigan promised to have an improved team from the previous year, but not enough to be a threat for the conference title.[37]

Damer's opinion was shared by Dan Jenkins, the respected sportswriter for *Sports Illustrated*. In his long-awaited college football forecast, Jenkins wrote that Illinois and Ohio State were the class of the Big Ten. Jenkins was especially high on Illinois, "well equipped to repeat as the best in the Midwest," and Ohio State, where "the material is there," so that the Buckeyes were "sitting perfect" for a trip to the Rose Bowl. But, while Jenkins did not consider Michigan as a front-line contender for the Big Ten championship, he did not totally discount the Wolverines' chances, either. "[I]f the Big Ten has a dark horse, it is Coach Bump Elliott's young, hungry team. The Wolverines have the most, and the best-looking, backs in the conference," wrote Jenkins. "'Given the proper set of circumstances, we could do real well,'" Elliott said, and these words were interpreted by Jenkins to mean "victories over brother Pete's Illini, whom he always beats, and Ohio State."[38]

Elliott's guarded comments to Jenkins were about as far out as he was willing to stick his neck, however. Michigan "would have to have some fine performances from untested men to go places in 1964," Elliott told a group of sportswriters in September, stating that Illinois and Ohio State were the two strongest teams in the Big Ten going into the season.[39] Michigan began the 1964 season unranked in the national polls.

Once the season began, however, Michigan's fortunes improved quickly. Following its defeat of Air Force in the season opener, Michigan climbed to number 8 in the national polls, its first ranking in the top 10 since 1961. After the defeat of Navy the following week, the Wolverines moved up to number 6; and then, after the defeat of Michigan State in the third week of the season, Michigan advanced to number 5. Following its loss to unranked Purdue on October 17, however, Michigan dropped out of the top 10 and out of the national rankings until the Wolverines defeated Illinois on November 7. After the victory over Illinois, Michigan returned to the polls, ranked number 7. Then, victories over Iowa and Ohio State propelled Michigan to a final national ranking of number 4, its highest ranking of the season. The outcome of bowl games did not factor in the rankings for the national polls in 1964; therefore, Michigan's decisive victory over Oregon State had no effect upon its final ranking.

Regardless, Michigan's convincing victory over Ohio State on November 21, followed by its rout of Oregon State in the Rose Bowl, convinced at least one observer that Michigan belonged at the top of the national rankings. Sec Taylor, writing for the *Des Moines Register,* flatly declared, "Michigan was the best team in the country" after its shellacking of Oregon State.[40]

Second, the Michigan gridders in 1964 suffered, publicity-wise, from a lack of reporting coverage caused by a strike against the major newspapers in Detroit, the *Detroit News* and the *Detroit Free Press,* that began in mid–July and lasted until the end of November. The labor situation in Detroit's newspaper industry was especially tense between 1955 and 1964, with nine separate actions taken by newspaper unions against their managements over that period. In 1964, the labor situation deteriorated even further on July 13 when Freeman "Smoky" Frazee, the president of Detroit's Printer's Pressmen local, walked off his job at the *Detroit Free Press,* protesting the newspaper's failure to pay the pressmen time-and-a-half for rolling the Sunday edition. Frazee's fellow unionists joined in the walkout and the labor dispute dragged on for the next 131 days, despite the unsuccessful efforts of Governor George Romney to mediate a settlement. Eventually both sides settled their dispute, but the newspapers didn't return to Detroit's homes and streets until Tuesday, November 24, three days after the Michigan–Ohio State game, the final game of the regular season. Decades later, Brian Patchen, Michigan's starting center in 1964, acidly commented that the Detroit sportswriters who "were happy to write about us when we were losing were on strike when we were winning."[41]

The newspaper strike in Detroit, therefore, severely limited the sports reporting coverage of the Michigan football season in 1964. Wayne De Neff, reporting for the *Ann Arbor News*; Clank Stoppels, the sports editor of the *Grand Rapids Press*; and the talented student sports writers for the *Michigan Daily*—Bill Bullard, the sports editor; Tom Rowland, the associate sports editor; and reporters Thomas Weinberg, Nikki Schwartz, Scott Blech, Jim LoSavage, Gary Wyner, and Lloyd Graff, to name several—provided the most detailed coverage of Michigan's season. But admittedly, the reporting by De Neff, Stoppels, and the student journalists lacked the statewide impact that coverage by the major Detroit newspapers customarily provided.

Bump Elliott recognized that the newspaper strike was certain to affect the public's awareness of his team. In Pasadena for the Rose Bowl, Elliott told a group of reporters, "[T]he recent Detroit newspaper strike may be one of the reasons you don't know too much about us. We played the whole season without any coverage from the Detroit area."[42]

Years later, Elliott expressed some profound regret that the 1964 Michigan football team was the innocent victim of the lack of publicity caused by the newspaper strike. "The Michigan team in the 1965 Rose Bowl ... that was a good team," Elliott recalled. "It didn't get the recognition that it deserved. All fall the Detroit newspapers were on strike. We had Bob Timberlake, Mel Anthony, Bill Yearby, Rich Volk, Carl Ward, Bill Laskey, Frank Nunley, John Henderson—they all went into the pros. It was an excellent team that got lost in the shuffle. That's the power of the press."[43]

Third, the television schedule also worked against an enhanced recognition of the 1964 Michigan team. Given the reality of broadcast rules in effect at the time, the NCAA established its television schedule in advance of the season. The NCAA and the National Broadcasting Company (NBC) scheduled Michigan's allotment of two televised games for October 24 against Minnesota and November 7 against Illinois.[44] These games, while important for Michigan in terms of Big Ten competition, nevertheless were not against highly ranked teams. Michigan's games against teams ranked in the top 10—Navy on October 3, Michigan State on October 10, and most importantly, Ohio State on November 21—went untelevised on a nationwide or regional basis. The network schedulers apparently concluded, prior to the season, that the Michigan State–Illinois game, also on November 21, not the Michigan–Ohio State game, was to be the key contest of the weekend and therefore placed that game on the schedule. In 1963, the game between Michigan State and Illinois on the last weekend of the regular season decided the Big Ten championship and the television schedulers were preparing for a potential repeat of that situation in 1964.

But by the time Michigan and Ohio State squared off for the Big Ten championship on November 21, both teams had reached their allotted two televised games: Michigan against Minnesota and Illinois, and Ohio State against Illinois on October 10 and against the University of Southern California (USC) on October 17. Michigan was 6th-ranked and Ohio State was 7th-ranked going into the final contest, and yet the game was unavailable for viewing to a widespread television audience.

Nevertheless, some football enthusiasts did get the opportunity to watch the game on television, though they were limited either to a local broadcast, originating from WWJ-TV in Detroit and reaching viewers in southeastern Michigan, or to another broadcast originating from WOSU-TV, the public broadcasting affiliate of Ohio State that reached viewers in central Ohio.[45] Speaking of the limited television coverage, Wayne De Neff wrote that "thousands [of viewers] will watch the game on television," not the audiences of millions who tuned in to the Michigan–Ohio State game in subsequent years.[46] It was arguably the most important Michigan–Ohio State game to that point in the postwar era, and the one with the smallest television viewing audience! Michigan's victories over Navy, Michigan State, and Ohio State, had at least one been televised, would have increased Michigan's profile substantially in the minds of football observers across the country.

At this point, one can also speculate that the limited coverage of the 1964 Michigan team by the Detroit newspapers, and the modest national impact of Michigan's televised games, worked to Bob Timberlake's detriment as a Heisman Trophy candidate in 1964. In the final Heisman balloting, Timberlake finished fourth behind John Huarte, the Notre Dame quarterback and Heisman winner; Jerry Rhome, Tulsa's quarterback; and Dick Butkus, the two-way center/linebacker for Illinois.

In terms of all-around performance as a triple-threat player, however, Timberlake was clearly the nation's top performer in 1964, even though the newspaper strike and the limited television coverage of Michigan's games restricted the type of national publicity that he received. Furthermore, during the season, Bump Elliott and the other Michigan coaches, as well as the thinly staffed Sports Information Office at Michigan, were reluctant to promote the achievements of individual players as measured against the entire performance of the team. When pressed by reporters, however, Elliott certainly recognized Timberlake publicly for his impact on the success of Michigan's season.[47]

The Michigan athletic department did make one modest effort toward promoting Bob Timberlake's prospects as a potential Heisman recipient. On November 21, at halftime of the Michigan–Ohio State game, Bob Ufer broadcast an interview with Timberlake in which the two men discussed the Michigan quarterback's qualifications. "Bob, how do you personally feel about being considered for collegiate football's highest honor, the Heisman Trophy?" Ufer asked. In response, Timberlake acknowledged the talents of Roger Staubach, the 1963 Heisman recipient, and then explained that any Heisman winner needed to have a strong team around him. "If I should happen to win it this year," Timberlake answered, "it's because we have a great team."[48] Nevertheless, it is safe to assume that Michigan's absence from the national rankings in late October, coupled with the limited coverage from the newspaper strike and the television schedule, greatly handicapped Timberlake's opportunity to win the Heisman Trophy in 1964.

A fourth factor accounting for the relative lack of publicity for Michigan's football team in 1964 was the re-emergence of Notre Dame's football fortunes as a Midwestern and national football power. Under its first-year coach Ara Parseghian, Notre Dame shook off the dust of several sub-par seasons, dating back to the late 1950s, and came roaring out for the 1964 season with a renewed sense of purpose. Week after week, starting with their opening-game victory over Wisconsin by a score of 31-7, the Fighting Irish demolished their opponents by lopsided margins. In successive weeks, the Irish defeated Purdue, Air Force, UCLA, and Stanford. Over that five-game stretch, they outscored their opponents by a margin of 151-35, and climbed ever higher in the national polls as a result. On November 7, after defeating Pittsburgh 17-15 and being the beneficiaries of top-ranked Ohio State's loss to Penn State, 27-0, the Irish became the number 1-ranked team in the country. Notre Dame stood poised to win the mythical national championship if it were to close out the regular season with three more victories.[49]

In terms of publicity, the revitalized fortunes of the Fighting Irish was the football story of the year in the Midwest. Led by its enormously productive passing combination of quarterback John Huarte to split end Jack Snow, its powerful running game of Bill Wolski and Nick Eddy running behind a "massive (219 lbs. per man) [offensive] line," and a lockdown defense led by linebacker Jim Carroll and tackle Alan Page, the Irish gave their loyal faithful a taste of football prowess not seen since the teams of Frank Leahy.[50]

On November 20, 1964, Parseghian appeared on the cover of *Time* magazine, and the unbeaten team's season was featured in a glowing five-page article that highlighted the Irish's impressive 34-7 victory over Michigan State on November 14, played to a full house in South Bend and an estimated television audience of 35 million people.[51] Then, on November 21, Notre Dame defeated Iowa, 28-0, to set up a showdown the following week in Los Angeles with USC to determine whether the Irish would finish the year with a perfect 10-0 record, and thereby lay claim to the number-1 ranking and the national championship. Understandably, the attention of football enthusiasts in the Midwest moved in the direction of South Bend, and away from Ann Arbor and other Big Ten cities, as the season progressed.

Regardless, the Michigan Wolverines were the Champions of the West in 1964. It was a relatively unheralded team, at least at the beginning of the season, that nevertheless gained momentum throughout the campaign. As Rick Sygar later wrote, "Few thought Michigan was one of [the title contenders]. But Bump Elliott and his staff had assembled what turned out to be an undeniable combination of veterans, hardened by previous Big Ten warfare, with a gifted group of soph[o]mores to provide the blind zeal for the winning margin. The cool efficiency of Timberlake, Ward, Mack, Detwiler [and] Henderson on offense contrasted sharply with the often maniacal play of Conley, Volk, Nunley, Laskey, et al., on defense. I was a member of the maniacal group."[52]

Bump Elliott also sensed a quality of determination and cohesiveness in the 1964 Wolverines as the season progressed, a quality that he later termed Michigan's "fighting spirit." Game after game, Michigan displayed a persistence that set this team apart. "Very seldom will you find a college football team with this fighting spirit, the will to win, of this ball club," he observed. For the Wolverines in 1964, Elliott concluded, "Everybody just seemed to fit."[53]

So Michigan's championship in 1964 came as a surprise to most experienced Big Ten football watchers, most of whom had grown accustomed to seeing Ohio State, Michigan State, Wisconsin, Minnesota, and Illinois battle it out for the top spot. But the Michigan players stayed focused on the main prize, the Big Ten title, all season and even improved their performances on a weekly basis. By season end, no one could deny that Michigan was the best team in the Big Ten, and, perhaps just as importantly, one of the elite teams in college football in 1964.

One

Quickness and Agility: Building the '64 Michigan Team

After the Michigan Wolverines finished the 1964 season with a record of 8–1 and were preparing to travel to California for the Rose Bowl, Fritz Crisler, Michigan's legendary coach between 1939 and 1948, gave an interview to reporter Joe Hendrickson in which he described the qualities of the team. In Crisler's opinion, Michigan was "a quickness and agility team [more] than a big, bruising outfit."[1] Crisler's description was accurate: throughout the season, Michigan relied more on precision, execution, and conditioning than on size and straight-ahead power. Not to be misunderstood, the Michigan players were hard-hitting gridders, but they were also versatile, fundamentally sound, and mentally tough.

Michigan owed much of its success in 1964 to two factors: the culmination of an ambitious recruiting program begun by Bump Elliott when he took over the reins of the program in 1959, and the effects of a change by the National Collegiate Athletic Association (NCAA) in its rules regarding substitution in football competition. The effects of these factors were not evident at the outset of the 1964 season, but once Michigan continued to win convincingly as the campaign unfolded, it became clear that the Wolverines were enjoying the benefits of some profound changes in their football environment.

First, Elliott realized that the future success of the Wolverine program revolved around the establishment of a solid recruiting base, primarily in the three Midwestern states of Michigan, Illinois (especially in the area of Chicago), and Ohio. Simply put, by the late 1950s, if not before, successful recruiting and obtaining the best possible high school talent was the *sine qua non* of collegiate football success, not only in the Big Ten but nationwide.

During the 1950s, Michigan's level of football talent had fallen off noticeably by comparison with its opponents, especially at Michigan State under the leadership of Biggie Munn and Duffy Daugherty, and at Ohio State under the

Bump Elliott (left) and Fritz Crisler, Michigan's athletic director (Bentley Historical Library, University of Michigan).

leadership of Woody Hayes, where aggressive recruiting became a priority. Michigan was "up against the two best recruiters in the country in Duffy Daugherty and Woody Hayes," Elliott later observed.[2]

For his part, Duffy Daugherty understood the vital role that successful recruiting played in molding a top-flight college football program. As the Spartan coach once explained, "We have no secrets. We don't have any magic formula and neither does anyone else in the business. The reason you win is because you've got more good players than the next guy. Most football games aren't won on the field. They are won from December to September when the recruiting is done."[3]

Once he became Michigan's head coach, Bump Elliott recognized the deficiencies in Michigan's recruiting program. "It will take three to five years to rebuild and win a championship," he commented in 1959.[4] Michigan's football fortunes now depended, therefore, upon the success of the football staff's ability to raise the overall talent level of the Wolverine roster. "There is no question about it," Elliott said. "You've got to recruit nowadays. At one time, you didn't have to, but the competition from rival schools is so great that if you don't do your share, you don't get the better high school football players." Don Dufek, one of Elliott's assistant coaches, put the matter more emphatically: "Recruiting had become the guts of college football."[5]

Michigan's program for football recruiting occurred on several levels, although admittedly not with the organizational sophistication that later prevailed in college football. The recruiting process for prospective Michigan football players in the 1960s was essentially a never-ending series of continuous conversations, occurring on an annual basis, between three groups of people: Bump Elliott and his assistant coaches; high school football coaches, mostly in the Midwest, who were open to having their players choose the Michigan football program as their collegiate destination; and Michigan alumni who maintained contact with high school players (and, just as importantly, with their families) and coaches, and with the Michigan coaching staff.

Bump Elliott was a successful recruiter himself, a man with a "personality that would make most prep stars feel rude to say no" to him, according to one observer. Elliott and his assistant coaches essentially targeted outstanding high school football players who combined solid academic records and sound judgment.[6] Elliott was also a man who was willing to spend long, cold winter nights on the highway driving to various places to meet with prospective Michigan players.

Elliott and the members of the Michigan coaching staff also enjoyed a reputation for honesty and integrity in their recruitment of high school athletes, attributes that caused both Jim Detwiler, a heavily recruited player from Toledo, and John Henderson, a much sought-after athlete from Dayton, to attend Michigan. Detwiler chose Michigan over the service academies, while Henderson decided to attend Michigan instead of Ohio State. Henderson later wrote, "As a youngster growing up in Ohio, most boys had visions of catching the winning touchdown or throwing the key block for the Ohio State Buckeyes football team. I was no different than any other youngster." But the Michigan coaching staff impressed Henderson to the point that he chose to become a Wolverine. As Henderson concluded, "The [Michigan] coaching staff—Jocko Nelson, the end coach; Jack Fouts, who latter [*sic*] became the head coach at Ohio Wesleyan; Hank Fonde, the back field coach; and Bob Hollway, the defensive coach—were fine gentlemen who knew their business. This core of assistant coaches was headed by one of my all-time favorite people, 'Bump' Elliott.... The coaching staff and alumni shared the ethical and gentlemanly quality which spoke well for the university."[7]

As mentioned previously, Elliott and his coaching staff focused their recruiting efforts primarily on three states: Michigan, Illinois, and Ohio. Each of the coaches took responsibility for a particular state or region to "cover," in terms of identifying talented high school players and then beginning a process of persuading them to play for Michigan. Bob Hollway and Hank Fonde were responsible for recruiting in the state of Michigan. Because of his background as an outstanding high school player in Chicago, Don Dufek recruited extensively for Michigan in Illinois. Jack Fouts, and later Tony Mason, were responsible for recruiting in Ohio, as was Jocko Nelson, who also occasionally recruited in Pennsylvania and New Jersey.

Central to that effort was establishing a rapport with high school football coaches who were open to presenting Michigan as a logical choice for their outstanding players. One such coach, for example, was Tony Mason of McKinley High School in Niles, Ohio, who recommended Michigan to several of his players, including Dick Rindfuss, Rick Sygar, Charlie Kines, Dennis Flanagan, and Jim Seiber.[8]

Another important aspect of recruiting in the mid–1960s was the role played by Michigan alumni who were supporters of the football program. As Elliott remembered, "Alumni were involved in the recruiting of high school players in ways that were later prohibited by NCAA rules," and Michigan's assistant coaches regularly received information about outstanding high school players from Michigan alumni.[9] Such individuals, known in the football vernacular as "bird dogs," actively identified talented football players in their areas and kept the Michigan coaching staff informed about their achievements.[10]

In that respect, therefore, establishing a rapport with the "bird dogs" was as important for Michigan's coaching staff as establishing a rapport with high school coaches. The "bird dogs" kept the Michigan coaching staff informed about player performances, sent press clippings from the local newspapers to the Michigan coaching staff, and otherwise maintained contact with the players, their coaches, and their families. They performed the critically necessary function of being the eyes and ears of high school football talent before technology came along to perform that function. As Jim Conley once explained, "A lot of recruiting back then was done by [simple] word of mouth. Basically, the 'bird dogs' would do the work. Then [the coaching staff] get[s] a [high school] coach on [its] side, like Tony Mason, and then that coach would be telling you who the players were coming up and who to watch for."[11]

At this point, it is important to understand how the National Collegiate Athletic Association dealt with the matter of alumni and their involvement in the recruiting process. In the mid–1960s, the NCAA established a set of procedures that enabled alumni to function essentially as extensions of their institutions and, one might argue, even encouraged alumni to become partic-

Tony Mason (kneeling), assistant football coach, with four Michigan players that he previously coached at McKinley High School in Niles, Ohio. Standing, left to right, Dick Rindfuss, Rick Sygar, Jim Seiber, and Charlie Kines. Dennis Flanagan, another Michigan player from Niles, Ohio, was absent from the photograph (Bentley Historical Library, University of Michigan).

ipants in the athletic enterprise. For example, Article 6, Section 5: Recruiting—Contracts and Offers, of the *National Collegiate Athletic Association 1964-1965 Yearbook* read: "If an institution's staff member requests an alumnus or other friend of the institution to recruit a particular prospect, or the staff member has knowledge that the alumnus or friend is recruiting the prospect, then that alumnus or friend becomes a 'representative of athletic interests' of that institution."[12]

Within the language of that policy, alumni had wide latitude to promote an institution to high school players, including forming a relationship with the recruit and his family. Consider for example, the matter of official campus visits by recruits. The NCAA's policy stipulated that an institution "may finance one and only one visit to its campus for a prospective student athlete," a visit that could not exceed "two days and two nights."[13] That policy did not, however, prohibit one or more alumni representatives from bringing a recruited athlete to campus themselves, "provided that such person, at his own expense, accompanies the student-athlete on his visit." As a result, many of Michigan's recruits made more than one visit to Ann Arbor.[14]

The effect of these policies by the NCAA essentially placed alumni at the center of the recruiting process, a source of consistent information, communication, contacts, and support between the coaching staff and the high school recruit. The lesson was clear: coaching staffs that effectively mobilized the efforts of their alumni stood a better chance of landing prized high school talent than those who lacked that particular capability.

To cite an example, John Henderson acknowledged the importance of two Michigan alumni, Ben Sproat and Boarden Greathouse, in promoting Michigan to him. Henderson later wrote, "As I recall, my initial contacts [for Michigan] were with Ben Sproat and Boarden Greathouse, both members of the Dayton chapter of the University of Michigan alumni. These two men, and others, respected me and my family and had a sincere interest in my well-being. The University of Michigan boasted that 85 percent of its lettermen graduated. This made a tremendous impression on me and my parents."[15]

Occasionally, family connections even played a role in recruiting. For example, the father of Bill Laskey, Durward Laskey, and the father of Dick Wells, Robert Wells, were members of the Michigan football team, and Cass Kemp, the father of Stan Kemp, competed on the track team, for Michigan during the 1930s. In that respect, the sons were continuing their own unique family traditions by following in their fathers' footsteps to play for the Wolverines.

Sometimes, however, familial connections were no guarantee that Bump Elliott would land a recruit. Bill Laskey, for example, was a heavily recruited player from Milan, Michigan, who made his initial commitment to the University of Iowa and its coach, Jerry Burns, a former teammate of Don Dufek on the 1950 Michigan team. After informing Elliott of his decision to attend Iowa, Laskey nevertheless agreed to meet with Elliott to reconsider the matter. Elliott's intervention led Laskey to a last-minute change of heart but, unfortunately, he had already mailed his letter of acceptance to Iowa. The letter to Iowa needed to be retrieved. "Fortunately, my mother knew the local postmaster so she called him and explained my problem," Laskey remembered. "Like everyone else in Milan, our postmaster was a dyed-in-the-wool Wolverines fan and he was only too happy to relieve me of my predicament. So there I was with my mom, the head coach of the University of Michigan, and the postmaster fishing through the mailbox until we found that fateful letter, and I became a Wolverine. It was the best decision I ever made."[16]

But as far as the family connections for players on the 1964 roster were concerned, none could surpass the experience of Rick Volk. Rick Volk was recruited as a star quarterback from Wauseon, Ohio, and definitely wanted to play for Michigan. Bob Chappuis, one of the Mad Magicians and a backfield teammate of Bump Elliott on Michigan's national championship team in 1947, was Volk's uncle. Growing up, Volk had heard stories from his grandparents about his uncle's playing career at Michigan. Volk was candid in explaining his intentions: "[E]verybody in my hometown knew that, if I had the chance to go to Michigan, that's where I was going. I'd loved Michigan since I was a little kid because of Uncle Bob."[17] When Volk made his visit to Michigan as a recruit, Elliott offered him an athletic scholarship, knowing of his relationship to Chappuis. With no hesitation, Volk told Elliott, "I'm coming."[18]

In terms of recruiting priorities, Elliott and his assistants targeted the football talent in high schools in Michigan and Ohio primarily, with those in Illinois of slightly lesser importance but still considered vital to the program. During the 1950s, Michigan struggled in recruiting the top-flight football talent in its home state as Michigan State became the more successful program. "I'd have to say that one of the objectives of our staff when we came in was that we had to start beating Michigan State in recruiting before we could beat them on the field," Elliott said.[19]

By the early 1960s, Elliott's recruiting strategy was beginning to pay off as the Wolverines enjoyed increasing success in strengthening their roster with players from Michigan, especially in the Detroit area. The 1964 roster of players from Detroit and the wider area of southeastern Michigan included linemen Bill Yearby, Bill Laskey, Dave Butler, John Marcum, and Arnie Simkus; linebackers Tom Cecchini, Barry Dehlin, and Frank Nunley; defensive back Mike Bass; offensive halfbacks Jack Clancy and John Rowser; and offensive end Craig Kirby. Defensive back Dick Wells, offensive end Ben Farabee, and punter Stan Kemp came from the west Michigan area.

In Illinois, Michigan's recruiting efforts also bore considerable fruit in the early 1960s. With a strong alumni base in Chicago, as well as Evanston native Don Dufek's ties to the area, Michigan was able to attract the attention of some outstanding Illinoisans. The mainstays on the 1964 team from Illinois were offensive end Steve Smith, defensive end Jeff Hoyne, and interior linemen John Yanz, Jerry Mader, Bob Mielke, Bill Keating, and Charlie Ruzicka. It was these Illinoisans who provided much of the up-front muscle for the interior of the Michigan defensive front in 1964. For his part, Smith was a crushing blocker as an offensive tight end who contributed significantly to the success of Michigan's ground game.

It was in Michigan's arch-rival state of Ohio, however, that Elliott and his staff mounted an effort, every bit as concerted as their effort in Michigan, to attract top-notch football talent. The powerful high school programs in the Buckeye State presented a target-rich environment for Wolverine recruiters. The main effort to recruit Ohioans initially fell to Jack Fouts and Jocko Nelson, the assistant coaches with the most prior experience working in the state.

Fouts, in particular, knew the football landscape in the state of Ohio and, just as importantly, had a confidence-building recruiting demeanor that appealed to his potential recruits and their families.[20]

In retrospect, it was clear that Bump Elliott and his assistant coaches used their full arsenal of recruiting weapons to recruit Ohioans. One stratagem involved having the alumni in a particular community arrange for an alumni meeting—and then invite prospective high school players, their parents, and their coaches to attend as guests. Once again, such practices were fully in accord with existing NCAA policy, which did not "prohibit bona fide alumni organizations of an institution from sponsoring luncheons, teas or dinners at which prospective students (athletes and non-athletes) of that immediate locale are guests."[21]

The Michigan alumni invited either Bump Elliott or one of the assistant coaches to attend these meetings, usually held in the evening, and give the featured speech. "We had meetings in Cleveland, Dayton, and Cincinnati," Elliott remembered. "The [members of the audience] were exposed to us for the evening and the [high school] players could attend."[22]

The efforts by Elliott, Fouts, and the other Wolverine coaches paid off, and by 1964, Michigan's roster included a host of Buckeye standouts. In the offensive backfield were quarterback Bob Timberlake, fullbacks Mel Anthony and Dave Fisher, and halfbacks Jim Detwiler and Carl Ward. Three Ohioans started on the offensive line: center Brian Patchen and tackles Tom Mack and Charlie Kines. John Henderson, Michigan's starting split end, was from Ohio. Rich Hahn, another Ohioan, started on the defensive line until injuries forced him to the sidelines midway through the season. For most of 1964, Michigan's starting defensive secondary consisted of three Ohioans: Dick Rindfuss, Rick Sygar, and Rich Volk.[23]

In assembling this team, Elliott and his assistant coaches vigorously stressed the importance of Michigan's football tradition, combined with its outstanding academic reputation. The stress on Michigan's academic strength struck a responsive chord with several Ohioans who came across the border to become Wolverines. Mel Anthony, Michigan's highly recruited fullback from Cincinnati, was emphatic about the importance of the academic realm when it came to his selection of a university. "At Michigan, I can get one of the finest college educations and at the same time play the best quality college football in the country," Anthony wrote several years later. "Bump Elliott, our head coach, had convinced me that I would play fullback at Michigan and, just as importantly, would graduate. None of the other schools I visited stressed receiving a degree as much as Michigan," he added.[24]

Dave Fisher, a sophomore fullback from Kettering on the 1964 team, also was impressed with the stress on athletics and academics that Michigan presented to him during the recruiting period. As he later wrote, "[A]fter a brief meeting with Jack Fouts, line coach at the time, I soon sensed something special about Michigan." Recruited by more than 100 colleges and universities, Fisher wanted to study engineering, historically one of Michigan's strongest academic areas. During a visit to Michigan, Fisher recalled, "I remember Jack Borchardt (professor of civil engineering) and Dick Balzhiser (professor of chemical engineering and former football player) taking a major portion of a Saturday to show me around the Engineering School and introducing me to their colleagues."[25]

Finally, Bob Timberlake, Michigan's All-American quarterback and Heisman Trophy finalist in 1964, was the valedictorian of his high school class and also underscored the importance that he attached to Michigan's academic reputation. In a radio interview with broadcaster Bob Ufer, aired strategically during halftime of the Michigan–Ohio State game in 1964, Timberlake explained how he arrived at his decision to attend Michigan. In response to Ufer, Timberlake noted that he was impressed by Bump Elliott and the members of the coaching staff, the imposing Michigan Stadium, and "most of all with the fine academic standing here at the University of Michigan."[26] So for any Ohioans listening to Ufer's broadcast of the game on the Michigan football network, Timberlake's message came through loud and clear: the Michigan athletic program stressed success on the field and success in the classroom.

Michigan's success in recruiting front-line players from Ohio was satisfying to Bump Elliott and the rest of the Michigan coaching staff, even to the point of some astonishment. "Gee whiz," Elliott said, after the 1964 season, "were there that many Ohio preps who found their way to Michigan this year?" He added, "Michigan's fame as an academic institution must really be getting around."[27]

Regardless, Elliott savored the contributions that the Ohioans made to the Michigan program. "I don't think we should call these boys Ohioans. Once they crossed the state line and entered Michigan, we forgave them completely and absolutely. And, if you don't believe me, then you should hear them sing 'The Victors' [the famed Michigan fight song]. They know every word," Elliott said.[28] And, in fact, it was Ohioan Rick Sygar who mounted a bench in the locker room after Michigan's opening-game victory over Air Force, and led the team in singing "The Victors," a ritual that the team followed in 1964 after every one of its victories, a tradition that continues to this day.[29]

From Ironman to Two Platoon Football

The second factor in Michigan's success in 1964 came from a change in the rules for substitution, adopted by the NCAA's Football Rules Committee in January, 1964. On January 12, the Rules Committee adopted a rule that a coach could substitute any number of players (including a full "platoon" of purely offensive or defensive players) at any time when the clock was stopped.[30] In addition, coaches were permitted to substitute as many as two players when the clock was running, such as a long snapper and a punter on fourth down in punting situations, for example. The rules change in 1964 shifted the college game back to so-called "two-platoon" football that had characterized play between 1941 and 1953. The platoon system in use at that time had some variations, however.

At Army in the 1940s, Coach Earl ("Red") Blaik substituted different teams for each quarter, with the players going "both ways" for the full quarter before another "team" entered the game as its substitute. In 1945, Michigan coach Fritz Crisler, facing an Army team that physically overmatched his Wolverines, substituted his players in the more customary fashion of an offensive unit and a defensive unit. Michigan lost to Army in 1945, 28–7, but Crisler's innovation, and the tenacity with which the Michigan offensive and defensive units competed against the more powerful Army team, nevertheless caught the attention of college football coaches throughout the United States who immediately adopted his version of the two-platoon system.[31] As Crisler stated some years later, "many coaches wrote and phoned to know what we were doing. By the following season, many of the colleges and high schools had begun to adopt platooning."[32]

Then, on January 15, 1953, the Rules Committee abruptly adopted a rules change that essentially brought back the Ironman, or "both ways," system, by ruling that no player withdrawn from a game could re-enter the contest until the next period after he was withdrawn. Ironically, one of the leading proponents for the return to Ironman football was Fritz Crisler, who argued that "specialization was becoming too pronounced and the all-around skills and objectives [of preparing players] were being overlooked."[33]

General Bob Neyland, the athletic director at the University of Tennessee in 1953, was more graphic in his denunciation of two-platoon football, and he applauded the return of the Ironman system. Two-platoon football, according to Neyland, also the former football coach at Tennessee, was "chicken ---- football," not the optimum way of playing the college game.[34]

Fritz Crisler had other objections to two-platoon football, however. Now the athletic director at Michigan, Crisler was witnessing an escalation in the costs of collegiate sports and came to believe that should more specialization enter college football, the process inevitably would lead to larger player rosters, larger coaching staffs, and ever-increasing budgets for recruiting, three trends that he viewed with increasing alarm. In Crisler's estimation, the recruiting dynamic had reversed itself, and not necessarily to the good. "It used to be that the young man recruited the school. Now it's the other way around," Crisler once told Michigan broadcaster Tom Hemingway. "I really wonder which is best."[35] The overemphasis on recruiting had driven him from coaching in the late 1940s, and with costs on the rise, he was understandably concerned about how to find the increasing revenues needed to cover these growing expenses.

Over the years, in fact, Michigan's athletic facilities in football had fallen behind those of its competition, and Bump Elliott and his coaching staff operated in an environment of near-austerity. The coaches lacked meeting rooms and the locker rooms inside Michigan Stadium were in need of serious renovation. The plumbing leaked and players hung their clothes on pegs on the walls, sources of irritation for visiting teams. Bob Devaney, coach of the University of Nebraska, looked at Michigan's cramped locker room when his team came to play Michigan in 1962, and asked, "Wouldn't you think that the University of Michigan could do a little bit better for visiting teams than this?"[36]

These deficiencies did not go unnoticed by the Michigan players, either. "[In] the shower room below Michigan Stadium, half the shower heads didn't work ... and a light bulb hung from two wires in the ceiling," Brian Patchen observed in 2004. The only difference between "our locker room [at Michigan Stadium] and Fielding Yost's was that his was brand new and ours was forty years old."[37] If the continuation of Ironman football promised some potential cost savings for the athletic program, Fritz Crisler was not one to question its value.

Notwithstanding Fritz Crisler's preferences, the return to Ironman football became unworkable over the course of the next decade. Gradually, the NCAA tried to relax these stringent rules for substitution but, in the process, created an even more confusing environment in which officials needed to monitor substitutions continuously and coaches became focused more on the rules for substitution than on their responses to game situations. "Under the revived rules," said Red Blaik, "the game became less fun for the coaches, less fun for the players and cluttered with bookkeeping for the officials."[33]

By 1963, the college football coaches clamored for change. Jack Curtice, the football coach at the University of California–Santa Barbara and the rules chairman of the American Football Coaches Association (AFCA), submitted a proposal to the NCAA for the provisions outlined above. According to Curtice, 90 percent of the college football coaches wanted "an end to rule restrictions" and a return to "two platoon football." Marv Levy, the football coach at the College of William and Mary, supported the change, claiming, "Now maybe the coaches will be able to concentrate on the progress of the game instead of staying occupied with whom they can substitute and when."[39] Duffy Daugherty, Michigan State's coach, also agreed with the rules change. "If nothing else, it should take a great burden off the officials," Daugherty argued. "Anyone can understand the new rules. You just have to know when to substitute and for what reasons. It certainly is a step in the right direction...."[40]

John McKay, whose Southern California team had defeated Wisconsin, 42–37, in the 1963 Rose Bowl, was another prominent voice in support of the rules change. "I think the rules change will help us quite a bit," McKay stated. "In spring practice, we'll try to develop boys who work both ways, then decide in the fall who will play mostly offense or defense. You are still going to have the boys ready to play a little offense and a little defense in case they get caught in there."[41]

Even with what appeared to be overwhelming support for the rules change from the football coaching fraternity, the return to *de facto* free substitution still had its critics. The NCAA Council, for example, made a last-ditch, unsuccessful effort in 1964 to preserve Ironman football, writing to the subcommittee of the Rules Committee that was considering the rules change that it "further believe[s] that college football—which is the original game—always should remain true to its basic educational function and purpose, and also retain its own distinct identity and image."[42]

Some coaches also viewed the move as an effort to imitate the National Football League, where teams consisted of offensive specialists and defensive specialists. Ralph "Shug" Jordan, the Auburn University coach, announced that he "was utterly opposed to free substitution. College football is now out of the educational field and into the entertainment field. Football is now a game where coaches will strictly exploit the talent of a particular boy without having to particularly teach him anything."[43]

Despite these conflicting views, the fact remained that the substitution changes adopted by the NCAA in 1964 transformed the game of college football—permanently. Once a game of endurance played by generalists, college football became a vigorously played contest that pitted a talented unit of offensive players against a talented unit of defensive players and, in time, talented units of special teams players. No longer would a player "who was average on offense and average on defense get more playing time than a player who was outstanding on offense but weak on defense," according to Jim Conley.[44] For football coaches, specialized ability replaced all-around skills in terms of deciding upon the players who went onto the field at any given time.

Once two-platoon football returned to the college gridiron, Bump Elliott and his coaching staff embraced the change, and began laying the groundwork in spring practice, 1964, for the development of a new system, one that promised to use the specialized talents of many more players than those who previously saw action on Saturday afternoons. Publicly, Elliott supported the concept of training well-rounded football players who could play on both sides

Jim Conley (82), Michigan's team captain, and coach Bump Elliott (Bentley Historical Library, University of Michigan).

of the ball, but he also left no doubt as to the direction for Michigan's team in 1964. "We're still going to teach boys to go both ways," Elliott stated when the new rules came out. "But, basically, this is a return to two platoon football."[45]

In responding to the rules change and the advent of two-platoon football, Bump Elliott and the Michigan assistant coaches devised an ingenious system. "We had what we called three teams: an offensive team, a defensive team, and a team that played both ways," Elliott recalled. "We practiced them that way: one team practiced on offense (primarily), one team practiced on defense (primarily), and the other [practiced] half and half [on offense and defense]."[46] In fact, when Michigan published its program for its opening game against Air Force on September 26, the "probable order of substitutions" showed the members of the three separate units: offense, defense, and two-way.[47]

Starting with spring practice in April, the coaches instituted this new system, basically starting from scratch, under the broader rationale of protecting the team against the inevitable injuries that were bound to occur in any football season. "The reason [that we adopted this system] was this: if we had an injury to an offensive tackle, for example, we could move a person over from the defense to offense and then move a person over from the two-way team to take the place of the defensive player," Elliott recalled.[48]

The system also had other, somewhat unexpected, benefits. For example, a player from the two-way unit often became the in-game substitute for a player on the offensive unit or the defensive unit when a coach wanted to rest a specific player during a contest. More specifically, the two-platoon system enabled two key players, Tom Cecchini and Rick Sygar, who had suffered season-ending injuries in 1963, to make their way back into the lineup as defensive specialists, rather than having to master both the offense and the defense.

In Tom Cecchini's case, he incurred a season-ending knee injury in the game against Purdue, the fourth game of the season, in 1963. From Detroit, Cecchini had realized a long-sought ambition of playing for Michigan, and he earned a starting position as a center and linebacker while only a sophomore in 1963. His performance against Michigan State, the third game of the season, was magnificent. He intercepted a pass in the second quarter and then essentially made a game-saving tackle in the fourth quarter to preserve Michigan's 7–7 tie with the Spartans. These exploits earned Cecchini the Lineman of the Week honors from the UPI.[49] Following his injury against Purdue, however, Cecchini underwent surgery and then an extensive regimen of rehabilitation.

In 1964, Cecchini rejoined the team and the coaches slated him for a linebacking position on defense. Although somewhat small for the assignment at 6'0" and 200 pounds, Cecchini was one of the hardest hitting players in the Big Ten. In addition, as Tom Hemingway pointed out, Cecchini was a "brilliant student of the game ... who could smell a football a mile away."[50] In 1964, Cecchini had a dual role as the long snapper on the punt team and an inside linebacker on defense. In that capacity, he anchored Michigan's defense for much of the season and called the team's defensive signals prior to each play.

In Rick Sygar's case, he had come to Michigan in 1962 as a highly recruited running back from Niles, Ohio, where he excelled under Coach Tony Mason. Slated to start at right halfback as a sophomore, Sygar suffered a broken leg in practice just before the start of the season, ending any chance of playing football in 1963. The injury put him on crutches for most of the winter. Then, while walking on campus, he fell on an icy street and broke the leg again, this time in a different place.

The injury to his leg forced Sygar to miss spring practice, but he held out hope of rejoining the football team in time for the preseason workouts in August. "Sure, I felt I'd be able to play football again," Sygar said. "Guys have had broken legs before."[51] With the admiration of his teammates and coaches, he put himself through an extensive conditioning program in the summer designed to strengthen the leg, but when the preseason drills began, he was still limping. By this point, Tony Mason, his former high school coach, had joined the coaching staff and assiduously worked with Sygar to maintain his morale and encourage him to keep making progress in practice. By the end of the preseason, Sygar had made the team and the coaches slated him for a spot in the defensive secondary. As the leg continued to heal and strengthen, Sygar likewise became a mainstay on defense for the Wolverines.

On January 15, 1964, Wayne De Neff, the sportswriter who covered the Wolverine football program for the *Ann Arbor News*, filed a story that served as a prescient indicator of how the Michigan team would appear in the fall. Titled "M Appears to Have Depth for Two Platoons," De Neff's article pointed out that Elliott had 18 of his top 22 players returning from the 1963 team, a nucleus by itself for potentially separate units on offense and defense. Michigan's strengths, De Neff argued, were at the ends, the backfield, and at center.[52] The platoon system, therefore, enabled Elliott to move senior ends Jim Conley, the Wolverine team captain, and Bill Laskey permanently to the defensive unit while assigning John Henderson, Michigan's leading pass receiver in 1963, and Craig Kirby (from the two-way unit), to split end; he then alternated Steve Smith and Ben Farabee at tight end.

The division of the talent at the end position paid instant dividends for both units. As described by Michigan radio broadcaster Tom Hemingway, Conley was a "sure and punishing tackler who lived for the thrill of clobbering enemy ball carriers." Jocko Nelson, Conley's position coach, acknowledging his prejudice, still considered the Michigan captain as the best "defensive end in the Big Ten." Laskey, likewise, was agile, mobile, and versatile. He proved to be equally adept at closing the flank on running plays and covering receivers off the line of scrimmage or coming out of the backfield. A photograph of Laskey catching a pass, stored in his individual file at the Bentley Historical Library, carried the caption: "Bill Laskey didn't catch many passes but hit a lot of people who did."[53]

For their parts, Henderson, Kirby, and Smith were able to concentrate exclusively on their roles with the offense. Henderson and Kirby were valuable receivers and Smith was more than a prototypical Big Ten tight end whose blocking ability strengthened the Wolverine ground game. At 6'3" and 192 pounds, Henderson was fast, athletic, sure-handed and acrobatic, the perfect go-to receiver, a player whose natural physical abilities in football were complemented by the coordination that he developed as a champion high hurdler. At 6'5" and 230 pounds, Smith was the largest of Michigan's offensive linemen. Walking by practice one day, Fritz Crisler pointed out Smith and commented to a reporter, "Look at that boy there—a real fine specimen. And he moves pretty well on the basketball court, too."[54] Tom Hemingway put it more succinctly: when Smith combined with one of Michigan's tackles to block "a poor unsuspecting linebacker," the linebacker was in "for a miserable afternoon."[55]

In the offensive backfield, Michigan returned its starters from 1963: Bob Timberlake at quarterback; Mel Anthony at fullback; left halfback Jack Clancy; and right halfback Dick Rindfuss. Also competing for starting spots in the backfield were returnees John Rowser, Dick Wells, and Rick Sygar. But, in 1964, Michigan also had a bevy of incoming sophomores, led by four Ohioans: Jim Detwiler, Carl Ward, Rick Volk, and Dave Fisher, as well as Mike Bass, from nearby Ypsilanti, who were clear challengers for playing time.

No one was certain how Elliott and his offensive coaches would sort out the embarrassment of riches that the Wolverines enjoyed with these talented performers, but by the end of the pre-season practice, Clancy and Rowser were lost to injury, and Detwiler and Ward (slated already to be a starter, even as a sophomore) joined Timberlake and Anthony in the starting offensive backfield, giving Michigan its first-ever all–Ohio backfield.[56] In turn, Sygar, Rindfuss, and Volk became starters in the defensive secondary, with Wells (from the two-way unit) filling in for Rindfuss when Rindfuss was occasionally sidelined by injury. Bass (also on the two-way unit) became another valuable contributor to the secondary in special situations.

With the linemen, De Neff noted the presence of several returning lettermen, led by Bill Yearby, a powerful tackle who was able to play either on offense or defense. Bump Elliott, Tony Mason, and Bob Hollway were able to choose from several other returning interior linemen: Charlie Kines, Dave Butler, Rich Hahn, John Marcum, John Yanz, and Jerry Mader in particular. Then, during spring football and fall camp, other linemen were added to the mix. Tom Mack, a converted end who played exceptionally well in the spring; Arnie Simkus, a returning senior; and junior Bill Keating and sophomore Bob Mielke (from the two-way unit) joined the ranks. Tony Mason, the incoming offensive line coach, explained the simplicity of placing the linemen according to their respective skills: "If a man goes quicker forward," the coaches assigned him to the offense. "If he goes quicker laterally," the coaches assigned him to the defense."[57] Mason also asked Mack to switch from end to tackle and Mack leaped at the chance. "The coaches told me they wanted to make me an offensive tackle instead of a two-way offensive end who couldn't catch," Mack later recalled. "I was thrilled."[58]

When the starting lineups were announced in the fall, Mack, Kines, Butler, and Marcum were on the offensive front line along with Brian Patchen, a returning center. Yearby, Hahn, Yanz, Mader, Simkus, and Keating were assigned to the defensive front line. Tom Cecchini, another player with experience at center, moved full-time to the defense at one of the linebacker positions. Joining Cecchini at linebacker was Barry Dehlin, a returning letterman, and Frank Nunley, a talented incoming sophomore who started the season on the two-way unit but moved up as a starter after Dehlin suffered a season-ending knee injury in the Purdue game.

By virtually every account, the Michigan players responded enthusiastically to the prospect of two-platoon football. Tom Mack, perhaps the most instant beneficiary of the change, recalled 1963 as "the last year of complete, one-platoon football. As one of the numerous bench-warmers on the team, I had watched with some awe as players like Tom Keating, Joe O'Donnell, Rich Hahn, and Dick Rindfuss played both ways in the rugged games of that fall." Players and coaches alike witnessed the effects of the end of the Ironman system almost immediately. During the games, play on the field became more intense and the utilization of two platoons enabled the Michigan coaching staff to exploit the talents of more of its players. "The advent of two-platoon football came at the right time for Michigan.... In one year, Michigan had gone from the depths to the pinnacle of the Big Ten."[59]

Elliott also agreed with the popularity that the two-platoon system, as well as the three-team concept, enjoyed with the team. "It meant that a lot more players got to play," Elliott observed years later. In that connection the two-platoon concept introduced a new element of opportunity into the Michigan system and gave the talented incoming sophomores, especially, the chance to make their contributions much earlier in their football careers than would have taken place under the Ironman system. Elliott also observed, "We even had times in some games where we substituted the two-way unit" in its entirety because its level of proficiency was such that Michigan lost no effectiveness with that team on the field. "I don't know if other programs followed this approach but it fit our personnel very well."[60]

Even the skeptical Fritz Crisler set aside his reservations about the rule change once he saw how effectively the Wolverines adapted to the platoon system. Speaking to reporters before the Rose Bowl game in Pasadena, the Michigan athletic director observed, "In 18 years of changing rules, this is the soundest substitution rule we've had yet. It best satisfies the largest number of interests."[61]

Another aspect of the players on Michigan's roster in 1964 was that many of them were talented performers in sports other than football, and had even come to Michigan with the intention of participating in more than one sport. Keen to maintaining the morale of these players, Bump Elliott's attitude toward their participation in other sports, even though on football scholarships, reflected his years at Michigan as a three-sport performer in football, basketball, and baseball himself. The attitude of his football coach, Fritz Crisler, also helped: "[The] philosophy of Fritz Crisler [was that] you became a better athlete if you were participating in more than sport, *if* [emphasis Elliott's] you were contributing," Elliott stated. "So, if you were [on] another team in the spring, and you were contributing, you were gaining more than if you were in spring football practice. I thought that [our players] were fresher and more ready to play football [in the fall] after they had participated in a spring sport."[62]

It is often overlooked that several of the players on Michigan's 1964 football roster were standouts on other Michigan athletic teams, sometimes even with a higher level of success than they enjoyed as football players. Steve Smith and Clayton Wilhite, a reserve end on the 1964 team, were standout basketball players for the Wolverines before deciding to concentrate full-time on football. The versatile Bill Yearby also played basketball for Michigan in his freshman and sophomore years. Frosty Evashevski was a Big Ten championship–caliber golfer. Rick Sygar earned three varsity letters as a baseball player.

Several of the Wolverine gridders were also standout lettermen in track and field. Bill Yearby was a talented performer in the weight events. Dick Wells was a fine pole vaulter. John Henderson was one of the best high hurdlers in the Big Ten. John Rowser participated in the long jump. Carl Ward and Dorie Reid (one of Michigan's reserve halfbacks) were Big Ten–level sprinters.

In conclusion, a silent transformation took place in Michigan football during the first six months of 1964. Bump Elliott and the coaching staff began the implementation of two-platoon football, and the three-team approach, during spring practice and refined the concept in the preseason drills. A host of talented, but largely unheralded, newcomers, such as Detwiler, Ward, Nunley, Volk, and Fisher, were poised to make their mark on the team, along with the experienced upper classmen.

This silent transformation in Michigan's football fortunes early in 1964 went largely unnoticed by the team's observers in the media. Reporting for the *Ann Arbor News*, Wayne De Neff was one of the few sportswriters who saw a profound difference in the potential for Michigan's upcoming season. Due to the two-platoon system that Elliott and the Michigan coaches were implementing, De Neff wrote, "[T]he season ahead could be [Michigan's] most serious championship bid in years."[63]

Two

A Solid Start

MICHIGAN 24—AIR FORCE 7
MICHIGAN 21—NAVY 0

The Michigan Wolverines began the 1964 season by defeating their two non-conference opponents, Air Force and Navy. The first two games of the season were hard-nosed, fast-paced, exciting—and sloppy. On September 26, Michigan beat Air Force, 24–7, in Ann Arbor, in a game marked by numerous turnovers on both sides. While Michigan clearly held the upper hand throughout the game, the two teams battled until well into the third quarter, when Jim Detwiler rushed for a touchdown that gave the Wolverines a commanding lead of 24–7, a margin that they never relinquished.

On October 3, the second week of the season, Michigan beat 6th-ranked Navy, 21–0, once again in Ann Arbor. Roger Staubach, the 1963 Heisman Trophy winner, led the Navy attack and a crowd of more than 70,000 turned out to watch what was billed as a rematch of the 1963 Michigan–Navy game, when Staubach dazzled the crowd with his running and passing artistry. Among the spectators at the game in 1964 were former Michigan All-Americans Benny Friedman and Tom Harmon.[1]

In playing the Air Force Academy for its season opener, and Navy for its second game, Michigan was following a tradition of regularly scheduled games against the military service academies, a practice initiated by Michigan's athletic director Fritz Crisler in 1945. In fact, few universities, with Notre Dame being one exception, had more experience than Michigan when it came to playing the service academies. Between 1945 and 1963, Michigan played Army (the United States Military Academy at West Point, New York) and Navy (the United States Naval Academy at Annapolis, Maryland) twelve times. Michigan played Army nine times, with the West Point Cadets winning five of those contests. Michigan played Navy three times over that period, with the Midshipmen winning two of the games.[2]

The success that Army and Navy enjoyed against Michigan was one indication of the quality of the teams fielded by the service academies in the first two decades after World War II. Army and Navy generally ranked in the top tier of college football teams throughout the country, and several of their players, such as Army's Doc Blanchard, Glenn Davis, and Pete Dawkins, as well as Navy's Joe Bellino and Roger Staubach, were Heisman Trophy winners. Michigan certainly took its games against Army and Navy seriously, and in Bump Elliott's estimation, when the Wolverines played either Army or Navy, it was often the most important game on the non-conference schedule.[3] By the mid-1960s, however, as the effects of recruiting and the institution of two-platoon football began to take hold, the service academies began to fall from their once-lofty perches.

Michigan's performances in the first two games revealed the strengths that Bump Elliott's team continued to display throughout the 1964 season: a powerful running attack complemented by efficient passing, and a hard-hitting defensive unit that forced turnovers and played its best once the opponent threatened the Michigan goal line. On the negative side, the results of the games against Air Force and Navy also demonstrated two Michigan weaknesses: a worrisome tendency by the offensive unit to commit turnovers, and a somewhat leaky pass defense. In its first two games, Michigan fumbled four times and lost three of them. Bob Timberlake also threw two costly interceptions against Navy. In terms of the pass defense, Michigan's defenders gave up more than 400 yards through the air, although they held Air Force and Navy, combined, to less than 200 yards on the ground.[4]

Still, Michigan unmistakably showed in the first two games that it was a well-balanced and talented team. After the Air Force game, Michigan cracked the Top 10 in the national football polls with a number 8 ranking. Then, after defeating Navy, Michigan moved up one place to number 7.[5] After the Navy victory, it was clear: the 1964 Michigan team was for real.

Laying the Groundwork: Spring Practice and the Preseason

Michigan went into its spring practice in April 1964 with a healthy supply of talented players, albeit many of them untested, as well as a host of question marks as to where the coaches intended to assign their players within the two-platoon system then being devised. At least one Big Ten observer was not fooled about the level of Michigan's football talent going into the 1964 season. Woody Hayes, the Ohio State coach, remarked at the end of the 1963 season that Michigan "was the best team in the Big Ten for the last four games of the [1963] season. They beat the first-place team [Illinois], tied the second-place team [Michigan State] and just got beat by another second-place team [Ohio State, who scored a touchdown in the final moments to win, 14–10]."[6]

Bump Elliott's major concern throughout spring practice was establishing the personnel on the offensive line. But that task was accomplished easily with the move of Tom Mack to the right tackle position and the emergence of senior Dave Butler as the left guard and Charlie Kines as the left tackle, three men who, Bump Elliott observed, had never won a varsity letter. Largely overlooked until his senior season, Dave Butler exploited the opportunity that the transition to two-platoon football provided him. Given his big chance under Tony Mason, Butler took advantage of his speed and intelligence to become an exemplary blocking technician, the prototypical Michigan pulling guard. He also had the best sense of humor on the team and frequently kept his teammates in stitches with his comic routines and impersonations. As Tom Hemingway wrote, Butler "came out of the pack [in spring practice] to seize the left guard spot. He was the center of attention with his Friday night performances as Coach Rudy Bazoote or a South American dictator recruiting players as mercenaries."[7]

Elliott's other major task was the integration of the talented freshmen-soon-to-be-sophomores into the respective units. These players worked their ways into the offense and defense, and in mid–April, Elliott divided the squad into a White team and a Blue team for the final scrimmage of the spring. Unlike the 1963 spring scrimmage, a "game" that ended in a scoreless tie, the 1964 contest was an offensive display, with the White pulling out a 32–29 win. The standout of the scrimmage, interestingly enough, was freshman (soon to be sophomore) quarterback Dick Vidmer, from Jeannette, Pennsylvania. Vidmer passed for two touchdowns and ran for two others. Dave Fisher (another sophomore-to-be) ran for 86 yards on 16 carries, while Mike Bass and Mel Anthony scored two touchdowns each for the Blue team.[8]

Altogether, five players—Vidmer, Bob Timberlake, Rick Volk, Pete Hollis, and Wally Gabler—saw action at quarterback as the two teams showed a level of offensive proficiency that had been lacking in the two previous spring games. It was also important to note that several players the coaching staff counted on for major roles in the fall did not attend spring practice, either because of their commitment to other sports or because they were recovering from injuries. Frosty Evashevski, in line to be the backup quarterback, was playing with the Michigan golf team. Bill Yearby, John Henderson, Dorie Reid, John Rowser, and Dick Wells were standouts on the track team. Tom Cecchini, Rick Sygar, and John Yanz were recovering from season-ending injuries that they had experienced in 1963.[9]

```
                                            320 East Madison
                                            Apt. #9
                                            Ann Arbor, Michigan
                                            July 20, 1964

Dear Teammates,

Guess what? Approximately a month from now the fun will begin.
And believe me, if your aspirations are similar to mine, fun is
exactly what this season will be. In order to have an excep-
tional ball club, we should attempt to eliminate one of the
"ifs" that could hinder its success. The "if we don't have any
injuries" clause should be eliminated. In plain words, it's
about time to start getting in top condition. You'd be
surprised at the tan one can get by working out in the hot sun.

Most of the fellows that I have come in contact with have
already been working out for weeks. It's important that we all
report in top shape so we can get right down to business. Be
sure and make yourself tired and sore now, especially your legs.
Try pushing a car or running up and down steps. As you probably
realize from past experience, no matter how good a condition you
report in, that week of two-a-day practice is hell.

To sum this all up, I hope you all are as enthused as I am. We
should all resolve to give that "little bit extra" this year.
Those of you who ended spring practice with a different color
jersey than the one you expected will have to work even harder.
There will be plenty of opportunity to play at every position.
No one has it made, and some who think they do had better wake
up in a hurry.

If anyone has any questions or would care to drop me a line,
please do. I hope your summer vacations are passing in a
socially desirable and romantically pleasant manner. Hoping
to see you soon, I remain

                                        Sincerely yours,

                                        Jim Conley

P.S.: If running interferes with your dating, find a girl
      who likes to run and chase her.
```

Jim Conley letter to teammates, July 20, 1964. Before the beginning of fall practice, Jim Conley, Michigan's captain in 1964, sent out this letter to his teammates. Conley's letter captured the spirit of the 1964 season: conditioning, enthusiasm, and commitment (James P. Conley).

Matters turned more serious for the Michigan football team in the summer. In early August, Bump Elliott sent out invitations to 75 players, notifying them that pre-season drills would begin on Monday, August 24, at 9 a.m. Once pre-season drills were underway, the players went through morning and afternoon sessions until the beginning of classes for the autumn term.

In the first week, Elliott and the assistant coaches slotted the players into the offensive and defensive units and then finished the week with a top-speed scrimmage. Bob Timberlake was held out of the scrimmage because of an ankle injury, so Frosty Evashevski and Rick Volk split the time at quarterback.[10]

In the second week of practice, Bump Elliott and the assistant coaches began cementing the starting lineups for the season opener against Air Force on September 26. They also made a key position shift designed to strengthen the defensive line. The big news to come out of the second week was that Elliott and Bob Hollway moved Arnie Simkus over to a defensive tackle position. The coaches did not hand Simkus the position outright, however, noting that "whether this experiment will pay off has not been determined as yet." Plus, the coaches signaled that Rick Sygar was being "kept chiefly for defense," a recognition that, while Sygar was making progress in his recovery from a broken leg, his role would be restricted to one platoon.[11]

On September 22, Bump Elliott released Michigan's starting lineup for the Air Force game. On the offensive unit, Steve Smith started at left end, the tight end position; Charlie Kines at left tackle, Dave Butler at left guard, Brian Patchen at center, John Marcum at right guard, Tom Mack at right tackle, and John Henderson at right end, the split end position.

Starting in the offensive backfield were Timberlake at quarterback, Anthony at fullback, Ward at right halfback, and John Rowser at left halfback. By game day, September 26, Jim Detwiler had replaced Rowser after he was sidelined by injury. As mentioned previously, the combination of Timberlake, Anthony, Detwiler, and Ward gave Michigan its first all–Ohio backfield. Bump Elliott called it the "I-75 Backfield" since all of the players came from communities that lay along the route of this major interstate highway as it wound through Ohio.[12]

On the defensive unit, Jim Conley started at left end, Bill Yearby at left tackle, Rich Hahn at left guard, Arnie Simkus at right guard, alternating with Bill Keating, John Yanz at right tackle, and Bill Laskey at right end. Breaking back into the starting lineup was especially gratifying for John Yanz. Yanz came to Michigan as an end from De La Salle High School in Chicago. But, given his size and especially his speed, Yanz moved to the interior line and earned a varsity letter in 1962. Bulked up to 6'2" and 220 pounds, Yanz impressed the coaches to the point that they considered starting him at tackle in 1963. But Yanz suffered a knee injury, requiring surgery, and missed the entire 1963 season. With his college career in jeopardy, Yanz worked to strengthen the injured knee in the off-season and was granted another year of football eligibility. He came to fall practice, determined to make his mark, and won a starting position on the defensive line.[13]

Tom Mack's move to offensive tackle paid another dividend for Michigan, since it allowed Elliott and Hollway to place Bill Yearby permanently at a defensive tackle position where he was so dominant that most teams needed to double-team him to keep him away from their ball carriers. As Tom Hemingway described him, Bill Yearby was "quick enough to play basketball, agile, fast, [and] tremendously strong, he could have played about anywhere he wanted. He certainly wreaked enough damage from the tackle slot."[14] Yearby had been a mainstay as a two-way player in 1963 and the Wolverine coaches knew that he had the potential to be one of the outstanding linemen in the country.

Surveying the composition of both lines, Elliott knew that he was placing his confidence in some inexperienced players. Like Mack, Kines, and Butler, Simkus and Keating were non–letter winners. Bump Elliott presciently told a group of sportswriters before the Air Force game, "Three interior linemen on our offensive team and two on our defensive team did not earn a letter last year. These five men hold the key to any success that we might achieve this season."[15]

Michigan's two starting linebackers were Tom Cecchini and Barry Dehlin. Dehlin, likewise, was a proven player from 1963 who made his mark with a sterling effort in Michigan's defeat of Illinois, 14–8, Illinois' only defeat of the Big Ten season. Dehlin made nine tackles in the Illinois game and fit easily into the defensive scheme that Bob Hollway had established. Relatively unknown when he came to the university, Dehlin had been a quarterback in high school in Flushing, Michigan; but his hometown supporters urged him to concentrate on playing defense in college, which turned out to be a wise decision on his part.[16]

Playing in the secondary were Rick Volk, the left corner; Dick Wells, who was substituting for the injured Dick Rindfuss, at right corner; and Rick Sygar at safety.[17] One year after sustaining his leg injuries, Sygar had finally made it into Michigan's starting lineup, but as a defensive, not an offensive, contributor.

The members of the two-way unit, most of whom saw extensive action in the game against Air Force, were linemen Charlie Ruzicka, Bob Mielke, Jerry Mader, and Jeff Hoyne. The linebacker was Frank Nunley and the backs were quarterback Frosty Evashevski, fullback Dave Fisher, and halfbacks Louis Lee and Mike Bass. Evashevski and Fisher were offensive specialists while Lee and Bass were able to go both ways.

"We're just going to go in and knock 'em down"

The Air Force Academy Falcons were relative newcomers to the college football scene, with 1964 being only their ninth year of competition. Nevertheless, the Falcons were a worthy opponent in their first-ever contest against Michigan, and Bump Elliott took them seriously. Ben Martin, a 1945 graduate of the Naval Academy, coached the Falcons; he was an experienced football man who was an assistant coach at Navy between 1947 and 1955 and the head coach at Virginia in 1956 and 1957 before taking the Air Force position in 1958. The Falcons entered 1964 with some momentum after a solid 7–4 season in 1963, a record that earned them a trip to the Gator Bowl, where they lost to North Carolina, 35–0.

Going into the Michigan game, Air Force enjoyed at least one advantage: the Falcons had already played one game, upsetting the University of Washington, 3–2, on September 19 in Seattle. The fact that Washington was heavily favored in that game was further evidence that Michigan faced a rugged test in its home opener.

Don Dufek and Dennis Fitzgerald, two of Michigan's assistant coaches, scouted Air Force in its game against Washington and came away impressed with the Air Force defense, which stopped Washington five times, without giving up any points, when the Huskies were in scoring position. "They've got a quick, hard-hitting defensive line and they never let up," Dufek reported. "Defeating Washington two years in a row will bring them here with their morale very high."[18]

Bump Elliott also gave a gesture of respect to his opponent. "This is going to be a real tough opener for us," Elliott told the press. "Any team with a game under its belt has a real advantage—especially when they win. We'll need to improve considerably this week to face this Falcon team."[19]

But Michigan was ready to play, too, and a crowd of 66,000 gathered in Michigan Stadium to watch the opener. For Rick Volk and Stan Kemp, two Michigan sophomores, it was their first experience with running down the eastern tunnel and crossing the field over to the home bench on the western sideline. Volk and Kemp decided to remain in the rear of the squad and savor the moment as they made their playing debut for the Wolverines. As Volk later recalled:

> I remember preparing for the game. One of my roommates throughout college, Stan Kemp, who later married my twin sister, Marsha, and I thought of what we would do the first game at Michigan and we thought the neatest thing to do would be to stay in back of the line of players as we came out of the tunnel and see the fans rise across the field, [and] watch the sun shine down on the jerseys of our players. We didn't want to lead the team out, we wanted to stay in back so we could see what was happening. I remember as we ran down the tunnel that is what we were thinking about—it was just a great feeling to be part of that team at Michigan and be experiencing some of the things that I had thought about for a long time. We did win the game and I got my first interception so that was very memorable for me.[20]

Once the game began, Michigan won the coin toss and chose to take the wind. Air Force elected to receive and Bob Timberlake kicked off for Michigan, sending the ball flying out of the end zone. Air Force started Jim Greth and Fritz Greenlee at the ends, Ed Rebitz and George Hanseth at the tackles, Scott Jackson and Mike Lanagan at the guards, and Bill Nemeth at center. In the Falcon backfield were Tim Murphy, a left-handed passer, at quarterback, Paul Wargo at left halfback, Dick Czarnota at right halfback, and Steve Amdor at fullback.

On its first series, Air Force took over on its 20 and promptly began moving the ball. Two running plays by Czarnota gained 12 yards and a first down for Air Force on its 32. Then, on the third play from scrimmage, Paul Wargo carried to the Air Force 35, where Jim Conley delivered a devastating hit, forcing a fumble that Arnie Simkus recovered for the Wolverines. Michigan had its first turnover of the season.

Air Force sent its defensive unit, known as the Hunters, into the game. Starting for Air Force on its defensive unit were ends Joe O'Gorman and Wendell Harkleroad, tackles Phil Bacigalupo and John Puster, and guards Don Heckert and Gary Fausti. The linebackers were Tom Gorges and Larry Tollstam. In the secondary were Jeff Jarvis, Ken Jaggers, and Lloyd Duncan.[21]

For Michigan, the I-75 Backfield took the field for the first time as a unit. Starting on the Air Force 35, Anthony, Ward, and Timberlake carried for a first down to the Air Force 25. After Anthony carried once more for 2 yards, Timberlake passed 7 yards to John Henderson to the Air Force 16. On 3rd and 1 from the Air Force 16, Detwiler carried the ball 3 yards for a first down. Timberlake took it from there, running 12 yards down to the 1, and then sneaking the ball for a touchdown on the next play. On its first possession of 1964, Michigan had scored a touchdown. Before the game, Tony Mason was asked if the offense was going to try anything special in its attack. "No," Mason replied. "We're just going to go in and knock 'em down."[22] Mason's comment was an almost perfect description of Michigan's first scoring drive of 1964.

On Air Force's next possession, the Falcons gained a first down, starting from their own 20 up to the Air Force 31. They were well within reach of another first down but quarterback Tim Murphy fumbled on his 37, losing five yards and ending the series. Ken Jaggers, Air Force's outstanding punter, entered the game and punted down to the Michigan 28.

On Michigan's next possession, the Wolverines made a first down up to their 42, courtesy of a 15-yard personal foul (grabbing the face mask) penalty against the Falcons. But on the next series, Mel Anthony ran for 15 yards down to the Air Force 42 and fumbled, with Air Force recovering. The Falcons began their next possession with improved field position.

From his own 45, Tim Murphy methodically moved the Falcons down the field. The biggest plays of the drive were two passes to Rick Czernota that gained 29 yards. But, facing a 3rd and 2 from the Michigan 15, Paul Wargo fumbled once again and Tom Cecchini recovered for Michigan. The Wolverine defense had stopped the first scoring threat of the season.

The Michigan offense came back onto the field for its third possession of the game. On 3rd and 8 from the Michigan 15, Timberlake passed complete to John Henderson, who caught the ball at the Michigan 28, circled back to the 22, and then was hit by Lloyd Duncan of Air Force. Henderson fumbled the ball and Air Force recovered on the Michigan 15. Would Air Force finally be able to capitalize on another Michigan turnover?

Starting from the Michigan 15, Air Force attempted one running play before deciding to pass for a touchdown. Looking for his end Bill Landes in the end zone, Murphy threw into coverage and Rick Volk intercepted the pass, thwarting another scoring opportunity for Air Force. Volk's interception in the end zone resulted in a touchback, and Michigan started its next possession on its own 20.[23]

The I-75 Backfield now went to work again for Michigan. In short order, Anthony ran inside for 7 yards, but then Carl Ward, on his third carry as a Wolverine, took a pitchout from Timberlake and scampered 34 yards to the Air Force 39. After two plays gained little, Timberlake looked at a 3rd and 8 from the Air Force 37. He then passed to tight end Steve Smith for a 25-yard gain to the Air Force 12. The first quarter ended with Michigan in the lead, 7–0, but threatening to score its second touchdown of the game. The first quarter of the Michigan–Air Force game had been sloppy, but also exciting. Air Force had committed three turnovers, two fumbles and an interception, while Michigan had lost two fumbles.

The second quarter began with Michigan on the Air Force 12. Timberlake wasted no time, first giving the ball to Jim Detwiler, who powered down to the 5, and then to Mel Anthony, who ran the last five yards for Michigan's second touchdown. Timberlake successfully kicked his second extra point and Michigan led 14–0.

For Michigan's long-suffering fans, the second touchdown drive of the 1964 season must have appeared like a thing of beauty. Timberlake had taken the offense down the field for 80 yards in only 8 plays, mixing in the pass to Steve Smith with the hard-charging rushes of Anthony, Detwiler, and Ward. On that 80-yard drive, Ward gained 35 yards, Anthony 19, and Detwiler 7. Timberlake had shown off the well-balanced character of the Michigan attack for the first time.

Down 14–0 early in the second quarter, Air Force mounted an 80-yard drive of its own. Relying mostly on the pass, Tim Murphy ran off 14 plays and had Air Force with a 3rd and 9 from the Michigan 18. From that spot, Murphy passed complete to his end Paul Stephens, who carried the ball down to the Michigan 5, and then fumbled. In the scramble for the loose ball, Rick Sygar recovered for the Wolverines, giving the inspired defenders their fourth turnover of the game, and all this before halftime. Air Force had squandered three solid scoring opportunities.

Taking over on its own 1-yard line, Michigan was in a slightly precarious situation, ahead 14–0 but backed up deep in its own end. The Wolverine offense entered the game determined to move away from the shadow of its goal line. Timberlake carried for 4 yards on 1st down and Detwiler went for 3 on second down. On 3rd and 3, Anthony charged off tackle for a first down, but then a late personal foul call on Michigan penalized the team back to the Michigan 6. On 3rd and 5 from the 6, Timberlake decided to live dangerously and passed to Henderson. But the pass fell incomplete, and Stan Kemp entered the game for his first punt as a Wolverine.

Taking a high snap from center, Kemp stepped into the ball and boomed a punt 48 yards down the field. Jeff Jarvis, Air Force's punt returner, fielded the ball on his 46 and ran 10 yards down to the Michigan 44. Once again, Air Force had excellent field position and a golden opportunity to score and cut into Michigan's lead, provided that its players hung onto the ball. Purposefully, Tim Murphy once again moved the Falcons forward, relying mostly on short passes, and helped along by a pass interference call against Michigan on the 6-yard line. From that point, Air Force had a first and goal, but could gain only 3 yards on the next 3 plays. Facing 4th and goal from the Michigan 4, Air Force coach Ben Martin sent in his field goal unit. Bart Holaday, the Air Force place kicker who had scored the team's only points against Washington the previous week, lined up for the attempt. But Ben Martin crossed up the Wolverine defense by calling for a fake field goal. Tim Murphy was the holder for Air Force's field goal attempts, but on this play, he took the snap from center, rolled out, and threw to Rick Czernota in the end zone for a touchdown. After Holaday's successful extra point, Air Force trailed Michigan 14–7, with 2:03 left in the first half.[24]

With scarcely two minutes left in the first half, the expectation in Michigan Stadium was that the Wolverines would run out the clock and take a 14–7 lead into the locker room. But instead, the Michigan offense chose a course that it followed throughout the season: it kept relentless pressure on the opposing team's defense. Well rested after the long Air Force drive, the Michigan offense came back onto the field determined to score before time ran out. Jim Detwiler ran the kickoff out to the Michigan 35. Eight plays later, through a combination of running and passing, Timberlake had the Wolverines on the Air Force 18. Bump Elliott decided to settle for a field goal with almost no time left on the clock. Timberlake attempted a field goal from the Michigan

25, and missed. But Air Force was offside on the play and Michigan received another chance from its 20. Timberlake attempted another field goal, and missed. Air Force once again jumped offside and the officials moved the ball to the Air Force 15. On his third attempt, Timberlake sent the ball through the uprights and Michigan led 17–7 at the end of the first half.

Air Force decided to take the ball at the beginning of the third quarter. As he had all afternoon, Timberlake kicked into the end zone and Air Force started on its own 20. Air Force was unable to move the ball, however, and Michigan resumed its diversified attack on its second possession of the second half. Starting on its 20, Michigan went on a 15-play, clock-eating drive that resulted in a touchdown by Jim Detwiler, effectively putting the game out of Air Force's reach. The key play on the drive was Timberlake's 31-yard scramble for a first down on a 3rd and 30 play from the Michigan 45. As Tom Hemingway described the play, "With 11 Falcons and 70,000 fans looking to see how far Bob could throw the ball, Timberlake simply tucked it away and rambled for 31 yards up the middle to get Michigan a first down by a foot."[25] Six plays later, Detwiler bounced off several Air Force tacklers from the 10 yard line and scored the touchdown that gave Michigan an unsurmountable lead.[26]

In the fourth quarter, Bump Elliott emptied the bench, giving virtually every player on the roster the chance to play in the game. The game ended with Michigan on top, 24–7, for a convincing victory in its home opener. As the Wolverines trooped into their locker room, Rick Sygar jumped onto a bench and hollered out, "OK, let's all sing 'The Victors.'" A tradition had begun. Ever after, the Wolverines sang "The Victors" in the locker room when they won, never when they lost. "We used to sing in high school," Sygar remembered. "We had a lot of loud guys who did a lot of singing. I thought it'd be a good thing to do at Michigan, and got up after that first game and got them singing."[27]

"We stopped them when we had to"

After the game, both coaches spoke with the press. "Michigan presented a diversified attack. I think they can go a long way once their team jells," Air Force Coach Ben Martin said. "I think some of the breaks were against us and the turning point for us was that early fumble [in the first quarter]."

While underplaying the convincing nature of the victory over Air Force, Bump Elliott acknowledged that he was impressed with his team's performance. "[W]e're certainly glad to have this one behind us," Elliott told the reporters after the game. "We should never be satisfied but I think our boys played a pretty good first game. I think the game was in doubt until the third quarter when Bob Timberlake, on a third down pass play, ran to get the first down by a yard. I think that gave us the lift we needed."[28]

By virtually every statistical measure, Michigan controlled the game. First, Timberlake's field generalship and overall performance was remarkable. He rushed for 72 yards, completed 7 of 14 passes with no interceptions, made one of two attempted field goals (Air Force blocked his second attempt early in the third quarter), was a perfect three-for-three on extra points, and sent four of his five kickoffs into the end zone for touchbacks.

Second, Michigan's ground game was a force to behold, especially with the numbers put up by the I-75 Backfield. For the game, Michigan rushed for 311 yards, its highest total under Bump Elliott's leadership. Timberlake ran for 72 yards, Mel Anthony gained 79, Jim Detwiler 72, and Carl Ward 51. On Michigan's two 80-yard touchdown drives, the backfield demonstrated its ability to control the ball, and the clock.[29]

Third, Michigan's defense only gave up the touchdown in the second quarter and thwarted a host of Falcon scoring drives by forcing key, timely turnovers. When Air Force approached the Michigan end zone, the Wolverines prevented a score, with the exception of the Falcons's lone touchdown. After

Bob Timberlake (28) showed his passing ability in Michigan's opening game victory against Air Force, 24-7 (Bentley Historical Library, University of Michigan).

the game, Elliott lamented the fact that Michigan had given up 240 yards in the air, most of the yardage coming in the first half. But reading Elliott's comments, one receives the impression that he was searching for one aspect of the team's performance that he could criticize, at least mildly. "We need a lot of work on pass defense," Elliott told the reporters. "But even with inexperience, we were able to stop them when we had to and I think that our pass defense improved in the second half."[30] Throughout the season, Elliott's remark became a distinguishing feature of the Michigan defense: "We stopped them when we had to."

Fourth, Stan Kemp left little doubt in anyone's mind that he had locked up the punting job. Kemp punted three times for an average of 43 yards, and the special teams gave up only 28 yards on Kemp's three punts and 32 yards on Timberlake's five kickoffs. If Elliott was searching for any negatives, about the only ones that he would find from the game against Air Force were Michigan's three 15-yard penalties, two for personal fouls and one for holding. Presumably those penalties received the attention of the players and coaches in the next week's preparation.

The Lingering Memory of the 1963 Michigan–Navy Game

Michigan's impressive victory over Air Force and the expectation about the upcoming game against Navy created a renewed sense of excitement for Wolverine football in Ann Arbor. At the weekly meeting with the University of Michigan Club at the North Commons Union, Bump Elliott and Jocko Nelson spoke to more than 160 club members, showing film from the Air Force game and generally answering questions. It was the largest-ever gathering of the Club for that purpose.[31] Michigan's solid performance against Air Force raised hopes among the Wolverine faithful that the Wolverines would make a strong showing in 1964 against Navy quarterback Roger Staubach, their nemesis from 1963, and a front-runner for another Heisman Trophy.

In 1963, Navy had one of the most successful teams in its history. Coached by Wayne Hardin, whose teams had defeated arch-rival Army five consecutive times since 1958, Navy went 9–1 during the 1963 regular season and were ranked second in the country before losing to Texas, 28–6, in the 1964 Cotton Bowl.[32] The cause of Michigan's heightened expectations in 1964, however, was Staubach's performance against the Wolverines on October 5, 1963, in Ann Arbor. Staubach's performance in that game was the stuff of legend, where the eventual Heisman Trophy winner ran for 70 yards and completed 14 of 16 passes, to eight different receivers, for 237 yards.[33] The play of the game for Staubach and the Midshipmen was a 50-yard completion to halfback Johnny

Sai on the last play of the first half. On that play, Staubach stood tall in the pocket, escaped a strong rush by Michigan's defensive line, and connected with Sai on a deep pattern for a touchdown that gave Navy a 20–0 lead. "Roger was as fantastic as usual today," Navy Coach Wayne Hardin told reporters after the game, conceding that "half the time [he doesn't] know what Staubach will do next."[34]

While the football media tended to view the Navy victory in 1963 as an embarrassment bordering on humiliation for Michigan, the fact remained that the Wolverines actually outscored the Midshipmen, 13–6, in the second half of the game. More disappointing for Michigan was the blizzard of injuries that the Wolverines suffered, injuries that had a greater impact on their fortunes in the Big Ten season than any temporary embarrassment that Staubach's performance may have caused. As Jerry Green, the respected sportswriter for the *Detroit News*, put it: "Navy's forward wall dished out a severe physical beating to the Wolverines a week before their traditional game with Michigan State."[35]

In the Navy game, eleven Wolverines went to the sidelines with injuries: Joe O'Donnell, Bill Keating, Rich Hahn, Jack Clancy, Dick Wells, Dick Rindfuss, Barry Dehlin, Bill Laskey, Bill Yearby, Bob Timberlake, and Frosty Evashevski.[36] O'Donnell and Yearby both suffered head injuries midway through the second half and were out of the game for good. "They never got back [in the game]," Bump Elliott explained afterward. "We'd never play a boy with any kind of head injury."[37]

After the game, Michigan was "shell shocked," according to Hal Schram, the sportswriter for the *Detroit Free Press*.[38] Mike Block, associate sports editor for the *Michigan Daily*, also noted the numerous head injuries inflicted on the Michigan players by the vicious contact in the game. "The Wolverines' casualty list was an extremely lengthy one," Block wrote. "For the most part, it amounted to a player getting hit in the head and being dazed enough to miss the rest of the game. This was the case for O'Donnell, Evashevski, fullback Dehlin, and starting tackle Bill Yearby, who had to be helped from the field apparently badly hurt, but who recovered shortly thereafter."[39]

Navy's Early Season Fortunes

Navy began its 1964 season by defeating Penn State, 21–8, on the road at Happy Valley, on September 19, and then William and Mary, 35–6, in its home opener in Annapolis on September 26. Against Penn State, the Midshipmen moved out to a 14–0 lead by the third quarter and never trailed in the game. Navy's first touchdown came on a one-yard sneak by Roger Staubach, after Navy recovered a Nittany Lion fumble on the Penn State 12-yard line.

The second touchdown came on a 57-yard pass interception for a touchdown by defensive back Duncan Ingrahan. Penn State closed the gap to 14–8 with a touchdown and a two-point conversion, but Navy responded with another touchdown in the fourth quarter to cement its victory.

But Navy's victory over Penn State came at a twofold price. First, the Penn State defense managed to contain Roger Staubach all afternoon and prevented him from inflicting the running and passing damage feared by the opposition. Penn State's defensive line rushed Staubach fiercely, sacking him on several occasions and forcing him to hurry his passes to his receivers. For their part, Staubach's receivers dropped a number of his passes, thereby hampering the establishment of any kind of sustained offensive attack. For the game, Navy finished with only 155 yards of total offense and Staubach completed only 5 of his 13 passes. It was the Navy defense, not the offense, that played the critical part in its victory.[40]

Second, and more important for the longer term, Staubach injured his left ankle in the second quarter and briefly left the field for some medical attention. He returned to play the remainder of the contest, but he was clearly restricted in his movements. The injury occurred on a play in which Staubach had scrambled from the pocket, and in searching for a receiver, was hit by a Penn State defender. On the play, Staubach, the Penn State defender, and Bruce Kenton, Navy's center, collided and fell to the ground. Staubach sprained his ankle and also strained his Achilles tendon. Immediately, Navy's season and Staubach's college career were in jeopardy. As Carlton Stowers, Staubach's biographer, wrote: "And from that moment, the high expectations for his final season as a collegian turned into a frustrating week-to-week struggle just to play."[41]

The following Saturday, September 26, Navy played the College of William and Mary in the home opener in Annapolis. Staubach started the game on the sidelines. In a far closer contest than anyone expected, Navy carried only a 14–0 lead into the fourth quarter. Then, Tom Feola, a defensive back for William and Mary, intercepted a pass thrown by Navy quarterback Bruce Bickel and returned it 15 yards for a touchdown to cut the Navy lead to 14–6. Shortly afterward, Bickel was hit and suffered a broken nose. He was out of the game.

With his ankle heavily taped and withheld from practice for the previous week, Roger Staubach entered the game. "Virtually immobile," in the words of Carlton Stowers, Staubach nevertheless went to work. On his first play from scrimmage, Staubach handed off to his fleet running back, Skip Paskewich, who ran 71 yards for a touchdown. On the next series, Navy recovered a William and Mary fumble on the visitors' 12-yard line. Staubach then threw three consecutive completions, the final one to John Michelosen for a 7-yard touchdown. Staubach had participated in four plays and produced two touchdowns. With the game safely in hand, Staubach left the contest, and Navy scored another touchdown to make the final score 35–6.[42]

In the game against William and Mary, Staubach's ailing ankle seriously restricted his mobility—and the threat that he presented to opposing defenses. With Michigan next on the schedule, Navy's trainers and team doctors "worked feverishly to make Staubach ready to play."[43] But for two weeks, the national media had openly discussed Staubach's injury, and the Michigan defense knew that the Navy quarterback, potentially at least, posed less of an offensive threat in 1964 than in 1963.

"Keep Staubach in front of you"

Prior to the Navy game, the Michigan coaches made only one position change from the week before. On offense, Bump Elliott and Jocko Nelson inserted Craig Kirby into the split end position to alternate with John Henderson, the only change from the game against Air Force. Craig Kirby had taken an interesting route to front-line playing status at Michigan. He was a fine performer at Royal Oak Kimball High School, outside of Detroit, but never achieved the all-state recognition that normally applied to Michigan recruits. He strongly considered attending a smaller college or university until Ron Kramer, Michigan's All-American tight end from the 1950s, approached him. "Rather than being a starter on a small college football team, give Michigan a try," Kramer advised him. "Ron told me that if Michigan offered me a scholarship, I should accept it because it meant that the Michigan coaches felt that I could play Big Ten football. When they approached me, I accepted."[44]

Before Kirby began his studies at Michigan, Kramer, then with the Green Bay Packers in the National Football League, worked with him to strengthen his skills as an end. In 1963, Kirby played mostly at tight end but moved over to split end in 1964. "Ron gave me a lot of help in down-field blocking and pass receiving," Kirby noted, explaining that Kramer tutored him in the summers once he made his decision to attend Michigan. In the season opener against Air Force, Kirby came off the bench to catch 2 passes for 22 yards, and Jocko Nelson gave him the starting nod for the Navy game.[45]

Compiled by Don Dufek, Michigan's scouting estimate of Navy held that the Middies, even with Staubach as an offensive threat, were weaker on offense in 1964 by comparison with 1963. But the Navy defense was stronger. Regardless, the Michigan coaches could not afford not to prepare assiduously for stopping Staubach. Bump Elliott naturally wanted to avoid a repeat of 1963, when Staubach repeatedly scrambled out of the pocket to find open receivers or run the ball himself. "In 1963, [Staubach] beat us with his running," Elliott recalled. "Keep Staubach in front of you," Elliott, Bob Hollway, Jocko Nelson, and Don Dufek told the defense. Throughout the week, "'Keep him in front of you' was the theme song, so to speak, and we practiced it that way," Elliott said. "That's what we did. But we were a better team [in 1964 than in 1963]."[46]

It was an intense week of practice, therefore, for Michigan's "Red Shirts," the players on the demonstration team that included Wally Gabler, Tom Parkhill, Bruce Allison, Michael Gorte, ("the unofficial captain of the Red Shirts"), Gary Schick, Tom Briggstock, and others, whose job it was to simulate the Navy attack. For the week, Wally Gabler became Roger Staubach. Elliott also devised a daily drill where he had the entire defense run 100 yards in reverse, while containing a scrambling back. Bob Hollway and Elliott outlined a plan whereby Michigan was able to utilize two schemes: its standard 6–2–2–1 alignment, or a 5–3–2–1 alignment to provide an additional pass defender. The key, Elliott recognized, was to keep enough pressure on Staubach to disrupt Navy's passing attack while not allowing him to escape the pocket and scramble. As the game approached, Elliott was apprehensive. "You prepare the best you can, go over all the fine points, you run the game films of last year's game a hundred times, run the film of a Navy game this year a couple of hundred times," he told Clank Stoppels of the *Grand Rapids Press*. "You know in your mind there's nothing more to take care of—and yet...."[47]

"Not a revenge game but still a game we wanted to win"

With 70,000 in attendance at Michigan Stadium, Michigan and Navy took the field on an almost perfect football afternoon on October 3, 1964. Navy won the coin toss and elected to receive. Starting for the Midshipmen on offense were Neil Henderson at split end, Doug McCarty at tight end, Pat Philbin and Jim Freeman at the tackles, John Connelly and Fred Marlin at the guards, and Bruce Kenton at center. In the backfield for Navy were Roger Staubach at quarterback, Pat Donnelly at fullback, Tom Leiser at left halfback, and Ed ("Skip") Orr at right halfback. The Michigan defense for Navy was identical to the unit that started against Air Force.

Navy's Pat Donnelly, considered by his coach as the best fullback in the country, took Bob Timberlake's kickoff on his own 15 and returned the ball to the Navy 32. Staubach came onto the field for Navy's first series. To prepare him for Michigan, Navy's trainers had outfitted Staubach's ankle with a special brace, resorted to a new taping design, and injected the ankle with painkillers.[48] Passing on first down, and immediately rushed hard by John Yanz and Bill Yearby, Staubach threw incomplete to Skip Orr. Pat Donnelly then carried for a first down to the Navy 44. After two running plays lost 2 yards, Staubach went back to the air. Looking for Neil Henderson, his primary receiver, Staubach faced another fierce rush by the Wolverine front line. He missed Henderson at mid-field, and Tom Cecchini intercepted for Michigan, returning the ball to the Navy 37. Michigan had its first turnover and the Wolverines had a golden opportunity to take the lead.[49]

Michigan's offense took the field, led by Bob Timberlake and the other members of the I-75 Backfield. Navy had not adopted the platoon system, and played essentially an alternating number of players in a two-way unit. The exceptions were Staubach and Orr, who were replaced by defensive safety Steve Szabo and halfback Duncan Ingrahan.[50] As the game progressed, the effectiveness of Michigan's platoons, and Navy's lack of depth, quickly became evident.

Mel Anthony carried first for Michigan, gaining 3 yards off right guard. Then it was Detwiler's turn, and the big Ohioan rambled 21 yards around right end to the Navy 13. After a carry by Carl Ward and a 5-yard offside penalty, Timberlake faced a 3rd and 8 from the Navy 11. Looking to pass, Timberlake threw to Craig Kirby at the goal line, but Navy linebacker Bruce Kenton intercepted his pass at the 5-yard line. Kenton returned the interception to the Navy 16 and Navy had thwarted Michigan's first drive.[51]

On their next possessions, neither Navy nor Michigan could move the ball and wound up punting back to each other. Nevertheless, it was clear to all those watching that the 1964 Michigan–Navy game was not going to be a repeat of 1963. The Michigan defense was containing Roger Staubach, frustrating the Navy ball carriers, and drilling its pass receivers.

Regardless, Navy took the ball on its 4-yard line after Stan Kemp's first punt. Navy then mounted its first serious drive of the afternoon. The key play of the drive occurred on a 2nd and 12 play from the Navy 2, when Staubach scrambled from his end zone and ran 25 yards for a first down to the Navy 27. Unknown at the time, of course, was that Staubach's dash to the Navy 27 turned out to be his only escape from the clutches of the Wolverine defenders, as well as Navy's longest play from scrimmage, for the entire afternoon.[52]

But mixing his passing and running plays, Staubach moved the Midshipmen down to the Michigan 39. Facing 3rd and 5, Staubach threw to Jim Ryan, one of his ends, but Ryan fumbled the football on contact, and Rich Hahn recovered for Michigan on their 35.[53] The crowd erupted in a prolonged cheer after Michigan's second turnover of the game. The Wolverine defense was gaining confidence with each Navy possession.

With time starting to run down in the first quarter, the Michigan offense went to work. Facing 3rd and 5 from the Michigan 40, Timberlake passed to Craig Kirby for 11 yards and a first down just across midfield. Then Carl Ward carried the ball for 30 yards on 2 carries to the Navy 17 as the first quarter came to an end.[54]

Beginning the second quarter, Detwiler carried twice and Anthony once. Michigan had the ball on the Navy 2-yard line, poised to score the first touchdown of the game. On 3rd and goal, Ward blasted off left tackle into the end zone. Michigan led 6–0, but Frosty Evashevski fumbled the snap on the extra point attempt and Michigan failed to convert.[55]

On the ensuing kickoff, Bob Timberlake sent the ball out of the end zone, negating a Navy return. Navy took over on its 20-yard line, needing a score to keep pace with the Wolverines. Once again, Roger Staubach methodically moved the Midshipmen down the field, mixing in passes to Skip Orr, Skip Paskewich, and Doug McCarty with runs by Pat Donnelly. On 2nd and 6 from the Michigan 38, Staubach threw incomplete to Orr, but Michigan was called for pass interference and Navy received a first down at the Michigan 19. After Donnelly carried for 2 yards to the Michigan 17, Staubach passed to Neil Henderson at the Michigan 11. Henderson caught the pass and was immediately hit by Rick Sygar, whose jolting tackle sent the football "flying halfway across the field," in the words of Michigan broadcaster Tom Hemingway.[56] Tom Cecchini recovered Henderson's fumble for Michigan, another Navy drive thwarted.

Starting at its own 6-yard line, the I-75 Backfield began moving the ball. After one first down, and facing 3rd and 4 from the Michigan 34, Timberlake handed off to Detwiler, who gained three yards to the 37. Michigan faced 4th and 1 from its own 37, logically a punting situation so early in the game and with the Wolverines holding onto a slim 6–0 lead. But Bump Elliott, showing great confidence both in his offense and his defense, decided to go for the first down. On 4th and 1 from the Michigan 37, Timberlake gave the ball to Carl Ward, and the Navy defenders threw him for a 1-yard loss! Behind 6–0 midway through the second quarter, Navy had the ball on the Michigan 36.[57] On the first down the Middies gained four yards. Then, on 2nd and 6, Staubach went back to pass and released the ball, only to have it batted up into the air, and an alert Bill Yearby, who had been pummeling Navy's offensive line all afternoon, snatched the ball out of the air for Michigan's second interception.

At this point in the game, Michigan's long-suffering fans must have wondered how long the Wolverine defense could keep rising to the occasion when the offense left the opposition in such enviable field position. But, even by this early point in the 1964 season, it was obvious to everyone—players, coaches, fans, and the media—that the Michigan defense was the bedrock element of the team. Bob Hollway, Jocko Nelson, and Don Dufek had assembled a defensive unit that yielded yardage grudgingly. Scoring against Michigan was a difficult task.

Michigan took over on its 30. Once again, Timberlake found holes in the Navy defense. Mixing in runs by Anthony, Detwiler, and Ward, with passes to Kirby and Detwiler, Timberlake drove Michigan down to the Navy 21. But in this game, turnovers were contagious, and on 3rd and 7 from the Navy 21, Mel Anthony fumbled Timberlake's pitchout, and Navy's defensive tackle James Taylor recovered for the Midshipmen.[58] The Navy defense knew how to force turnovers, too.

On Navy's subsequent possession, the Michigan defense overwhelmed the Middies. After an incomplete pass on first down, John Yanz pursued a scrambling Roger Staubach and sacked him for a 12-yard loss down to the Navy 5. Trying to play it safe, on 3rd down Staubach handed off to Pat Donnelly on a draw play, hoping to gain enough space to give Navy's punter, end Tom Williams, a decent chance to punt the ball away on fourth down. But Donnelly fumbled on the Navy 10-yard line, and in the ensuing scramble, the loose ball was recovered by—who else?—Tom Cecchini.[59] With enough time remaining in the second quarter, Michigan had its most golden of scoring opportunities and the chance to grab the upper hand, firmly, against the 6th-ranked Midshipmen. Could the Michigan offense take advantage of this latest gift from Navy?

The answer was no. Once again, the Navy defense stiffened. On first and second downs, Detwiler and Anthony carried the ball to the Navy 6. On 3rd down, Timberlake retreated to pass, looking for Craig Kirby near the goal line. But for the second time in the game, Bruce Kenton intercepted Timberlake, this time in the end zone, giving Navy a touchback out to its 20.[60] In football vernacular, the Midshipmen had dodged another bullet and the Wolverines had squandered at least three priceless scoring opportunities. After Kenton's interception, Navy ran out the clock and the first half ended, Michigan 6, Navy 0.

At halftime, three salient facts stood out to those who were watching the first thirty minutes of the Michigan–Navy contest. First, both teams had stout, opportunistic defenses that elevated their level of play once the opponent came within scoring distance. Navy had lost three fumbles and two interceptions. Rick Sygar's hard tackle on Neil Henderson at the Michigan 11 ended one Navy drive and Bill Yearby's interception ended another. Michigan's offense was no better, or worse, depending on one's perspective, when it came to exploiting the opponent's mistakes. Bruce Kenton had prevented two Michigan touchdowns with interceptions around the goal line. James Taylor recovered Mel Anthony's fumble at the Navy 17, ending another scoring chance.

Second, Michigan gained 156 yards rushing on 29 carries in the first half. Navy managed only 70 yards on 19 carries, and 25 of those yards had come on Staubach's scramble in the first quarter. Michigan was averaging more than 5 yards per carry; Navy was averaging fewer than 3 yards per carry.⁶¹ The lesson was clear: Michigan possessed the offensive power to control the football and score points, provided that the Wolverines managed to hang onto the football.

By contrast, Navy's prospects were much less hopeful. For the second week in a row, the Michigan defense had shut down its opponent's rushing attack, forcing it to resort to a much more risky passing offense. In addition, Navy clearly lacked the depth, on both sides of the ball, that the Wolverines enjoyed with their two platoons. How much longer would the players on Navy's two-way unit be able to contend with Conley, Yearby, Yanz, Cecchini, and Sygar on defense and Tom Mack, Dave Butler, and the pounders in Michigan's I-75 Backfield on offense?

Third, it was obvious that Roger Staubach was undeniably not the passing and running threat in 1964 that he was in 1963. Staubach's first half performance had been solid; he was 10 for 16 passing for 109 yards, but the two interceptions ended Navy scoring drives. More important, with his injured ankle, he was unable to run, and the Wolverine defense took proper account of that fact as it made its halftime adjustments. Still, for Navy, there was all to play for. Despite being outplayed by the Wolverines in the first half, Navy remained very much in the game. Could Staubach work his magic against Michigan one more time?

Navy kicked off to Michigan to start the second half. Rick Volk returned the kickoff 27 yards from his own 17 out to the Michigan 44. With good field position, the I-75 Backfield started Michigan's first offensive series of the third quarter. The series did not last long as Carl Ward fumbled on second down and Navy's Patrick Philbin recovered the football on the Michigan 44. How long did Michigan expect to live this dangerously before the Midshipmen finally took advantage?

Behind 6–0, Roger Staubach led Navy out for its first possession of the second half. As in the second quarter, Staubach moved Navy forward, mixing runs by Pat Donnelly and Skip Paskewich with passes to Skip Orr and Doug McCarty. Navy had a first down at the Michigan 17 when the Middies took a costly 5-yard penalty for offside, moving the ball back to the Michigan 22. From that point, the Michigan defense came charging at Navy. Arnie Simkus and John Yanz sacked Staubach for a 9-yard loss on second down. On 3rd and 22, Rich Hahn and Bill Yearby threw Paskewich for a 2-yard loss. Navy now faced a 4th and 24 from the Michigan 31 and Tom Williams came in to punt the ball into the Michigan end zone. The Michigan defense had thwarted yet another Navy threat from deep in Wolverine territory.

Michigan went back on offense from its 20, and then got serious. Facing 3rd and 6 from his 24, Bob Timberlake rolled to his right to pass, stopped, reversed his field and took off down the field. Helped by a crushing downfield block by Craig Kirby, Timberlake ran 27 yards to the Navy 49. Ron Kramer's tutelage had paid off big for Craig Kirby and Michigan. After the game, Kirby explained to reporters that his downfield block, springing Timberlake for his long gainer, gave him more satisfaction than his four pass receptions in the game.[62]

Keeping the drive moving, Timberlake moved the Wolverines into Navy territory. Facing 3rd and 9 from the Navy 36, Timberlake hit Ben Farabee, his tight end, and Farabee set off for the end zone. Two Navy defenders finally tackled Farabee at the 4 yard line. On the next play, Carl Ward drove off left tackle for the touchdown. Bump Elliott chose to go for the two-point conversion, which Timberlake executed with another pass to Farabee. With 8:28 gone in the third quarter, Michigan led 14–0.[63]

Down by two touchdowns, Navy now faced an uphill struggle to get back in the game. But the Middies again came up empty in their next two possessions as Yearby, Hahn, Yanz, and the rest of the Michigan defense repeatedly hit Roger Staubach. By this point, the painkillers in Staubach's ankle were starting to lose their effect, and the Navy quarterback was limping noticeably as he ran on and off the field.[64] The third quarter ended with Michigan holding a 14–0 lead, and Navy pondering the mystery of its game-long futility.

Michigan began the fourth quarter on offense from its own 20. At this point, the I-75 Backfield produced another of its patented 80-yard drives, the second one of the second half. The Wolverines went 80 yards in only 8 plays for their third touchdown of the game. With the exception of one completion to Craig Kirby for 15 yards, Timberlake, Anthony, Detwiler, and Ward gained the rest of the yardage on the ground. On the drive, Anthony carried three times, Ward twice, Detwiler once, and Timberlake once as the Michigan offense pounded away at the weary, beleaguered Navy defenders. Dave Fisher, backing up Mel Anthony, ran 4 yards for Michigan's third and final touchdown. From Dayton, Ohio, Fisher felt right at home in the I-75 Backfield. Timberlake kicked the extra point, and with 11:30 remaining in the game, Michigan had built an insurmountable lead, 21–0.[65]

The rest of the game was anticlimactic. Michigan substituted freely throughout the fourth quarter as both Frosty Evashevski and Wally Gabler took turns running the offense. Mike Bass, Louis Lee, and Dave Fisher were Michigan's running backs. Roger Staubach's misfortunes continued. On Navy's next series after Fisher's touchdown, Staubach was sacked for an 8-yard loss by Charlie Ruzicka and left the game. He returned for a couple of plays in the next series, threw an incompletion, failed to get a first down, and exited the game for good.

On the Michigan sideline, the thoughts of some of the players went back to the 1963 game. After that game, Wayne Hardin, the Navy coach, went into the Michigan locker room and diagrammed some of the offensive plays that Staubach used in the game, apparently to show the Wolverines how they might have defended them. Not surprisingly, Hardin's presence in the Michigan locker room in 1963 offended a good number of the Wolverines. Now, in 1964, with the defense pitching a shutout against the Middies, the players started approaching the Michigan coaches, suggesting that they go into the Navy locker room after the game and "diagram [Hardin] a few defenses."[66]

The game ended with the final score Michigan 21, Navy 0, "as a thunderous ovation rocketed through Michigan Stadium."[67] The Michigan defense had recorded its first shutout of 1964. For Jim Conley and the Michigan seniors, the victory over Navy was especially satisfying, coming the year after the painful experience of 1963. Even so, Conley did not dwell on the supposed "revenge factor" of the game. "It *was not* a revenge game," Conley asserted. "But it *was* [emphasis Conley's] still a game we wanted to win."[68]

"Those boys came ready to play and they showed it"

After the game, the opposing coaches met with reporters. Wayne Hardin addressed Navy's performance as well as Roger Staubach's condition. "Michigan had no surprises for us," Hardin said. "But they were a vastly improved team over last year."[69] He also admitted that Staubach played injured and was "not able to run. Staubach isn't well at all.... But we played him, hoping he could drop back and throw."[70]

Nevertheless, the Michigan game was costly for Navy. The numerous tackles delivered by the Michigan defense on Staubach aggravated his ankle injury to such an extent that Staubach was hospitalized when he returned to Annapolis. His leg was put in a cast, immobilized for the next 10 days. Before leaving Ann Arbor, Hardin declared that Staubach would not play against Georgia Tech, the next game on Navy's schedule.[71]

On the Michigan side, Bump Elliott expressed satisfaction with the Wolverines' performance. Despite the five turnovers, certainly a worry for any head coach, Michigan still racked up almost 400 yards in total offense against Navy, 272 yards on the ground in 59 carries, and 121 yards passing. In this important game, the I-75 Backfield excelled for the second week in a row. Detwiler led the way with 77 yards on 11 carries, followed by Ward with 71 yards on 18 carries. Timberlake ran for 51 yards on 6 carries. Anthony ran for 38 yards on 10 carries. "Staubach isn't much of a problem if we've got the ball," Elliott observed. The Michigan players awarded game balls to Mel Anthony and Brian Patchen. Anthony expressed some surprise as to the reason for his selection, "[but I] accepted it as graciously as the victory."[72]

Timberlake completed 7 of 11 passes for 106 yards. Craig Kirby led the receivers with 4 catches. Stan Kemp also had another fine day, with 3 punts for a 41-yard average. The special teams surrendered no points and Timberlake sent two more of his kickoffs into the end zone. Even Clayton Wilhite, an end on the two-way unit, kicking off to Navy in the fourth quarter after Dave Fisher's touchdown, sent the football into the end zone, negating a return by the Midshipmen.[73]

In his post-game remarks, Bump Elliott emphasized that Michigan's performance on defense was the difference in the game. "Our defense is coming along fine," Elliott told the reporters.[74] He may also have added, paraphrasing the defense's performance against Air Force, that it stopped Navy when it had to, despite the Middies' numerous penetrations of Michigan territory. The Michigan defense's opportunism, its ability to force turnovers and otherwise stop drives by the opponent, was emerging as a distinguishing characteristic.

Then, Elliott added a comment that he had not mentioned previously: that another noticeable feature of the Michigan defense was its capacity to hit hard. Michigan had no intention of allowing the Midshipmen to administer a physical beating on the Wolverines for a second consecutive year. "Navy had a fine football team," Elliott said. "But those early fumbles hurt them [and] I feel sure [that] our hard tackling caused those fumbles.... I was especially pleased with the kind of hitting we did out there. We learned a lot about our limitations in the first game and our key to victory today was our improvement on defense. Those boys came ready to play and they showed it."[75]

After defeating Air Force and Navy, Michigan entered the Big Ten season with a record of 2–0, and holding their place as a Top 10 team in the national polls. Michigan State, the next opponent, a team Michigan had not beaten since 1955, was a key rival and one of the most important games of the early Big Ten season. Furthermore, Michigan was to play the Spartans in East Lansing, where the Wolverines had not won since 1948.

Burt Smith, Michigan State's freshman coach, scouted the Michigan–Navy game for the Spartans in anticipation of the following week's showdown in East Lansing. "Michigan is a fine football team and those aren't just words," Smith told reporters after the game. "They have fine speed, good line play, and Timberlake seems to have really found himself.... Believe me, they're going to be tough for any team to handle this year."[76]

Then, after playing Michigan State on October 10, Michigan was scheduled to return to Ann Arbor and play the Purdue Boilermakers on October 17. For the Wolverines, the Boilermakers were every bit as difficult an opponent as the Spartans. Michigan had lost two of its past three games against Purdue, and the Boilermakers enjoyed a well-earned reputation within the Big Ten as a hard-nosed, fundamentally sound, and opportunistic team.

Jim Detwiler (48), carrying the ball against Navy, was a key part of Michigan's ground attack in its victories against Air Force and Navy (Bentley Historical Library, University of Michigan).

For the moment, however, the Wolverines enjoyed the afterglow of defeating Roger Staubach and Navy. The victory over Navy, and the fact that Michigan pitched a shutout against the vaunted Middie offense, provided a much-needed boost in morale as the Wolverines entered the Big Ten season. In retrospect, the Navy win was a signature victory, the first real prize of the 1964 season. It also provided a healthy measure of confidence-building for Michigan, who now knew it was a solid team, a much improved version of recent Wolverine squads. It was their first triumph over a Top 10–ranked team, and a clear indication that Michigan was well on the way to challenging for a Big Ten championship and a trip to the Rose Bowl.

Three

One Step Forward, One Step Back

MICHIGAN 17—MICHIGAN STATE 10
PURDUE 21—MICHIGAN 20

Following its impressive victory over Navy on October 3, Michigan began the Big Ten season with games against its arch-rival Michigan State on October 10 in East Lansing, followed by its encounter the following week, on October 17, against Purdue in Ann Arbor. Both games promised to be hard-hitting contests in the tradition of 1960s-era Big Ten football, and the Wolverines realized that victories in both games would give them an inside track to the conference championship and a trip to the Rose Bowl. Michigan State and Purdue were potential rivals for the Big Ten crown, and Michigan's convincing victory over Navy, with its near-total domination of the Midshipmen, gave the Wolverines a tailwind of confidence as they faced the conference season.

"After the Navy game, we knew we were a pretty good team," Bump Elliott later observed, and in fact, the national polls reflected Michigan's impressive beginning to the season.[1] Michigan advanced to the number-7 position in the national polls after the Navy game, and the Wolverines had ample reason to believe that they were heading for a memorable season.

Michigan's rivalry against Michigan State, however, had been one-sided in favor of the Spartans throughout the 1950s and early 1960s. Since 1953, Michigan State's record against Michigan was 7–2–2 (the ties occurring in 1958 and 1963), and the football consciousness within the state of Michigan, and throughout the Big Ten, reflected the belief that the Spartans were the superior program. In fact, going into the 1964 contest, Michigan's last victory over Michigan State had occurred in 1955, and the Wolverines had not won in East Lansing since 1948.[2]

In 1953, the Michigan–Michigan State rivalry added a new dimension when Michigan's Governor G. Mennen Williams "put into circulation" the Paul Bunyan Trophy, given to the annual winner of the game.[3] The trophy was a "four-foot wooden statue of Paul Bunyan astride an axe with feet planted on a map of Michigan. Two flags—one with the Michigan 'M' and the other with the Michigan State 'S'—are planted on either side of Bunyan."[4] With the introduction of the Paul Bunyan Trophy, the Michigan–Michigan State game entered the realm of trophy games and with only two exceptions, the trophy remained in possession of the Spartans for most of its early history. Now, in addition to bragging rights, the winner of the Michigan–Michigan State game had a trophy to show off.

By the early 1960s, moreover, the game between the Wolverines and the Spartans had become essential from the standpoint of recruiting. With Bump Elliott and Duffy Daugherty, Michigan State's veteran coach, and their coaching staffs engaged in a vigorous, never-ending competition for the best high school football talent in the state, the outcome of the annual rivalry game played a key role in convincing prospective recruits of the superiority of one football program over the other.[5]

Entering the 1964 game against Michigan State, the Wolverines had more reason for optimism than at any time in recent history, despite the old saw that when the two teams played, you could throw out their current records as a predictor of the game's outcome. The source of at least some of that optimism was Michigan's 7–7 tie with the Spartans in 1963 in Ann Arbor. That year, coming off the previous week's disheartening loss to Roger Staubach–led Navy, the Wolverines battled the heavily favored Spartans to a 7–7 draw in Michigan Stadium on October 12. Michigan scored first in the game on a 15-yard pass from quarterback Bob Chandler to John Henderson in the first quarter to give the Wolverines a 7–0 lead, their first lead over the Spartans in three years. Michigan State did not score until the third quarter, when State's quarterback Steve Juday hit fleet halfback Sherman Lewis on a 7-yard scoring pass.

After Michigan State's touchdown, the game became downright hairy. Michigan State had a prime scoring opportunity in the fourth quarter, but Lou Bobich missed a field goal attempt from the Michigan 15. Then, on its final possession, Michigan reached the Michigan State 27, but Bob Timberlake missed a field goal with 55 seconds left. On State's next possession, a fight broke out on the field between Michigan State's fullback Roger Lopes and Michigan's Mel Anthony, playing linebacker at that time in the game. Both players took swings at each other and were ejected from the game, although Lopes clearly appeared to be the instigator of the fracas. Unfortunately for the Spartans, the officials did not stop the clock as Lopes and Anthony went to the sidelines. The altercation between the two players began with 45 seconds left on the game clock, and the clock continued to run even though play was stopped on the field. Duffy Daugherty hollered at the officials from the Michigan State sideline to stop the clock, but the clock ran until only 10 seconds remained in the game, insufficient time to make a scoring play.[6]

Michigan State's hard feelings about the game's final minute carried over into the post-game press conferences. Although Duffy Daugherty chose not to pursue the matter in his comments to reporters, Michigan State's Athletic Director Clarence "Biggie" Munn was not so charitable. "Did you see that?" Munn thundered to the reporters after the game. "They [the officials] let the clock run for 35 seconds after the penalty was called on the players for fighting. They didn't stop it until there were ten seconds left."[7]

In the Michigan locker room, Bump Elliott expressed considerable pride in the Michigan effort, if not the result, when he spoke to the press. He praised the resilience of his players, especially after the disappointment of the previous week's game against Navy. "I have to be satisfied with the way the [players] played. My team hasn't hit as hard as it hit today in quite awhile," Elliott said. "My kids came out of [the game] realizing that they can beat any team they play."[8]

Following their 7–7 tie, however, Michigan and Michigan State went in different directions for the remainder of the 1963 season. Michigan lost its next two games to Purdue and Minnesota, then rallied to defeat Northwestern and Illinois, before tying Iowa and then losing the season finale to Ohio State. Michigan finished the 1963 season with a record of 3–4–2, an improvement over the previous season's record of 2–7, but still only an average season at best.

By contrast, Michigan State put together a fine season in 1963. The Spartans finished the 1963 campaign with a record of 6–2–1, ending the season with a 22–0 defeat at the hands of Illinois, who won the Big Ten championship. Illinois then went to Pasadena and won the Rose Bowl, defeating the University of Washington, 17–7. En route to their showdown with the Fighting Illini, the Spartans reeled off four successive conference victories against Indiana, Northwestern, Purdue, and Wisconsin, along with a non-conference victory over Notre Dame. The Spartans finished 1963 in a second-place tie with Ohio State in the final Big Ten conference standings and a number–10 ranking in the final national football polls.

"Michigan State would rather defeat Michigan than any other opponent on its schedule"

In 1964, pre-season hopes for the Spartans were obviously high, for good reason. Duffy Daugherty was entering his eleventh season as the head coach of the Spartans, and under his leadership, Michigan State had emerged as one of the elite programs in the Big Ten. Daugherty's coaching staff, consisting of Henry Bullough, the defensive line coach; Dan Boisture, the offensive backfield coach; Cal Stoll, the ends coach; Gordon Serr, the offensive line coach; Vince Carillot, the defensive backfield coach; John McVay, the assistant backfield coach; and Burt Smith, the freshman coach, was experienced and battle-tested.[9] Tom Krzemienski, a tight end on Michigan State's 1964 team, admired the members of the Michigan State coaching staff. "Duffy was the guy that ran the show," Krzemienski observed. "He was a very active coach, to put it bluntly. [But] what made Michigan State so good was the quality of the assistant coaches."[10]

After the 1963 season, the Spartans lost a number of key players to graduation, including All-American halfback Sherman Lewis and Earl Lattimore, their outstanding guard. Still, Michigan State returned a solid nucleus of 22 experienced letter winners that Daugherty and the assistant coaches molded into two solid platoons of offensive and defensive players. Michigan State's offensive unit included linemen Rahn Bentley, Jerry Rush, John Karpinski, Don Ross, and Krzemienski. The Michigan State backfield also contained some experience in junior quarterback Steve Juday, the returning starter from 1963, and running backs Eddie Cotton, Harry Ammon, and Dick Gordon, as well as Dave McCormick, an all-purpose back who could play quarterback, running back, and receiver.

On the Michigan State defense, several players returned from 1963 including defensive linemen Buddy Owens, Don Bierowicz, Harold Lucas, and Bob Viney, linebackers Ron Goovert, Ed Macuga, John Walsh, and Steve Mellinger, and defensive backs Don Japinga, Charlie Migyanka, Herm Johnson, and Lou Bobich.

In the 1964 pre-season, however, experienced Spartan observers directed a great deal of their attention to several highly touted sophomores who saw their first playing time in 1964 and then became standouts in the next two years. These sophomores included two Ohioans, offensive back Clinton Jones and defensive back Larry Lukasik; two recruits from Texas, wide receiver Gene Washington and defensive lineman Charles "Bubba" Smith; two recruits from South Carolina, defensive lineman George Webster and defensive back Jimmie Summers; Charlie Thornhill, a running back/linebacker from Virginia; and Dick Kenney, a punter/placekicker from Hawaii who kicked the ball with a barefoot style. Don Dufek, who handled the major scouting responsibility for Michigan, was quick to notice the talent in Michigan State's sophomore class. "They have good sophomore strength," Dufek told Clank Stoppels, the sports editor of the *Grand Rapids Press*, at the beginning of the season, "[and] that's usually a tipoff on how good any team will be with a few games under its belt."[11]

Jones, Washington, Webster, Smith, and Kenney worked their way into the offensive and defensive units almost immediately.

The addition of Gene Washington, Bubba Smith, George Webster, Charlie Thornhill, and Jimmy Summers was evidence of the enormous success that Duffy Daugherty achieved in recruiting talented African American players from the South who, due to racial segregation, were denied admission to Southern universities at the time. In fact, as Randy Roberts and Ed Krzemienski point out in their book *Rising Tide: Bear Bryant, Joe Namath, and Dixie's Last Quarter,* "Daugherty was one of the first coaches to vigorously and systematically recruit southern black players." In that regard, Daugherty and Paul "Bear" Bryant, the coach of the University of Alabama, engaged in a quiet, below-the-radar enterprise to recruit players who were potential contributors at either school. As Roberts and Krzemienski wrote, "In the late 1950s and early 1960s, Bear and Duffy continued their informal exchange, Bryant sending names of southern black prospects who might want to head north and Daugherty doing the same with northern white recruits who might be a better fit in the south." In 1962, for example, Bryant actively recruited Charlie Thornhill, one of the most sought-after players in Virginia—for Michigan State. Thornhill went to Michigan State largely because of Bryant's encouragement. Thornhill recalled that he was affected by the overwhelming personality of Bear Bryant.[12] For his part, Daugherty helped to steer Tom Krzemienski's teammate from Beaver Falls, Pennsylvania, a quarterback named Joe Namath, to Alabama.

Despite the high expectations of the 1964 pre-season, Michigan State stumbled in its first game, losing to North Carolina in Chapel Hill, 21–15, on September 26. But the Spartans regained their footing the following week at home, defeating the University of Southern California in an upset, 17–7.[13] The victory over USC, ranked number 2 in the country at the time, propelled the Spartans into the top ten in the national polls with a number-9 ranking, and Duffy Daugherty won national coach of the week honors for the victory over the Trojans. Anticipating another stellar year for Michigan State, Biggie Munn also exulted in the upset victory over USC. "Last Saturday's victory over Southern Cal was one of the finest football victories I've ever seen," Munn told the Downtown Coaches Club in East Lansing on the Wednesday after the game.[14]

But as the Michigan–Michigan State game approached on October 10, neither team was thinking about its non-conference schedule. Both teams were focused on the more immediate task of winning this major intrastate rivalry. As Duffy Daugherty told reporters in the week prior to the game, "Michigan State would rather defeat Michigan than any other opponent on its schedule."[15] In short, Michigan State expected to beat Michigan, every year.

For the first time in several years, Michigan was the pre-game favorite in 1964. Going into the game, Michigan held the statistical advantage over the

Spartans, something of an unusual circumstance given the recent history between the two teams. For Duffy Daugherty, being an underdog to Michigan, especially at home, was not normal. Bob Hoerner, sports editor for the *Lansing State Journal*, sized up the teams accordingly: Michigan had the better record, 2–0, to Michigan State's 1–1. In its two games, Michigan scored 45 points to Michigan State's 32, with sophomores Clinton Jones and Gene Washington scoring all four of the Michigan State touchdowns. Michigan had accumulated 795 yards of total offense to Michigan State's 406. Michigan led Michigan State in first downs, 40 to 18, and had a better rushing average of 4.8 yards per carry to Michigan State's 3.2. In addition, Michigan held the edge over Michigan State in most of the defensive categories, including defense against the run.[16]

Duffy Daugherty was willing to concede the pre-game advantage to Michigan, as least as far as the offense was concerned. "We can't possibly hope to match Michigan's great offense and must rely on our defense," Daugherty told reporters at midweek. "We hope to get our attack moving more than we have in the first two games but the Wolverines have a tremendous running game plus a strong passing attack and it's doubtful if we can match it in an offensive battle."[17]

The Capulets and the Montagues

The Michigan–Michigan State game in East Lansing on October 10, 1964, exemplified the pageantry of Big Ten football. An all-time record crowd of 78,234 gathered in Spartan Stadium to watch the contest. Among the spectators were the governor of Michigan, George Romney, and his wife Lenore, who followed the custom of observing the game from one side of the field for the first half and then moving to the other side to watch the second half. The weather on game day was unseasonably cold, 39 degrees, with a slight breeze of 8 miles per hour coming from the northwest.[18]

The hustle and bustle of the pre-game festivities, however, did not obscure the fact that the Michigan–Michigan State rivalry created its own unique set of tensions. As R.W. Apple, Jr., covering the game for the *New York Times*, reported: "The intrastate rivalry means to the people of Michigan what the struggle between the Capulets and Montagu[e]s did to the citizens of 15th century Verona."[19] For some spectators, the pre-game tension turned to tragedy. Three men in attendance at Spartan Stadium were stricken with heart attacks; two died before the game, and the third man died afterward. These individuals were Almond T. Norton, 59, of Grawn; Peter Harig, 70, of Wyoming; and Paul V. Miller, 46, of Pontiac.[20]

For the players, the bad feelings that existed between the two teams after the 1963 game boiled to the surface during the pre-game activity in 1964. In

Michigan's midweek preparations, the players were reminded of Michigan State's practice of running onto the field while the opponent was doing its pre-game drills. Michigan's scouts had noticed that the Spartans had performed that particular ritual the previous week against Southern Cal, in an obvious attempt to disrupt the concentration and preparation of the Trojans. The scouts warned the Michigan players to be aware of a particular Spartan *provocateur,* a lineman named Pat Gallinagh.

True to form, as the Wolverines were going through their pre-game drills, the Spartans came running onto the field. For the Michigan players the question was whether Michigan State intended to follow their pre-game ritual, disrupt Michigan's preparations, and, in the process, try to establish an early psychological edge. As Rick Volk recalled, "When we arrived at East Lansing, we were the first team on the field to warm up...." The Wolverines kept their eyes out for Patrick Gallinagh, who quickly emerged from the Spartans players and headed in the direction of Michigan's defensive backs. Gallinagh "started to come into our drills and Rick Sygar saw [him] coming and struck him right under his chin [with his helmet] and knocked [him] right on his back." Now what? As Volk recalled, one of Michigan State's players rushed in and restrained Gallinagh and prevented him from fighting with Sygar. But Volk saw the Gallinagh-Sygar episode as a good omen; "I think it proved that we were ready to beat Michigan State that day and we did beat them."[21] If Michigan State intended to use its pre-game ritual to gain a psychological advantage, the encounter backfired, giving a psychological advantage to the Wolverines, not the Spartans. The episode also proved that the battle between Michigan and Michigan State was not confined to the sixty minutes on the field.

The Gallinagh-Sygar dust-up gave new meaning to the term Backyard Brawl, later used to describe the Michigan–Michigan State game. Nevertheless, Bump Elliott and the other Michigan coaches rushed to the scene of the disturbance and calmed the situation. "We thought we were going to have a brawl [between the players] before the game," Elliott later recalled. "The tensions were [that] high."[22] As subsequent events were to prove, Sygar's belt to the chin of Patrick Gallinagh was only the first instance of the damage that he was to inflict on the Spartans on October 10.

A Game Marred by Fumbles but Highlighted by Spectacular Performances

Michigan won the coin toss and elected to receive, defending the north goal. Michigan State kicked off, defending the south goal. Lou Bobich kicked off for the Spartans to Jim Detwiler, who took the kick four yards deep in the end zone and returned the ball to the Michigan 20. From that point, the Michigan offense took the field, with its regular starting lineup of Steve Smith and John Henderson at the ends, Tom Mack and Charlie Kines at the tackles, John Marcum and Dave Butler at the guards, Brian Patchen at center, and the I-75 Backfield of Bob Timberlake, Mel Anthony, Jim Detwiler, and Carl Ward. Facing the Wolverine attack was the stout Spartan defense that consisted of George Webster and Bob Viney at the ends, Bubba Smith and Don Bierowicz at the tackles, Buddy Owens at middle guard, Ron Goovert and Ed Macuga at the linebackers, and Charlie Migyanka, Don Japinda, Herm Johnson and Lou Bobich in the secondary.[23]

Michigan started its first drive on its own 20 and promptly lost the ball. On second and 6 from the 24, Mel Anthony fumbled a pitchout from Bob Timberlake, and Ed Macuga recovered the loose ball for Michigan State on the Michigan 17. Michigan obviously had not been cured of its bad habit of committing dangerous fumbles deep in its own end.

The Spartan offense began work with tremendous field position on the Michigan 17. On offense for Michigan State were linemen Tom Krzemienski at tight end, Gene Washington at split end, Jerry Rush and Dick Flynn at the tackles, Rahn Bentley and John Karpinski at the guards and Don Ross at center. In the backfield were Steve Juday at quarterback, Eddie Cotton at fullback, and Clinton Jones and Harry Ammon at the halfbacks.[24] To meet the Spartans, Bob Hollway sent out the same 11-man defensive unit that started the week before against Navy.

Michigan State began its first possession with a 5-yard penalty for illegal motion. Then Juday went to work. After two plays gained 8 yards, Juday hit Dave McCormick, who had entered the game as a receiver, for 10 yards and a first down to the Michigan 4. On first down, Harry Ammon carried to the 1, and on second down, Juday sneaked in for the touchdown. Lou Bobich kicked the extra point and Michigan State had drawn first blood, 7–0, with more than eleven minutes to go in the first quarter.[25]

After its inauspicious start, Michigan showed some strength on its second possession. On second and 10 from the 20, Timberlake hit Steve Smith for a 29-yard gain to the Michigan 49. Five consecutive running plays, one by Carl Ward and four by Mel Anthony, brought the ball down to the Michigan State 18 and a first down. Thus far, it was a typical Michigan drive, featuring power running and a timely pass completion that put the Wolverines in position to tie the game. But then misfortune struck again as Jim Detwiler, in his first carry from scrimmage, fumbled on the 18 and Ron Goovert recovered for the Spartans. Michigan's first serious scoring threat of the game had ended with another turnover.[26] Unlike in their first two games against Air Force and Navy, the Wolverines were getting off to a terrible start.

Taking over on their 18, Michigan State began its second possession of the game. The Michigan defense stopped the Spartans and forced a punt, with Lou Bobich punting to the Michigan 45. But the Wolverines were called for holding on the play and Michigan State received a first down at its 41. With a fresh set of downs, the Spartans resumed their attack. On second down, Dave McCormick took a pitchout from Juday and, on a halfback option, threw to Gene Washington, who carried the ball 43 yards down to the Michigan 15 before Dick Rindfuss forced him out of bounds. For the second time of the game, the Spartans stood at the doorstep of another score. But Michigan's defense rose to the occasion as Tom Cecchini forced a fumble by Juday, and Bill Yearby recovered for the Wolverines at the 15.[27]

Michigan went back on offense but the Wolverines were unable to move the ball. On fourth down, Stan Kemp entered the game and punted the ball to the Michigan State 42. After an 11-yard punt return, the Spartans took over on the Michigan 47, with excellent field position once again. On the next three plays, Michigan State gained twelve yards and a first down at the Michigan 35. Then came the play that Duffy Daugherty considered the turning point of the game. On first and 10 from the Michigan 35, Steve Juday, keeping the ball on the ground, handed off to Clinton Jones for a sweep to the right. But Tom Cecchini, the hero of Michigan's 1963 game against State, blitzed and hit Jones, forcing a fumble that Barry Dehlin, Michigan's other linebacker, recovered on the Wolverine 46-yard line. "If we could have scored another touchdown there," Daugherty said after the game, "I don't think they'd have caught us."[28]

For the remainder of the first half, Michigan's offense continued to sputter, unable to crack the Spartan goal line. Midway through the second period, Michigan advanced from its 48 to the Michigan State 14, but Bob Timberlake's attempt for a field goal was wide right. Then the Wolverines got another scoring opportunity, late in the first half. Taking over at mid-field with less than three minutes left in the second quarter, Timberlake took advantage of a personal foul call against the Spartans and a 22-yard pass to John Henderson to advance the ball to the Michigan State 13. On the last play of the first half, Timberlake kicked a 29-yard field goal and reduced Michigan State's lead from 7 points to 4.[29]

In the Michigan locker room at halftime, the Wolverines were frustrated and even bewildered, facing a deficit for the first time all season. "At halftime all of us were down," Jim Conley later wrote. "We wanted to win so badly, but we were having doubts about how good we really were."[30] Bump Elliott reassured the players, telling them that they were the better team and that they had worked too hard to lose the game now.[31] Elliott had good reasons for his optimism. Michigan had outgained the Spartans, 133 yards in total offense to

A fumble by Michigan's State's Clinton Jones (26) was a key play in Michigan's victory over Michigan State. Defending for Michigan are Bill Laskey (83) and Tom Cecchini (53) (Bentley Historical Library, University of Michigan).

Michigan State's 72, and had made more first downs, 11 to 4. If the Wolverines could only manage to play without losing fumbles to the Spartans, they stood a good chance of overtaking them in the second half.[32]

Regardless of Elliott's optimism, the second half started badly for Michigan. Carl Ward took Lou Bobich's kickoff in the end zone, fumbled it, and then ran out to the 18, where Michigan State's Phil Hoag hit him, causing a fumble that Bobich recovered. Just like the first half, the Spartans were back in business at the Michigan 18. But the Wolverine defense, playing "with reckless abandon," according to Jim Conley, once again stopped the Spartans when it had to.[33] Michigan State only managed to gain four yards on three downs and Dick Kenney entered the game for his first (barefoot) field goal attempt. But, from the Michigan 21, Kenney pushed his kick to the right and the Spartans squandered a golden opportunity to add to their slim lead.

Kenney was soon to get another opportunity, however. On Michigan's next possession, the Wolverines only managed one first down before they were forced to punt. The Michigan State defense was unquestionably the best defensive unit that Michigan had faced to that point in the season. After Stan Kemp punted to the Michigan State 36, the Spartans mounted a drive. Unable to move the ball effectively on the ground against Michigan, Steve Juday went to the air. He completed one pass to Dave McCormick for 8 yards on the first

Arnie Simkus (70) and Rick Volk (49) close in on Michigan State's quarterback, Steve Juday (23) (Bentley Historical Library, University of Michigan).

series, then hit McCormick for 23 more yards on the second series down to the Michigan 28. But the Michigan defense regained its footing and pressured Juday into two incompletions on second down and third down. Dick Kenney entered the game for a second time for another field goal attempt, this time from Michigan's 34, which, if successful, would have been a 44-yard field goal. Against Southern California, Kenney had kicked a 49-yard field goal (a Michigan State school record), so his second attempt against Michigan was well within his range. But Kenney missed again, this time pushing his kick to the left.[34] The Wolverine defense had stopped Michigan State five times in its own territory.

Still, the third quarter of the 1964 Michigan–Michigan State game remained unkind to the Wolverines. After Kenney missed his second field goal attempt, Michigan went three and out on its next two possessions against the stout Spartan defenders. By now, Rahn Bentley and Jerry Rush were going both ways for Michigan State in the effort to stop Michigan's ground game. With time running down in the third quarter, Michigan State took over on Michigan's 49 after Stan Kemp's sixth punt of the game. Thus far in the second half, all of the momentum in the game belonged to the Spartans.[35]

On State's last possession of the third quarter, Duffy Daugherty reinserted Dave McCormick at quarterback, replacing Steve Juday. Relying on the running of Harry Ammon and his own quarterback keepers, McCormick moved the Spartans to the Michigan 25, where they faced third and one as the quarter ended, with Michigan State still holding a 7–3 lead. Resuming the drive at the beginning of the fourth quarter, McCormick stayed on the ground. Two running plays by Clinton Jones, and two running plays by McCormick, brought the Spartans to the Michigan 9, where they faced 4th and 5. Daugherty sent Larry Lukasik, not Dick Kenney, into the game to attempt a field goal. Lukasik's kick was good and the Spartans now led, 10–3. The clock showed 12:30 left in the game.[36]

As Michigan broadcaster Tom Hemingway wrote, the Michigan offense now faced a near "make or break" situation.[37] If Michigan was to win the game, it needed to score some points, and at this critical juncture, three players—Bob Timberlake, Rick Sygar, and John Henderson—assisted by the down-and-dirty determination of the Michigan offensive linemen, took over the game. The Michigan offense, dormant throughout most of the first half and the entire second half, suddenly sprang to life.

On Michigan's next possession, Dick Rindfuss ran the kickoff back to the Michigan 27. Then Timberlake went to work. Sygar and Rindfuss entered the game at the halfback positions to give Michigan better, sure-handed passing options out of the backfield. First, Timberlake kept the drive alive by passing for 11 yards and a first down to Sygar from the Michigan 29. Then Sygar caught another pass for eight yards on first down, but the Wolverines failed to convert

Three. One Step Forward, One Step Back 81

Jeff Hoyne (88) and Barry Dehlin (31) pursue Michigan State's Steve Juday (23) (Bentley Historical Library, University of Michigan).

a first down on the next two plays. They faced 4th and inches from their own 48. Bump Elliott told Timberlake to go for the first down, instead of sending in Stan Kemp for a punt. Timberlake sneaked two yards for a first down. The drive stayed alive.

Then, the pace of the offense accelerated. On first down from mid-field, Timberlake hit Henderson for 29 yards down to the Michigan State 21. The Wolverines were on the move. On the next play, as Timberlake tried an option right, two Spartans grabbed his right arm, but before he hit the turf of Spartan Stadium, Timberlake back-handed the ball to Sygar, who gained 9 yards around the right side. Two running plays by Mel Anthony gave Michigan a 3rd and goal at the Spartan 5. On 3rd and goal, Timberlake calmly fired to Sygar, "who tucked in the ball like a mother cradles her baby." Sygar made it into the end zone and the Wolverines suddenly were within one point, 10–9, of tying the game.[38] Sygar was so excited after scoring the touchdown that he fired the ball toward the Michigan State bench, barely missing Duffy Daugherty.[39]

Bump Elliott immediately called for a two-point conversion attempt. "We went for the two points after the first touchdown because we wanted to

Rick Sygar (18) catches a touchdown pass from Bob Timberlake in the fourth quarter against Michigan State (Bentley Historical Library, University of Michigan).

win the game right there and then," Elliott told the reporters after the game. "We weren't too confident that we could score again."[40] But Mel Anthony, taking a pitchout from Timberlake, failed to elude Michigan State's Charlie Migyanka, who tackled him inches short of the goal line. The score remained 10–9, Michigan State, with 8:18 left in the game. On Michigan's scoring drive of 73 yards, Timberlake, Sygar, and Henderson accounted for 62 of the total.[41] Maurice Shevlin, the veteran sports reporter of the *Chicago Tribune*, later described the game as a contest marred by fumbles but highlighted by spectacular performances, a perfect description for the action that had transpired through the first 52 minutes of the game.[42]

The Niles Special

After Michigan's first touchdown, Michigan's first score in East Lansing since 1960, both teams knew what was necessary with eight minutes left in the game. Michigan needed to get the ball, and Michigan State needed to keep the ball and either score or run enough time off the clock to prevent Michigan from scoring. So, with the tension almost unbearable, Bob Timberlake kicked off for Michigan into the Michigan State end zone, where the Spartans took a touchback. From its 20, Michigan State went to the ground game with Dave McCormick at quarterback. On first down, Harry Ammon ran off left tackle and John Yanz stopped him for no gain. On second down, McCormick tried a sweep to the right but Barry Dehlin shot through to tackle the Spartan quarterback after a gain of only one yard. State now faced 3rd and 9: would Duffy Daugherty call for a pass to get the first down? No. Daugherty stayed on the ground with McCormick trying another sweep but Jim Conley brought him down after a gain of two. After a 5 yard delay-of-game penalty (which Daugherty used to send in his defensive unit), Michigan State faced a 4th and 12 from its 18. Lou Bobich came in to punt and Dick Rindfuss dropped back for the return. Rindfuss fielded Bobich's punt at the Michigan 43 and returned it 16 valuable yards down the sidelines before Don Japinga forced him out at the Michigan State 41.[43] For most of the game, Michigan State had controlled the tempo, but now Michigan had all the momentum—and the ball. Could the Wolverines capitalize on what was almost certainly their final possession?

Starting at the MSU 41 with 4:55 left in the game, the Wolverines knew they only needed a score, either a touchdown or a field goal by Timberlake, to win the game. Timberlake started the possession on the ground. Carries by Timberlake, Ward, and Anthony gave the Wolverines a first down at the Spartan 31, with the clock running.

Then Rick Sygar entered the game to replace Ward, who had been playing with an injured hand. The State defenders were obviously keying on Sygar, whose running and pass catching had helped to produce Michigan's first touchdown just moments earlier. On first down, Sygar took a pitchout from Timberlake and ran to his right on a play that resembled the play in which Sygar had carried for 9 yards on the previous possession. But on this play, specifically sent in from the sidelines by Tony Mason, Sygar stopped, planted his feet and threw downfield to John Henderson, who was all alone at the Michigan State 5-yard line. Henderson caught the pass, well behind Don Japinga, the Michigan State safety, and ran in for the touchdown. With less than three minutes to play, Michigan took the lead, 15–10. Bump Elliott chose once again to go for the two-point conversion, successful this time, as Timberlake threw to Steve Smith in the end zone to make the score Michigan 17, Michigan State 10.[44]

The Sygar-to-Henderson touchdown pass became known as the "Niles Special" because both Tony Mason, the coach who called the play, and Rick Sygar, who executed the pass, came from Niles, Ohio.[45] The coaches inserted

John Henderson (81) catches the game-winning touchdown pass from Rick Sygar against Michigan State (Bentley Historical Library, University of Michigan).

the Niles Special into the playbook especially for the Michigan State game. John Henderson recalled, "We executed a halfback option pass and I was supposed to decoy my activities as if I were a blocker. When the defensive back came up to make the play on the halfback, I would break into the open to receive the pass from Rick Sygar. Rick got the pass to me and I managed to drag the defender into the end zone for a touchdown."[46]

Duffy Daugherty admitted that the play caught the Spartans unprepared. "There [sic] play fooled us completely," the Spartan coach admitted after the game. "It was very well executed."[47] In fact, the play was the perfect call, at the perfect time, with perfect execution. And, in a bit of irony, the play was almost identical to Michigan State's halfback option pass from Dave McCormick to Gene Washington in the first half that went for 43 yards and a near touchdown.

But, in this game, Michigan State still had one last opportunity with less than three minutes left in the contest. Michigan State returned the ensuing kickoff to its 32 and Steve Juday replaced McCormick at quarterback. State needed to pass and the Wolverine defenders knew it. On first down, Juday threw incomplete to McCormick. On second down, Arnie Simkus sacked Juday for a loss of two yards. On third down, Juday threw incomplete to Dick Gordon. On fourth down, he threw downfield to Gene Washington, who leaped for the ball, but Washington was surrounded by the entire Michigan secondary: Volk, Rindfuss, and, of course, Sygar. Volk and Sygar broke up the pass and the Wolverines took over on downs. Timberlake ran out the clock and the game ended with a Michigan victory, 17–10. The jubilant, and relieved, Wolverine players ran onto the field, hoisted Bump Elliott and Tony Mason onto their shoulders, and headed to the locker room to celebrate an historic victory, punctuated by the singing of a lusty rendition of "The Victors." In the dimly lit locker room, the players awarded the game ball to Elliott. Said John Henderson, "I remember after the game that Bump was so happy he came over to me and gave me a big bear hug.... I remember feeling extremely proud because I had contributed to something [he] really wanted, a victory over Michigan State."[48]

Both coaches met with reporters after the game. In Bump Elliott's estimation, it was the Michigan defense that won the game for the Wolverines. "We were able to contain them three or four times in absolutely critical situations," Elliott said. "The defense really deserves a lot of credit for winning the ball game. They really did a job."[49] Once again, the Michigan defense had stopped its opponent when it had to.

Then Elliott somewhat uncharacteristically singled out several players for outstanding individual performances. He praised Tom Cecchini for the tackles on two plays that resulted in fumbles that ended Michigan State drives in the first quarter. He also praised the Michigan defensive line, saying, "[Bill] Yearby had one of his finest games but, for that matter, you can't take anything away from the rest of the defensive line. John Yanz had a fine game and Arnie Simkus and Jim Conley were real effective, too. Conley hurt his knee and had to come out but he was right back in there and did an excellent job." Years before, Bump Elliott had said that if he managed to recruit Bill Yearby and John Rowser, his classmate at Eastern High in Detroit, to Michigan, he "would win a Big Ten title." Those words were starting to appear prophetic.[50]

Michigan had its share of unsung heroes in the game, too. Rick Volk shadowed the dangerous Gene Washington all game and largely prevented him from getting open for a long score. Dick Rindfuss ran back a kickoff and a punt in critical situations that enabled the Wolverines to begin scoring drives in good field position. The entire team played the game with only 18 yards in penalties. And the list went on.

In the Michigan State locker room, Duffy Daugherty complimented Michigan while noting that the Spartans had failed to capitalize on their opportunities. "I felt our boys played real hard all the way," Daugherty said. "We contained Michigan's ground power quite well but it was their passing late in the game that hurt."[51] Admittedly, the game went down to the final minutes, and Daugherty lamented the numerous times earlier in the contest when the Spartans failed to score. "It was a game of inches," Duffy remarked. "We certainly had plenty of opportunities. We'll never have better field positions than we did on several occasions, but we stopped ourselves. Michigan was a very fine team. You have to speak well for any team that comes back after being behind like they were."[52]

The victory over the Spartans was pivotal, and was Michigan's most important win of the season to that point. Certainly a defeat of the Spartans was satisfying, especially after a nine-year drought, in come-from-behind fashion, and on the road in East Lansing. But undoubtedly the hero for Michigan was Rick Sygar, who executed the big plays down the stretch: his rushing and pass catching on the drive leading to Michigan's first touchdown, and then his Niles Special to Henderson for the winning touchdown. Clank Stoppels wrote, "For a few brief moments, [Sygar] looked like a Tommy Harmon, Bob Chappuis, and Jimmy Pace—all rolled into one."[53]

After the game, Elliott praised Sygar, the versatile player whom he once doubted would ever play for Michigan after suffering the two leg fractures during his sophomore year. "The kid who really stuck with it is Sygar," Elliott said.[54] It was Sygar, "feisty Rick Sygar, equally adept on offense and defense," according to his photograph in the football files, who showed his determination to contribute. From the time of his pre-game altercation with Pat Gallinagh to his game-winning touchdown pass to John Henderson, Sygar was the player who made the difference in the outcome.[55]

So the Wolverines won the Backyard Brawl in 1964, easily winning the statistical battle over the Spartans despite the narrow margin of the final score. Michigan made 20 first downs to Michigan State's 8, rushed for 124 yards to Michigan State's 73, passed for 153 yards to Michigan State's 83 (with 43 of the yards coming on Gene Washington's lone reception of the game), and importantly, were only penalized for 18 yards to Michigan State's 60. The Michigan State game marked the third consecutive contest that the Wolverine defense held its opponent to fewer than 200 yards in total offense and fewer than 100 yards on the ground.[56]

Years later, Tom Krzemienski agreed that Michigan outplayed the Spartans in 1964. "We did our best to beat them, but we couldn't handle them," Krzemienski said. "It was a tough game and nobody was going anywhere. The defenses controlled the game. But Michigan was the better team that year."[57]

Michigan incurred no major injuries in the contest, although the team did receive a big scare. During the game, James F. Conley, father of Michigan's captain Jim Conley, suffered a heart attack, but it was not diagnosed by his doctor until he returned to Pennsylvania the following week. The thrilling finish to the game was "so exciting," Jim Conley later wrote, "that my dad had a heart attack in the stands. But he was as tough as Michigan," and recovered but not enough to continue being a spectator at his son's games later in the season.[58]

The game against Michigan State was "a tremendously bruising affair," Bump Elliott admitted afterward, "and we'll need some time to recover. But I'm afraid Purdue isn't going to allow us much rest on Saturday."[59] Elliott did not need to wait long to see the accuracy of those remarks realized.

The Spoilermakers

Michigan returned to Ann Arbor after its defeat of Michigan State, undefeated at 3–0, undefeated in the Big Ten at 1–0, and by midweek, elevated to number 5 in the national polls.[60] Purdue University, the next opponent, entered its game against the Wolverines on October 17 with a 2–1 record, having defeated Ohio University from the Mid-American conference, 17–0, on September 26, losing to Notre Dame in South Bend, 34–15 on October 3, and defeating Wisconsin in its Big Ten opener, 28–7, on October 10. So, like Michigan, Purdue was 1–0 in the Big Ten and realized the impact that this early-season tilt with the Wolverines would have on the outcome of the Big Ten race.

In terms of recent history, Purdue was every bit as formidable a foe for the Wolverines as Michigan State. Prior to the 1961 season, Purdue and Michigan had played only three games against each other since World War II, with Michigan winning all three contests. Beginning in 1961, the two schools began playing each other annually throughout the decade of the 1960s. Michigan defeated Purdue, 16–14, in Ann Arbor in 1961, but Purdue won the next two games, 37–0 in West Lafayette in 1962, and 23–12 in Ann Arbor in 1963.[61]

Purdue's head coach was Jack Mollenkopf, who had directed the fortunes of the Boilermakers since 1956 but had also previously served as the Boilermakers' line coach between 1947 and 1955 under his predecessor Stu Holcomb, who left Purdue to become athletic director at Northwestern. Like Duffy Daugherty at Michigan State, Murray Warmath at Minnesota, and Milt Bruhn at Wisconsin, Mollenkopf became a head coach in the mid–1950s, and by 1964, he was a recognized fixture in the Big Ten coaching fraternity. Under Mollenkopf's leadership, Purdue experienced only two losing seasons and usually finished the season in the top half of the Big Ten standings.

Perhaps more important, however, Purdue (before, during and after Mollenkopf's tenure as head coach) thrived on its reputation as the "Spoilermakers," the team capable of scoring upset victories over highly ranked opponents and, in the process, delivering a devastating setback to their seasons. Purdue was especially tough on Notre Dame and Michigan State, ending Notre Dame's 39-game winning streak in 1950 and Michigan State's 28-game unbeaten streak in 1953. Then, in 1957, Purdue beat Michigan State 20–13, ending any chance for the Spartans to have an undefeated season, a Big Ten championship, a trip to the Rose Bowl, and a possible national championship.[62]

Mollenkopf's coaching staff included nine assistant coaches: John Jardine, Al Parker, Allen Hager, Don Foss, Ned Maloney, Bob De Moss, Ernie Zwahlen, Bernie Crimmins, and Len Jardine. Several of these assistant coaches—De Moss, Hager, John Jardine, and Len Jardine—had coached at Purdue for several years or were recent additions to the staff after completing their playing careers with the Boilers.[63] Among the assistant coaches, however, a definite hierarchy of authority existed, as Randy Minniear, the fullback on Purdue's 1964 team, recalled: "Bob De Moss was like a second head coach. He was the *de facto* offensive coordinator and coached the quarterbacks."[64] De Moss had played quarterback at Purdue in the late 1940s, and once on the coaching staff, he developed the outstanding Purdue quarterbacks of the postwar era: Dale Samuels, Lennie Dawson, Bernie Allen, and Ron DiGravio. Largely due to De Moss's tutelage, Purdue became known as "the cradle of quarterbacks" in the postwar period.[65]

But Jack Mollenkopf's teams were also known for their stout defenses, and in six of his eight years at the helm of the Boilers, Purdue ranked among the leaders in the Big Ten in total defense.[66] The implementation of the platoon system enabled Mollenkopf to construct an experienced defensive unit that consisted of Harold Wells and Jim Long at the ends, Jerry Shay and Jim Garcia at the tackles, Bob Hopp at middle guard, Bill Howard and Larry Kaminski at the linebackers, and Ken Eby, Charlie King, John Kuzniewski and John Charles in the secondary. All of the players in Purdue's starting defensive unit were returning letter winners.

On offense, Purdue was also an experienced team in 1964. Starting at the ends were Rich Ruble at tight end and Bob Hadrick at split end. The tackles were Lou De Filippo and Karl Singer. The guards were George Pappas and Sal Ciampi and the center was Ed Flanagan. In the Purdue backfield were two highly recruited running backs from Indianapolis, halfback Gordon Teter and fullback Randy Minniear, and the flanker was Jim Morel. Rich Ruble, a sophomore, was the only player on the Purdue offense in 1964 who was not a returning letter winner.[67]

Except for one other player. The Purdue quarterback in 1964 was a highly recruited sophomore from Evansville named Bob Griese. Griese was a triple-threat player whose *forte* was definitely passing and field generalship, but who also handled the place-kicking duties for the Boilermakers. Much to the dismay of the Wolverines, Griese burst onto the national scene with a performance against Michigan in 1964 that marked him as a future star in the Big Ten, the latest addition to Purdue's "cradle of quarterbacks."

Purdue prepared carefully for its game against Michigan on October 17. Each Purdue player received a thorough, written scouting report on the Wolverines that analyzed, in detail, the Michigan performances against Navy and Michigan State. The scouts drew charts that showed Michigan's defensive personnel, its offensive personnel, running plays, passing plays, and perhaps just as important, the formations and plays that Michigan used to score inside the so-called red zone. These plays also included the formations that Michigan used to score their two-point conversions against both Navy and Michigan State.

Purdue's offensive game plan against the Wolverines depended on establishing an effective balance between running and passing, a different emphasis from that of Michigan, which relied primarily on its strong running attack. "We were shooting for balance, run and pass," Randy Minniear recalled. "We felt that we could do both [against Michigan]. We were going to try to control the ball, limit turnovers, and take advantage of any mistakes by Michigan. We did a lot of work [in practice] on the short passing game [between Griese and Bob Hadrick]. Bob De Moss said, 'Let's complete a lot of short passes.'"[68]

The Niles Special: II

Michigan and Purdue squared off at 1:30 p.m. on October 17, 1964, a near-perfect autumn day for football. An announced crowd of 60,424 gathered in Michigan Stadium to watch the game, more than 10,000 fewer spectators who were in the stands to watch Michigan's games against Air Force and Navy. Michigan received the ball first and returned the kickoff to its 29. Starting for Michigan on offense were the usual members of the offensive line and the I-75 Backfield, minus Carl Ward. Dick Rindfuss started at right halfback in place of Ward, and the Michigan faithful soon found out the reason. On first down, Rindfuss took a pitchout from Bob Timberlake and ran to the left. Then he stopped, and facing two Boilermaker defenders bearing down on him, threw a pass to Jim Detwiler, who caught the pass on the Michigan 35 and ran down to the Purdue 24 before he was tackled by Ken Eby, a Purdue safety. Like Rick Sygar, Dick Rindfuss came from Niles, Ohio, and he executed the same play (but to a different side of the field with a different receiver) that went for a touchdown against Michigan State.[69] The Rindfuss-to-Detwiler version of the Niles Special caught Purdue by surprise, gained 47 yards, and put Michigan in position for the first score of the game.

For the rest of the drive, the Wolverines stayed on the ground. After carries by Carl Ward (back in the game after the first play), and Mel Anthony, Timberlake went around the right side from the 4-yard line, broke a tackle by a Purdue defender at the 2, and dived into the end zone for a touchdown. Timberlake kicked the extra point and Michigan led 7–0, with less than four minutes elapsed in the first quarter.[70]

For the remainder of the quarter, however, neither team moved the ball successfully. Purdue's game plan of mixing the pass with the run was showing only modest results.[71] Near the end of the first quarter, though, Purdue struck with lightning quickness. Taking over on its 10 following a punt by Stan Kemp, Purdue started a drive. Two running plays by Minniear and Teter gave Purdue a first down at the 21. Then Bob Griese hit Bob Hadrick for nine yards and Teter carried for another first down to the Purdue 34. Bob Hadrick was a converted quarterback who displayed a knack for getting open and was the perfect receiver for the efficiency-minded Griese. "Hadrick had the hands," Rich Ruble remembered. "He was Bob's 'go-to guy' and I don't ever remember anyone in the film room yelling at Bob Hadrick."[72]

By this point in the game, the Griese-to-Hadrick combination was starting to frustrate the Michigan defenders. "They kept hitting these short passes out in the flat," Jim Conley recalled. "Griese would throw a little pass, 7–8 yards, and I was always stuck in the middle [between Griese and the receiver]. Griese was no threat to run but I still had to protect my side of the field [against a possible scramble by Griese]."[73]

A Bomb and a Turnover

On the next play, from the Purdue 34, Griese rolled to his left, once again looking for Hadrick on a short route. Rindfuss and Volk moved up and blanketed the Purdue receiver. Immediately sensing an opening for the deep route, Griese stopped, set his feet firmly in the turf of Michigan Stadium, and lofted a perfect pass 50 yards downfield to a streaking Jim Morel, who had gotten behind Rick Sygar and Tom Cecchini. Morel caught the pass in full stride at the Michigan 18 and ran untouched into the end zone, leaving the Wolverine defenders "eating drag dust."[74] Morel's touchdown was his only catch of the day, but after Griese kicked the extra point, Purdue had tied the score, 7–7.

Michigan struck back on its next possession. Starting from the Michigan 33, Timberlake completed two passes, one to Steve Smith and the other to John Henderson, that gained 38 yards to the Purdue 29. Timberlake stayed on the ground until he faced 3rd and 9 at the Purdue 17 and then threw a strike to Steve Smith in the end zone. After Timberlake's successful PAT, the Wolverines regained the lead, 14–7.[75]

The Michigan defense stopped Purdue on its next possession and then took over after a Purdue punt which pinned the Wolverines deep in their own territory. On the next series, Timberlake ran for a first down up to the Michigan 23. Then, disaster struck. On the next play, Timberlake retreated to pass but John Charles, one of Purdue's defensive backs, blitzed the Michigan quarterback and forced a fumble. Charles recovered the fumble on the Michigan 16. Once again, the Michigan offense's unfortunate tendency to fumble deep in its own territory, previously on display against Navy and Michigan State, reared its ugly head. The fumble in the second quarter against Purdue was the first of three fumbles committed by the Michigan offense against Purdue, and each fumble had devastating consequences.

Purdue wasted no time taking advantage of the Wolverine turnover. Facing a key third down from the 14, Griese passed to Hadrick for seven yards to the Michigan 7. Purdue faced a 4th and 2 from the 7, and Mollenkopf called for Griese to go for the first down. On fourth down, Griese rolled to his left, looking for a receiver. Finding no one open, he then cut to the middle and scrambled five yards for a first down at the Michigan 2. From there, Randy Minniear "black jacked in" for the touchdown. After Griese's successful PAT, the score was tied, 14–14, and the first half ended with the two teams deadlocked. While the Wolverines had outplayed the Boilermakers in virtually every offensive and defensive category, they could not escape the effects of "a bomb and a turnover," in the words of Michigan broadcaster Tom Hemingway.[76]

In other respects, the first half of the game against Purdue proved costly to the Wolverines. Rich Hahn, a starter at guard on defense, and Barry Dehlin, Cecchini's counterpart at linebacker, went to the sidelines with knee injuries that effectively ended their seasons. They both faced surgery the following week. Bob Hollway inserted two sophomores from the two-way unit, Bob Mielke and Frank Nunley, as the substitutes for Hahn and Dehlin, respectively.[77]

The game against Purdue was puzzling for Michigan as it contemplated making adjustments at halftime. Against Air Force and Navy, Michigan asserted its dominance early in the game and maintained its strength through the remainder of the contests. Against Michigan State, the Wolverines staged a furious come-from-behind rally in the fourth quarter to gain the victory. Against Purdue, however, it was back-and-forth with the Boilermakers who, while clearly being outplayed, were taking advantage of every opportunity to stay in the game against the Wolverines. With Griese throwing to Hadrick, and Jeter and Minniear gaining valuable yards on the ground, Purdue was showing Michigan a more diversified attack than any that it had seen thus far in 1964.

The Harold Wells Show

Michigan was unable to move the ball on its first possession of the second half, and Stan Kemp punted to Purdue. Starting from their own 22, the Boilermakers mounted an impressive drive that resulted in the touchdown that gave them their first lead in the game. Two running plays by Gordon Teter and Randy Minniear gave Purdue a first down at the 32. Then Griese displayed his best passing of the afternoon, first hitting Bob Hadrick up on the Purdue 49. Uncharacteristically, the Wolverines were penalized for a personal foul on the play, and the Boilers moved down to the Michigan 36. Then Griese-to-Hadrick clicked again with Hadrick carrying the ball down to the Michigan 16. From that point, Minniear and Griese took turns carrying the ball until Purdue reached the Michigan 3-yard line. Then, Minniear caught a short pass from Griese in the end zone, and with Griese's successful PAT, Purdue went ahead 21–14.

Purdue had obviously made the half-time adjustments necessary to hold Michigan, and the Wolverines were unable to put together a drive until early in the fourth quarter. Moving into Purdue territory, Michigan made a first down from the 36 when Timberlake ran 25 yards to the Purdue 11. It was here that Michigan became snake-bit. From the 11, Jim Detwiler took a handoff from Timberlake and plowed through a hole on the right side and into three Purdue defenders near the 5-yard line. The ball popped out of Detwiler's grasp and into the end zone. John Marcum, Michigan's right guard, was the closest player to the football and went to smother it. At almost the same instant, Purdue's defensive end Harold Wells dived for the ball and apparently wrestled it away from Marcum for a touchback. The Michigan players signaled for a touchdown, believing that Marcum had secured the fumble, but the officials ruled otherwise. When the officials called for the touchback, Dave Butler waved his arms in protest and pleaded his case with the officials. To no avail. Purdue had the ball and Michigan had failed to tie the score.[78]

Harold Wells, Purdue's playmaker on Detwiler's fumble, was, at age 26, the oldest player on the field and a veteran of the United States Air Force who enrolled at Purdue after being discharged from the military. He was a quick, enthusiastic, talented performer who "was always around the football," according to Randy Minniear.[79] As the rest of the game was to prove, Wells reserved his biggest moments for the Wolverines.

Bob Griese (12) kicks the extra point that gave Purdue a 21–14 lead against Michigan. Griese's PAT was the deciding point in Purdue's 21–20 victory against the Wolverines (Bentley Historical Library, University of Michigan).

Still, Michigan was not finished and the defense stopped the Boilermakers on the next possession. The Wolverines took over on their 35. Timberlake ran for a first down up to the 46, but then brought the crowd to its feet on the next play. On first down from the 46, Bump Elliott called for Timberlake to sweep to the left, instead of to the right, a different call from the normal practice. Running left, and with blockers sealing off the Purdue defenders who were desperately trying to get back into pursuit, Timberlake broke a tackle, used his elusiveness to split two defenders, and ran 54 yards for the touchdown. The score was 21–20 with more than 6 minutes left in the game.[80] As he had against Navy and Michigan State, Bump Elliott called for a two-point attempt for the conversion that would put the Wolverines ahead.

Then ensued the most controversial play of Michigan's 1964 season. On the two-point attempt, Timberlake took the snap and rolled to the right, with the option to pass or run. No Michigan receivers had worked free in the end zone and Timberlake was forced to cut to his left where three Purdue defend-

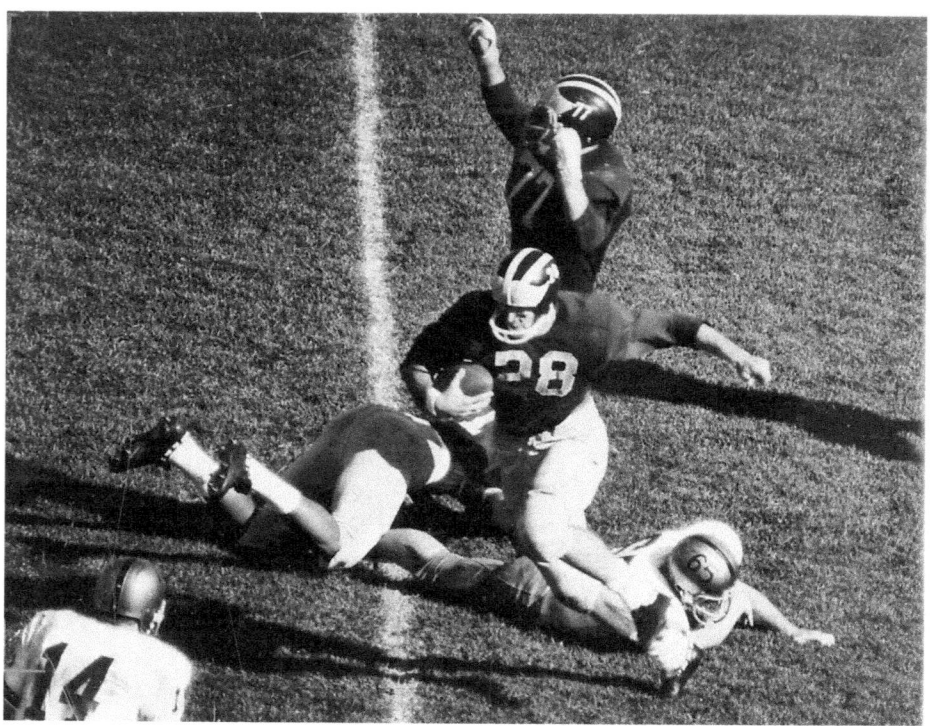

Helped by a block from Dave Butler (77), Bob Timberlake breaks through the Purdue defense (Bentley Historical Library, University of Michigan).

ers, led by stout defensive tackle Jim Garcia, met him inside the 2-yard line and stopped him 2 feet short of the goal line. The score remained Purdue 21–Michigan 20. Whatever limitations the Purdue defense had shown in stopping the Michigan attack as it moved downfield, it defended the two-point conversion attempt perfectly.

Michigan needed to get the ball back and the Michigan defense responded once again. Purdue went three-and-out, and Russ Phahler punted to the Michigan 42. The powerful Michigan offense took the field with three and a half minutes to go, more than enough time to score another touchdown or maneuver into field goal range for an attempt by Timberlake to win the game. The scene was eerily reminiscent of the previous week against Michigan State when Michigan scored a touchdown to come within one point, failed on a two-point conversion attempt, and then regained the possession of the ball, with good field position, and sufficient time on the clock to score the game-winning points.

Michigan stayed on the ground against a Purdue defense that had already given up more than 200 yards rushing to the Wolverines. Two carries by Timberlake, one by Carl Ward, and one by Mel Anthony brought the Wolverines to the Purdue 35, where Michigan faced a 2nd and 6. Two minutes remained in the game and the Wolverines stood poised to make another fourth-quarter comeback for the second week in a row.

At that point, Bump Elliott inserted Dave Fisher into the game for Mel Anthony, a substitution that Elliott later explained as an attempt to give Anthony a rest before the final push for a score. But on the next play, Fisher bobbled a slightly awkward pitchout from Timberlake and fumbled. Diving for the loose ball, Harold Wells recovered for the Boilermakers at the Michigan 46.

Although Michigan managed to get the ball one final time in the game, the Wolverines had squandered their best chance with the second fumble recovery by Harold Wells, who almost single-handedly had snuffed out two scoring drives by the Wolverines.[81] The game ended with Purdue in possession of the ball, walking off the field as the final seconds ticked off the clock. The Spoilermakers had staged another major upset, Purdue 21–Michigan 20.

Lost Opportunities

On October 17, 1964, Michigan lost to Purdue, despite making more first downs than the Boilermakers, 22 to 15, and outgaining them in total offense, 435 yards to 234. Bob Timberlake gained 300 yards in total offense, running and passing, and scored 14 of Michigan's 20 points.[82] But the three fumbles, two recovered by Harold Wells and one by John Charles, made the difference in the outcome. Without question, the Purdue defense had stopped Michigan when it had to.

After the game, Bump Elliott faced the unavoidable question of whether he should have had Timberlake kick the almost certain extra point (Timberlake was perfect on extra-point attempts for the year) and tied the score, hoping to get another possession and then go for the victory. But, as at Michigan State the previous week, Elliott did not hesitate to attempt the two-point conversion. Elliott believed that the decision reflected the preferences of his players. "People wonder why coaches go for two points," Elliott recalled. "You have to be out there with the boys to understand. Winning means so much at the time that you don't think about ties."[83]

Years later, given a near-lifetime to reflect on the decision, Elliott continued to express no regret for deciding to go for two points and the victory—with one caveat. "The thing that I didn't take into account [at the time] was that Timberlake had just run 54 yards for a touchdown and he was tired. He needed to rest for at least the next play. But that wasn't in my mind at all," Elliott remembered. "You don't think of those things when you've got 30 seconds to make a decision. I don't regret [the decision]; I just regret that maybe we would have had a different play called that would have been better. I'm not sure what [that play would have been] because that's the best two-yard offensive play that we had."[84]

Almost as open to second-guessing was Bump Elliott's decision to substitute Dave Fisher for Mel Anthony with two minutes left in the game and Michigan on the Purdue 35. Fisher's fumble on the ensuing play made the substitution even more questionable. But Anthony had just carried for 10 yards on one of the previous plays, and Elliott's post-game explanation about wanting to give Anthony a quick rest needs to be viewed in that light. Anthony and some of the other Michigan players questioned the decision, nevertheless.[85]

Fisher's substitution for Anthony even surprised the Boilermakers—not the substitution itself, but the fact that Fisher was given the ball on his first play after entering the game. Watching the play from the Purdue sidelines, Randy Minniear asked himself, "Why did they give the ball to a fresh back on the first play? Why didn't they let him get used to the game? Normally, you let a back get knocked around for a few plays before you give him the ball."[86] The answer, of course, was that Elliott did not intend to leave Fisher in the game for more than a play or two before sending Anthony back into the lineup.

Statistical analysis and second-guessing aside, the fact remained that the Michigan–Purdue game featured ferocious hitting. As mentioned earlier, Michigan lost Rich Hahn and Barry Dehlin to knee injuries in the first half. Dave Butler played the second half with bruised ribs and Jim Detwiler suffered a broken nose.[87] On the Purdue side, Bob Griese experienced dizziness after the game and was admitted to the University of Michigan Hospital for observation. He spent the night in the hospital before being released to join the team in West Lafayette the next day. Bob Timberlake visited Griese in the hospital before he left Ann Arbor.[88]

Randy Minniear's memories of the game echoed its hard-nosed physicality. "I remember it was about as hard-hitting a game as I'd been in in a long time. [The Michigan] defensive line, to me, seemed awfully quick. They got to you quicker than anyone else. They'd hit you hard, knock you down, and then turn around and walk back to their huddle," the Purdue fullback said.[89]

In their post-game comments to reporters, both coaches appeared to be weary. Asked if Michigan had suffered a letdown after the two previous, emotional victories over Navy and Michigan State, Bump Elliott replied, "I don't think that we had let down after the Michigan State game. It was just a hard-fought football game. Purdue is a real good football team and you simply cannot give anything away to a team like that."[90]

But Elliott's matter-of-fact explanation to the reporters did not hide the near-despair in the Michigan locker room, once the players realized that they had lost a game to a rival contender that should have been a victory. "We skipped [singing "The Victors"] on October 17 [the only time during the year that the team didn't sing the Michigan Fight Song]," Elliott said after the regular season. "Nobody wanted to talk after that one, let alone sing." Dave Fisher was especially upset, understandably. Tony Mason got sick to his stomach and vomited after the game.[91]

On the Purdue side, Jack Mollenkopf praised the performance of his team but also paid his compliments to Michigan. "When we played Notre Dame," Mollenkopf said, "We didn't play nearly as well as we played today. I still think Michigan could go all the way. They have a fine team. [The game] was a toss-up all the way."[92]

In fact, while Michigan faced the reality of a disheartening loss, the Purdue contingent was not exactly in a celebratory mood. "It was such a gut-wrenching game," Randy Minniear recalled. "I can remember thinking, 'Oh thank God, this one's over.' There were so many highs and lows. I thought Michigan, in my opinion, was the best team we played all year."[93]

Back in West Lafayette, Jack Mollenkopf was not in an overly optimistic frame of mind, either. "Jack was all over us after Michigan," Minniear remembered. "He told us we got lucky, we had barely squeaked by, [and] without their mistakes, we wouldn't have won the game. We didn't beat them. They beat themselves. If we expected to win the Big Ten, we had to play better."[94]

Still, Mollenkopf had to be impressed with what Wayne Fuson, sports editor of the *Indianapolis News*, described as the "Herculean efforts" of the Boilermakers. Bob Griese played "with the savvy of a veteran and the bravado of a burglar." Bob Hadrick gave "125 percent" and the backfield of Gordon Teter and Randy Minniear provided "plenty of zing." Harold Wells and John Charles were "simply fabulous."[95] Perhaps Michigan broadcaster Tom Hemingway said it best: "It was obviously not Michigan's day."[96]

It fell to Jim Conley, and the Michigan seniors, to rally the Wolverines after the loss to Purdue. "The thing that we got together and talked about after the Purdue game was that we had to win all our games in order to win the Big Ten championship. If we had beaten Purdue and gone down and lost to Ohio State, it wouldn't have changed anything."[97] Bump Elliott simply told the Wolverines to "get your heads up. I promise you, we are going to Columbus to play for the Big Ten championship."[98] Still, the fact remained: with five games left in the Big Ten season, the road to Pasadena had just gotten considerably more rocky for the Wolverines.

Four
Two Steps Up the Ladder

MICHIGAN 19—MINNESOTA 12
MICHIGAN 35—NORTHWESTERN 0

The Michigan Wolverines entered the final two weeks of October 1964 in an uncomfortable and even unfamiliar position. For the first time all season, Michigan had dropped out of the top 10 in the national polls and, worse from a Big Ten perspective, were one game behind both Purdue and Ohio State in the race for the conference title. The 21–20 loss to Purdue on October 17 also rekindled some apprehensions among the Wolverine faithful about what lay in store for the remainder of the season. Would Michigan be able to rebound from a damaging loss and escape the mid-season swoon that had ruined so many recent campaigns? Michigan's next two opponents, Minnesota on October 24 and Northwestern on October 31, had inflicted such losses on the Wolverines on several occasions, and in the process, knocked them out of the race for the Big Ten title. Was 1964 going to be different from those previous unfortunate seasons?

After the loss to Purdue, however, Bump Elliott rallied his team, telling the players that they needed "to climb a ladder one step at a time," and keep their focus on victories over each of their five remaining opponents: Minnesota, Northwestern, Illinois, Iowa, and Ohio State.[1] Admittedly, the task ahead was daunting: another loss, or even a tie, meant the end of Michigan's chances of claiming its first Big Ten championship since 1950. Moreover, even if the Wolverines went undefeated the rest of the way, they still needed two teams to defeat Purdue in order to claim the title outright.

But the Wolverines rose to the occasion and began a five-game stretch in which, with the exception of a tension-filled fourth quarter in their game against Minnesota on October 24, they played their best football of the season,

Program cover: Michigan vs. Minnesota, October 24, 1964. Henry Hatch, Michigan's equipment manager for 44 years, was featured on the cover of the game program for the Michigan–Minnesota game in 1964. Hatch, who had a special affection for the Little Brown Jug, unfortunately passed away in April 1964, and did not witness Michigan's victory over Minnesota and the return of the Little Brown Jug to Ann Arbor for the first time since 1960 (Bentley Historical Library, University of Michigan).

in effect improving their performance with each successive game. Under Bump Elliott's leadership, the Wolverines went back to their basics in the last half of the 1964 season. The offense continued to feature a bone-crushing running attack, spearheaded by the I-75 Backfield and complemented by the efficient passing of Bob Timberlake. The defense stayed stingy, depriving opponents week-after-week of any semblance of a ground game and stopping opposing offenses when they had to, down near the Michigan goal line. Finally, Michigan continued to derive vast benefits from Stan Kemp, whose punting excellence repeatedly kept the opposition bottled up in its own end.

Michigan climbed the first two steps of the ladder by defeating Minnesota, 19–12, on October 24, followed by a shutout of Northwestern, 35–0, on October 31. In both games, Michigan clearly outplayed the Golden Gophers and the Wildcats, and only a courageous fourth-quarter rally by Minnesota prevented the Wolverines from registering a lopsided victory. Against Minnesota and Northwestern, Bob Timberlake demonstrated once again why he was the outstanding player in the Big Ten, as the Wolverine offense continued to pulverize opposing defenses.

Reclaiming the Little Brown Jug

When Michigan played Minnesota on October 24, it went into the game as a two-touchdown favorite. Such odds were hardly indicative of Michigan's recent record against Minnesota, however, a team that it had not defeated since 1959. Moreover, in three of Minnesota's four victories over Michigan during that period—1960, 1962, and 1963—Minnesota registered a shutout, a further embarrassment to the Wolverines. And since the winner of the Michigan–Minnesota game kept the cherished Little Brown Jug, the prized trophy had remained in Minneapolis for four consecutive years, the longest era of Minnesota success against Michigan since the 1930s.

Reclaiming the Little Brown Jug, therefore, provided sufficient motivation for the Wolverines to bounce back from their disheartening loss to Purdue a week earlier. The oldest and most prestigious trophy awarded to the winner of a rivalry game in college football, the saga of the Little Brown Jug traced its origins to the Michigan–Minnesota game of 1903, played in Minneapolis. That game ended in a 6–6 tie, with Minnesota breaking Michigan's 29-game winning streak.

Prior to the game, Michigan's legendary coach Fielding H. Yost dispatched Tommy Roberts, the team's equipment manager, to purchase a container in which the Wolverines were to keep their drinking water for the game in order, so the legend went, to prevent Minnesota from contaminating the team's water supply. Roberts returned with a five-gallon jug that he had purchased in a local store.

Minnesota tied the game, 6–6, with two minutes left in the contest and its delirious fans rushed the field in celebration. The officials called the game, amidst "the ensuing pandemonium," and the Michigan team headed for the train station, leaving the jug behind in the post-game confusion in Minneapolis. Oscar Munson, the Minnesota equipment manager, discovered the jug after the game, and painted the score of the game on the jug, with the Minnesota "6" being three times larger than the Michigan "6." He then hung the jug from the ceiling of his office to commemorate the occasion.

But Fielding H. Yost wanted the jug returned, according to legend, and wrote a letter to L.J. Cooke, Minnesota's athletic director, requesting that the jug be sent to Ann Arbor, a reasonable request since Roberts had purchased the jug for the Michigan team. At this point, accounts differ as to how the Little Brown Jug became the traditional prize for the winner of the Michigan–Minnesota game. One account holds that Cooke wrote back to Yost, "If you want it, you'll have to come and win it." The Wolverines then returned to Minneapolis in 1909, defeated the Golden Gophers, 15–6, and reclaimed what had become the Little Brown Jug.

A second account of the tradition, probably more reliable than the first, maintained that Cooke and Yost met in Cooke's office prior to the 1909 game and discussed the idea that playing for the Jug, in Cooke's words, "might be material to build up a fine tradition" for the Michigan–Minnesota game. Yost agreed, and after Michigan's victory in 1909, the Little Brown Jug returned to Ann Arbor and became the prize for the winning team in the annual matchup.[2]

Both accounts lack historical veracity, however, as Wolverine historian Greg Dooley has pointed out in a recent article, "Exploring the Myths." As Dooley wrote, Yost bought the jug for 30 cents in Minneapolis because he did not want to carry a container all the way from Ann Arbor, not because he was concerned about a possible contamination of the team's drinking water by Minnesota. Furthermore, Yost was unaware that he left the jug in Minneapolis after the game and never requested that Minnesota return it.[3] The Little Brown Jug did, however, for whatever reason, become the prize for the winner of the Michigan–Minnesota game, and Michigan defended its possession of the crockery by defeating Minnesota, 6–0, in Ann Arbor in 1910. The series experienced a ten-year hiatus when Michigan left the Western Athletic Conference, and then resumed in 1919, when Michigan lost to Minnesota, 34–7, in Ann Arbor.[4]

Moving ahead to 1964, when the Wolverines and Golden Gophers squared off in Michigan Stadium, it was the 49th game of the rivalry between the two teams. Michigan had dominated the series except for the 1930s, when the Gophers won every game between the two teams.

Minnesota's head coach was Murray Warmath, 51, a seasoned veteran of the Big Ten coaching fraternity. Warmath became Minnesota's head coach in 1954, won a Big Ten championship in 1960, and went to the Rose Bowl in 1961 and 1962. Warmath's teams lost to Washington in the 1961 Rose Bowl, 17–7, but defeated UCLA in 1962, 21–3. Warmath also had an experienced coaching staff consisting of Don Grammer, Denver Crawford, Jerry Annis, Robert Bossons, Dick Larson, Butch Nash, Wallace Johnson, and Joe Salem. Warmath's staff was richly represented with former Minnesota players, including Annis, Larson, Nash, Johnson, and Salem.[5]

Minnesota had proved to be a difficult opponent for Michigan since Bump Elliott took over as Michigan's head coach in 1959. Although Elliott's 1959 team had defeated Minnesota, 14–6, losses to Minnesota in 1960 and 1961, coming at the midpoint of the season, derailed two potentially promising seasons for the Wolverines.[6] Then, in 1963, the Gophers shut out Michigan, 6–0, in Minneapolis, in part due to a controversial call by the officials. The questionable call occurred on the last play of the first quarter of a scoreless game after Michigan had stopped Jerry Pelletier, one of Minnesota's running backs, for no gain on a 1st and 10 play at the Michigan 41 yard line. After the teams changed sides, however, the officials placed the ball at the Michigan 39, not the 41, and Minnesota faced a 2nd and 8 situation, not a 2nd and 10. Jocko Nelson, one of Michigan's assistant coaches, recalled the confusion: "When the Gophers got the ball, they had no gain on first down. [At] that point the whistle blew ending the first quarter. When the chains were switched, I looked up and saw Minnesota had second down with eight yards to go. We lost two yards somewhere. Minnesota eventually made a first down by inches."[7] On that drive, Minnesota kept the ball and scored on a rushing touchdown by Pelletier, the only points scored in the game.[8]

But the 1963 Minnesota game was now only a memory for the Wolverines. Coming out of the Purdue game on October 17, Michigan's most immediate task was filling the positions on defense created by the loss of Rich Hahn, the right guard, and Barry Dehlin, one of the linebackers, both of whom had suffered knee injuries that ended their seasons. To replace Hahn, Bob Hollway called on Bob Mielke, who had been playing on the two-way unit. Mielke entered the lineup in the Purdue game after Hahn exited with his injury. Mielke was a sophomore from Chicago with the versatility to play either fullback, linebacker, or a guard position in the interior line.[9] He quickly became a mainstay.

To replace Dehlin at one of the linebacking positions, Hollway inserted Frank Nunley, a sophomore from Belleville, Michigan, who also had been playing on the two-way unit. Like Mielke, Nunley was also a versatile player, able to play center on offense as well as linebacker on defense. Growing up in

Michigan, Nunley had idolized Joe Schmidt, the All-Pro middle linebacker for the Detroit Lions, and Nunley approached the assignment with the same intensity as his idol. "I rooted for the Lions," Nunley said. "Joe Schmidt was always my idol [when] I was playing linebacker in high school at Belleville."[10]

Minnesota entered the game with a 2–2 record, with wins over California and Northwestern and losses to Nebraska and Illinois. Like Michigan, Minnesota had a Big Ten record of 1–1 and its hope for a Big Ten title made its game against Michigan critically important. As Les Etter, Michigan's publicist, wrote, the Michigan–Minnesota game "was a showdown struggle to get back in the Big Ten race."[11]

Regionally televised, the Michigan–Minnesota game began at 1 p.m. in Michigan Stadium on October 24. With the wind blowing at 23 m.p.h. from the west-southwest, Michigan won the coin toss and elected to defend the south goal. Minnesota chose to receive and Bob Timberlake's kickoff reached the goal line where Bill Bevan, Minnesota's backup quarterback, returned the ball to the Minnesota 19. Minnesota's starting lineup included Kent Kramer and Aaron "Tiny" Brown at the ends, Don Rosen and Gale Gillingham at the tackles, Paul Faust and Randy Staten at the guards, and Frank Marchlewski at center. The most talented of the linemen was Aaron Brown, who played both ways, offense and defense, for Minnesota.

In the backfield for the Gophers were John Hankinson at quarterback; Mike Reid at fullback, Fred Farthing at left halfback, and Ray Whitlow at right halfback. Like Michigan, Minnesota had suffered some key injuries in its previous game as one of its leading ball carriers, Bill Crockett, was sidelined with a foot injury and Fred Farthing moved over from the fullback position to left halfback and Mike Reid started at fullback.[12]

Bump Elliott's decision to start the game on defense paid instant dividends. On Minnesota's first possession, two runs by Hankinson and an incomplete pass yielded only two yards and the Gophers were forced to punt from deep in their own end. Bruce Van De Walker, Minnesota's punter, kicked from near his end zone to Michigan's Dick Rindfuss, who signaled for a fair catch at the Wolverine 48.

With excellent field position, the I-75 Backfield entered the game for the first time. Michigan's starting lineup listed Steve Smith as the starting tight end, but Ben Farabee actually started the game and played for most of the contest. Minnesota's starting defensive unit consisted of Bob Brueggers and Kenny Last at the ends, John Staebler and Fred Nord at the tackles, and Willie Costanza and Brian Callahan at the guards. The linebackers were Joe Pung and Jerome Newsome. In the Gophers secondary were halfbacks Larry Peterson and Stan Skjei. The safety was Kraig Lofquist.[13]

Starting on its own 48, Michigan stayed entirely on the ground for the next ten plays with Mel Anthony (7 carries) and Carl Ward (3 carries) doing the heavy lifting, down to the Minnesota 1-yard line. On 2nd and goal from the 1, Anthony dived over left guard for the first touchdown of the game. Timberlake kicked the extra point and Michigan led, 7–0, halfway through the first quarter.[14]

On Minnesota's next possession, Timberlake again kicked off into the end zone, but Fred Farthing unwisely decided not to take a touchback. Michigan stopped Farthing on the Minnesota 9-yard line and the Gophers took over from that point. The Gophers managed to move out to their own 38, but the Michigan defense stiffened and forced another punt by Van De Walker. Dick Rindfuss made his second fair catch of the game, this time at the Michigan 33.

In its second possession, with time running out in the first quarter, the Wolverines mounted another bone-crushing drive. In an 11-play drive, Timberlake moved the Wolverines from their own 33 to the Minnesota 10. With the exception of a short, 7-yard completion to Ben Farabee on a 3rd and 4 play from the Michigan 39 to keep the drive going, Michigan gained all of its yardage on the ground. Once again, Timberlake, Anthony, and Ward shared the load. Still, Minnesota managed to stop Michigan inside its 10-yard line, and Michigan faced a 4th and goal on the Minnesota 6. At that point, Frosty Evashevski entered the game for a field goal attempt by Bob Timberlake. Bump Elliott decided to try a fake field goal, however, with a play that called for a pass from Evashevski to Ward.[15] The attempt failed, and Minnesota took over on its 10-yard line. The Gophers still trailed the Wolverines, 7–0, but they had prevented a potentially game-crippling score that would have given Michigan a two-touchdown lead midway through the second quarter.

Hankinson moved the Gophers to a first down at their 38 on the next series. Then the Michigan defense slammed the door. On first down, Farthing carried for three yards. On second down, Frank Nunley swatted away one of Hankinson's passes. On 3rd down, Bill Laskey blitzed and threw Hankinson for a 6-yard loss. On fourth down, Van De Walker came in for another punt, which Rick Sygar returned five yards from the Michigan 20 to the 25.[16]

With plenty of time left in the second quarter, Timberlake brought out the Michigan offense for another crack at the Gophers. Showing his almost-total mastery of the Michigan attack, Timberlake ran through the Minnesota defenders for 33 yards on this series. The author of the game rundown recorded Timberlake's two carries using the following words: on 2nd and 10, "Timberlake ran out of maze of Minn players for 24" until the Gophers defensive back Andy Haines brought him down. On 1st and 10 from the Michigan 40, "Timberlake did it again, this time for 9."[17] On the next six plays, mixing runs by

Ward with an 11-yard pass to John Henderson, Timberlake moved the Wolverines to a 3rd and 6 from the Minnesota 11. The Gophers stiffened once again, and prevented a first down. Evashevski entered the game for another field goal attempt. Timberlake successfully booted a 29 yard field goal and Michigan led 10–0. The first half ended with the Wolverines leading by that score, and the oddsmakers who had established Michigan as two-touchdown favorites looked to be almost entirely on the mark.

As the teams went to their locker rooms at halftime, Michigan's loyal supporters at Homecoming must have been pleased by the Wolverines' domination of the game. Michigan clearly had shown no letdown after the Purdue loss, and if ever a team appeared to be overmatched and overwhelmed on the basis of a first-half performance, Minnesota certainly qualified. In the first half, Michigan had rushed for 202 yards compared to Minnesota's 36, made 11 first downs to Minnesota's 6, and held the ball for 41 plays to Minnesota's 29. From the standpoint of Michigan's coaching staff, an especially gratifying aspect of the first half was that, for the first time all season, Michigan played 30 minutes of turnover-free football.[18] Tom Hemingway, the Michigan broadcaster, summarized Michigan's first half: "The first half domination was pointed up by the fact that [Carl] Ward had outgained the entire Gopher running attack by better than two to one margin with [Mel] Anthony close to doing the same. And for the first time on the season, Michigan had gone through a half of errorless ball. The Purdue loss was starting to recede into memory as the second half began."[19]

Bob Timberlake started the second half by kicking off to Minnesota's Bill Bevan, who downed the ball in the Gophers' end zone. Then, the Michigan defense pushed the Gophers backward from their own 20. On first down, Bob Mielke sacked Hankinson for a 9-yard loss to the Minnesota 11-yard line. On second down, Hankinson got 8 of those yards back with a pass to Aaron Brown, who carried up to the Minnesota 19. On third down, Hankinson missed his other tight end, Kent Kramer, and Minnesota faced a 4th and 11 from its 19. Terry Van De Walker entered the game for another punt. Van De Walker stood in his end zone waiting for the snap from Rian Tellor, the Gophers' long snapper. But Tellor snapped the ball over Van De Walker's head and out of the end zone for a safety. With two more points, Michigan now led 12–0.[20]

To compound Minnesota's frustrations, Michigan's first scoring opportunity of the second half occurred on its second possession after Rick Sygar made another fair catch of a Terry Van De Walker punt at midfield, halfway through the third quarter. From that point, Michigan went on a 12-play drive, culminating in a 1-yard quarterback sneak by Bob Timberlake. Every member of the I-75 Backfield contributed to the drive. With the exception of a 6-yard completion from Timberlake to Farabee from the Minnesota 22-yard line, Michigan stayed on the ground for the entire drive. Mel Anthony carried once for 14 yards; Detwiler carried once for 5 yards; Ward carried twice for 2 yards, Dave Fisher carried 4 times for 14 yards, and Timberlake carried twice for 7 yards, including the touchdown.[21] With Frosty Evashevski holding, Timberlake kicked the extra point and Michigan increased its lead to 19–0, with slightly less than 4 minutes left in the third quarter. Michigan was in total control and the Wolverines were within 20 minutes of reclaiming the Little Brown Jug.

Michigan's offensive proficiency against Minnesota also saw the introduction of an unexpected feature. One week earlier, Michigan's offensive unit came away chastened by the numerous mistakes that it had committed in the game against Purdue. Bob Timberlake believed that those mistakes occurred because the "Machine" was "out of tune." So, in the practices leading up to its game against Minnesota, if the offense committed a mistake, Timberlake gathered the players in the huddle, and then began to hum, with the players joining him, until they were "in tune." Once the players were "in tune," they broke the huddle and ran the next play.

Tony Mason liked the idea and encouraged the players to continue humming during the practices when they felt that they were "out of tune." Not surprisingly, the players wanted to continue the practice during the game, and just prior to converting one of their drives into a touchdown, Timberlake had the players hum in the huddle to get themselves "in tune." As Brian Patchen recalled, "[W]hen I broke out of the huddle, the Minnesota team was looking at us like we were from Mars because they could clearly hear us. We scored easily on the next play...."[22]

On the Ropes

Appearances in college football are occasionally deceiving, as Minnesota's effort in the fourth quarter was about to prove. Unbeknownst to Michigan, and perhaps even Minnesota, the Golden Gophers were poised to launch a memorable fourth-quarter comeback that almost enabled them to keep the Little Brown Jug and knock Michigan out of contention for the Big Ten championship. As Michigan broadcaster Tom Hemingway wrote, "Oddly enough, the Michigan march [culminating in Timberlake's touchdown in the third quarter] seemed to do more toward inspiring the Gophers than demoralizing them."[23]

The Minnesota rally began on its next possession after the Michigan touchdown. Not wanting to risk injury to Bob Timberlake, Bump Elliott sent in Clayton Wilhite to handle the kickoff duties.[24] Fred Farthing took Wilhite's kickoff on the Minnesota 13 and returned it to the 20. From that point on the field, the Gophers mounted their first scoring drive of the game. Mixing runs by Farthing with passes to his split end Kenny Last and his tight end Kent Kramer, Hankinson moved the Gophers across midfield into Michigan territory, and down to the Michigan 10-yard line as the third quarter came to an end. The key play on the drive was a 9-yard completion from Hankinson to Farthing on 3rd and 7 from the Michigan 48 that kept the drive alive.[25]

The fourth quarter began with Minnesota facing 3rd and 3 from the Michigan 10. Hankinson tried to run for the first down but lost a yard back to the 11. Facing 4th and 4 from the Michigan 11, and down 19–0, Minnesota had no choice but to try for the first down. The Michigan faithful rose to cheer on the defense: would the stout Wolverine defenders thwart another scoring opportunity by its opponent?

The answer was no, not this time. On 4th and 4, Hankinson went back to pass, found his tight end Kent Kramer in the end zone, and then fired a pass through three Michigan defenders for the touchdown. As the game recorder noted the play, Hankinson "threaded the needle on pass to Kramer in end zone" for the touchdown.[26] Needing a two-point conversion, Hankinson tried another pass, and threw to Minnesota's other tight end Aaron Brown, who was open in the end zone but dropped the pass. Minnesota was on the scoreboard, but Michigan still held a comfortable lead, 19–6, and the game had moved to the fourth quarter.

Following Minnesota's touchdown, Mike Reid kicked off for the Gophers, and Jim Detwiler returned the kick from his 10-yard line up to the 36. Michigan had good field position and the I-75 Backfield came out for the next Wolverine possession, hoping to score and negate the effect of the Minnesota touchdown. Any score by Michigan, either a touchdown or even a field goal, would put the game out of Minnesota's reach. Staying on the ground with Timberlake, Anthony, Ward, and Fisher, the Wolverines moved down the field to a first down at the Minnesota 17-yard line. The next two plays gained four yards, but Michigan took a costly 5-yard penalty for offside that moved the Wolverines back to the 18, where Michigan faced a passing situation on second and 11. Rolling out to pass, Timberlake spotted Craig Kirby coming across the middle of the field and fired the ball in his direction. But Minnesota safety Kraig Lofquist, anticipating a pass, stepped in front of Kirby and intercepted the pass, in full stride, at the Minnesota 9-yard line. Lofquist did not stop running until he crossed the Michigan goal line 91 yards later.[27] This unexpected turnover completely changed the momentum of the game. Behind 19–12, after another two-point conversion attempt failed, the Gophers were charged up, wanting another chance at the ball.

When Lofquist intercepted Timberlake's pass and took off toward the Wolverine end zone, Dave Butler tried valiantly but unsuccessfully to catch the Gopher safety. During their practices, the Michigan linemen had a drill ("that we all hated," according to Brian Patchen) in which they ran around Michigan Stadium, alternating every ten yards between a sprint and a trot. When the team gathered on Sunday to watch the film of the Minnesota game, Tony Mason good-naturedly chided Butler about his failure to catch Lofquist. "I did just like you coached me," Butler responded to Mason, "I ran 10 yards and trotted 10 yards." As Brian Patchen recalled, Butler's comment "broke up the meeting in laughter!"[28]

On the ensuing kickoff, Jim Detwiler returned the ball from the Michigan 5 to the 33. Now the Wolverines needed the I-75 Backfield to grind out some yardage, get some first downs, and run out the clock. But the Michigan offense stalled out, gaining only three yards on the next series. With 4 and 7 from the Michigan 36, Stan Kemp entered the game to punt the ball downfield and out of danger. On this occasion, however, Kemp got off a poor kick, and his punt rolled out of bounds at mid-field. Minnesota now had the ball in excellent field position, and with four minutes remaining either to tie the score or potentially even take the lead.

John Hankinson came onto the field to direct the Gophers' attack. Mixing runs by Farthing and Reid with passes to Last and Brown, the Gophers quickly had a 1st and goal at the Michigan 7. What had once appeared to be a certain Michigan victory now became a struggle to preserve a slim 7-point lead. In the Michigan huddle, Jim Conley took charge. Grabbing Bill Yearby by his jersey, Conley challenged the big tackle: "You've gotta make a play! You've gotta make a play! Here is where we win!"[29] Yearby responded. On 1st and goal from the Michigan 7, Mike Reid tried the left side of the Michigan line, where he gained one yard before he "hit a stone wall" led by Yearby and Tom Cecchini. On 2nd and goal from the 6, Hankinson tried to sweep to the right but Conley stopped him on the 5. On 3rd and goal, Hankinson tried to sweep left, where Yearby harassed him and Rick Volk fired through to make the tackle at the 3-yard line.

On 4th and 3, Murray Warmath inserted Kraig Lofquist into the offensive backfield for the first time in the game. The play that Minnesota called was designed to be a halfback option: Lofquist was to take a handoff from Hankinson, run to his right, and either keep the ball or throw to an open receiver in the end zone. But once Lofquist took the handoff, Conley, Yearby, and John Yanz swarmed after him and Lofquist lateraled the ball to Aaron Brown, who was to have been the lead blocker on the play. Now Brown had the ball and Rick Volk, gambling on a corner blitz, tackled Brown securely by the ankles for a 4-yard loss at the Michigan 7-yard line.[30] Drive thwarted: the Wolverine defense had once again stopped them when they had to. The sense of relief in Michigan Stadium was palpable.

Still, the game was not over and the Michigan offense needed to produce one first down to run out the clock. It failed. The I-75 Backfield only managed to gain seven yards on three running plays before Stan Kemp came on to punt from the goal line. Kemp punted to mid-field and the Gophers had one last opportunity with less than two minutes remaining in the game. But now the Gophers had no alternative but to pass and the Michigan defenders knew it. On first down, a short pass from Hankinson to Last gained only three yards. On second down, Bill Laskey sacked Hankinson for a five-yard loss. On third down, Minnesota committed an offensive pass interference penalty and went back fifteen yards. The Gophers were unable to convert a first down on the next play, and the game ended with Michigan defeating Minnesota, 19–12.

So, Michigan reclaimed the Little Brown Jug and Minnesota left Ann Arbor Jug-less for the first time in five years. For the players on both teams, the Jug was "the most coveted piece of football crockery in the world," according to Michigan broadcaster Bob Ufer, and definitely not "that ugly bit of bric-a-brac," as Bruce Morrison, the sports reporter for the *Chicago Sun-Times*, used to describe it.[31]

After the game, Bump Elliott expressed the sense of relief felt in the Michigan locker room. "We're thankful we won," Elliott said. "Minnesota had us on the ropes late in the game but the way our defense held for those four downs decided the outcome."[32] In a curious fashion, the game's final statistics revealed the closeness of the game. Michigan outgained Minnesota in total offense, rushing and passing, by a margin of 336 to 247, but when Kraig Lofquist's 91-yard pass interception was added, the Golden Gophers actually finished the game with more total yardage than the Wolverines.[33]

After the game, the big question mark in the minds of the Minnesota faithful was why Murray Warmath resorted to such conservative play-calling when the Gophers had a first-and-goal inside the Michigan 10-yard line late in the game. By that point, Minnesota had accumulated more than 160 yards passing, but less than 100 yards rushing, yet Warmath chose to run the ball on three consecutive downs before attempting a pass, and then with Lofquist, not Hankinson, throwing the ball. Warmath's play-calling, in effect, worked to Michigan's defensive advantage.[34] Minnesota had scored its first touchdown on a perfectly executed pass from Hankinson to Kent Kramer, but Warmath chose not to attempt a pass to his tight ends on the most critical series of the game. For Michigan, therefore, it was an "odd win," in the words of broadcaster Tom Hemingway, "[b]ut a win nevertheless at an all-important juncture for Bump and his boys."[35]

The Niles Special Without the Niles

Still alive in the Big Ten race, Michigan turned its attention to the next game, against Northwestern. Bump Elliott's teams had experienced some success against Northwestern during his tenure as head coach, defeating the Ara Parseghian-coached Wildcats, 14–7, in 1960 and 27–6 in 1963, after losing to them, 20–7, in 1959. By 1964, however, Parseghian had moved on to become the head coach at Notre Dame, and Alex Agase, an assistant coach at Northwestern under Parseghian since 1956, took over the reins of the program.

In 1964, Northwestern came into its contest against Michigan in the midst of a four-game losing streak. The Wildcats began the season with a 14–13 victory over Indiana, but then lost on consecutive weekends to Illinois, Minnesota, Miami of Ohio, and Michigan State.[36] Michigan entered the game against Northwestern with no serious injuries coming out of the Minnesota contest, although Ben Farabee continued to alternate with Steve Smith at tight end and Craig Kirby and John Henderson alternated at split end.[37]

To begin the game, Northwestern won the coin toss and elected to receive. Bob Timberlake kicked off for Michigan and Northwestern's Ron Rector returned the kick from his goal line to the 28. Northwestern's offensive unit came onto the field with Dick Smith and highly touted sophomore Casimir Banaszek at the ends, Jim Burns and Mike Schwager at the tackles, Rich Olson and Don Robinson at the guards and Joe Cerne at center. In the Northwestern backfield were Tom Myers, an outstanding passer and veteran quarterback, Ron Rector at left halfback, and Woody Campbell at right halfback, and Steve Murphy at fullback.[38] On its first series, Northwestern failed to gain a first down and Tom Myers punted to Rick Sygar, who took a fair catch at the Michigan 24.

On its first possession, Michigan moved down almost effortlessly behind the running of Jim Detwiler and Carl Ward. The Michigan drive stalled out, however, at the Northwestern 26, and Bob Timberlake attempted a field goal from the Northwestern 33. Timberlake's attempt missed, wide right, and the Wolverines came up empty on their first drive.

Northwestern went three and out for the second consecutive time, and Myers punted back to Michigan. Starting from its own 39, the I-75 Backfield went back to work. The Wolverines advanced the ball downfield behind the running of Timberlake, Detwiler, and Mel Anthony. Timberlake kept the drive alive with two key passes, the first to Detwiler on a 3rd and 5 from the Northwestern 41, down to the Northwestern 17, and the second to John Henderson on a 3rd and 6 that carried down to the Northwestern 2. On 1st and goal from the 2, Timberlake carried the ball into the end zone for the first touchdown of the game. Timberlake's touchdown was the final play of the first quarter, and after he successfully kicked the extra point, the Wolverines led, 7–0.[39]

Bob Timberlake kicked off to Northwestern to begin the second quarter, and Woody Campbell returned the ball to the Northwestern 27. From that point, Northwestern began its first serious scoring drive of the game. Myers mixed up runs by Rector, with passes to Campbell, Cas Banaszek and Dave McKelvey, to reach the Michigan 37. The Michigan defense stiffened, however, and Myers was forced to punt for a third time in the game, booting into the Michigan end zone, and the Wolverines took possession on their 20.

Ahead 7–0, Michigan and the I-75 Backfield mounted another patented 80-yard scoring drive. The touchdown occurred with two quick strikes. First, on a 3rd and 10 play from the Michigan 31, Carl Ward took a pitchout from Timberlake and dashed 36 yards off left tackle down to the Northwestern 33. Then, Elliott inserted Rick Volk into the game. Up to this point in the season, Volk had played little on offense. On the next play, however, Volk took a pitchout from Timberlake and ran to his right on a play that initially appeared to be a sweep. Then Volk stopped suddenly and threw downfield to John Henderson, who was all alone at the Northwestern 10. Henderson caught Volk's

Bill Laskey (83) tackles Ron Rector (29) in Michigan's 35–0 victory over Northwestern. Also defending for Michigan on the play are Dick Rindfuss (17), Frank Nunley (59), and John Yanz (72) (Bentley Historical Library, University of Michigan).

pass and ran untouched into the end zone. The Niles Special had once again worked to perfection, except that Volk came from Wauseon, Ohio, instead of Niles, Ohio.[40] It was a Niles Special without the Niles, and Michigan took a 14–0 lead in the game.

On Northwestern's next possession, the Wildcats again threatened to score their first touchdown of the game. Tommy Myers mixed in runs by Rector and Campbell with passes to Campbell and moved the Wildcats to the Michigan 32. Then, Northwestern got greedy. On 2nd and 9 from the Michigan 31, Myers attempted to throw for a touchdown, but Rick Sygar intercepted his pass in the end zone for a Michigan touchback, thereby thwarting another Northwestern scoring opportunity.

Michigan then put together another 80-yard scoring drive. On this drive, Northwestern helped Michigan with a 15-yard face mask penalty at the Michigan 43 which brought the Wolverines into Wildcat territory. Timberlake then passed twice to Steve Smith, but mostly carried the ball himself, including a 6-yard carry for a Michigan's third touchdown. At the end of the first half, Michigan led 21–0, and the game was basically decided by that point.

In the second half, Michigan continued to demonstrate its offensive prowess and its hard-nosed, stifling defense. In the third quarter, Mel Anthony scored Michigan's fourth touchdown on a 30-yard dash along the right sideline. In the fourth quarter, Dave Fisher scored Michigan's fifth touchdown on a short 3-yard run that culminated a short drive from the Northwestern 36 after a short punt. The Michigan defense also stopped two Northwestern drives inside the Michigan 10-yard line in the fourth quarter, but by this point in the game, Bump Elliott had emptied his bench, and every player on the Michigan sideline saw action that day. All totaled, Michigan used 61 players against Northwestern. The game ended with a final score of Michigan 35-Northwestern 0, and the Michigan defense had recorded its second shutout of the season.[41]

The Best Combination of Effort All Year

After the game, both coaches spoke to the press. "We had the best combination of offensive and defensive effort we've had all year," Bump Elliott said. "We got the upper hand early and when we got those three touchdowns [in the first half], we simply went on from there." Alex Agase, the Northwestern coach, praised the Michigan performance while also acknowledging that mid-season injuries were taking a toll on the depth of the Wildcats. "We were a different team than we were when we played Illinois four weeks ago," Agase said. "We were much stronger then and didn't have all these injuries." As for

Michigan, "Michigan leads the conference in offense and they showed their prowess today. Their offensive skills showed up very well today and they showed us four fine running backs and a halfback who can also throw."[42]

A glance at the game's final statistics revealed the veracity of Elliott's observation. Against Northwestern, Michigan piled up 453 yards of total offense: 336 yards rushing and 117 yards passing. Michigan's rushing performance against Northwestern, 336 yards, was its highest total of the season and the fourth time in five games that the I-75 Backfield rushed for more than 200 yards in a game. Against Northwestern, Timberlake rushed for 81 yards on 14 carries, Detwiler for 50 yards on 10 carries, Ward for 57 yards on 11 carries, Anthony 50 yards on 6 carries, and Fisher for 44 yards on 8 carries.[43]

The Wolverine defense also stood out against Northwestern, holding the Wildcats to 153 yards of total offense. "Michigan's defense is tremendously underrated," Alex Agase told reporters after the game. "Those kids are strong and fast."[44] Bob Hollway, Michigan's defensive coordinator, was also effusive in his praise of the defense's performance, not only against Northwestern but throughout the season. He heaped praise on several of the standouts on the defensive unit. Jim Conley "was a great leader" and John Yanz "has done a tremendous job." Bill Yearby, according to Hollway, was "the best defensive tackle I've seen since I've been coaching here, a relentless hard worker who takes pride in playing in a quiet, workmanlike fashion." Tom Cecchini and Frank Nunley were "a combination [that] gives us two of the finest linebackers in the country."[45]

For Bump Elliott, the play of Bob Mielke and Frank Nunley was especially gratifying since both players were newcomers who were asked to step in and perform at a level consistent with that of the two experienced players, Rich Hahn and Barry Dehlin, whom they replaced on defense. As with Jim Detwiler, who replaced Jack Clancy and John Rowser at left halfback earlier in the season, Elliott had sufficient depth on the team to keep playing at a high level, even when injuries began to take their inevitable toll on the roster. As Elliott observed later in the season, "In many cases, the boy who got off the bench to become a starter became better than the regular [player], simply because he was up to the challenge presented him."[46]

Michigan's victories over Minnesota and Northwestern kept alive its hopes for a Big Ten title. Its record of 3–1 in conference play kept Michigan in second place in the league standings. The victory over Minnesota was especially satisfying. Not only did the Wolverines return the Little Brown Jug to Ann Arbor, but it marked the first time since 1955 that Michigan had defeated its arch-rivals Michigan State and Minnesota in the same season.

Even so, any realistic observer of the Big Ten race in 1964 had to conclude that Purdue and Ohio State remained in the driver's seat as conference play entered the month of November. Purdue and Ohio State both had unbeaten 4–0 records in the Big Ten and were well positioned to enter the stretch run. After defeating Michigan on October 17, Purdue beat Iowa, 19–14, on October 24 and Illinois, 26–14, on October 31. Purdue had three games remaining on its schedule: at Michigan State on November 7, at Minnesota on November 14, and at home against Indiana on November 21 in its traditional rivalry game for the Old Oaken Bucket.

Ohio State, also unbeaten at 4–0 in the Big Ten and as well as unbeaten on the season, held the number–1 ranking in the national polls. After defeating Wisconsin 28–3 on October 24, and Iowa, 21–19, on October 31, Ohio State followed up with a non-conference game against Penn State on November 7, and then played Northwestern on November 14 and Michigan on November 21. All of Ohio State's remaining games were scheduled for Columbus, giving the Buckeyes a considerable home-field advantage for the rest of the season. Michigan may have climbed two steps up the ladder, but its chances were dwindling with each passing week.

Five

Back in the Big Ten Race

> MICHIGAN 21—ILLINOIS 6
> MICHIGAN 34—IOWA 20

As the 1964 Big Ten football season entered the month of November, the Michigan Wolverines were in second place behind Purdue and Ohio State, who were undefeated in conference play and tied for the top spot. With three games left in the season, the Wolverines had to keep winning and hope that Purdue would encounter at least one setback that would enable Michigan to play Ohio State for a share of, if not the outright, Big Ten championship on November 21, the last game of the season.

Michigan did its part, defeating Illinois in Ann Arbor on November 7, 21–6, and then outlasting Iowa in Iowa City on November 14, 34–20. Just as important, however, Michigan's fortunes improved dramatically over that two-week stretch in early November when Purdue lost to Michigan State, 21–7, in East Lansing on November 7 and then lost to Minnesota, 14–7, in Minneapolis on November 14. For the Wolverines, whose season appeared dangerously precarious at the beginning of November, by mid-month they found themselves in the thick of the race for the Big Ten championship. As Charles Bartlett wrote in the *Chicago Tribune* after Michigan defeated Illinois, "Make no mistake, football fans, Michigan's Wolverines are very much in the Big Ten championship picture."[1] The 1964 Big Ten football season showed every indication of going down to the final week of play before a champion emerged to claim the trip to the Rose Bowl.

Bump vs. Pete

When Michigan played Illinois on November 7, it marked the fifth consecutive time that Bump Elliott coached against his younger brother, Pete

Elliott, the coach of the Fighting Illini since 1960. Bump Elliott and Pete Elliott were the sons of Dr. J. Norman Elliott and his wife, Alice. They grew up in Bloomington, Illinois, during the 1930s and 1940s; their father was an eye, ear, nose and throat specialist, as well as the head football coach at Illinois Wesleyan University. Both Elliott brothers inherited their father's love of athletics and became outstanding high school performers in multiple sports, especially football, basketball, and baseball.

While in high school, Bump Elliott enlisted in the Marine Corps' V-12 Navy College Training Program. He was later assigned to Purdue University, where he became an instant contributor to Purdue's football, basketball, and baseball teams in 1943 and 1944. Late in 1944, he entered active military service and served during World War II with the Marines in China.

One year younger than Bump, Pete Elliott entered the Navy training program and spent a year at Park College in Missouri before enrolling at the University of Michigan in 1945. Elliott went on to an illustrious athletic career at Michigan, becoming the school's only 12-letter winner, after earning four varsity letters in football, basketball, and golf between 1945 and 1948.[2]

After World War II, once discharged from military service, Bump Elliott enrolled at Michigan, instead of returning to Purdue, and played on Michigan's football teams in 1946 and 1947. Bump went to Michigan rather than Purdue for a simple reason: "I wanted to play on the same teams with my brother."[3] And, in fact, the Elliott brothers were virtually inseparable at Michigan, rooming together, coordinating their class schedules, and, significantly, playing on the great Michigan teams of the Fritz Crisler era, including Michigan's national championship team of 1947.

In 1948, both Elliott brothers traveled to Oregon State, where they became assistant football coaches under Kip Taylor, another former Wolverine standout. After coaching briefly at Oregon State, the brothers went in different directions. In 1952, Bump Elliott moved to Iowa, where he joined the staff of Forest Evashevski for the next four years. Like Kip Taylor, Evashevski was a former Wolverine standout who played in the same backfield with Tom Harmon in the late 1930s. As an assistant coach at Iowa, Elliott coached the offensive backfield and also acquired experience as Evashevski's defensive coordinator. In 1957, he joined Bennie Oosterbaan's staff at Michigan as the offensive backfield coach.

Pete Elliott stayed at Oregon State until 1951, when he joined the staff of Bud Wilkinson at the University of Oklahoma. Elliott coached at Oklahoma for five seasons before he accepted the head coaching position in 1956 at the University of Nebraska, Oklahoma's chief rival in the Big Eight conference, ironically. In 1957, the following year, he accepted the head coaching position at the University of California, where he remained until 1959. Elliott's

Bump Elliott and Pete Elliott (l), his younger brother, were coaching rivals in the Big Ten between 1960 and 1966 when Pete Elliott was the head coach of the Fighting Illini (Bentley Historical Library, University of Michigan).

California team played Iowa in the 1959 Rose Bowl, losing to the Hawkeyes, 38–12. The Hawkeyes were heavily favored in the Rose Bowl, especially because of their powerful running attack. "We didn't want Iowa to go around us—we worked on that, and they didn't," Elliott told reporters after Iowa had decisively beaten his team. "They went inside us."[4] In 1960, at age 33, Pete Elliott became the head coach of the University of Illinois and thereby began his Big Ten coaching career, and his rivalry with his older brother Bump, the first such coaching rivalry between brothers in the Big Ten.

In this rivalry of coaching brothers, Bump Elliott clearly enjoyed the upper hand, defeating Illinois four consecutive times: 8–7 in 1960, 38–6 in 1961, 14–10 in 1962, and 14–8 in 1963. The Elliott brothers went to considerable lengths to play down their competition, of course. "My basic thought always has been this is the Michigan football team and the kids on it playing the Illinois football team and the kids on it," Bump Elliott observed before the game in 1963. "It's not Pete against me. And Pete feels exactly the same way."[5]

Official niceties aside, Bump Elliott wanted badly to beat his younger brother Pete. Perhaps in an unguarded moment, Elliott revealed his inner feelings on the rivalry to Rich Hahn, who was visiting Michigan as a recruit in 1961. As Hahn recalled many years later:

> I was watching the [1960] game of Michigan vs. Illinois [on television] ... and Illinois scored midway in the first quarter and they kicked [the extra point]. Score was Illinois 7 and Michigan 0. And at the end of the first quarter, Michigan puts together a drive and scores. [Michigan lined up] for the PAT, faked it,

went for two, the end of the first quarter.... And guess what, [Michigan] converted. Score, Michigan 8, Illinois, 7. Second quarter was a battle. Halftime score, Michigan 8, Illinois 7. Third quarter, tough battle, end, Michigan 8, Illinois 7. End of the game, guess what the score was? Michigan 8, Illinois 7. So, I came here for my visit that winter ... and in our interview on Sunday morning, [Coach Elliott] said, "Rick [he called me Rick], do you have any questions?" And I said, "Ah, yeah, I do have a question, Coach." I said, "Why, against Illinois, when they scored so early and kicked the [extra] point, you scored and went for two?" He looked me right in the eye and he said, "Rick, do you have a brother?" And I said, "Yes, yes I do." And he said, "Well, I'll tell ya, I never wanted to lose to my brother and more importantly, I never wanted to be behind him."[6]

To no one's surprise, the Elliott brothers as coaching rivals created some emotional tugs of loyalty within the family. Alice Elliott, for example, found it very difficult to attend the Michigan–Illinois games when her two sons were on the opposing sidelines. In 1963, she chose not to attend the game in Champaign-Urbana, even though it was only 50 miles away from her home in Bloomington. "I'm not going to attend the game. I couldn't win either way," Alice Elliott told Wayne De Neff of the *Ann Arbor News*. "I don't think they'll play to a tie, although that would solve my feelings. Someone will have to lose. I'll feel sorry for him. And I'll feel happy for the winner. I don't want to be there to show my emotions. I'll listen [to the game] at home in Bloomington."[7]

In 1963, the Michigan–Illinois game took on a special significance as Illinois was in the midst of an outstanding season, contending for the Big Ten championship, and ranked number 2 in the country when it played Michigan on November 9. Illinois had defeated Northwestern, Minnesota, and Purdue, while tying Ohio State, to go along with non-conference victories against California and UCLA. The Illinois offense featured the power running of sophomore fullback Jim Grabowski, supplemented by the passing of quarterback Fred Custardo. The Illinois defense was anchored by junior linebacker Dick Butkus. Illinois needed a victory over Michigan to keep pace with Michigan State in the race for the Big Ten title.

Michigan's fortunes were far less desirable in 1963. In the middle of the Big Ten standings, Michigan had defeated Northwestern, tied Michigan State, and lost to Minnesota and Purdue. The Wolverines needed a signature victory over a highly ranked opponent to inject some respectability into what had been, thus far, a mediocre season.

"We won that one for you, Doc!"

In 1963, the Wolverines responded with their best performance of the season against the heavily favored Fighting Illini. Michigan took its first lead of the game in the second quarter on a short run by Dick Rindfuss and went into halftime with a 7–0 lead. In the third quarter, Illinois regained the lead on a quick, 2-yard burst by halfback Al Wheatland after a 93-yard drive. Pete Elliott chose to attempt the two-point conversion and quarterback Mike Taliaferro swept for two yards to give Illinois an 8–7 lead.[8]

The two teams battled it out in the middle of the field well into the fourth quarter. Then, midway through the final period, Michigan mounted a drive that took the Wolverines from their own 12 yard line to the Illinois 38 as Bob Timberlake mixed in passes to John Henderson and Dick Rindfuss, combined with his quarterback keepers and the running of Mel Anthony. The drive stalled out at the Illini 38, however, and Michigan's punter Joe O'Donnell punted to Illinois' Mike Dundy, who made a fair catch on his 13.

Two plays later, disaster struck for Illinois. On 2nd and 10 from the 13, Illinois halfback Jim Warren took a pitchout from quarterback Fred Custardo and fumbled. John Rowser recovered the loose ball for Michigan at the 11. From there, it took Michigan five plays to score the go-ahead touchdown when Mel Anthony plunged for a touchdown on first and goal from the 1-yard line. Timberlake kicked the extra point and Michigan led, 14–8. Illinois had one final possession, but John Rowser ended it with another fumble recovery. Michigan's upset victory was undoubtedly the highlight of its season and earned Bump Elliott national Coach of the Week honors, and Rowser national Back of the Week honors, from the United Press International (UPI).[9]

Michigan's upset victory over Illinois may have yielded some longer-term benefits as well. For example, Jim Conley traced the improvement in the Wolverines' football fortunes in 1964 to its defeat of Illinois in 1963. "We entered Champaign as a heavy underdog," Conley later wrote, noting the significance of the game. "From then on, we knew we could win."[10]

The Wolverines also had an intangible factor working for them in this big Michigan victory, although that factor became known only afterward. Michigan's game against Illinois in 1963 was the last road trip for Dr. William Coxon, Michigan's team physician since 1938, who planned to retire at the end of the academic year. Dr. Coxon had looked after the players on the teams of Fritz Crisler, Bennie Oosterbaan, and Bump Elliott, making so many friends that, as Wayne De Neff wrote in the *Ann Arbor News*, "he finds it best to purchase wedding gifts in wholesale lots." Dr. Coxon treated the whole patient, and some of his biggest battles each fall came with keeping injured athletes out of the game, for their own good. "Most football players want to play, injured or not. Some of them would be in there with a broken leg if you'd let them." Regardless, Dr. Coxon always adhered to the firm rule that a player's health could not be jeopardized, especially any player with a head injury. During his tenure as the team physician, he never missed a game and only one practice—due to a death in the family. In the jubilant Michigan locker room after the victory over Illinois, Mel Anthony threw his arms around Dr. Coxon, and exclaimed, "We won that one for you, Doc!" John Henderson, Bill Dodd, captain Joe O'Donnell, and Tom Keating joined in the celebration.[11]

The Home Stretch

When Michigan and Illinois met on November 7, 1964, however, the situations for both teams were reversed from the previous year. In 1964, Michigan was contending for the Big Ten title, and Illinois, the defending champion and a pre-season favorite to repeat, was playing for respect. By losing to Ohio State and Purdue in October, Illinois had lost its chance to win a second consecutive Big Ten championship. Still, Pete Elliott's Fighting Illini were a formidable team, with many of the players on its 1963 team, such as Grabowski, Custardo, and Butkus, returning as key contributors in 1964. Elliott's coaching staff was also experienced, including his assistants Burt Ingwessen, Jack Hart, Bob Herndon, Lou Baker, Jim Brown, Gene Stauber, Buck McPhail, and Bill Taylor.[12] All of the coaches on Pete Elliott's staff, except Ingwessen, had prior experience with Elliott, either at Nebraska, California, or Illinois. Furthermore, Illinois had the added motivation of wanting to beat Michigan, the only team which had defeated the Fighting Illini in 1963.

For Michigan, the motivation was of an entirely different nature. For the long-suffering Wolverine seniors, the game against Illinois was their final appearance in Michigan Stadium, the last time that Jim Conley, Bill Laskey, Ben Farabee, Dick Rindfuss, Bob Timberlake, John Marcum, Dave Butler, Brian Patchen, John Henderson, Jerry Mader, Arnie Simkus, John Yanz, Frosty Evashevski, Bill Muir, Michael Gorte and Nick Frontzczak played before the home crowd. They most assuredly did not want to lose their final game in Michigan Stadium. As part of the weekly preparation, Jim Conley, as team captain, called a players-only meeting. "There was nothing dramatic about the meeting," Conley later recalled. "I just reminded everybody that this is the home stretch and we need to win. As a team, we had done everything together and we couldn't afford to let up now."[13]

When Michigan and Illinois squared off on November 7, the weather was again ideal for Big Ten football: 54 degrees and overcast with a slight wind. Michigan won the coin toss and elected to start the game by kicking off to Illinois. The offensive unit for Illinois consisted of Bob Trumpy and Eddie Russell at the ends, All-America candidate Archie Sutton and Brian Duniec at the tackles, Dave Powless and Ed Washington at the guards, and Dick Butkus at center. In the Illini backfield were Fred Custardo at quarterback, Jim

Grabowski at fullback, and Sam Price and Ron Acks at the halfbacks. When Butkus started the game at center, it was an indication of the importance that Pete Elliott attached to the game by having Butkus go both ways on offense and defense.[14]

To meet the diversified attack of the Fighting Illini, Bob Hollway made no adjustments to the Michigan defense. The Michigan defense remained the same: Jim Conley and Bill Laskey at the ends; Bill Yearby and John Yanz at the tackles, Bob Mielke and Arnie Simkus at the guards, Tom Cecchini and Frank Nunley at the linebackers, and Rick Volk, Dick Rindfuss, and Rick Sygar in the secondary.[15] Hollway was confident going into the game, convinced that he knew the tendencies of Pete Elliott's offense and was able to anticipate the play-calling of the Fighting Illini.[16]

To begin the game, Bob Timberlake kicked off to Tony Parola, who returned the ball to the Illinois 18. Then the Illini began a drive that carried them to the Michigan 44, where it stalled out with a 4th and 8. But Pete Elliott and the Illinois coaches could take some satisfaction with the first possession, which produced two first downs before George Donnelly punted to the Michigan 22.

Then the Illini sent their defense onto the field to meet the Wolverines. Illinois deployed the same basic structure as the Michigan defense with two ends, Dave Mueller and Rich Callaghan; two tackles, Bill Minor and Gary Eickman; and two guards, Lynn Stewart and Greg Schumacher on the front line. Dick Butkus and Don Hansen were the linebackers. In the secondary were George Donnelly, Wayne Paulson, and Dick Kee.

On Michigan's first possession, the Wolverines went three and out, hardly a good omen. Two runs by Timberlake and one by Mel Anthony netted only five yards for the Wolverines and Stan Kemp punted 41 yards to the Illinois 32, where Wayne Paulson returned the punt to the 38. It was Kemp's first punt of the afternoon. More were to follow.

On their second possession, the Illini made a first down and then presented Michigan with its first gift of the game. On 1st and 10 from the Michigan 49, Jim Grabowski fumbled and John Yanz recovered the football for the Wolverines at the Michigan 48. But, once again, Michigan was unable to move the ball and soon faced a 4th and 4 from the Illinois 44. Not inclined to gamble at this point of the game, Bump Elliott dispatched Stan Kemp into the game for his second punt. Kemp sent the Illini deep into their own territory with a punt that rolled out of bounds on the Illinois 10.

On their first two possessions, the Illini had moved the ball against Michigan, but were unable to sustain the drives. On their third possession, the Illini made two quick first downs and had the ball, 1st and 10, from their 40 with time running out in the first quarter. Then the Michigan defense stiffened.

Dick Rindfuss threw Sam Price for a six-yard loss on first down. On second down, Jim Conley stopped Jim Grabowski for no gain. On third down, Fred Custardo went back to pass, looking for Bob Trumpy, his go-to receiver. An alert Frank Nunley stepped in front of Trumpy, intercepted Custardo's pass, and returned the interception to the Illinois 35. The first quarter ended with no score, but with Michigan solidly in Illinois territory.[17]

From that point, the Michigan offense turned to Bob Timberlake and Mel Anthony. Virtually alternating carries, the two backs moved the ball to the Illinois 23, where the Wolverines faced a 3rd and 12. Timberlake kept the ball on the ground and pitched back to Carl Ward for Ward's first carry of the game. Ward swept to the right and "weaved through [the] Illini" for the touchdown. After Timberlake's successful PAT, Michigan led 7–0.[18]

On the ensuing kickoff, Sam Price returned the ball to the Illinois 30. Then the Illini moved quickly in an attempt to tie the contest. Four consecutive running plays for Illinois brought the ball to mid-field. On 1st and 10 from the 50-yard line, Pete Elliott went for the touchdown, with Custardo throwing downfield to a streaking Bob Trumpy, who caught the football on the Michigan 15 and ran the rest of the distance for the touchdown. The score was 7–6 and Custardo awaited to kick the extra point. But Custardo missed, wide right, and the Wolverines clung to a slim one-point lead, 7–6.

After the game, Bump Elliott stated that he believed that Custardo's missed attempt for the extra point was the turning point of the game. After such an important touchdown, the failure to tie the game was a serious letdown for the Illini. "It left them flat," Elliott said.[19]

With the score 7–6, Carl Ward returned the next kickoff to the Michigan 31. The Wolverines managed to make one first down, but once again found themselves stopped by the Illinois defense. Dick Butkus was performing superbly for the Illini, making tackles, pursuing Timberlake, and otherwise frustrating the Michigan offense. Michigan faced a 4th and 15 from mid-field when Bump Elliott once again called on Stan Kemp to pin the Illini in their own end. On his fourth punt of the afternoon, Kemp punted out of bounds deep in Illinois territory at the 15.

On the next possession, Illinois lost its poise, perhaps the result of Custardo's missed extra point. On 2nd and 8 from the 17, Custardo hit halfback Ron Acks out of the backfield for a gain up to the 32, but Acks fumbled and an alert Brian Duniec recovered for Illinois on the 29. On the next play, Custardo fumbled, attempting to pass, but he recovered his fumble while losing three more yards. Two plays later, Custardo found Trumpy again, who caught the pass and ran to the Illinois 40 before he was hit hard by Frank Nunley and also fumbled. Jerry Mader, in the game to replace an injured John Yanz, recovered the loose ball, and the Wolverines had their third gift of the game.

Carl Ward (19) carries the ball against Illinois. Ward gave Michigan the break-away threat needed to complement the power running of Bob Timberlake, Mel Anthony, Jim Detwiler, and Dave Fisher (Bentley Historical Library, University of Michigan).

Michigan wasted no time adding to its slim one-point lead. First, Timberlake passed to John Henderson for a first down at the Illinois 29. Then, on first down, Timberlake ran to the 24. On second down, Timberlake went back to pass and then hit Jim Detwiler, who was coming out of the backfield on a crossing route. Detwiler caught the ball at the 1-yard line and crossed the goal line for an easy touchdown. Timberlake kicked the extra point and Michigan led 14–6, the score that remained when the teams went to their locker rooms at halftime.[20]

At halftime, the Wolverines received some bad news: John Yanz had suffered a knee injury that required surgery. His season was over, an especially bitter blow for Yanz, who had already battled a serious knee injury to get back onto the field and into the starting lineup. To replace Yanz, Bob Hollway inserted Jerry Mader from the two-way unit at the right tackle position on defense.[21]

Although Michigan held the lead at halftime, Illinois was curiously winning the game's statistical battle, holding the edge in total offense, 168 to 95, and even out-rushing the Wolverines, 58 to 54. It was the first time all season that one of Michigan's opponents had outperformed the Wolverines in the first half in those two categories.²² Still, the Illini had committed two costly turnovers and Michigan had capitalized on each turnover by moving in for the two touchdowns that provided the lead. As Michigan learned to its dismay on October 17 against Purdue, winning the statistical battle is meaningless if the opponent takes advantage of your mistakes.

The Silent Count

To begin the second half, Timberlake kicked off to Illinois and Sam Price returned the ball to the Illinois 23. The Michigan defense had made its adjustments at halftime, however, and the Illini soon discovered that moving the ball in the second half was going to be a difficult task. After making one first down, the Illini attack stalled out and Illinois faced a 4th and 9 from its own 37. George Donnelly came in to punt and boomed the punt of the year in Michigan Stadium down to the Michigan 6, where Dick Butkus tackled Dick Rindfuss, Michigan's punt returner.

The Wolverines went to work on their first possession of the second half deep in their own territory. They then proceeded to grind out a 14-play, 94-yard drive that culminated in Bob Timberlake's quarterback sneak for a touchdown at the 9:15 mark of the third quarter. On this impressive drive, Timberlake completed two passes, one to Ben Farabee for 4 yards and a near-first down, and one to John Henderson for eight yards and a first down. Otherwise, Michigan stayed on the ground for the entire drive with Timberlake carrying eight times, Detwiler six times, Ward four times, and Anthony once. The key play on the drive was a 23-yard burst by Carl Ward around left end from the Illinois 46 down to the 23.²³

Michigan's touchdown drive in the third quarter was unique for reasons other than its length, however. On this possession, Michigan set up its attack to neutralize Dick Butkus, who was having one of his better games in the first half against Michigan. In preparation for Illinois, Bump Elliott, Bob Timberlake, and Brian Patchen, Michigan's center, devised a stratagem designed to keep Butkus off-balance. The scheme essentially called for Michigan to run its plays without an audible signal. Timberlake received the snap from Patchen without a snap count, in effect sending the play into action without any audible cadence.

Elliott and the Michigan coaches had noticed that Butkus had a tendency to favor one side or the other when the opposing offense came to the line of scrimmage. Timberlake's responsibility was to run the play away from Butkus. So once he set the team at the line of scrimmage, Timberlake touched Patchen either on the left hip or the right hip, the signal to the backfield as to the direction of the play. Patchen, in turn, devised a series of head movements designed to inform John Marcum and Dave Butler, Michigan's two guards, about the

Bob Timberlake sets the Michigan offense in its game against Illinois. During the game, Michigan often snapped the ball without an audible signal in order to neutralize the impact of Dick Butkus, Illinois' All-American linebacker. On this play, Michigan's center is Brian Patchen (51). To Patchen's left is Dave Butler (77). Standing to the right of Timberlake is Carl Ward (19) (Bentley Historical Library, University of Michigan).

direction of the play. Once Patchen snapped the ball to Timberlake, with no cadence, he flew out to block Butkus and was joined by either Marcum or Butler on a double-team block of the Illini linebacker.

In retrospect, the key to the successful execution of the silent count was Brian Patchen's ability to fire off the line and maintain his block on Dick Butkus.[24] Patchen succeeded. The silent count neutralized Butkus, handicapped his pursuit of the play, and enabled Timberlake, Detwiler and Ward, running from the backfield, to reel off sizable chunks of yardage on sweeps, either to the right or to the left. As Jim Conley remembered, the stratagem worked to perfection against Butkus, who was "out of his mind" in frustration.[25]

After Timberlake scored Michigan's third touchdown and successfully kicked the extra point, the Wolverines led, 21–6. With Michigan's defense able to hold the Illinois offense in check, Michigan was in a strong position with a two-touchdown lead. After the game, Pete Elliott stated that he considered Michigan's long touchdown drive of the third quarter to be the game's turning point. "We matched them pretty well until that score," Elliott said. "Our first half play was as good as we've produced at any time this year."[26]

Timberlake's touchdown ended the scoring for the game, as Michigan's defense continued to stymie the Illinois attack. In addition, Stan Kemp kept up his punting artistry to prevent Illinois from getting good field position at any point in the second half. Midway through the fourth quarter, Michigan almost scored its fourth touchdown, after taking over on the Illinois 40 following a short punt by George Donnelly and a 15-yard personal foul penalty called against the Illini. Frosty Evashevski took over at quarterback for Michigan on this drive and called on Dave Fisher to carry the ball. Six carries by Fisher and a quarterback keeper by Evashevski gave the Wolverines a 4th and 1 from the Illinois 4-yard line. Rather than attempt a field goal, Elliott chose to go for the first down, but Evashevski fumbled the snap from center and George Donnelly recovered the loose ball for Illinois on the 1-yard line. In the scramble for the ball, tempers flared as players from both teams started throwing punches at each other. Dennis Flanagan, one of Michigan's offensive linemen, and Gary Eickman, a defensive tackle for Illinois, were ejected from the game and Michigan received a 15-yard "non-contact" penalty. This "fist-swinging brawl," in the words of Michigan broadcaster Tom Hemingway, was the last of the game's excitement, and the Wolverines finished the contest with a hard-earned, well-deserved, and workmanlike 21–6 victory.[27]

In his post-game comments, Bump Elliott singled out Stan Kemp for his contribution to the Michigan victory over Illinois. "The punting really helped us," Elliott observed. "Kemp hit some really good ones." For the game, Kemp punted seven times, with four of his punts going out of bounds inside the Illinois 15-yard line at the 15-, 13-, 10-, and 3-yard lines.[28]

Elliott's recognition of Stan Kemp was well earned. By this point in the season, Stan Kemp and his punting artistry had emerged as one the key strengths of the Wolverines. Depending on the situation, Kemp was able to punt long or short. Kemp was an assiduous player who prepared meticulously for each game. Each week in practice, Kemp placed cones out on the field at varying distances, and practiced hitting the cones with his punts. The Michigan offense knew that if it managed to reach its 40-yard line, but was forced to punt, Kemp was able to pin the opponent deep in its own end, sometimes by kicking the ball out of bounds inside the 10-yard line. Since Kemp was only a sophomore, his punting contribution turned out to one of the most unexpected, and pleasant, surprises of the 1964 season.[29]

"Let's go, State! Let's go, State!"

As the crowd of more than 62,000 watched the Michigan–Illinois game in Michigan Stadium, a curious, almost unheard-of chant began to be heard throughout the stands. "Let's go, State! Let's go, State!" went the crowd as Wolverine fans, transistor radios to their ears, were listening to the broadcast of the Michigan State–Purdue game from East Lansing. And Purdue was losing. Throughout the second half, Steve Filipiak, Michigan Stadium's public address announcer, regularly broke in with updated scores from East Lansing.[30] Followers of Big Ten football were well aware of Purdue's habit of inflicting season-deflating losses on its favored opponents, especially their upsets of Michigan State, but now the Spartans were turning the tables, and convincingly so.

On November 7, Michigan State defeated Purdue, 21–7, giving the Boilermakers their first Big Ten loss. Although the score of the game remained close until well into the fourth quarter, the Spartans were clearly getting the better of the Boilermakers, racking up 21 first downs to 11 for the Boilers, and out-gaining Purdue on the ground, 302–91, with Dick Gordon pounding through the Purdue defenders for 145 yards. Michigan State had played a strong defensive game against Michigan, and against Purdue, the Spartan defenders harassed Bob Griese all afternoon. The Michigan State defense also scored the Spartans' first touchdown on a blocked punt by Charlie Thornhill, recovered by Harold Lucas, who ran in for an easy score.[31]

Worse for the Boilermakers was the loss of Bob Hadrick, Purdue's leading receiver and Griese's favorite target, who left the game in the second quarter with a severely sprained ankle. After Hadrick's departure, Michigan State keyed on the Purdue running attack and the Boilers entered Spartan territory only once in the rest of the game.[32]

Following the crushing defeat, Purdue's coach Jack Mollenkopf summarized the abrupt change in his team's performance. "Sure, the loss of Hadrick hurt us. It hurt the morale and spirit as well as the offense," Mollenkopf said. "But I can't blame it all on that. We just didn't perform up to what we have been doing. Michigan State came harder after us than any team this year and that includes Notre Dame. State is the finest team we have played yet. They had everything today, speed, desire, and effort."[33]

Like their coach, the Purdue players were deflated by their loss to Michigan State, as well as its implications for the rest of the Big Ten season. Randy Minniear, who gained 82 hard-fought yards rushing against Michigan State, retained a vivid memory of the game. State "just popped our bubble," Minniear recalled. "Hadrick was so much of our go-to guy. When Hadrick went down, it affected the [entire] Purdue game plan."[34] Moreover, the loss to Michigan State was even more discouraging to Purdue's players since they had already defeated Michigan and Illinois, arguably the two teams that stood in their path to the Rose Bowl. "The loss to State was the one that killed us," Minniear added. "It took the wind right out of our sails. We really thought that we were the better team. It was like, 'Here we go again, we beat Michigan and then we falter.' It just seemed like..." and then his voice trailed off.[35]

Purdue's first loss had an immediate effect on the Big Ten race and put Ohio State firmly in the driver's seat. Even so, Michigan now faced the prospect of being able to claim at least a share of the championship if it won its final two games, against Iowa and then Ohio State. Even if Michigan did not receive a Rose Bowl invitation (almost a certainty to go to Purdue if the two teams finished tied for first place), a co-championship was certainly a worthy accomplishment for the season. But the cold, hard fact still prevailed: to win the championship outright, the Wolverines needed another team to defeat Purdue.

On to Iowa City

On November 14, Michigan played its eighth game of the 1964 season against Iowa on the road in Iowa City. The victory over Illinois, one week earlier, combined with Ohio State's loss to Penn State, 27–0, in Columbus on the same day, gave Michigan an enormous bump in the national football polls. Michigan entered the game against Iowa ranked number 6 in the country, the first time that Michigan had cracked the Top Ten since the loss to Purdue on October 17. Michigan even passed Ohio State in the polls as the Buckeyes, previously ranked number 1 in the country, fell to number 7 after being shut out by Penn State, 27–0, in Columbus on November 7. Michigan, therefore, went into the game against Iowa with a renewed sense of confidence as well as a sense of urgency.

In the postwar period, Michigan and Iowa were regular opponents, playing each other on ten separate occasions between 1951 and 1963. The Michigan–Iowa games were usually close, hard-fought matches, with Michigan winning six of the contests, Iowa winning two, and two games ending in ties. Between 1951 and 1960, Forest Evashevski was Iowa's head coach and Hawkeye supporters considered his coaching tenure as the Golden Era of Iowa football. Evashevski's record was 52–27–4, and his teams won two conference championships, and two Rose Bowls, during his tenure as the head coach.

Evashevski stepped down as head coach to become Iowa's athletic director after the 1960 season, and Jerry Burns, one of his main assistants, succeeded him as head coach. Like Evashevski, Burns was an alumnus of the University of Michigan, playing for the Wolverines between 1947 and 1950, where he was briefly a teammate of Pete Elliott. Once the head coach at Iowa, Burns assembled an experienced coaching staff that, by 1964, included "Whitey" Piro, Ray Jauch, Archie Kodros, Wayne Robinson, Bill Happel, and Andy McDonald.[36]

Michigan's previous game against Iowa, on November 16, 1963, in Ann

Arbor, ended in a 21–21 tie. Michigan scored the first touchdown in the game, but Iowa scored twice in the second quarter to take a 14–7 lead into halftime. In the third quarter, Michigan regained the lead, 21–14, on two rushing touchdowns by Mel Anthony. But the lead failed to hold up as Iowa's quarterback Gary Snook passed to his leading receiver, Paul Krause, who scored on a 25-yard pass to tie the score. Both teams missed field goals in the fourth quarter and the game ended in a deadlock, the second tie game for each team in 1963.[37]

In 1964, Iowa became the Big Ten's hard-luck team. Before playing Michigan, Iowa had lost its three previous games by a total of eight points, losing to Purdue, 19–14, Ohio State, 21–19, and Minnesota, 14–13. Led again by Gary Snook, the Big Ten's leading passer, Iowa's "record was deceiving and the Hawkeyes possessed one of the finest passing teams in the country," Bump Elliott observed before the game. "They'll be shooting the works to break out and we'll have to be at our very best to beat them."[38]

Jocko Nelson, Michigan's ends coach, scouted the Hawkeyes in their games against Ohio State on October 31 and against Minnesota on November 7. "Nobody's looking beyond Saturday. We'll have our hands full with Iowa," Nelson said. "Iowa looks like a pro club and they put the ball in the air a lot. They are very, very dangerous."[39] Iowa built its attack around the passing of Snook to his primary receiver, Karl Noonan, augmented by the running of two quick halfbacks, Dalton Kimble and Craig Nourse. Interestingly, both Noonan and Kimble were recruited to Iowa from their high schools in Flint, Michigan.[40]

Regardless of their record, the Hawkeyes knew that a victory over 6th-ranked Michigan would be a signature win on their season, and the Iowa supporters turned out in huge numbers for the game. A packed house of almost 57,000 jammed Iowa Stadium on Dad's Day for the contest. The weather was unseasonably warm, with temperatures in the mid–70s and a strong west southwest wind blowing between 15 and 25 miles per hour.

Michigan won the coin toss and elected to receive the first kickoff. Gary Simpson kicked off to Jim Detwiler, who returned the ball to the Michigan 35.[41] Bump Elliott sent out the I-75 Backfield and the usual starters on the offensive line, except for Ben Farabee, who started at tight end in place of Steve Smith, out nursing a shoulder injury. Iowa's starting defensive unit consisted of Dave Long and Cliff Wilder at the ends, Phillip Deutsch and Robert Mitchell at the tackles, Stephen Hodoway at nose tackle. Daniel Hitsabeck and Delbert Gehrke were the linebackers. The secondary consisted of Ivory McDowell, Russell Ferance, Daniel Moreland, and Karlin Ryan.[42] The game started off poorly for Michigan as the Hawkeye defense stopped the Wolverines with a three-and-out. Stan Kemp entered the game on fourth down and kicked out of bounds at the Iowa 37.

Iowa started its first possession with good field position on the 37. The Hawkeyes started Rich O'Hara at split end and Tony Giacobazzi at tight end; Robert Ziolkowski and Leo Miller at the tackles; John Niland and Bernard Budzik at the guards; and David Recher at center. In the backfield were Gary Snook at quarterback, Dalton Kimble and Craig Nourse at the halfbacks and Karl Noonan at flanker.[43]

To face the Hawkeye offense, Bob Hollway sent out a defensive unit that made some changes from the game against Illinois. Following the injury to John Yanz, Jerry Mader started at right tackle. Dick Rindfuss seriously sprained an ankle against Illinois and was unable to play against Iowa. Dick Wells took Rindfuss's place in the secondary. Other less perceptible changes quickly became evident, however, as Hollway used Mike Bass and John Henderson in the secondary on obvious passing situations. Michigan's defensive objective in the game was to stop Iowa's passing attack, and Hollway used several combinations in the secondary to keep Snook off-balance, and occasionally to double-team the Hawkeye receivers.[44]

On Iowa's first possession, the Hawkeyes provided quick evidence of their intentions: they were going to pass. On first down, Snook threw incomplete to Noonan. But on second down, Noonan took a pitchout from Snook and, on a flanker option, threw to split end Rich O'Hara for a gain of 45 yards down to the Michigan 18. On the second series of the possession, however, the Hawkeyes were unable to move past the Michigan 10, where they faced 4th and 2. Jerry Burns called on Gary Simpson to attempt a field goal from the Michigan 17. Simpson's kick was unsuccessful, however, and the game remained scoreless.[45] The Hawkeyes had squandered a golden opportunity to take the first lead in the game.

But Iowa quickly received another opportunity. On Michigan's next possession, Carl Ward fumbled on a 2nd and 6 play, trying to sweep left end, and Dave Long recovered for the Hawkeyes at the Michigan 11. The Michigan offense, thus far in the game, looked terrible: two possessions had only yielded a three-and-out and a turnover. Iowa wasted no time taking advantage of Michigan's mistake as Craig Nourse, on first down, carried the ball for an 11 yard touchdown at the 8:29 mark of the first quarter.[46]

Michigan continued to sputter on offense. In their next series, the Wolverines once again failed to gain a first down and Stan Kemp was forced to punt for the second time in the game. On Iowa's next possession, though, the Michigan defense stiffened and forced a three-and-out. But Iowa's punter Mickey Moses pinned Michigan down on its 11 after his first punt of the game.[47]

With slightly less than six minutes left in the first quarter, the Michigan offense found its bearings. Timberlake expertly moved the Wolverines downfield on runs by Mel Anthony and Carl Ward, and passes to Jim Detwiler and

Ben Farabee. The big gain on the drive was a 29-yard completion from Timberlake to Detwiler that brought the ball from the Michigan 41 to the Iowa 30. The Michigan drive reached the Iowa 6 yard line and it looked as though the Wolverines were about to tie the score. But, on first and goal, Timberlake fumbled the ball on a sweep to the right. Anthony recovered the fumble, but Michigan lost ten yards on the play. The Michigan offense's tendency to fumble, mostly absent in the three previous games, was rearing its ugly head once again. Michigan failed to gain any yardage on the next two plays, and Bump Elliott called for Timberlake to attempt a field goal from the Iowa 24. He missed the kick and the first quarter ended with Iowa holding onto a 7–0 lead.[48]

Iowa took over on its 20 after Timberlake's missed attempt for a field goal. On first down, the Hawkeyes became generous. Trying to carry off left tackle, Craig Nourse fumbled, and an alert Jerry Mader recovered the ball for Michigan at the Iowa 23. With 14:43 left in the first half, the I-75 Backfield wasted no time evening up the score. A completion from Timberlake to Farabee brought the ball to the Iowa 12. Runs by Timberlake and Ward gained six more yards. On 3rd and 4 from the Iowa 6, Timberlake calmly passed to John Henderson for Michigan's first touchdown. Timberlake kicked the extra point and the score was tied, 7–7.[49]

On their next possession, the Hawkeyes were generous once again. On third down, Craig Nourse fumbled for the second time and Dick Wells fell on the loose ball at the Iowa 24. Courtesy of another Hawkeye turnover, Michigan had an invitation to take the lead. But after a 14-yard completion from Timberlake to Henderson, the Wolverines were penalized 15 yards for holding, back to the Iowa 26. Soon it was 4th and 21 for Michigan from the Iowa 22. Elliott called for a field goal. Timberlake missed again and the Wolverines had squandered an opportunity.

Fortunately for Michigan, though, Iowa was not finished with turnovers. On the next possession, one of Gary Snook's passes was deflected by Bob Mielke and picked off by Bill Laskey at the Iowa 29. Laskey ran the ball to the Iowa 10, where Michigan took over. The Iowa defense barely had time to breathe on the sidelines before the offense's turnovers sent them back onto the field. On the next play, Mel Anthony bolted over right guard for a touchdown and the Wolverines took the lead, 13–7.

Following Anthony's touchdown, the Wolverines lined up for the extra point. But Brian Patchen, medicated for a severe cold, snapped the ball to Bob Timberlake, the kicker, instead of to Frosty Evashevski, the holder. Surprised to get the snap, Timberlake scrambled, looking for a potential receiver, and threw in the direction of John Henderson in the end zone. The pass was incomplete and the score remained 13–7 in Michigan's favor.

On the sideline after the failed extra point attempt, Tony Mason went up to the obviously disappointed Brian Patchen. "Tony told me not to worry about it," Patchen recalled. "Ohio State will spend a couple of hours in practice defending it," Mason said, because they would be fooled into thinking that Michigan had a new two-point play in its offensive arsenal.[50]

Iowa showed its resilience, however, even after the offense committed its fourth consecutive turnover when Mike Bass intercepted one of Snook's passes on the next Hawkeye possession. The Hawkeye defense snuffed out another scoring opportunity by Michigan and Iowa got the ball back on its 24, with 7:15 left in the first half. After making two first downs, Iowa had a 1st and 10 at the Michigan 49 when Snook hit Noonan on a 40-yard strike to the Michigan 9-yard line. The Michigan defense kept the Hawkeyes out of the end zone on the next three plays and Iowa faced 4th and goal from the Michigan 5. With one missed field goal already in the books, Jerry Burns decided to go for the touchdown. His gamble paid off as Snook found Rich O'Hara in the end zone. Iowa had tied the score, but Simpson missed the extra point attempt.[51] Despite the disappointing missed PAT, the enthusiastic Iowa fans in Iowa Stadium sensed an upset, a gigantic upset.

Michigan started its final possession of the first half from its own 20 with

Bill Laskey intercepted a pass against Iowa, which turned out to be a key turnover for Michigan in its defeat of the Hawkeyes, 34–20. Also defending for Michigan are Arnie Simkus (70), Bob Mielke (63), who deflected the pass that Laskey intercepted, Frank Nunley (59), and Tom Cecchini (53) (Bentley Historical Library, University of Michigan).

3:42 left on the clock. For the packed house gathered in Iowa Stadium, the question was whether Michigan intended to stay conservative and go into halftime content with the score tied. Mel Anthony provided the answer to that question. The Wolverines intended to score and break the deadlock, just as they had in the waning moments of the first half against Air Force in the first game of the season. The offense intended to keep the pressure on the opposing defense. On first down from the Iowa 20, Timberlake ran a quarterback option play to the right, then pitched the ball back to Mel Anthony, who broke through a hole on the right side and ran into the clear for 62 yards to the Iowa 18. Al Randolph, one of Iowa's defensive backs, pulled him down from behind, saving a touchdown. Two plays later, Timberlake swept around left end for 14 yards and the go-ahead touchdown. Michigan had gone 80 yards in three plays, all of them on the ground, in less than one minute. Timberlake kicked the extra point and the Wolverines had the lead, 20–13.[52] When the first half ended, the Wolverines headed to the locker room confident and the Hawkeyes went to the locker room, deflated.

A Game of Turnovers and Missed Opportunities—On Both Sides

At halftime, the game's statistics revealed the strategies that each team had adopted. For Michigan, the plan was to pound the ball on the ground with the I-75 Backfield running behind the talented offensive line. The Wolverines had already rushed the ball for 147 yards at the mid-point of the game. For Iowa, the strategy was to pass the ball effectively against a Michigan defense that could stop the run but was vulnerable to the pass. At halftime, the Hawkeyes had gained 142 yards through the air, as Snook managed to find Noonan and O'Hara consistently.[53] Except for the unusually warm weather, the Michigan–Iowa contest was a typical, hard-hitting, bruising, mid–November game in the Big Ten.

Iowa elected to receive in the second half and Timberlake kicked off to Dalton Kimble, who returned the ball to the Iowa 24. At this point in the game, the contest turned clearly in Michigan's favor. On Iowa's first play from scrimmage in the third quarter, Gary Snook fumbled, and Arnie Simkus, like Jerry Mader and Dick Wells in the first half, fell on the ball for the Wolverines. Once again, Michigan had the ball deep in Iowa territory at the 24.

It took Michigan five plays to score and expand the lead to two touchdowns. The key play on the short drive was a 12-yard completion from Timberlake to Henderson that gave Michigan a first down at the Iowa 12. Two plays later, Anthony went over left guard for Michigan's fourth touchdown.

Timberlake kicked the extra point and the Wolverines led, 27–13, with 12:42 left in the third quarter.[54] Almost half the game remained to be played, but for the moment at least, Michigan held the upper hand.

The Hawkeyes appeared to have lost their focus. On the next possession, Iowa managed to gain a first down, but on the ensuing series, Rick Volk intercepted a pass thrown by Snook and Michigan regained possession at the Iowa 12. Two plays later, Timberlake ran seven yards around the right end for a touchdown, but Michigan was penalized 15 yards for holding, nullifying the score. Michigan was forced to settle for another field goal attempt by Timberlake, his third of the game, but like the first two, Timberlake missed again. The Iowans could breathe slightly easier; a Michigan touchdown at that point would have put the game out of reach.

When Iowa began its next series, Snook fumbled again, this time on second down. Bill Keating recovered the fumble for Michigan at the Iowa 8-yard line. With time still left in the third quarter, Iowa had already committed seven turnovers, four fumbles and three interceptions. But the battered Hawkeye defense rose to the occasion and forced a fumble by Jim Detwiler, recovered by Iowa's Terry Mulligan at the Iowa 7. Even given opportunity after opportunity, the Wolverines were unable to slam the door on the Hawkeyes.[55]

In the second half, the one constant for Michigan was the stout play of its defense, which, by now, had figured out the Iowa attack. On Iowa's next possession, the Wolverine defenders forced a three-and-out, and Mickey Moses only managed to punt the ball to the Iowa 44. With 8:33 left in the third quarter, Michigan went back to work on offense. Two runs by Ward, two by Timberlake, and one by Anthony brought the ball to the Iowa 30, where the Wolverines faced a 3rd and 10. Timberlake then fired another strike to Henderson, his favorite target all season, and Henderson carried the ball to just outside of the 10-yard line. From that point, it took two carries by Timberlake and two by Anthony, the last from the 1-yard line, and Michigan had its fifth touchdown of the game. After Timberlake's successful PAT, Michigan led by a commanding margin, 34–13, with 3:35 left in the third quarter.

But Iowa refused to give up. On the first series of the next possession, Iowa kept its drive alive after a personal foul penalty on Michigan. Soon the Hawkeyes had the ball at midfield, and then Snook hit Noonan for 30 yards down to the Michigan 20. On the next play, Snook ran 20 yards around right end for the touchdown. After Gary Simpson's successful PAT, the score was Michigan 34-Iowa 20, with 10:06 left in the game.[56]

With a two-touchdown lead, Michigan grasped the necessity of the moment: control the ball, score if possible, but above all, take time off the clock. Bump Elliott decided to lower the blade on the Michigan ground game. With victory in sight, the I-75 Backfield took over. From the Michigan 15, Timberlake, Anthony, and Detwiler took turns carrying the ball, along with another 10-yard completion from Timberlake to Henderson, and Michigan soon had a first down at the Iowa 48. Then Dave Fisher entered the game and carried the ball four consecutive times to the Iowa 25. Two more carries by Fisher, one by Timberlake, and one by Ward brought Michigan to the Iowa 15. But then the Wolverines faltered. Through a combination of tackles-for-loss and a 5-yard penalty for offside, Michigan was back at the Iowa 18, where the Hawkeye defense held and its offense took over. But for Michigan, the I-75 Backfield, with an assist from Dave Fisher, had marched almost 80 yards in 22 plays and, more important, had taken more than 9 minutes off the clock. Iowa took possession with 46 seconds left in the game, hardly enough time to do any further damage. The game ended, Michigan 34–Iowa 20, the seventh victory for the Wolverines in eight games.

But the big boost in the Wolverines' spirits came on Michigan's last possession, when Iowa's public address announcer gave the final score of the Minnesota-Purdue game at Minneapolis: Minnesota 14–Purdue 7. Michigan's linebacker Tom Cecchini remembered the moment vividly: 'It was in the midst of the Iowa game that I realized how far we had come. Our offense was on the field when the announcement blared from the loudspeaker: Minnesota had beaten Purdue, 14–7. The picture was clear—beat Iowa and the next week we would take on Ohio State for [the Big Ten] title. I doubt that anything short of a national disaster could have stopped our momentum."[57]

The Minnesota victory came as a relief to Bump Elliott also. "We were playing pretty well against Iowa," Elliott remembered. "But hearing that score sent our bench into jubilation. That was a great stimulus [when we knew Purdue had lost]."[58]

Although it only became clear afterward, Purdue had become seriously handicapped by injuries by the eighth game of the season. Bob Hadrick was knocked out in the Michigan State game, as well as Ken Eby, one of the starting safeties.[59] Rich Ruble, the starting tight end, was out with an injury and his replacement, Ed Snitger, left the Minnesota game early. Most important, both Gordon Teter and Randy Minniear were badly shaken up in the first half in Minneapolis. "Gordy got his ribs busted up early in the game," Randy Minniear remembered. "He could barely breathe and the pain was so bad that he could hardly stand it." Minniear was injured in the first quarter, came out of the game briefly, and then returned hurt to play the rest of the contest.[60]

Minnesota took an early lead, 7–0, in the first half before Purdue tied the game late in the third quarter. In the fourth quarter, Minnesota struck again on a pass from quarterback John Hankinson to end Kent Kramer. The scoring occurred on a 43-yard strike from Hankinson, who hit Kramer between two Purdue defenders and then outraced them into the end zone.[61]

Curiously, Purdue easily won the game's statistical battle in terms of making more first downs and more total yardage than Minnesota, but three interceptions of Bob Griese by the Golden Gophers ruined the Boilers' scoring opportunities. After the game, a dejected Jack Mollenkopf concluded, "It was not one of our better games. But in the end, Minnesota wanted it more than we did."[62]

Years later, Randy Minniear expressed the frustration and disappointment felt by the Purdue players after the losses to Michigan State and Minnesota: "What was so different about the Big Ten was that, I don't care if you played the worst team in the Big Ten, [all the games] were head-knockers. The other conferences had weak teams [but not the Big Ten]. *We were so beat up by the end of the year*" [Minniear's emphasis]. We were very down, very down. That game against Minnesota, we just couldn't get it going. It was all terribly frustrating."[63]

"It hurt me worse than it hurt him"

In his post-game comments, Bump Elliott spoke in terms of relief, saying, "Boy, that was the longest game I've been in. I thought it would never end. I didn't want to breathe easy until late in the fourth quarter. An explosive team like Iowa can score from anywhere. In a helter-skelter game like this, anything can happen."[64]

For Michigan, once again the keys to victory against Iowa were the play of Bob Timberlake, Mel Anthony, and John Henderson, as well as the opportunism of the Michigan defense. Timberlake ran for 106 yards, passed for 136, and scored one touchdown. Anthony ran for 124 yards and scored three touchdowns. Henderson caught six passes for 74 yards and scored a touchdown.[65] With his size and strength, Timberlake presented a daunting problem for the smaller Hawkeye defenders. In the third quarter, Iowa's defensive back Terry Foley left the game on a stretcher after "getting the wind knocked out of him," the result of a collision with Timberlake. "I dove at Timberlake," Foley recalled, "and I thought that I was getting him from the blind side. I hit him all right, but he's hard as a rock. It hurt me worse than it hurt him."[66]

For the Michigan defense, the Hawkeyes were the toughest opponent of the season. Iowa managed to gain 324 yards of total offense and 19 first downs against Michigan. Even so, Michigan held Iowa to less than 100 yards rushing and forced seven turnovers, thereby limiting the damage that the Hawkeyes could do.[67] In his post-game comments, Elliott paid the defense some compliments. "We used double coverage and kept switching defenses the entire game," Elliott said. "It seemed to keep them off-stride. Credit should go to our defensive coach, Bob Hollway, who planned our defense this week."[68] Once again, the Michigan defense had stopped them when it had to.

The combination of Michigan's victory over Iowa and Purdue's loss to Minnesota was felt all the way back to Ann Arbor. When the Michigan team's plane landed at Willow Run Airport outside Detroit after the flight from Iowa City, a crowd estimated at 400 to 500 supporters waited to welcome and cheer on the players. After the team filed out of the plane, broadcaster Bob Ufer introduced Michigan's captain Jim Conley to the cheering Maize and Blue assemblage as "the fans cheered and yelled."[69] As Doug Mintline wrote in the *Flint Journal*, "There's no avoiding the strong scent of roses as the Wolverines shoved aside an undermanned Iowa band, 34–20."[70] The final test of the season awaited the Wolverines the next weekend, against Ohio State in Columbus. Before leaving Iowa City, Bump Elliott was asked by reporters for a prediction on the following week's game against the Buckeyes. Elliott gave a quick reply: "We'll be ready."[71]

Six

"We gotta beat Ohio! We gotta beat Ohio!"

Michigan 10—Ohio State 0

For the Michigan Wolverines, their victory at Iowa on November 14, combined with Purdue's loss to Minnesota on the same day, opened the door to a Big Ten title. Michigan had received its long sought-after second chance, and Bump Elliott and his players knew that they needed to capitalize on it. After the loss to Purdue on October 17, the Wolverines realized that their only realistic hope of salvaging their championship ambitions rested on winning the remainder of their games, including the game against Ohio State on November 21, and then hope for some help from Purdue's opponents. Somehow Elliott sensed that Michigan was to get its second chance, but that a win over the Buckeyes was essential. After the Purdue game, Elliott recalled, "I finally got to sleep [that night] by repeating, 'We gotta beat Ohio! We gotta beat Ohio!' Just like a fellow counting sheep."[1]

The Michigan players got the message, too. After the Purdue game, "Beat Ohio State" became the team chant until the two teams squared off on November 21. The mood of the Michigan team for the Ohio State game was captured by Rick Sygar, who recalled more than twenty years later, "Rarely, if ever, do I recall preparing for an important game, against a strong team like Ohio State, with the unshakeable belief that we would not lose. We will win. They will lose. Simple. Such was our confidence going into Columbus."[2]

So the season finale between Michigan and Ohio State in 1964 was played for the Big Ten's highest stakes. Michigan had an overall record of 7-1 and a Big Ten conference record of 5-1. Michigan was ranked 6th in the country in the national polls. Of Michigan's six Big Ten opponents prior to the Ohio State game, only Iowa and Northwestern had conference records below .500.

For its part, Ohio State entered the Michigan game with an overall record of 7–1 and a 5–0 record in conference play. The Buckeyes were ranked 7th in the national polls. In Big Ten play, however, Ohio State had played only one opponent, Illinois, whose record in the conference was above .500. As the Big Ten conference schedule clearly showed, Ohio State had the easier route to the championship. Not only did the Buckeyes play one less conference game than Michigan, but the records of their opponents were clearly inferior by comparison. Three of Michigan's toughest opponents, Michigan State, Purdue, and Minnesota, were off the Ohio State schedule. Nevertheless, the Big Ten championship, and a trip to the Rose Bowl, went to the team with the best overall winning percentage in conference play. To secure the championship, Michigan needed a victory over Ohio State on November 21. Ohio State, by contrast, could claim the conference title with a victory or a tie.

At this point, it's helpful to remember that few football observers, prior to the season, expected Michigan and Ohio State to play for the Big Ten championship in the final game of the season. Unlike the Michigan–Ohio State games of the 1970s, when Michigan's teams, coached by Bo Schembechler, and Ohio State's teams, coached by Woody Hayes, dispatched their conference opponents with regularity, setting up a long-anticipated showdown in the season finale, the Big Ten season throughout the 1960s was highly competitive without any single team dominating the conference. It was most assuredly not the Big Two and Little Eight, reminiscent of the 1970s, but instead a conference where four or five teams remained in contention throughout the season with the outcome usually in doubt until the final two or three weekends of play. In that context, the results of several different games often determined the final outcome and league champion.[3] In terms of the importance of the Ohio State game to Michigan's entire season in 1964, Bump Elliott even admitted, "It sort of snuck up on us. Nobody realized that was going to happen. All of a sudden here we are, playing for the conference championship."[4]

The Brutish Buckeyes

For Ohio State, the 1964 football season, its 75th, began both with a sense of apprehension and a sense of optimism. The Buckeyes returned 23 lettermen from the 1963 team that finished behind Illinois and Michigan State in the final Big Ten standings. Even so, the Buckeyes still lost several key players from 1963: Paul Warfield, their All-American wide receiver; Matt Snell, their stalwart fullback; and Dick Van Raaphorst, their all-time leader in field goals and extra points.

Like the Michigan coaching staff, the Ohio State coaches were experienced football men who were familiar with the Big Ten wars. Woody Hayes was beginning his fourteenth season as Ohio State's head coach and he had suffered only one losing campaign (1959) during his tenure as the Buckeye leader. The assistant coaches under Hayes were a mixture of veterans combined with some newcomers. Esko Sarkkinen, the ends coach, was beginning his nineteenth season at Ohio State. Harry Strobel, who coached the guards and centers, had been at Ohio State since 1949. Lyal Clark, the defensive line coach, started on the Ohio State staff in 1954.

The relative newcomers were Lou McCullough, the offensive backfield coach, who was in his second season; Frank Ellwood, the defensive coordinator and a member of the staff since 1962; Hugh Hindman, who coached the tackles and joined the staff in 1963 after another Hayes assistant, Bo Schembechler, left Ohio State to become the head football coach at Miami University of Ohio; Max Urick, who joined the staff in 1963; and Glenn Ellison, the freshman coach, who also came along in 1963. Sarkkinen and Ellwood were Ohio State alumni; the other coaches received their playing experience at other colleges.[5]

For a season outlook, Ohio State's strength was clearly on defense and the major problems facing the Buckeyes were rebuilding the offensive line and strengthening the offensive backfield. Like the other Big Ten teams, Ohio State planned to adopt the platoon system, and even went so far to inform the media that "[t]he liberalized substitution rule will permit the Buckeyes to employ the platoon system, favored by the Buckeye coaching staff."[6]

By the time spring practice ended in 1964, Ohio State had established its offensive and defensive units. Leading the offense were three returning lettermen: quarterback Don Unverferth, the starter in 1963; fullback Willard Sander; and left halfback Tom Barrington. Right halfback Bo Rein, a highly touted sophomore from Niles, Ohio, was the newcomer in the backfield.

The leaders of the Ohio State defense were the ends Bill Spahr and Tom Kiehfuss, linebacker Ike Kelley, and defensive safety Arnold Chonko, all of whom were returning lettermen. Steve Dreffer, a starter in the defensive backfield, was the Ohio State punter, and Bob Funk was the team's place kicker. The Buckeyes' *1964 Media Guide* summed up the preseason succinctly: "With the defense strong, the offense must shoulder its share of the burden by breaking away for occasional long gainers. If the offense achieves this consistency, the Buckeyes may well put up a stiff challenge for the coveted Big Ten championship."[7]

Ohio State began the 1964 football season on September 26 at home against Southern Methodist University (SMU), coached by Hayden Fry. The large crowd of 80,737 was not disappointed by the result as the Buckeyes rolled to an easy 27–8 victory. Ohio State put on "a crushing display of the power football which is a Woody Hayes trademark," so that "the small sophomore-dominated Mustangs put up a scrap, but never had a chance," according to one account of the game.⁸

Ohio State's next opponent was Indiana University on October 3. Unlike in their opening contest, the Buckeyes needed to contend for the entire game before emerging with a 17–9 victory over the stubborn Hoosiers. The hero for Ohio State was defensive safety Arnold Chonko, who intercepted three passes by Indiana quarterback Rich Kadar, two of them deep in Ohio State territory, including one in the fourth quarter that ended a drive that conceivably could have tied the game.⁹ While Buckeye fans could take some heart in the team's undefeated record after two games, the fact remained that Ohio State had played two relatively weak opponents to begin the season. The next two opponents, Illinois and the University of Southern California (USC), promised to offer much stiffer competition.

On October 10, the Buckeyes traveled to Champaign-Urbana to take on defending Big Ten champion Illinois. Then, on October 17, they returned to Columbus, where they faced 7th-ranked USC. The outcomes of these two games promised to determine the degree of success that the Buckeyes were to experience in 1964. In both games, Ohio State rose to the occasion and turned in its most dominating performances of the season, shutting out the Fighting Illini, 26–0, and then holding USC scoreless, 17–0.

Ohio State's victory over Illinois gave the Buckeyes a 2–0 record in conference play, good for a first-place tie in the Big Ten as well as a push upward in the national polls. The Ohio State–Illinois game, an early-season clash of the two preseason favorites for the Big Ten championship, raised expectations throughout the Midwest for its potential impact on the outcome of the conference season. But the Buckeyes held the upper hand from their first possession, when quarterback Don Unverferth embarrassingly fooled the Illini with a 23-yard naked bootleg run for a touchdown. Woody Hayes was thrilled with the play itself, as well as its impact: "I called the play in the dressing room before the game," Hayes exulted in his postgame press conference.¹⁰

The following week, October 17, the Ohio State–Southern Cal contest in Columbus was nationally broadcast as a "Game of the Week." But this much-anticipated showdown between a Midwestern football power, and a West Coast football power, turned out to be no contest as the Buckeyes shut out John McKay's Trojans, 17–0. Ohio State controlled the line of scrimmage on both sides of the ball and "the brutish Buckeyes," in the words of *Chicago Tribune* sportswriter Robert Markus, showed the nation why they were ranked first among the country's best teams.¹¹

After these impressive victories over two highly rated opponents, however, Ohio State mysteriously lost some of the sharpness and precision that it had displayed against Illinois and Southern Cal. On October 24, the Buckeyes capitalized on several Wisconsin turnovers to defeat the Badgers in Columbus, 28–3. But a lack of concentration the following week against Iowa in Iowa City almost cost the Buckeyes a victory. Playing an inspired Hawkeye team that had lost its previous two games, Ohio State managed to squeak out a 21–19 victory, but only by stopping Iowa quarterback Gary Snook's two-point conversion attempt after Iowa had scored a touchdown with less than two minutes remaining in the game.[12] Even though Ohio State retained its number-one ranking in the national polls, as well as holding the top spot in the Big Ten standings, the Buckeyes no longer resembled the powerhouse juggernaut of the first four games.

Ohio State's next opponent was Penn State, a team coming into Columbus on November 7 with an overall record of 3–4, hardly a team to raise much concern among the Buckeye faithful. In this case, however, Coach Rip Engle's Nittany Lions were a better team than their record indicated. Penn State started the season woefully, losing to Navy, the University of California–Los Angeles (UCLA), and Oregon on successive weekends. Then Penn State narrowly defeated Army but lost to Syracuse. After the loss to Syracuse, however, Penn State's fortunes improved markedly as the Lions convincingly defeated West Virginia and Maryland.

Confident after two consecutive victories, Penn State did not approach the Ohio State contest with any apprehension. "We're going to shut out Woody [Hayes]," Joe Paterno, Engle's assistant coach, predicted before the game, although Paterno offered no clues as to how he intended to make good on his prediction.[13]

But the game proved Paterno correct. "The Nittany Lions had upset on their minds from the start, and played like it," wrote Roy Damer in the *Chicago Tribune*.[14] Penn State scored once in the first half and three times in the second half to defeat the Buckeyes, 27–0. Penn State's total domination of the game was reflected in the post-game statistics. Penn State racked up 22 first downs to Ohio State's 5, had 349 yards of total offense to the Buckeyes' 63, and outgained Ohio State on the ground, 201–33.[15]

Following the game, Woody Hayes gave full credit to Penn State for outplaying his Buckeyes. "That was the soundest trouncing we ever have had," Hayes told the reporters. "They have a well balanced attack and they sure used it. They were a great team today and they were tremendous on defense."[16]

So the question deserves to be asked: how did Joe Paterno know that Penn State had completely figured out the Ohio State attack? "Actually, Woody had gotten into a pattern with his offense," Paterno said later. "After studying the films and our scouting reports, we felt we could tell which side they were going to run to, without error."[17] That brief comment was the extent of

Paterno's explanation, however. He left unsaid the clue (or clues) that tipped off the Lions to the inner secrets of the Ohio State offense.

Despite the loss to Penn State, the day was far from a total loss for Ohio State, although the defeat was to cost the Buckeyes their number one ranking in the national polls. In East Lansing, Michigan State defeated Purdue 21–7, giving the Boilermakers their first loss in conference action. Purdue's loss left the Buckeyes all alone atop the Big Ten, with two games to play. Told about the Purdue defeat after the Penn State game, Hayes simply commented, "Somebody else seems to be having trouble today."[18]

After the shutout loss to Penn State, Ohio State faced two Big Ten opponents, Northwestern on November 14 and Michigan on November 21. Both games were in Columbus, giving Ohio State the home-field advantage for the rest of the season. Purdue's loss put the Buckeyes atop the Big Ten all by themselves, but since the Boilermakers had never played in a Rose Bowl game, Ohio State knew that it needed victories in its final two games to lock up the Big Ten championship and a trip to the Rose Bowl. If Purdue went undefeated in its last two games, against Minnesota and then Indiana, the Boilers would finish with a conference record of 6–1. If Ohio State were to lose one of its final games, its record would be 5–1 and Purdue would become the undisputed Big Ten champion and win the trip to the Rose Bowl on the basis of a better winning percentage in conference play.

On November 14, the Buckeyes played Northwestern in Columbus. A troublesome foe for Ohio State in recent years, Northwestern had defeated Ohio State 18–14 in 1962 and 17–8 in 1963. In fact, Ohio State's loss to Northwestern in 1963 deprived the Buckeyes of an opportunity to win the Big Ten title. In 1964, however, Northwestern was a weaker team and also one ravaged by injuries by the end of the season. Ohio State defeated Northwestern, 10–0, the third shutout of the season pitched by the stout Buckeye defense. The Wildcats managed only 144 yards in total offense and 9 first downs on the afternoon.[19]

After the game, Ohio State learned that Minnesota had defeated Purdue, 14–7, ending the Boilermakers' chance for a Big Ten championship and a place in the Rose Bowl. Ohio State's next game, against Michigan on November 21, would settle the matter for good. "Well, one more ... sure is a big one," Woody Hayes told the reporters after the Northwestern game. Asked about Ohio State's injury situation for the Michigan game, Hayes said that Tom Barrington had reinjured himself and that Leon Lindsey would replace him "against our opponent next week," taking care not to mention the identity of the opponent.[20] Like most Big Ten observers, Hayes had probably not expected the Michigan–Ohio State game to determine the championship, but that was the circumstance that now presented itself. It was another Michigan–Ohio State game for all the marbles.

"Every game was a 'must' game"

After the loss to Purdue on October 17, Bump Elliott realized that the Wolverines had no margin for error if they expected to win a Big Ten championship. For Michigan, every game after the Purdue defeat was a "must game," Elliott told reporters in the week before playing Ohio State.[21] The Wolverines had risen to the occasion with four consecutive victories and, perhaps more importantly, showed consistent improvement in each game. Michigan's renewed sense of purpose, and Purdue's misfortunes, nevertheless did not obscure the fact that the Wolverines faced their toughest conference opponent, Ohio State, on November 21.

Michigan had a solid week of practice, understanding that its major task in the game was the penetration of the Ohio State defense. Don Dufek, who had scouted the Buckeyes on the two previous weekends, came away convinced that Ohio State was solid in every aspect of the game. "You have to completely disregard the Penn State game," Dufek told Nikki Schwartz and Lynn Metzger, two reporters for the *Michigan Daily*. "They save their best efforts for the Big Ten games."[22]

After scouting Ohio State on the previous two weekends, Dufek believed that the strength of the Buckeyes was on defense. But at the same time, Michigan's defense had played well all year and entered the contest equally confident about its prospects. Bob Hollway pored over the Ohio State offense and devised "16 different buffers and seals" designed to contain the Buckeye ground attack and its tendencies to run out of unbalanced line formations. By game time, Hollway had the scheme in place to his satisfaction. As Tom Cecchini recalled, "Coach Bob Hollway had told [the defense] to aim for a shutout," secure in the belief that the Ohio State offense was not going to present any major problems.[23]

For their part, the Michigan players focused ceaselessly on the Buckeyes in the week before the game. "We all sat around all week and talked about their players, every one of them, and how we were going to handle them," Jim Conley remembered. "We went down [the Ohio State roster] one by one by one. [T]he fact was that we had all these Ohio players [on our team] who knew those players down there. [They would say] 'this guy does this and this guy does this.'"[24]

Still, the actual game preparation was paramount, and while looking at game footage of Ohio State's recent games, Tom Cecchini and the Michigan coaches found a magic bullet. "We watched the Ohio State game films over and over," Cecchini recalled. "During one of those film sessions, we discovered [that] the Ohio State's offensive halfback, Bo Rein, did something unusual. When he got into his stance and put his right hand down, their play would move to the left. If he put his left hand down, the play developed to the right.

I always wondered if Woody Hayes was aware of Rein's quirk. It gave us a definite advantage, because during the game, I would watch Rein's hands and call our defensive slants accordingly."²⁵ Tony Mason, who had coached Rein at McKinley High School in Niles, Ohio, was also aware of Rein's tendency and alerted the Michigan defenders accordingly.

As a consequence, Jim Conley and Bill Laskey, Michigan's defensive ends, deciphered the tendencies of the Ohio State ground game once the Buckeyes came to the line of scrimmage. If the play was going to the left, Conley yelled out "Kill," and then blitzed from that side. If the play was headed to the right, Laskey yelled out "Kill," and blitzed from that direction.²⁶

Meanwhile, in Columbus, a certain wariness had crept into the Buckeye preparations. After the Northwestern game, the Ohio State coaches expressed concern not only about the injury to Tom Barrington, but also to fullback Willard Sander, raising some questions about the health of the backfield. By midweek, however, both players were declared ready and cleared for the game. And, within the Ohio State coaching staff, it was clear that Michigan's performance throughout the season had impressed them. Esko Sarkkinen, the Ohio State assistant who had scouted Michigan previously, told reporters that Michigan's team was the "best since the Fritz Crisler era." Sarkkinen praised the Michigan offense. "The thing is that the offense keeps the ball so much, that the defense really hasn't been under too much pressure," Sarkkinen told the press. "Against Iowa, Michigan had the ball for 93 plays—93!"²⁷

So, the priority in the Buckeye camp during the week before the game was slowing down the Michigan ground attack, and that meant stopping Bob Timberlake. On November 19, the *Columbus Dispatch* featured a story, complete with a photo of Timberlake, in the caricature of a "Wanted" poster, with the title, "This Man Is Dangerous." Describing Timberlake as a "resident of Franklin, Ohio, during [the] summer but at present is a prominent citizen of Ann Arbor, Mich., ... armed with a rifle arm and legs of iron; [the] smell of roses may draw him to Ohio Stadium [on] Saturday, November 21." The poster concluded with the ominous words: "If Seen, Please Hold."²⁸

The reporting in Ohio before the Michigan game also drew attention to the strong Ohio influence on the Michigan team. In his article in the *Columbus Dispatch* on Monday, November 16, reporter Paul Hornung wrote, "Michigan looks like some former Ohio State teams—and not just because its four starting backs and 19 other squadmen come from Ohio. It's a quarterback-fullback attack with Timberlake running and Mel Anthony supplying the power from fullback. But ... the Wolverines also threaten with Carl Ward and Jim Detwiler ... [and] Dave Fisher ... and one of the Big Ten's most dangerous pass catchers in John Henderson. All of the players herein mentioned are Ohioans, which should add a little more fuel to the fire."²⁹

Another reminder of the Ohio connection occurred when the *Columbus Dispatch* ran a story on November 17, identifying the eight Michigan starters on offense who came from Ohio and comparing that number with the nine starters on Ohio State's offense who hailed from the Buckeye State.[30] In the minds of the Columbus reporters, at least, the game was going to feature a match between Ohioans, some of whom played for Ohio State and the others who played for Michigan.

The Michigan practices ended on Thursday, November 19. That night, the players and coaches attended a send-off pep rally organized by the M Club and held on the Michigan Diag on the central campus. As Bill Laskey recalled, "The Ohio State week was an experience I'll never forget. The enthusiasm and electricity on campus were overwhelming. We covered the huge tree in front of the Sigma Chi house with cartons of toilet paper—it looked like a snowstorm in bloom. I don't think that any of us slept a quiet night all week and I know that few of us made many classes." Some players, perhaps not Laskey, did attend class, though. Those who attended wore cardboard signs "plastered with the words, OPERATION HARDNOSE: Beat Ohio State."[31]

The rally's master of ceremonies was Wally Weber, the former Michigan player and coach, who led the crowd of 4,000 Wolverine supporters in cheering while the Michigan Marching Band belted out numerous refrains of "The Victors" and the other familiar songs heard in Michigan Stadium on Saturday afternoons. Dr. Harlan Hatcher, president of the University of Michigan and an enthusiastic supporter of the football team, also spoke to the crowd and casually remarked that one of the reasons that Michigan had changed its academic calendar from quarters to semesters was "so that the students could attend the Rose Bowl without missing having to miss any classes." Hearing Hatcher's comments, Bump Elliott winced, certain that the president had just provided some pre-game fodder for Woody Hayes's bulletin board in the Ohio State locker room. For his part, Elliott was content to tell the cheering crowd, "It may be cold out here tonight, but it's going to be hot [in Columbus] on Saturday."[32]

The highlight of the festivities was a spirited address by Dr. Hazel "Doc" Losh, one of the team's favorite professors and a "red-hot football fan," who spoke movingly about the Michigan football tradition, Michigan's big victory over Michigan State on October 10, its impending victory over Ohio State, and the great pep rally to come when the Wolverines went to the Rose Bowl. The crowd relished the passion and fervor demonstrated by "Doc" Losh, an astronomy professor whose grading scale reputedly was A-B-C: A for athletes, B for boys, C for coeds. The slight, gray-haired professor brought the crowd to its feet with her concluding remarks: "Remember this: Scholarship is not the only important thing at Michigan. Go Blue." "'Doc' Losh's words," Tom Cecchini recalled, "brought a chill of expectation."[33]

Six. "We gotta beat Ohio! We gotta beat Ohio!" 147

Bump Elliott addresses a crowd estimated at more than 3,000 at a pep rally held on Thursday evening, November 19, in the Diag on Michigan's central campus. The following day, November 20, Elliott and the Wolverines left for their showdown game against Ohio State in Columbus (Bentley Historical Library, University of Michigan).

On Friday morning, the Michigan team and coaches left Willow Run Airport outside of Detroit for the short flight to Columbus. Publicly, Bump Elliott expressed satisfaction and optimism about his team's prospects for the Ohio State game. "I have confidence they will play their best," Elliott told reporters earlier in the week.[34] Privately, he knew that the players were tense and anxious, emotions that the players also recognized. It was time, therefore, for some lighthearted comedy to break the tension. Dave Butler, who had entertained his teammates throughout the season with his impersonations of Wolverine coaches, Fidel Castro, and other famous personalities, broke the ice. As Cecchini remembered, "When we gathered for our film that night, we were too tight. People were not their usual selves. Laughter had been replaced by gnashing teeth. Coach Elliott's usual businesslike approach, his self-instilled confidence, had been joined by a creeping stress—an atmosphere Dave Butler [offensive guard] recognized when he addressed the team. He began, 'Gentlemen, you are probably wondering why I called this meeting tonight. I have to ask why in the world our waxed animal crackers are not selling!' The room shook with laughter. As his comic routine continued, our tensions eased."[35]

In other respects, however, the traditions of the Michigan–Ohio State game soon manifested themselves. The Buckeye faithful found out the location of the hotel where the Wolverines were staying on Friday night, the Lincoln Lodge, and kept up non-stop noise until the morning hours, attempting to deprive the Michigan players of a good night's rest before the game. Miles away, in downtown Columbus, the Ohio State fans kept up the festivities throughout the night. The Michigan players also discovered when they arrived at the visiting locker room at Ohio Stadium that Ohio State had heated the locker room to a stifling, suffocating temperature.[36] The two universities had not played for the Big Ten championship in almost a decade, but no one in Columbus or Ann Arbor had any doubt, on November 20, that they were to play for it tomorrow.

"This game may well be decided by a break"

Game time: Columbus, Ohio, November 21, 1964. Michigan vs. Ohio State for the Big Ten championship and a trip to the Rose Bowl. The day was cold and windy, a stark difference from the unseasonably warm 70-degree weather that the Wolverines had experienced in Iowa City one week earlier. The weather in Columbus was clear but cold, 15 degrees with a 20 mph wind. To the players, coaches, band members, and spectators alike, it felt frigid. Tom Hemingway, who broadcast the game on WUOM Radio, recalls that wind-chill factors had not been introduced yet, but everyone knew that the weather felt colder than the actual temperature indicated. To combat the cold, Bill Laskey rubbed his limbs with Vaseline in order to retain his body heat.[37]

The frigid weather gave Tom Cecchini a sharp stab of anxiety. Cecchini was assigned the long-snapping duties and wondered how the chill would affect his hands when he snapped the ball to the punter, Stan Kemp. Elliott had told the players earlier in the week, "This game may well be decided by a break."[38] Most assuredly, Cecchini did not want Ohio State to get a break caused by an errant snap from center in a punting situation. "When we left the visitors' locker room to begin our specialty drills," Cecchini recalled, "the manager handed me a ball for my duties as long snapper on the punting team.... The wind hit me for the first time. A cold, stiff wind that I remember to this day. My first concern was my hands. How could numb fingers deliver a football 15 yards to a punter? And in a game that meant so much!"[39]

Despite the apprehensions, Michigan's players were ready for the game,

Six. "We gotta beat Ohio! We gotta beat Ohio!"

charging out of their locker room for the pre-game drills chanting "Go-Go-Go," a refrain that they kept up throughout the preliminaries. Then, at game time, Cecchini recalled, "[W]e went onto that field with a spirit of togetherness that I could never recapture in words ... and the flow of adrenaline in my veins."[40]

Then the game began. Ohio State won the coin toss but elected to take advantage of the wind and kicked off to Michigan. Michigan's end Ben Farabee fielded the ball on the Michigan 21 and returned it 10 yards to the 31. On its first possession, Michigan showed no hesitation about going to the air. On 2nd and 13 (Michigan had been penalized five yards on first down for jumping offside), Bob Timberlake hit John Henderson for 12 yards to the Michigan 39. On 3rd down, Mel Anthony carried for the necessary yardage for a first down.

On the next series, Michigan made another first down on three consecutive carries by Timberlake. But on the third series, the Wolverines sustained another offside penalty, and two of Timberlake's passes to Henderson fell incomplete. In came Stan Kemp, and Tom Cecchini, to punt on fourth down. Kemp's first punt of the afternoon went out of bounds at the Ohio State 23.

Now it was Ohio State's turn. On 1st down, Tom Barrington carried for no gain after being tackled by Jerry Mader, but Don Unverferth picked up 8 yards on 2nd down. On 3rd and 2 from the Ohio State 31, Willard Sander broke through the Michigan defensive line for a 1st down. On the next series, the Buckeyes made another first down, but then stalled out on their third series. Steve Dreffer came in to punt for Ohio State and he kicked down to the Michigan 29. Coming off the field after giving up two consecutive first downs to the Buckeyes, Michigan's defensive unit, and Bill Laskey and Frank Nunley in particular, felt the wrath of Michigan's defensive coordinator Bob Hollway. "Nunley, what the hell's going on out there?" Hollway shouted. "We're just feeling them out," Nunley said, faking a certain amount of confident anxiety.[41]

In possession of the ball once again, the Wolverines failed to sustain an attack. Timberlake made a 1st down on a 15-yard run up to the Ohio State 44, but Michigan went nowhere on its next series. In came Stan Kemp to punt, kicking to Bo Rein on the Ohio State 23. Rein fumbled the punt but recovered the loose ball and Ohio State took over in its territory. Back on offense, the Buckeyes ran twice for 7 yards. On 3rd and 3, Sander took the handoff, broke through the Wolverine defensive line and into the secondary. At that point, Frank Nunley raced over from his linebacker position and delivered a ferocious hit on Sander, causing a fumble and shattering the Buckeye fullback's face mask. Still, Bob Stock, Ohio State's split end, alertly recovered the fumble and Ohio State retained possession on its own 46. But Nunley's tackle typified the action on the field in what had become a standard Michigan–Ohio State game, later described by Nunley as "a typical throat-to-throat struggle for the Rose Bowl."[42]

After the Michigan–Northwestern game in October, Bob Hollway told reporters, "When Nunley hits [someone], the [Michigan] Stadium rocks."[43] On Nunley's tackle of Sander, Ohio Stadium probably rocked, too, at least a little. After Sander's fumble, Ohio State's next three plays stalled out and the first quarter ended in a scoreless tie. Ohio State could feel some relief, though; it had fumbled twice in its own territory and managed to keep the ball both times.

In the second quarter, Michigan established the upper hand in the game, thanks largely to inspired play by its defense, opportunistic work by its special teams, Stan Kemp's continued punting artistry, and Ohio State's inability to exploit its scoring opportunities. Both teams failed to move the ball on their first two possessions of the second quarter, but on Michigan's second possession, Timberlake was hit hard by Buckeye middle guard Bill Ridder on a 3rd and 2 play from the Michigan 28. Timberlake fumbled and Ohio State's end Tom Keihfuss recovered. Was this the "break" that Elliott had spoken of that might determine the outcome of the game? Not this time and not this break.

Penalized five yards on first down, the Buckeyes were unable to make a first down on their next three plays as the Wolverine defenders rose up and thwarted the Ohio State attack. On 4th and 8, Bob Funk entered the game to attempt a field goal from the Michigan 27-yard line. Funk's kick was short and, at least in Michigan's view, crossed the goal line for a touchback. The officials thought differently, however, and gave Michigan the ball on the 1-yard line after it was downed by an alert Dan Poretta, one of Ohio State's offensive linemen.

With their backs to the goal, Michigan turned to Mel Anthony to wedge the ball away from the end zone. The Buckeye defenders dug in for a potential safety. Anthony responded, however, even escaping the clutches of Buckeye tacklers who thought they had him trapped in the end zone on 1st down. Still, the Wolverines could manage no better than a 4th and 5 from their own 6-yard line after Anthony's three rushes. Stan Kemp came into the game and boomed a punt with the wind to mid-field, where Bo Rein fielded the ball and ran down to the Michigan 33-yard line. To the deafening noise of the Buckeye partisans, it appeared that Ohio State was poised to take the lead.

But the Michigan defense stiffened for the second time in the quarter and stopped the Buckeyes again. After the first two plays of the drive gained only two yards, Ohio State went to the air on 3rd and 8. Unverferth threw to Tom Barrington coming out of the backfield, but Dick Rindfuss, playing on an injured ankle, flew into the coverage and broke up the pass. Earlier in the week, Rick Sygar had predicted that "no way Ryn [sic] was going to miss this game," and his prediction proved accurate.[44] Once again, Ohio State sent in its field goal unit. But Hayes had called for a fake and Arnold Chonko, the holder, tried to fool the Wolverine defenders with a pass to Barrington out of the formation. Barrington made 8 yards to the Michigan 25, 2 yards short of a first down. Michigan took over on downs. The game remained scoreless.

On Michigan's next possession, Timberlake passed 14 yards to Ben Farabee, his tight end, for a 1st down on the Michigan 39. Timberlake's pass to Farabee was more consequential than anyone realized at the time. To that point in the game, Timberlake had completed only one pass, to John Henderson in the first quarter for a 1st down. Timberlake's three other passes to Henderson fell incomplete. Farabee entered the Ohio State game with 7 pass receptions on the season, fourth on the team behind Henderson, Jim Detwiler, and Steve Smith, the other tight end. The completion to Farabee in the second quarter was the first time that Timberlake had thrown to his tight end, a fact that the Buckeyes would have to account for on subsequent Michigan possessions. When Farabee went out on a pass route, one of the Ohio State linebackers or defensive backs would have to cover him.

The 1st-down pass to Farabee did not result in any momentum for the Wolverines, however. Michigan lost 8 yards on the next three plays, and Bump Elliott sent Stan Kemp into the game for his fifth punt of the afternoon—and it was here that the tide of the contest turned in favor of the Wolverines. On

Jim Conley (82) stops Ohio State halfback Bo Rein for a loss. Pursuing on the play for Michigan is Bill Yearby (75) (The Ohio State University Archives).

4th and 10 from the Michigan 31, Kemp punted with the wind, standing on his own 17. Already, the swirling winds in Ohio Stadium had created problems for Bo Rein, Ohio State's punt returner, who had fumbled a punt in the first quarter. Now Rein was back on the Ohio State 30, awaiting another punt, and possibly another long return that would put the Buckeyes in good field position with time running out in the first half. Kemp got the snap from Tom Cecchini and pounded the punt down to Bo Rein. Rein circled under the ball, took a slight, hesitant step backward, and then dropped the kick. The ball bounced to the left, behind Rein, and away from Tom Barrington, the other Buckeye positioned back to receive Kemp's punt. John Henderson, streaking down the field on punt coverage, flew past a diving Barrington and fell on the football at the Ohio State 20. Only 1:15 remained in the first half, but the Wolverines now had their first serious scoring opportunity of the game.[45]

On the Michigan sideline, Bump Elliott was worried, however. Thus far in the game, after each defensive possession, Jim Conley went up to Elliott and told him, "Coach, hang in there, we'll hold 'em." And, after each offensive possession, Bob Timberlake came up to Elliott, and told him, "Don't worry, Coach, just stick with us. We'll break this thing open if you just give us enough time." "About that time, I had something to say, too," Elliott recalled, "Let's go now, then, let's not wait around."[46]

So Timberlake and the Michigan offense went on the attack. On 1st down from the Ohio State 20, Timberlake ran to the right, then changed direction and cut back to his left for 3 yards down to the Ohio State 17. With 44 seconds left in the half, Timberlake called time out and went to the sidelines to confer with Bump Elliott. In the pre-game preparation, Elliott, Hank Fonde, and Tony Mason had noticed a flaw in the Buckeye defense: its quick linebackers tended to follow the tight end across the middle of the field on pass routes, creating an opening for the wing back coming out of the backfield. It was time to exploit that weakness. As Michigan broadcaster Tom Hemingway recalled, Elliott decided to go for the touchdown on the next play. "Let's try double wing special," he told Timberlake. "But be sure of it before you throw. We're in field goal range if we can't move it in."[47]

The "double wing special," or "trailer," was a play that Elliott and the offensive coaches had devised specifically for the Ohio State game. Inserted into the playbook for the first time all season, the play had the advantage that it had never appeared on Michigan's game films, nor had it been seen by an opposing scout. The play called for Timberlake to roll to his right and then pass back to Jim Detwiler, who had lined up in the left slot and gone ten yards downfield. Ben Farabee, the tight end on the left side, was to come off the line, break to his right and draw coverage, a split second after which Timberlake was to release the pass to Detwiler.

Six. "We gotta beat Ohio! We gotta beat Ohio!" 153

The entire Michigan offensive unit executed their assignments perfectly on this play. Taking the snap from Brian Patchen, Timberlake rolled to his right with perfect pass protection from the offensive line. Farabee took three steps from the line of scrimmage, broke to his right across the middle, and raised his arms slightly as if to prepare for a pass reception. Arnold Chonko, one of the Ohio State defensive backs, moved up to cover Farabee. Trailing behind, Detwiler went downfield ten yards, broke to his right, and Timberlake hit him on the numbers and on the run. Don Harkins, the Ohio State defensive back

Stan Kemp's punting against Ohio State helped Michigan prevent the Buckeyes from scoring. Here Kemp punts from the Michigan end zone in the first half of the game (Bentley Historical Library, University of Michigan).

covering Detwiler, bumped him while the ball was in the air, but Detwiler caught the pass at the three-yard line, where he took a terrific jolt from linebacker Ike Kelley, who had closed instantly once Timberlake released the ball. "The play wasn't wide open," Detwiler recalled, "but Timberlake squeezed it in and I held on as the linebacker's tackle carried me into the end zone."[48] Carl Ward came running over and jumped into Detwiler's arms. Detwiler triumphantly threw the ball in the air in celebration as the Michigan Marching Band jubilantly struck up "The Victors." Touchdown Michigan, and after Timberlake kicked the extra point, the Wolverines led 7–0 as the first half came to a close.

The Michigan players and coaches went into their locker room at halftime brimming with confidence. Not only did they hold the lead, but they had managed to thwart two Ohio State possessions deep in Michigan territory. For the Buckeyes, though, it was a moment of frustration. They had two opportunities in the second quarter to score and possibly take the upper hand in the game before Michigan even had a realistic scoring chance. But penalties, faulty offensive execution, and the fumbled punt had turned the game's momentum clearly in Michigan's favor.

To start the second half, Timberlake kicked off to Ohio State's Tom Barrington, who returned the ball to the Buckeye 28. On their first possession of the second half, the Buckeyes managed one first down before the Michigan defense forced a punt. On their first possession, however, the Wolverines failed to move the ball and Stan Kemp came onto the field for his sixth punt of the game, driving Ohio State back to its 15. But the Buckeyes failed to make a first down and Steve Dreffer entered the game for another punt. Now, it was Michigan's turn to drop a punt, as Rick Sygar fumbled the kick and Ohio State recovered on its own 45. Could the Buckeyes capitalize on Sygar's miscue in the same fashion that the Wolverines had capitalized on Rein's fumble?

Since the Michigan defense had completely stopped the Ohio State ground attack to that point in the game, Woody Hayes changed his strategy. On first down, Unverferth threw to wide receiver Bob Stock, but Rick Volk broke up the pass. On second down, Unverferth threw again to Stock, who caught the pass, crossed into Michigan territory, was hit hard and fumbled. Always in motion, Frank Nunley dashed after the loose ball along the Michigan sideline and covered the ball before it rolled out of bounds. The Wolverines had thwarted another Ohio State drive.

With good field position near the Michigan 45, the Wolverine offense went to work. Detwiler ran twice for a first down to the Ohio State 32. Then Anthony and Detwiler carried for another first down to the Ohio State 22. Then it was Anthony and Detwiler again to the Ohio State 15, where the Buckeyes stiffened and Michigan faced a 4th and 3. Elliott chose to go for a field goal but Timberlake's attempt missed, wide left.

Jim Detwiler scored Michigan's only touchdown against Ohio State on a pass from Bob Timberlake shortly before halftime (Bentley Historical Library, University of Michigan).

Michigan was to get another scoring opportunity soon enough, however. On Ohio State's next possession, the Buckeyes once again failed to get a first down and were forced to punt, into the wind, from their own 23. Rick Volk and Rick Sygar went back into double safety to receive Steve Dreffer's punt. The punt went in Volk's direction, and he was initially inclined to signal for a fair catch around mid-field, but Sygar called out, "No, no, take it and run with it!"[49] Volk caught the punt on the Michigan 49 and ran into Ohio State territory. Breaking two tackles, he headed for the Ohio State end zone with Tom Cecchini out in front as a blocker. Only a tremendous play by Buckeye center Tom Federle, who went low to avoid Cecchini's block and then stuck out his arm to trip up Volk, prevented the Wolverine from returning the punt for a touchdown.

But now, late in the third quarter, Michigan possessed another golden scoring opportunity. As he had for the entire third quarter, Bump Elliott decided to stay on the ground. Mel Anthony ran for 12 yards and a first down at the Ohio State 12. On the next series, however, Anthony gained only three yards and Detwiler was tackled by Tom Kiehfuss for a 1-yard loss, ending the third quarter.

At the start of the fourth quarter, Michigan faced a 3rd and 8 from the Ohio State 10. Bump Elliott decided to pass for another touchdown. On the first play of the quarter, Timberlake retreated to pass and threw just beyond the outstretched hands of John Henderson in the end zone. On the play, Timberlake rolled out to his right, faced a strong rush, and then overshot Henderson, who had broken free on the right side of the end zone. Although it was not known at the time, of course, Timberlake's incompletion to Henderson early in the fourth quarter was to be Michigan's last pass attempt of the afternoon. On 4th and 8 from the Ohio State 10, Timberlake kicked a 27-yard field goal and Michigan led 10–0.

Still, the game was hardly over, although the Buckeyes certainly faced an uphill struggle if they expected to win. On their next possession, Ohio State drove down the field behind the running of Willard Sander and the passing of Don Unverferth. On first down from the Michigan 21, Unverferth rolled to his right, attempting to pass, and found himself being pursued by Bill Yearby, Michigan's superb defensive tackle. Yearby had played off two Ohio State blockers and began running Unverferth toward the eastern sideline. Needing to make a play, Unverferth threw on the run, hoping to hit Bo Rein near the Michigan 5-yard line, and Rein appeared to be open on the play. But Yearby's pressure forced Unverferth to throw the ball short, and Rick Volk, playing well back in coverage, intercepted the pass. Volk intercepted the pass around the Michigan 8-yard line, right in front of the Michigan band. The band members jumped with delight when Volk intercepted the pass—and then broke into a rousing refrain of "The Victors."[50]

Following Rick Volk's interception, the Buckeyes never seriously threatened to score, although Volk intercepted another of Unverferth's passes, this time on the Michigan 38 with 5:12 to go in the game. After Volk's second interception, along the sidelines and in the stands, "cautious enthusiasm ... spread to unrestrained joy" as the Michigan players, coaches, band members, and fans began to absorb the inevitability of their imminent historic victory.[51] Michigan will win. Ohio State will lose. Simple.

As reporter Jim Taylor described the scene in Ohio Stadium as the game clock wound down under three minutes, "band members could be seen pounding each other on the back, and fans lined the ropes and shouted encouragement at the players. One man yelled, 'God love you, Jim Conley.... God love

John Henderson stretches for a pass from Bob Timberlake in the Ohio State end zone in the fourth quarter (The Ohio State University Archives).

you, Bill Yearby.' ... With less than a minute to go, 'Rose fever' spread to the players and even coaches could be seen jumping up and down."[52] The game ended, fittingly, with Timberlake carrying the ball for a 5-yard gain.[53] Final score: Michigan 10–Ohio State 0. The players hoisted Bump Elliott and Bob Hollway onto their shoulders for the ride to mid-field and the post-game handshake with Woody Hayes. Bob Hollway had his shutout and Michigan's players were the Champions of the West for the first time since 1950

Bob Timberlake kicks a field goal early in the fourth quarter to give Michigan a 10-0 lead against the Buckeyes. The 10-0 lead held up for the final score of the game. Holding for Timberlake on the attempt was Frosty Evashevski (26) (Bentley Historical Library, University of Michigan).

After the game, the usual amount of pushing and shoving took place on the field as the spectators came down from the stands to mix in with the players. Dr. Bob Murphy, Ohio State's team physician, was knocked down by a "wildly enthusiastic group of [Michigan] fans" as he tried to leave the field. "I was knocked down," Murphy said, "and a couple fellows tried to help me up. Just about that time, here came some more fans and down I went again and got trampled in the melee." Dr. Murphy suffered a sprained ankle in the mishap and was scheduled for an X-ray on Sunday afternoon to determine the extent of his injury.[54]

Elsewhere on the field, Michigan's jubilant supporters who had made the trip to Columbus broke through a rope held by an angry Columbus policeman and rushed to congratulate the players. "One day of freezing is nothing com-

Six. "We gotta beat Ohio! We gotta beat Ohio!" 159

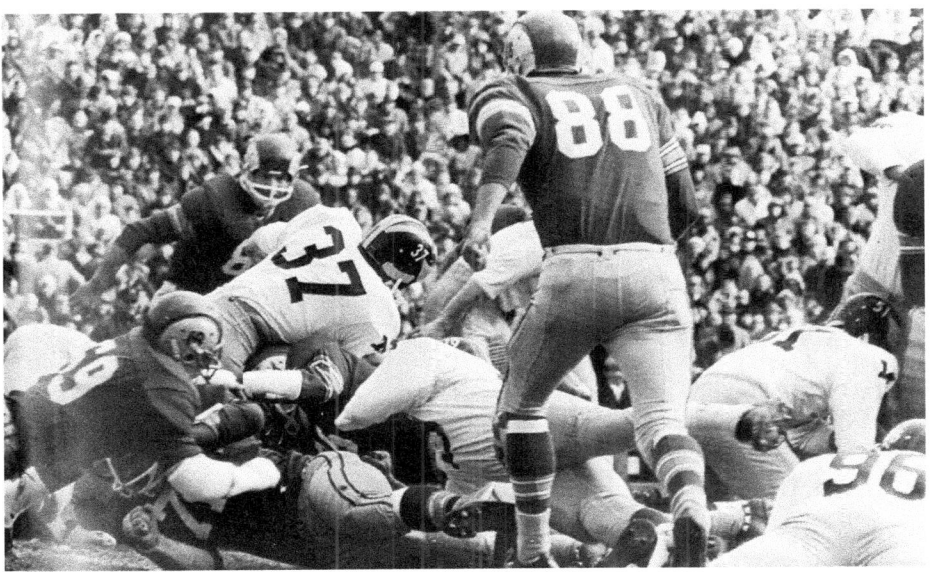

Mel Anthony's (37) tough running allowed Michigan to keep control of the ball in the second half of the game against Ohio State. Here Anthony attacks the Buckeye defense behind the blocking of Brian Patchen (51), Carl Ward (19), and Tom Mack (96) (The Ohio State University Archives).

pared to 14 years of waiting!" one supporter exclaimed. Another Michigan fan, "with tears in his eyes," declared, "I can't believe it. I can't believe it." Six other Wolverine alumni were determined to make their way to the 50-yard line, uncork their champagne, and celebrate the big victory, until they were stopped by a burly Ohio Highway Patrolman who prevented their celebration. "I sympathize with you [fans], though," the patrolman said. "I'm from Wauseon [Ohio] and I've known Rick Volk for a long time."[55]

There were other moments as well. In the locker room after the game, as Bump Elliott was talking to the press, an Ohio State supporter pushed through the crowd to speak with him. As Thomas Rivera, sports reporter for the *Chicago Tribune*, wrote: "Thrusting out his hand and saying, 'Bet you don't know what this is [,] Bump. 'Oh, yes, I do,' Elliott replied, reaching for the brown object in the man's hand. 'That's a Buckeye.' 'Will you take it to the Rose Bowl for good luck?' [the man inquired.] 'That's a promise,' Elliott told him."[56]

Elsewhere in the Michigan locker room, bedlam prevailed. "The revolution, she is here," thundered Dave Butler, standing on a bench and giving his best Castro impersonation.[57] Players sang "The Victors," led by Rick Sygar, of course, pounded each other on the back, posed for photographs, waved yellow roses in the air, and dragged the assistant coaches to the showers for a post-game celebratory dunking. The Michigan supporters who made the trip to Columbus gathered deliriously outside the Michigan locker room, singing "The Victors" over and over again, and preventing reporters from entering the locker room for twenty minutes.[58]

In his post-game interview, Bump Elliott enthused with praise for his Rose Bowl–bound Wolverines. "That, gentlemen, was a tough defensive game," Elliott told the reporters. "We were up against a pretty doggone tough defensive team."[59] But, he also added, "[Our] defensive team played awfully well. I've felt our defense has been underrated. I don't know what [Ohio State] got [in total offense] but I know they didn't score."[60]

Asked about Michigan's approach to the game, Elliott spoke about the team's preparations for Ohio State. "All week..., we were ready to play," he said. "Our only fear was that we might be too tight." Then, somewhat disingenuously in view of the touchdown pass from Timberlake to Detwiler, Elliott declared, "We didn't change anything. We knew Ohio State is a tremendous defensive team and we wanted to do the things that we do best. You aren't going to fool Ohio much."[61]

Following their 10–0 victory over Ohio State, the Michigan players and coaches staged a wild celebration, complete with roses, in their visitors' locker room. The most visible Wolverines, by uniform number, in the crowded scene are Carl Ward (19) and John Marcum (61). Bump Elliott is standing in the middle of the scene, surrounded by players (Bentley Historical Library, University of Michigan).

Elliott also agreed that the cold and the wind played a role in the outcome of the game, including being possible causes of Bo Rein's fumble in the second quarter. Not wanting to detract from his team's overall performance, however, Elliott singled out the play of Rick Volk and his "two great" interceptions, as well as Stan Kemp's punting performance as important keys in the Wolverine victory. Concluding his interview, Elliott called the victory over Ohio State his 'happiest moment" in football and then added, "We are pleased and proud of our football team.... The boys had great spirit and desire to be outstanding and they accomplished their goal."[62]

Following his meeting with the press, Elliott's players took him to the showers, too. After emerging, he met up with Fritz Crisler, now in the Michigan locker room to congratulate the players and coaches. Crisler gave Elliott "a crushing hug," in the words of Pete Waldmeir, the reporter for the *Detroit News*.[63] Given the state of Wolverine celebrations in the post-game environment, it appears that Fritz Crisler was the only member of the Michigan athletic staff who escaped the showers after the game.

On the Ohio State side, Woody Hayes met briefly with the press after the game. In response to questions from the reporters, Hayes admitted the obvious: Michigan's stout defense had stopped the Ohio State rushing attack in the first half, and Don Unverferth's passing in the second half had failed to rekindle the Buckeye offense. Then he added, "One of the things that hurt us was [Mel] Anthony's rushing late in the game. He consistently pounded through the center of our line" and enabled Michigan to keep possession of the ball.[64]

Mostly, however, Woody Hayes was disappointed by his team's four fumbles and two interceptions, especially costly turnovers in a game of this magnitude. Hayes summarized his view of the contest in simple terms: "They took advantage of the breaks and we were unable to make the most of ours." He also added, "The wind was a big factor. We elected to kick off [at the beginning of the game] even tho [sic] we won the toss and Michigan did the same thing in the second half." Did Hayes then consider the weather conditions to be the deciding factor in the game? "No," the Buckeye coach responded. "[Michigan] took advantage of the breaks and we were unable to make the most of ours. Bob Timberlake was a good quarterback today but the difference was that they outplayed us even tho [sic] our defense was superb. It is not a very happy day for Ohio State."[65] And with that, Woody Hayes turned and left the press conference.

Post-mortems on the game from the perspectives of Ohio's newspapers were not very heartening to Hayes, either. In his day-after report on the game, Paul Hornung of the *Columbus Dispatch* noted the Ohio connections of several Michigan standouts in the game. He identified Timberlake as "Michigan's versatile quarterback from Franklin, Ohio"; touchdown receiver Jim Detwiler, "from Toledo"; John Henderson, who recovered Bo Rein's fumble, saying "he's from Ohio"; and Rick Volk, "another Ohioan," who "wriggled 26 yards on a punt to the Ohio 25," in the third quarter.[66]

Certainly the Michigan coaching staff agreed with Hornung's sentiments about the contributions of the Ohioans on the Michigan roster. Reflecting on the Ohio State game and the entire 1964 season, Don Dufek once observed, "It was a shame, in a way, that Jack Fouts wasn't around [in 1964] because he recruited a lot of those players, offense and defense."[67] Fouts had, of course, made a sound professional decision to become the head football coach at Ohio Wesleyan University earlier in 1964, but the fact remained that he had played a major role in building the talent on Michigan's team in the mid–1960s.

The final statistics for the game showed a close contest. Michigan made 9 total first downs to Ohio State's 10; gained 115 yards rushing to Ohio State's 103; and 45 yards passing to Ohio State's 77. As the numbers showed, neither team mounted much of an offensive attack in the game, with both Michigan and Ohio State settling for less than 200 yards of total offense. What the statistics did not show, of course, was how Michigan capitalized on two of its three scoring opportunities. Bump Elliott had been correct all along: the game *was* decided by a break.[68]

The Wild Welcome at Willow Run

The Michigan football team flew back to Detroit in the early evening on Saturday, November 21. A crowd estimated at 7,000 students, alumni, supporters, and other fans gathered at Willow Run Airport to welcome the victorious Wolverines back to Ann Arbor. If anything, the weather had become colder since the game ended in Columbus, but the frigid temperatures did not dampen the enthusiasm of the gathered Wolverine faithful. "This whole thing is absolutely unreal," exclaimed one Michigan supporter in the crowd, holding her baby close to her body in the cold evening air.[69]

The flight was scheduled to land at Willow Run at 5:40 p.m., but it did not arrive until 6:19. Once the plane came into view, the celebrants ran out onto the runway, creating an instant safety hazard for the pilot and his crew. The pilot landed the aircraft, turned it around, and headed for the safety of a nearby hangar at the other end of the landing strip, instead of at the main gate. "The fans took off after the plane like convicts on a prison break," wrote Lloyd Graff of the *Michigan Daily*, describing the scene.[70] Among those in the rush was Michigan's president Harlan Hatcher, "who was almost trampled but made it to the safety of a heated bus." Commenting on the game to a reporter,

Hatcher said, "They held us to 10 instead of 21 as we planned. But I think 10–0 is a sportsmanlike score, don't you? I guess they were guarding against Ward's pitchout and Timberlake's rollout more than we planned," Hatcher offered with a bit of football insight.[71]

The crowd then sought the warmth of the United Airlines freight hangar before it heard an announcement on the loudspeaker that the team members were going to board two buses for the drive back to campus. An instantaneous chant broke out: "We want our team! We want our team!"[72] But the crowd quickly dispersed, disappointed that the team would not be making an appearance at the airport.

Then the two buses carrying the Michigan players and coaches traveled back to the terminal, setting off a mad rush. Michigan supporters who were about to pull out of the Willow Run parking lot stopped, parked their cars, and returned. The supporters who had left the airport, and happened to notice the team buses moving toward the terminal, parked their cars alongside the road, and ran across the wintry ground to reach the celebration. Those members of the crowd who had not departed began a raucous round of congratulations for the players and coaches. Then, shortly afterward, the players left the airport with family and friends, leaving just a few to return to campus on the two buses. One supporter carried a sign that simply read, "Pasadena."[73]

Years later, Bill Laskey described the welcoming scene at Willow Run from the perspective of the Michigan players:

> This was the biggest Michigan victory in 15 years, and we knew our fans would go crazy, but we were totally unprepared for the reception that we got when we landed at Willow Run Airport in Detroit that evening. After landing the plane, as we approached the terminal, we could see thousands of cheering fans gathered at the gate outside. As we got closer, the fans broke through the gate and headed for the plane. Fearing for people's safety [it was a propeller-driven aircraft], the pilot had to fire the plane back up and taxi several miles away before we could depart. After boarding us onto buses, we again approached the terminal, only to be mobbed by thousands of hysterical fans, who began crawling all over our bus.[74]

He added, "When we finally got to the crowd, there was absolute craziness. People yelling and screaming, throwing bunches of roses and dancing."[75]

The celebration worked its way onto the Michigan campus for the better part of the evening on November 21. "Back in Ann Arbor after the Ohio State game," Laskey wrote, "the town was caught up in victory hysteria."[76] Students paraded in the streets, turned up the volume on their phonographs, blew their car horns, and staged inter-dorm snowball fights. Even so, the Ann Arbor police reported no instances of disorderly conduct or unusual activity. "It's too cold," one Ann Arbor police officer said.[77] For his part, Bump Elliott later thanked the fans "for their tremendous display of enthusiasm," regretting that the reception hadn't worked out as planned.[78]

So the Michigan Wolverines were the Champions of the West in 1964. The unheralded team of August and September gained momentum in October and November to the point that Michigan was undeniably the best team in the Big Ten at the end of the season. Even after the tough loss to Purdue on October 17, Michigan's players stayed focused on their season-long goal and improved their performance game-by-game. When it came time to play Ohio State, the Wolverines were primed and prepared, whereas it could be argued that the Buckeyes never regained the level of performance that they had displayed in their games against Illinois and Southern Cal.

On a different level, Michigan's Big Ten championship was also a personal triumph for Jim Conley, the captain, the one player who never doubted that the Wolverines had the capacity to win a title and return to the Rose Bowl. It was Conley who galvanized the emotions and helped to build the confidence of the team from the spring practices in 1964 to the final triumph over the

Jim Conley was voted the game ball by his teammates after Michigan's 10–0 victory over Ohio State in 1964. In this photograph, taken in July 2012, he holds that game ball (Deborah L. Geelhoed).

Buckeyes on November 21, a game in which Conley made 12 tackles and assisted in 13 more. After the Ohio State game, the players voted the game ball to Conley, not only for his superlative play against the Buckeyes, but also for the leadership that he had demonstrated throughout the season.[79]

Michigan's success came as a surprise to most experienced Big Ten football watchers in 1964, most of whom had grown accustomed to seeing Ohio State, Michigan State, Minnesota, Illinois, and Wisconsin battle it out for the top spot. One person who was not surprised at Michigan's success, however, was Mel Anthony, whose strong running had been a staple of the rushing attack throughout the season. "There was no doubt in my mind that we would win [against Ohio State], only by how much," Anthony declared years later. "After all, that year the best players from Ohio were at Michigan."[80]

Now all that remained for Michigan in the 1964 season was the Rose Bowl, New Year's Day, 1965. The welcoming crowd at Willow Run on the evening of November 21 had serenaded the players and coaches by singing, "California, Here We Come!"[81] The Wolverines were California-bound, for the first time in fourteen years.

Seven

"We came to win and we did"

THE 1965 ROSE BOWL
MICHIGAN 34—OREGON STATE 7

After Michigan defeated Ohio State on November 21, the Wolverines had a brief respite to rest up and to prepare for the Rose Bowl in Pasadena on New Year's Day, 1965. The players and coaches also had ample time, finally, to reflect on their outstanding season, and the post-season statistics bore out the remarkable success of their yearlong efforts. Michigan dominated the Big Ten in virtually every offensive category. The Wolverines led the Big Ten in points per game (22.3), first downs per game (19.3), first downs by rushing per game (13.4), yards per game rushing (222.6), and were second to Iowa in total offense (325.6 to 346.0).[1]

On defense, the Wolverines more than held their own, too, finishing second to Ohio State in points allowed per game (6.8 to 9.9.), second to Ohio State in yards allowed per game by rushing (84.7 to 88.1), and number of plays allowed rushing (26.3). The last statistic was poignantly revealing: most of Michigan's opponents realized the futility of trying to run on the Michigan defense, so Michigan led the league in the number of passes thrown against it per game (25.3). Michigan's pass defense allowed 135.2 yards per game against it, placing the Wolverines toward the middle of the Big Ten, but that statistic needed to be measured against the fact that more teams chose to pass against Michigan than against the other teams in the conference. Michigan also ranked near the top in the final national statistics. Bob Timberlake finished fourth in the country, and first in the Big Ten, in individual scoring with 80 points on the season. Timberlake scored his 80 points, breaking a Big Ten season record, by scoring eight touchdowns, converting twenty points-after-touchdown, and kicking four field goals. It was a historic performance for Michigan's senior quarterback. The Wolverines also finished eighth nationally in total offense, averaging 341.6 yards per game, and fourth nationally in rushing offense, averaging 237.9 yards per game. In the defensive category, Michigan finished 9th, ahead of Illinois and Ohio State, in rushing defense.[2]

Individual honors also followed the Michigan players into the post-season. On November 26, the United Press International (UPI) announced its All-Big Ten team, to somewhat surprising results if you happened to be a Michigan supporter. On UPI's first team on offense, Bob Timberlake was selected as the Big Ten's offensive player of the year, but he was the only Michigan player selected to the first team. John Henderson, Dave Butler, and Carl Ward (but not Tom Mack or Mel Anthony, interestingly) were named to the second team. On defense, Bill Yearby made the first team and shared defensive player of the year honors with Dick Butkus, the outstanding linebacker from Illinois. Jim Conley was also voted to the first team on defense and Tom Cecchini and Rick Volk were named to the second team.[3] When the balloting for the All-America teams started appearing, Bob Timberlake and Bill Yearby were consensus All-Americans. Timberlake finished fourth, behind Notre Dame's quarterback John Huarte, Tulsa's quarterback Jerry Rhome, and Dick Butkus in the balloting for the Heisman Trophy.

For the 1964 Michigan football team, the trip to the Rose Bowl represented the realization of a long-sought dream. For the Michigan coaching staff, it likewise qualified as the realization of a dream, although not a new experience for several members of the staff. Bump Elliott and Hank Fonde, as seniors, were members of the 1947 Michigan team that defeated Southern California, 49–0, in the 1948 Rose Bowl, as was Bob Hollway, who played on that team as a sophomore. Elliott scored two of Michigan's seven touchdowns in its rout of the Trojans. Elliott returned to Pasadena for the 1957 Rose Bowl as an assistant coach under Forest Evashevski at Iowa. The Hawkeyes defeated Oregon State, 35–19, in their first visit to the Rose Bowl.

Don Dufek, Michigan's defensive backfield coach, was likewise no stranger to the Rose Bowl. In 1951, Dufek scored the winning touchdown in Michigan's 14–6 victory over California. But for Michigan's other assistant coaches, Jocko Nelson, Tony Mason, and Dennis Fitzgerald, the Rose Bowl was a treat to savor, and a fitting capstone to a memorable season.

Still, business was business. As Michigan's head coach, Bump Elliott faced the realization that three of his predecessors, Fielding H. Yost, Fritz Crisler, and Bennie Oosterbaan, kept alive Michigan's unbeaten streak in the Rose Bowl by winning in 1902, 1948, and 1951, respectively. Elliott intended to maintain that winning tradition. Michigan was going to Pasadena with the clear purpose of coming back to Ann Arbor with Michigan's fourth consecutive victory.

Michigan's Opponent: Oregon State or Southern Cal?

After Michigan defeated Ohio State, it was not clear who the Wolverines were to face in the Rose Bowl. As champions of the Big Ten, Michigan was slated to play the champion of the Athletic Association of Western Universities (AAWU), whose membership consisted of four universities in California, namely UCLA, Southern Cal, the University of California, and Stanford, plus Washington, Washington State, Oregon, and Oregon State. The AAWU came into existence in the early 1960s after a recruiting scandal led to the demise of the former Pacific Eight conference, which ironically consisted of the same previously mentioned institutions. But Oregon and Oregon State were added as members of the AAWU just before the 1964 season, and the schedule-makers were only able to assemble a four-game conference schedule by that point. Both Southern Cal and Oregon State finished the conference season with identical records of 3–1. In conference play, Southern Cal defeated California, Stanford, and UCLA, while losing to Washington. Oregon State defeated Washington, Washington State, and Oregon, while losing to Stanford. Significantly, Oregon State and Southern Cal did not play each other, so no ready indicator existed to identify the superior team.

In the event of a tie for the league title, the AAWU's policy required that the faculty representatives from the member universities vote to select the conference's representative in the Rose Bowl. And with the AAWU's conference season ending on November 21, the same day as the Michigan–Ohio State game, the faculty representatives could have selected either Southern Cal or Oregon State on that weekend and then publicly announced their choice for Michigan's opponent. But the AAWU's faculty representatives, to some surprise, chose to wait until after the outcome of Southern Cal's game against Notre Dame on November 28 before making their final choice. The rationale for the delay was that if neither Oregon State nor Southern Cal were able to receive unanimous support from the conference representatives, which happened to be the case, the decision would be made after USC's final game. So the signal appeared to be obvious and unmistakable: for Southern Cal, if it beat Notre Dame, it stood to win the vote for the Rose Bowl. Some have suggested that the AAWU's league office had even conveyed that signal covertly to USC.[4]

For Oregon State, its hopes for a Rose Bowl invitation apparently rested on the hope that Notre Dame would defeat Southern Cal and thereby give the Beavers their shot at Pasadena. But for Notre Dame, the AAWU's uncertainty in deciding its choice for a Rose Bowl opponent for Michigan revitalized the spirits of Southern Cal and gave the Trojans a powerful incentive not only to defeat the Fighting Irish and knock them from the top spot in the national rankings, but also to secure a highly prized invitation to the Rose Bowl.

"Father, it serves you right for hiring a Presbyterian"

John McKay, USC's head coach, knew the stakes involved, or at least what he perceived to be the stakes involved, in his team's upcoming clash against Notre Dame, caused by the delay in the balloting for the AAWU's Rose Bowl representative. Moreover, McKay was convinced that the Trojans could beat the Irish, even though he assiduously downplayed his team's chances in the week before the game. "I studied the Notre Dame–Stanford film for six hours last night and I have reached one conclusion: Notre Dame can't be beaten," he declared on the Monday of game week. But McKay devised a simple game plan, designed to maximize USC's strengths on offense, using its strong running game to open up its passing attack, while minimizing Notre Dame's strong passing attack of quarterback John Huarte to end Jack Snow.[5] By game time on Saturday, November 28, the Trojans were primed for the upset.

Notre Dame went into its game against Southern Cal as a 14-point favorite and played the first half accordingly. In quick order, Notre Dame scored on a 25-yard field goal by Ken Ivan in the first quarter, and then, in the second quarter, on a 22-yard touchdown pass from Huarte to Snow, and on a 5-yard carry by Bill Wolski on a quarterback option play. At halftime, Notre Dame led 17–0, looking virtually unbeatable and every bit like the number-one team in the country. Under Ara Parseghian's coaching, the Fighting Irish stood poised on the verge of an historic comeback: from winning only two games in 1963 to capturing an undefeated season and a national championship in 1964. In the Notre Dame locker room at halftime, Parseghian wrote four words in capital letters on the blackboard: JUST 30 MORE MINUTES.

Completely dominated by Notre Dame in the first half, the Southern Cal players and coaches could have been discouraged by their prospects. But, surprisingly, McKay was actually encouraged by the limited success that the Trojans had managed on the ground in the first half. In the second half, McKay planned to make some slight adjustments to the Southern Cal rushing attack while allowing Craig Fertig, his quarterback and, in McKay's opinion, "the best pure passer in college football," to loosen up the passing game. Injecting some humor into what appeared to be a bleak situation, McKay told the Trojans: "Gentlemen, if we don't score more than 17 points in the second half, we don't have a chance."[6]

So, instead of being by deflated by being on the wrong end of a 17–0 deficit, the Trojans came out confidently for the second half. USC took the opening kickoff of the third quarter and moved methodically down the field. Southern Cal's first possession of the second half ended with a one-yard run for a touchdown by halfback Mike Garrett, and the Trojans reduced Notre Dame's lead to 17–7.

When Notre Dame got the ball back in the third quarter, it failed to score, even though two drives took them deep into Trojan territory. One drive ended on a lost fumble. Another drive ended when the officials reversed a Notre Dame touchdown on a controversial holding call inside the USC one-yard line, a ruling that very well may have been the decisive call of the game.[7]

Both teams battled well into the fourth quarter, with Notre Dame hanging onto its 17–7 lead. Then, halfway through the final period, the Trojans struck for a second time. Fertig moved Southern Cal downfield on five straight completions to the Notre Dame 23. From there, he hit his end Fred Hill behind the Notre Dame secondary at the 3-yard line, and Hill crossed the goal line for USC's second touchdown. But Dick Brownell missed the extra point and the score was 17–13, Notre Dame.[8]

Hill's touchdown galvanized the Trojans. John McKay, who "paced the sidelines like a wild man" according to football historian Jim Dent, needed another possession. "I knew we had 'em," McKay told reporters after the game. "The momentum was all ours. In a situation like that, the No. 1 rating is a fairly suffocating thing."[9] But USC needed a touchdown: a field goal would do the Trojans no good.

On Notre Dame's next possession, McKay got his wish. The Fighting Irish only managed a three-and-out and then punted to Southern Cal. Mike Garrett returned the kick to the Notre Dame 42, where he fumbled, but his alert teammate Frank Lopez recovered the ball for Southern Cal at the Notre Dame 39. The clock showed 2:10 left in the game.

The Trojans wasted no time. Fertig completed another pass to Fred Hill, who ran to the Notre Dame 17. Garrett ran for 2 yards to the Notre Dame 15. Then Fertig threw two incompletions and the Trojans faced a 4th and 8 at the Notre Dame 15 with 1:37 left on the clock. In the Southern Cal huddle, Fertig called a pass known as 84-7. In the USC playbook, the 84-7 route called for a receiver, in this case Rod Sherman, who was split wide to the left, to delay one second after the snap, run five steps down the field, fake left, and then cut right, across the middle where the quarterback fires to him on the spot. The play worked perfectly. Sherman caught Fertig's pass at the 4-yard line, shook loose from Tony Carey, the Notre Dame defensive back, and ran into the end zone with the game-winning touchdown.[10]

So the game ended with Southern Cal pulling off the upset, 20–17. The Trojans hoisted John McKay onto their shoulders and carried him to midfield, where he shook hands with Ara Parseghian. The Fighting Irish headed for their locker room, devastated by the loss that ended their perfect season and deprived them of being the consensus number one team in the country. The Trojans exulted in their triumph, convinced that they had just punched their ticket to the Rose Bowl in Pasadena, where they would play the Michigan Wolverines for the second time in Rose Bowl history.

In the Southern Cal locker room, Notre Dame's president, Dr. Theodore Hesburgh, congratulated McKay on his victory and said to the religiously Roman Catholic coach, "That wasn't a very nice thing for a Catholic to do." To which McKay responded, with his well-known sense of humor, "Father, it serves you right for hiring a Presbyterian," the religious faith of Ara Parseghian.[11]

The Beavers, Not the Trojans

The faculty representatives of the AAWU met shortly after the conclusion of the USC–Notre Dame game to make their selection for the conference representative to face Michigan in the Rose Bowl. Few football observers doubted that the representatives would select Southern Cal after its dramatic victory over Notre Dame. But the faculty representatives shocked the football world by selecting Oregon State, and not Southern Cal. Actually, however, the representatives did not select Oregon State. Their vote was deadlocked at 4–4, with the representatives from the California institutions voting for Southern Cal, and the representatives from the Washington and Oregon institutions voting for Oregon State. In the event of a tie, the AAUW's policy stated, the first tie-breaker eliminated the school that had been to the Rose Bowl most recently. Southern Cal's most recent appearance was the 1963 Rose Bowl, when it defeated Wisconsin, 42–37. Oregon State's most recent appearance was in 1958, when it lost to Ohio State, 10–7.[12] On that basis, Oregon State became the AAWU's selection to face Michigan.

In California, the response to the selection of Oregon State was immediate—and brutal. Jess Hill, Southern Cal's athletic director, was incensed: "As far as I'm concerned, [the selection of Oregon State] is one of the rankest injustices ever perpetuated [*sic*] in the field of intercollegiate athletics."[13] The Southern California players learned that they would not be going to the Rose Bowl at their post-game dinner, just a few hours after the game ended in the Coliseum. Understandably, the news of the vote was met by the players with stunned silence. Craig Fertig, the quarterback who directed USC's memorable comeback in the second half against Notre Dame, expressed the players' acute sense of disappointment. "This is the worst of all," Fertig said. "We all thought if we beat Notre Dame we'd go to the Rose Bowl. I can't understand how the conference directors could have voted the way they did."[14]

For his part, John McKay took the high road and refused to inflame the situation, sort of. "I hope Oregon State does a real fine job [in the Rose Bowl],"

McKay said. "It is a well-coached team and I hope it justifies the conference decision that they are better than we are."[15] Tommy Prothro, Oregon State's coach, was less diplomatic than McKay, however. "I'm pleased that the faculty athletic representatives didn't get emotional over that 20–17 thriller," he said.[16]

Despite the protestations, the choice of Oregon State over Southern Cal was not overly controversial. Oregon State finished the season with an 8–2 record, better than Southern Cal's 7–3. Oregon State defeated two of its opponents who were Big Ten members, Indiana and Northwestern, while USC lost, convincingly, to Michigan State, 17–7, and to Ohio State, 17–0. Admittedly, Oregon State faced a far weaker set of Big Ten opponents than did Southern Cal. Nevertheless, a victory by Southern Cal over one of its Big Ten opponents might have been sufficient to sway at least one more vote in its direction, especially since it would have finished the season with a record identical to that of Oregon State.

Furthermore, Oregon State finished its regular season on November 21, the same date as the Michigan–Ohio State game, ranked number 8 in the national football polls. Even after its victory over Notre Dame, Southern Cal only managed to climb to number 10 in the same polls. And it must be pointed out that USC's victory over Notre Dame, dramatic and impressive though it was, occurred after Oregon State had finished its season and had no bearing on the conference records of either Oregon State or Southern Cal. Thus, the faculty representatives from Washington, Washington State, Oregon, and Oregon State did have at least the semblance of a rationale for their selection of Oregon State to face Michigan.

For Michigan, Bump Elliott wanted to be prepared to face either Southern Cal or Oregon State, and so sent Don Dufek to Los Angeles to scout Southern Cal in its game against Notre Dame. Like virtually every person who saw the game, Dufek came away convinced that Southern Cal was an outstanding team, but it was difficult to ascertain whether the Trojans were better than Oregon State. After scouting the game, Dufek returned to Ann Arbor, convinced that Michigan could defeat either opponent, Southern Cal or Oregon State.[17]

Once Oregon State was named as Michigan's opponent in the Rose Bowl, the oddsmakers apparently agreed with Dufek: they installed Michigan as almost prohibitive, 11-point favorites against the Beavers, a circumstance that was not exactly pleasing to Bump Elliott, who instructed his players not to comment on the outcome of the faculty vote in the AAWU. The line for the Wolverines was simple: they were pleased to be going to the Rose Bowl to play Oregon State. Elliott did not want the players to succumb to what he called the "Hollywood Trap," in which West Coast sportswriters treated a Michigan victory in the Rose Bowl as a foregone conclusion. For their part, however, the West Coast sportswriters did sense a Michigan blowout of historic proportions in the making. "Have your wife sew numbers on the uniforms, coach," the acerbic columnist Jim Murray wrote in the *Los Angeles Times*. "We'll want to identify your boys as they're carried off on stretchers."[18]

On to Pasadena

After holding some brief, unsatisfactory workouts in Ann Arbor, Bump Elliott decided to take the Michigan team to California on December 20 for pre–Rose Bowl workouts. Added to the Michigan roster for the Rose Bowl were Rich Hahn and Barry Dehlin, now healed from the knee surgeries after the Purdue game that ended their regular seasons on October 17. Jim Conley had visited both Hahn and Dehlin in the hospital after their surgeries and encouraged them to heal up because Michigan intended to go to the Rose Bowl and they needed to be ready. Elliott scheduled two workouts per day beginning on December 21 for the first week of practice, and then one workout per day leading up to the game. The workouts were vigorous, with lots of hitting. But the players had their evenings free—with no curfew—and they made the most of it. They won the roast beef–eating contest against Oregon State, sponsored by Los Angeles's famed Lawry's Restaurant, visited Disneyland, and otherwise embraced the attractions of the Hollywood night life. "Here we were, 20-year-old college men transplanted from the dead of a Michigan winter to sunny Southern California!" Bill Laskey later wrote. "Needless to say, we took full advantage of this rare opportunity to explore what we considered to be paradise between practices." Barry Dehlin echoed Laskey's sentiment: "I must admit that it was 'party on,'" he said.[19]

Apparently, at least more than a few of the players were having too much fun, in the opinion of some of the coaches and even of Jim Conley, Michigan's captain. During one pre-game practice, Tony Mason became incensed at the lackadaisical quality of the players' effort. He called the offensive team together and told the players that "they were reading the newspaper too much and getting the big head." Mason warned the players that if they did not "start getting [their] act together, start practicing like [they] should, and start thinking about what [they] were out there for," then Michigan would lose to Oregon State. "You are a bunch of good guys," Mason said, "you used to be good football players."[20] Mason's intervention convinced more than a few of the players that they "were just having a good time" and not paying proper attention to their preparation for the game.[21] For his part, Jim Conley was convinced that his teammates were getting soft on "too much Hollywood," and he also wanted to get their attention off the entertainment scene and get it refocused on the

Tom Harmon, left, Michigan's Heisman Trophy winner in 1940, speaks with Bob Timberlake at an event before the 1965 Rose Bowl in Pasadena, California (Bentley Historical Library, University of Michigan).

football game. He had no intention of coming out on the losing side in his only Rose Bowl game. The day before Christmas, Conley went to Bump Elliott and asked if he could schedule a "players-only" meeting for December 26. Elliott agreed and Conley called the meeting. Before the meeting with the entire team, though, Conley assembled the senior members of the team and told them: "We didn't come out here to lose and we need to get the team together to straighten some things out."[22] The meeting was held, and as Don Dufek recalled, the change in the players' attitudes became visible almost immediately. "Jim wasn't afraid to talk up to the guys on the team," Dufek remembered. "He was respected. He came to the realization that if we don't get a handle on this [lack of focus], we're going to get eaten up by all this Hollywood show scene. I think that some of the coaches were starting to come to the same conclusion so this meeting occurred at the right time."[23]

With the after-effects of the players-only meeting came a change in the routine for the Michigan team. As Brian Patchen recalled, "Bump took the team to a Catholic monastery in the hills a few miles away for the last several days before the game. The night life was over ... no TV or anything but football practice and team meetings. When game time came, we were ready."[24]

A Lackluster Start

Michigan went into the 1965 Rose Bowl rested and well prepared to face Oregon State. Admittedly, Coach Tommy Prothro's team had its strengths. Its punter, tight end Len Frketich, was ranked 13th in the country, and Steve Clark, its place kicker, was a reliable producer who scored 40 points on the season and kicked the game-winning field goal in Oregon State's 9–7 victory over Washington that helped to put the Beavers in the Rose Bowl. But the strength of the Oregon State team was its defense, known as the Mad Dogs, led by the linebacking duo of Dick Ruhl and Jack "Mad Dog" O'Billovich. The offense was led by the passing combination of sophomore quarterback Paul Brothers to ends Bob Grim and Frketich, as well as the ground attack led by halfback Cliff Watkins and fullback Booker Washington.[25]

To start the game, Jim Conley won the coin toss for Michigan and the Wolverines elected to receive. Carl Ward took the opening kickoff from Steve Clark three yards deep in the end zone and ran out to the 20, where he was hit and fumbled, but an alert Charlie Kines recovered the ball for Michigan. Playing on Michigan's kickoff return team was Barry Dehlin, playing in his first game since suffering the knee injury against Purdue on October 17 that sidelined him for the season. Before the game, one of Dehlin's uncles, who lived in Michigan's Upper Peninsula, asked him to tap his helmet three times when he entered the game so that his relatives in Michigan's far northern reaches would recognize him when he took the field. So, to what must have been the bewilderment of the Oregon State players, Barry Dehlin's gestures on the game's first play served as an indication that he had made it back into the Michigan lineup.[26]

In the first offensive series, Bump Elliott used the same starting lineup as he had in the game against Ohio State. Ben Farabee started at tight end, John Henderson at split end; the tackles were Charlie Kines and Tom Mack; the guards were John Marcum and Dave Butler; and the center was Brian Patchen. Elliott also started the I-75 Backfield intact: Bob Timberlake at quarterback, Jim Detwiler at left halfback, Carl Ward at right halfback, and Mel Anthony at fullback.

Oregon State's starters on defense were Greg Hartman and Al East at the ends; Dennis Rosario and George Carr at the tackles; Dave Gould and Doug John at the guards; Ruhl and O'Billovich at the linebackers; Dan Sieg at left halfback; Jim Smith at right halfback; and Dan Espelin at safety.[27]

On its first series, Michigan sputtered with a three-and-out, and Stan Kemp punted to Oregon State.[28] The Beavers began from their own 36 with Grim and Frketich at the ends, Ken Brusven and Rich Koeper at the tackles, Warren Cole and Al Funston at the guards, and Hoyt Keeney at center. The backfield consisted of Brothers at quarterback, Watkins at tailback, Washington at fullback, and Olvin Moreland at flanker. On defense for the Wolverines, Bob Hollway made one change along the front, starting Bill Keating at right tackle. Otherwise, the defensive unit was intact: Jim Conley at left end, Bill Yearby at left tackle, Arnie Simkus at left guard, Bob Mielke at right guard, and Bill Laskey at right end. The linebackers were Tom Cecchini and Frank Nunley. In the secondary were Rick Volk, Rick Sygar, and Dick Rindfuss.[29]

On Oregon State's first possession, Brothers threw complete to Olvin Moreland for a first down. Then, Michigan caught the game's first break. Charlie Shaw, in at tailback for Oregon State, carried the ball for a 5-yard gain before he was hit and fumbled. Tom Cecchini recovered for Michigan and the Wolverines had the ball, 1st and 10 at the Oregon State 41.

Three running plays by Sygar (in for Ward), Detwiler, and Anthony gave Michigan a first down at the Oregon State 30. But the Wolverines stalled out on the next three plays and Timberlake attempted a field goal from the Oregon State 30. The kick was short and Oregon State regained possession at its own 20 with the game scoreless. The Michigan defense, once again, held the Beavers to a three-and-out, and Frketich punted for the first time in the game, sending Michigan back to its 29.

On Michigan's third possession of the game, Bump Elliott opened up the offense. After a short gain by Anthony on first down, Timberlake threw for 11 yards to John Henderson for a first down at the Michigan 42. Then, two plays later, Timberlake found Henderson once again for a first down to the Oregon State 41. But, two plays later, Oregon State's defensive linemen Greg Hartman and George Carr sacked Timberlake for an 18-yard loss. On fourth down, Stan Kemp punted to the Oregon State 16. Thus far, in the 1965 Rose Bowl, the game belonged to the punters. Rusty from the layoff after the Ohio State game, the Michigan offense was finding it difficult to regain its physical and psychological edge.

In possession of the ball for the third time in the first quarter, Oregon State made a first down before Jim Conley and Bill Laskey sacked Paul Brothers for a 9-yard loss back to the Oregon State 18. Tommy Prothro called for a time out and when play resumed, Len Frketich surprisingly went back into punt formation on second down and punted to the Michigan 25. But Michigan's Dick Rindfuss was called for clipping on the play and the Beavers retained possession at their 33.[30]

The penalty on Michigan revitalized the Beavers' attack. Brothers threw 24 yards to Bob Grim for a first down at the Michigan 43. Then Brothers completed a pass to Moreland that gained another ten yards to the Michigan 33. At that point, the first quarter ended with the game scoreless but with Oregon State well inside Michigan territory and threatening to score.

Oregon State moved quickly at the start of the second quarter to score the first touchdown of the 1965 Rose Bowl. Two pass completions and a short run by Brothers gave Oregon State a first and goal at the Michigan five yard line. From there, Brothers threw to Doug McDougal, his tight end, who was wide open on the play, for a touchdown. Steve Clark kicked the extra point and the Beavers led, 7–0, at 2:27 of the second quarter. Bump Elliott later admitted: "It was touch and go in the early part of the game. Oregon State had the momentum at first."[31]

The Rose Bowl: A Game Built for Fullbacks

Following the Oregon State touchdown, Carl Ward returned the kickoff to the Michigan 28. On the ensuing series, Michigan looked like it was about to end its offensive lethargy. The Wolverines made a first down to the Oregon State 43 on runs by Timberlake and Anthony, and a pass completion from Timberlake to Farabee. But the Oregon State defense stiffened once again and Michigan advanced no further than the Beaver 38. On 3rd and 5 from the 38, Timberlake threw incomplete to Henderson, bringing on a fourth down. Stan Kemp came on for his third punt of the game and punted out of bounds at the Oregon State 16. In the contest between Michigan's offense and Oregon State's celebrated defense, the Mad Dogs were getting the better of it in the Rose Bowl's early rounds.

On Oregon State's next series, the Beavers gained a first down up to their 28 and then Michigan held Brothers to two incompletions. On 3rd and 10 from the Oregon State 28, Frketich came in to punt and boomed a kick down to the Michigan 18, which Rick Sygar returned to the Michigan 32. But, to Bump Elliott's dismay, Bob Mielke was called for clipping on the play and Michigan was penalized back to its 16-yard line.

On the Michigan sidelines, Bump Elliott and Tony Mason, along with Hank Fonde upstairs in the press box, were busily making adjustments in an attempt to get the sluggish Michigan offense untracked. They were about to make a game-changing adjustment. "We ran at the 2 and 8 holes [denoting the tackle positions] and then we found out that their ends were starting in," Bob Timberlake said after the game. "That gave us a sure 10 yards with the pitchout."[32]

Actually, a lot more than 10 yards. On first and 10 from the Michigan 16, Timberlake ran a fullback option, a play called Wing 1, and changed the flow of the momentum in the 1965 Rose Bowl. After taking the snap from Brian Patchen, Timberlake moved option right. Taking a hit from an Oregon State end (the only hit by an Oregon State defender on the play), Timberlake pitched the ball to Mel Anthony, who cut back to his left, received a block from Carl Ward, who drove the Oregon State cornerback out of the play, and ran across the middle of the field, with the Oregon State players trying desperately to get back into pursuit. One by one, the Michigan blockers cut down the Beavers' defenders as Anthony raced to the end zone. Breaking into the clear at the Michigan 40, Anthony picked up an escort in the person of Tom Mack, who ran virtually stride for stride with him until he crossed the goal line. Anthony scored on an 84-yard touchdown run, the longest in Rose Bowl history. Anthony's touchdown so thrilled one Michigan supporter that he threw a smoke bomb out onto the turf, temporarily stopping play until the offending firework was extinguished and removed from the field.

Anthony's long run was a textbook example of perfect execution. "Nobody touched me," Anthony admitted after the game. "I could see daylight after Carl Ward and John Henderson sprung me on that pitchout." Before the game, Anthony had spoken with assistant coach Don Dufek about the Rose Bowl.

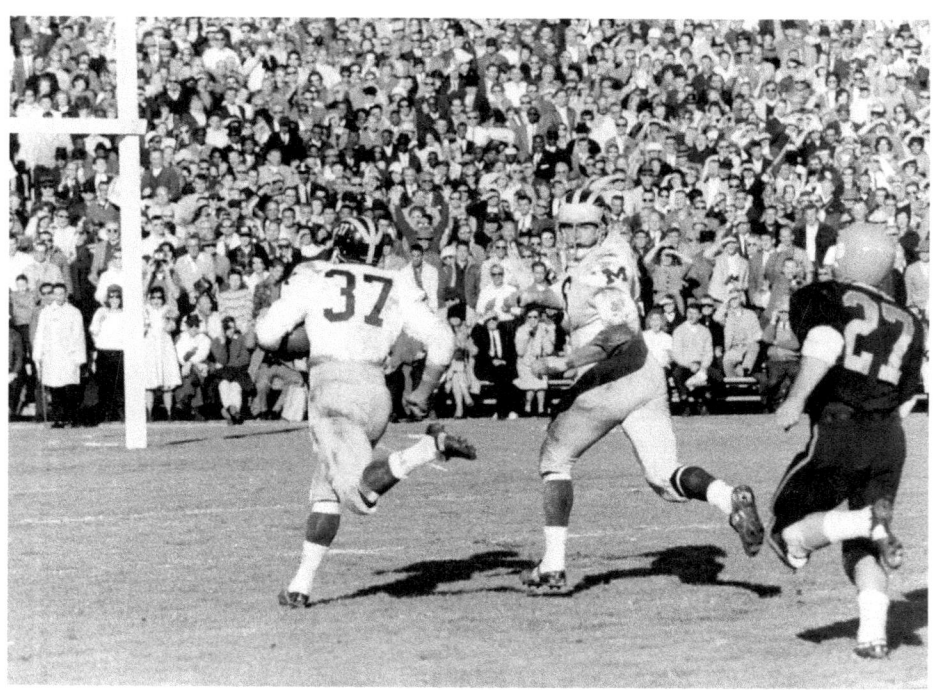

Accompanied by Tom Mack (96), Mel Anthony (37) dashes for the goal line *en route* to his record-breaking 84-yard touchdown run against Oregon State. Anthony scored three touchdowns in the Rose Bowl and was named the game's Most Valuable Player (Bentley Historical Library, University of Michigan).

"I told him just before the game started that this Rose Bowl game is just built for fullbacks," Dufek said, recalling his role as a fullback on Michigan's 1951 Rose Bowl team that defeated California 14–6 on his game-winning touchdown.[33]

After Anthony's record-setting touchdown, Bob Timberlake missed the point-after attempt and Michigan trailed Oregon State, 7–6. But the Wolverines had stemmed Oregon State's momentum with Anthony's quick strike. Anthony's touchdown appeared to shake the confidence of the Beavers. On the ensuing kickoff, Cliff Watkins returned the ball to the Oregon State 20 yard line. The next two plays gained only three yards and Prothro called for Len Frketich to punt on 3rd and 7. Frketich boomed another punt downfield that Rick Sygar caught on the Michigan 25 and returned to the 38. But the question remained: with an accurate passer like Paul Brothers on the field, why did Prothro punt on 3rd down, instead of 4th down? The Michigan defense had just recorded a two-and-out.

When the Michigan offense came onto the field for its next series, Dave Fisher replaced Mel Anthony at fullback, giving the senior a breather after his long touchdown run. Two running plays by Fisher, and a quarterback sneak by Timberlake near mid-field, gave Michigan a first down at its 49. Then, combining a completion to John Henderson with two runs of his own, Timberlake moved the Wolverines inside the Oregon State 30-yard line. Then Carl Ward was called for clipping on a scramble by Timberlake, and the Wolverines were penalized back to the Oregon State 43.

Carl Ward made amends for his penalty on the game's next play. Taking a pitch from Timberlake, Ward headed around right end. Two Oregon State defenders nearly had him trapped along the sideline, but Ward shook off a tackle, cut back to his left, and outran every defender on the field to the end zone. "It's just a quick pitchout to Ward," Bump Elliott said after the game, describing Michigan's second touchdown, "[and] it calls for sheer speed. We ha[d]n't used it much this year and thought Oregon State's defense might not be ready for it."[34] Michigan had taken the lead, 12–7. Bump Elliott called for a two-point attempt on the conversion, but Timberlake's pass to Ben Farabee was broken up by Oregon State's Al East. Michigan held its lead of 12–7 for the remainder of the first half.[35] When the teams went to their locker rooms at halftime, Michigan unmistakably had captured the momentum in the game.

"A hole big enough to drive a truck through"

In the early minutes of the second half, both Oregon State and Michigan responded tentatively. On its first possession of the third quarter, Oregon State moved as far as its 40 yard line before Len Frketich punted once again to the Wolverines. Michigan started its first series of the second half on its own 12-yard line but could not manage a first down. On fourth down, Stan Kemp punted back to Oregon State, which then took over on its own 43. With good field position near mid-field, Oregon State had an opportunity to score and either narrow the Michigan lead or take the lead itself. But the Michigan defense had made its halftime adjustments and knew the Oregon State tendencies. Bill Laskey and Bill Keating drove the Beavers back to their own 30-yard line with two tackles for loss. Len Frketich moved back into punting position and it was at this point that Michigan took control of the game and the 1965 Rose Bowl turned completely in its favor.

As on some of the other critical plays that had occurred during Michigan's regular season, it was meticulous coaching that paid the dividends. In the preparation for the Rose Bowl, Michigan's defensive coordinator Bob Hollway detected a fatal flaw in Oregon State's otherwise impeccable punting team. "It was when we were watching the movies in Ann Arbor," Hollway said, "and I noticed that the Oregon State center did something with the ball on punts. Well, he would lift the ball right off the ground—before passing it back. The rules say the defense can rush the minute the ball is snapped, and we figured that when he picked it up we could go.... So I went to the head linesman before the game and he said, yes, we could rush as soon as the center lifts it." Subsequently, Hollway obtained an understanding with the head linesman to watch the Oregon State center and the Michigan defensive linemen so that Michigan would not be penalized for being offside if they rushed the punter after the Oregon State center lifted the football.[36] While still in Ann Arbor, Hollway and Jocko Nelson devised a play for rushing the punter if the game situation called for it.

Michigan chose not to attempt to block a punt in the first half, nor on Frketich's first punt of the second half. But when Frketich went back for his second punt of the third quarter, Hollway left the defensive unit on the field rather than sending in the offensive unit to prepare for a punt return by Rick Sygar. When Oregon State's long snapper lifted the ball, the Wolverine defensive linemen charged ahead. Bob Mielke got to Frketich first and blocked the punt. The ball rolled free toward the Oregon State goal line until Mel Anthony, in the game at linebacker, recovered the ball at the Beavers' 16-yard line.

As the play unfolded, Mielke's assignment was to take out two opponents to allow Tom Cecchini to fire through and block the punt. But Mielke encountered little resistance and made it to Frketich before Cecchini arrived. "I line[d] up head-on-head with their right guard," Mielke said after the game. "Once I got past him, I'm supposed to draw a double block from two defenders, opening up an alley for Tom Cecchini ... to shoot in on them. However, they both went for him instead and I could go in with free sailing."[37] As far as the game was concerned, Mielke's block of Frketich's punt was not so much a turning point, as an exclamation point. "After that blocked punt," wrote Ollie Kneuchle for the *Milwaukee Journal*, "Michigan beat the hell out of the Beavers."[38]

Taking over on the Oregon State 16 yard line, the Wolverines stayed on the ground. Three runs by Anthony and Timberlake gave Michigan a 4th and 2 at the Oregon State 7. On the Michigan sideline, Elliott and Tony Mason wanted to attempt a field goal. On the field, the players wanted to go for a touchdown. The players won out: on the next play, Jim Detwiler plowed through the Oregon State line for four yards and a first and goal at the Oregon State 3. Two plays later, Mel Anthony recorded his second touchdown of the game and Michigan led 18–7. Anthony scored his touchdown on a play where Brian Patchen, John Marcum and Dave Butler "formed the apex of a wedge and I just follow[ed] them."[39]

Bump Elliott called for another two-point attempt and Timberlake converted on a sweep to the right. Or did he? Actually, Timberlake did not cross the goal line on the conversion, but the official on the play ruled that he had. "I didn't get over at all," Timberlake said after the game. "I wasn't as short of the goal line as I was in the Purdue game when we needed two points to win, but I definitely wasn't over It was a gift."[40] Regardless, Michigan led 20–7 midway through the third quarter and rout was on.

Michigan put its stamp of control on the game for the remainder of the contest as the Oregon State offense was unable to sustain any kind of attack against the stout Wolverine defenders. Oregon State also failed to withstand the pounding of the Michigan ground game that completely dominated the offensive show in the second half. Following Anthony's second touchdown of the game, Oregon State recorded another three-and-out, and Michigan took over on its own 22 after another booming punt by Len Frketich and a 12-yard return by Rick Sygar. From there, Michigan mounted another textbook drive. After a 7-yard gain by Carl Ward on first down, Timberlake crossed up the Oregon State defense with a pass to Detwiler out of the backfield, and the big halfback rambled for 30 yards to the Oregon State 41.

Six plays later, Anthony ran "through a hole big enough to drive a truck through" for his third touchdown of the game from 7 yards out. Anthony later said that his linemen "were a little mad at me before we scored the third one because they said the hole had been there all day."[41] Anthony's third touchdown enabled him to tie the Rose Bowl record of 18 points scored by an individual, held by fullbacks Elmer Layden of Notre Dame in 1933, and Jack Weisenberger of Michigan in 1948. After Timberlake's successful PAT, Michigan led 27–7 and the outcome of the 1965 Rose Bowl was no longer in doubt. The third quarter ended with Michigan holding onto its 20-point lead.

By now, the Michigan faithful in the Rose Bowl were enjoying themselves immensely. Michigan's fourth straight Rose Bowl victory was well in hand, and in sight. It was time for a bit of hijinks and one unknown Michigan supporter released a small pig onto the playing field. With a block "M" painted on its side, the pig took off for the end zone at the other end of the field, with a Rose Bowl attendant in hot pursuit. The attendant managed to grab the piglet and remove it from the field, to the howls of the crowd, who were, of course, cheering on the pig as he attempted to escape from the clutches of the attendant. One writer later described the scene: "Some fans thought the most exciting play of the game came when a tiny pig was turned loose on the field in the third quarter. The piglet ran the length of the field, with the fans chanting the countdown, before some lad came out of the stands to tackle the scrambling porker."[42] The episode with the pig caused a slight delay in the game, but, of course, to no one's disappointment.

Michigan scored its fifth touchdown of the 1965 Rose Bowl with five

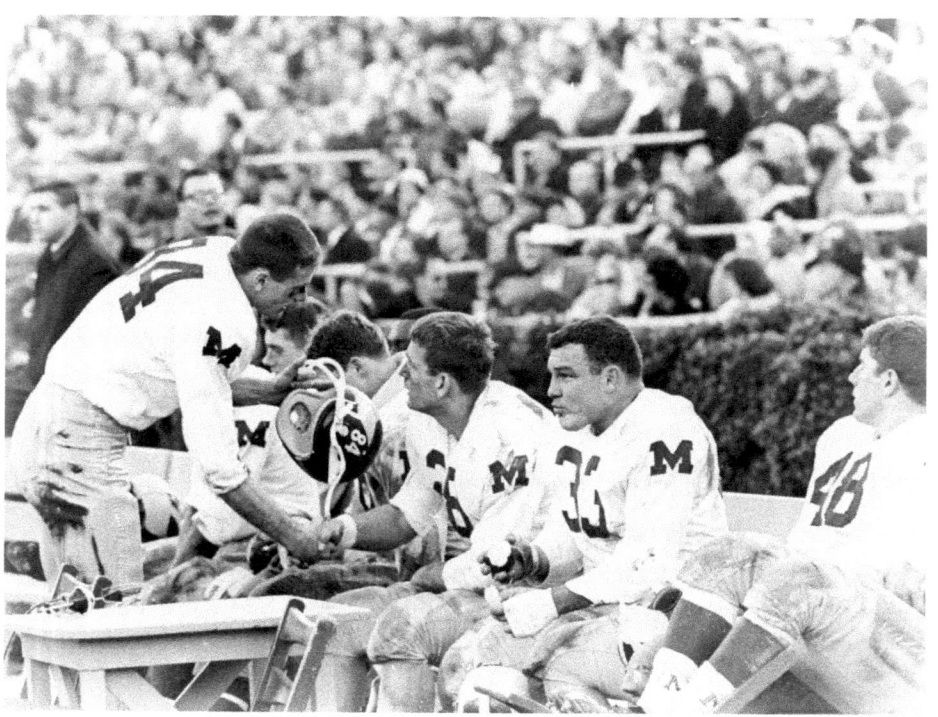

Craig Kirby (84) congratulates Bob Timberlake on the Michigan bench during the Rose Bowl. Seated to the left of Timberlake are Dave Fisher (33) and Jim Detwiler (48) (Bentley Historical Library, University of Michigan).

minutes gone in the fourth quarter on a 24-yard run for a touchdown by Bob Timberlake. Timberlake again kicked the PAT and the Michigan lead grew to 34–7. From that point to the end of the game, Bump Elliott emptied his bench, and several players who had played sparingly during the season had memorable experiences in the fourth quarter. Every member of Michigan's 44-man Rose Bowl roster saw action in the contest. Frosty Evashevski quarterbacked the Michigan attack for much of the final period. Dick Wells and Louis Lee took turns at halfback, and Barry Dehlin took a carry at fullback, unfortunately fumbling the ball and turning it over to Oregon State. Rich Hahn played most of the fourth quarter on the defensive line and recorded two tackles. For Dehlin and Hahn, both of whom feared their seasons, if not their careers, might be over after their knee injuries in the Purdue game, playing in the Rose Bowl was a dream come true.

In the final moments of the game, Oregon State moved down the field and reached the Michigan 5-yard line before turning the ball over on downs. The final score remained 34–7, and when the final gun sounded, 5,000 Michigan fans rushed the field, congratulating their victorious Wolverines and, of course, tearing down the goal posts. After the game, the Michigan players voted to give the game ball to Bump Elliott, "the man who deserved it," according to Tony Mason.[43]

"Crushing blocking and flashing speed"

In the post-game analysis, few observers doubted the totality of Michigan's convincing victory. The Wolverines outgained the Beavers in total yardage, 415–243, and in first downs, 18–14, with several of Oregon State's first downs occurring in the fourth quarter when Michigan's reserves were on the field. Perhaps the most telling statistic was Michigan's overwhelming rushing attack: 332 yards on the ground to only 64 for Oregon State. Once again, a Michigan opponent failed to gain 100 net yards rushing against the solid Wolverine defense.

To its credit, Oregon State outgained Michigan through the air, 179–83 on 19 completions in 33 attempts, but Oregon State's success in this aspect of the game only yielded one touchdown. Michigan's ground attack, as usual, was balanced and diversified between Timberlake, Anthony, Detwiler, Ward, and Fisher. Anthony gained 123 yards on 13 carries; Timberlake 57 yards on 12 carries; Ward 88 yards on 10 carries; Detwiler 16 yards on 5 carries; and Fisher, 30 yards on 5 carries. Michigan's yards-per-carry average in the Rose Bowl was a startling 6.5 yards. Timberlake also passed for 77 yards, giving him a total of 1,515 yards of total offense for the season, setting a new season record in that category, breaking the old record of 1,395 yards set by Bob Chappuis in 1947.[44] Michigan's performance was aptly characterized by "crushing blocking and flashing speed," wrote Mike Welds, who covered the game for the *San Jose News*. Frank Finch, a Los Angeles sportswriter, referred to the Wolverines as "Bump Elliott's Ann Arbor assassins."[45]

Michigan's performance drew its share of accolades from the opposing Oregon State, also. After the game, Tommy Prothro reiterated some of his previous comments about the Michigan team. "I said before the game that Michigan was the best team in the country," Prothro said. "Now I say they're close to being the best team I've ever seen. I don't think anybody could have beaten them in the Rose Bowl."[46] Paul Brothers, Oregon State's embattled quarterback, speaking about the Michigan defense after the Wolverine defenders had thrown him for 33 yards in losses, simply said, "I hope I never have to go through another afternoon like that one." Jack O'Billovich, the Mad Dog of the Oregon State defense, was also impressed with Michigan. "It was amazing that their backs were so big and could run so fast," he explained.[47]

"We didn't intend to lose"

Bump Elliott spoke candidly with reporters after the Rose Bowl. Acknowledging the magnitude of the victory, Elliott still expressed some sympathy for the Beavers. "I'm sorry it had to be Oregon State," Elliott said. "I have strong feelings for that school. That's where I started my coaching career."[48] In Elliott's estimation, two plays helped to determine the outcome of the contest: Mel Anthony's record-setting 84-yard run for a touchdown in the second quarter, and the blocked punt by Bob Mielke in the third quarter that set up Michigan's third touchdown. "It was touch and go in the early part of the game," Elliott recounted accurately. "Oregon State had the momentum at first. Then, with Anthony's run we held the momentum. It gave us a spark and a chance to get moving."[49]

Elliott's pride was evident: Michigan had capped off its season with a stellar performance and kept alive Michigan's unbeaten streak in the Rose Bowl. "I couldn't be prouder of our team," Elliott said. "This was as good a game as we've played all season. Oregon State is a good football team but we had a few breaks and it started to snowball to our advantage."[50] Simply stated, "We didn't intend to lose. We came out here to win and we did."[51] The mentality of the players, when it counted, remained focused on that objective.

In his comments to reporters, Bump Elliott chose to praise the Michigan team effort while soft-pedaling the largely disappointing performance turned in by Oregon State. In speaking with reporters, however, the Michigan players were not so generous, and their comments fueled the fires of the West Coast sportswriters, who produced a blizzard of criticism directed at Oregon State, even to the point of chastising the AAWU for its selection of the Beavers as the conference representative. Carl Ward minced no words when asked about the play of the Beavers. "[T]heir tackling was lousy," he said.[52] Bob Timberlake was scarcely more diplomatic. "[The Beavers] were a good team," Timberlake observed, "but not in the class of the Big Ten. I'm sorry to say it but it's true. We had a little trouble psychologically in the first quarter. It wasn't that we weren't ready for the game; it just took us a little longer to get started.... But it didn't bother us when they scored. We knew we could take them. We were just too strong for them."[53]

Bill Yearby echoed Timberlake's sentiments. "I played across from a guy who must have weighed about 250," Yearby said. "And he hurt me a little from time to time. On the other hand, I don't think they would have wound up with close to an 8–2 record in the Big Ten. They're a good football team, but not that good."[54]

Asked to comment on the Beavers, Mel Anthony expressed some more measured thoughts, although even his careful reply appeared to be on the side of damning with faint praise. "They were a good football team," Anthony said. "A lot people said they were rinky-dink, but they hit just as hard as anybody we've played."[55]

Not surprisingly, the free-flowing comments of the victorious Michigan players stirred the pot of the West Coast sportswriters, who began the chorus of "I told you so" that Oregon State should never have been invited to the Rose Bowl in the first place. The headline in the *Los Angeles Times* on January 2, "Michigan 34-AAWU Representative 7," captured the bitterness of the California sportswriters.[56] Not surprisingly, the Los Angeles sportswriters renewed their claim that Southern California, not Oregon State, should have been Michigan's opponent. "The football world will never know what the Trojans of USC might have done, but Oregon State proved beyond a doubt Friday that it was inadequate as an opponent for Michigan," wrote Paul Zimmerman in the *Los Angeles Times*.[57] Bud Furillo, writing in the *Los Angeles Herald-Examiner*, viewed the Oregon State defeat as a setback for the entire West Coast. Calling the game a "mismatch," Furillo wrote that the "Beavers had been warned to stay at home and let USC take the rap."[58]

Naturally, the sports reporters turned their attention to Tommy Prothro, Oregon State's coach, for his explanation of the debacle. "The offense operated as I thought it would, but the defense didn't hold up as we had anticipated," Prothro explained. "I thought it would be more of a defensive game. Our team seemed to let up after it scored in the second quarter and got the jump on Michigan."[59]

Prothro's play-calling prompted several questions from the reporters, such as his decisions in the first half to punt on second down and third down. Specifically, reporters challenged him for calling a punt on a 2nd and 19 situation in the first half. Commented Sid Ziff of the *Los Angeles Times*, "If Oregon State hadn't been so eager to punt on second and third down the score might have been closer. It was like sticking out your chin and inviting your opponent to take his best punch. Michigan did."[60]

In response, Prothro said, "We thought our best hope was to punt for field position and try to hold them." But, reporters inquired, had Oregon State punted on second down during the regular season? "No," Prothro replied, not exactly liking the tone of the question, "and we didn't have any 2nd and 19 situations in our own territory, either."[61] Also, trailing 12–7 with 17 seconds left in the first half and facing a 4th and 10 from their 41, why did Prothro decide to punt instead of try for the first down? "We hadn't given any indication that we could go 60 yards in one play, and they had," the coach replied.[62]

Finally, Prothro ran out of patience amidst the persistently critical questioning. Asked one more time whether USC might have been a more suitable opponent for Michigan than Oregon State, Prothro drew some laughter when he said, "No offense intended, but I think we could have beaten the hell out of the Los Angeles sportswriters today. But, of course, they're a little past their prime."[63]

The almost universal condemnation of Oregon State by the West Coast sportswriters unfortunately tended to diminish the magnitude of the Michigan performance. Pete Waldmeir, the respected sportswriter for the *Detroit News*, sought to restore some balance to the coverage, even if it meant taking on some fellow members of his journalistic fraternity. "It always pains to put the knock on somebody in your own business, since you work on the assumption you're all in the same sort of leaky boat," Waldmeir wrote after the Rose Bowl, "but the Los Angeles newspapers topped all their previous records for boorishness in recounting the Rose Bowl result.... Los Angeles has been pouting ever since the regular season ended over the fact that Oregon State and not Southern California was granted the right to represent the AAWU in the Rose Bowl.... To them, Michigan didn't win. Oregon State, the weak sister from the North that had not been dubiously blessed by residency in smoggy damp California, lost."[64]

In his column, written in the *Detroit News* on January 5, 1965, Waldmeir pointed out the statistically dominating nature of the Michigan victory, and in words that probably sounded blasphemous to his West Coast brethren, strongly argued that Southern Cal would have lost to Michigan, also. "About 'never knowing' whether Southern Cal might have beaten Michigan given the chance," Waldmeir pointed out that "USC lost badly to Michigan State in one of the worst games, if not the worst, played in East Lansing last fall. Now, ... what did Michigan do to Michigan State?"[65]

Likewise, the Michigan players entertained no doubt about their ability to defeat either Oregon State or Southern Cal. "We were too strong," Jim Conley stated years later. "Look at that [1964] team: seventeen of the players on that roster went on to play in the National Football League."[66]

"Captain Conley, what can I do for you?"

After the Rose Bowl, the Wolverines flew back to Ann Arbor to face the rest of the Michigan winter. But they also faced a sensitive issue. After Michigan's victory over Ohio State, the athletic department received a monetary donation from a family in Flint that had suffered the loss of a teenaged son who had been a keen and avid supporter of the Michigan football team. The family asked that the donation, in their son's memory, be directed toward honoring Michigan's 1964 championship football team. Bump Elliott, Jim Conley, and the other team members agreed to use the funds to produce an engraved charm, "designed by their teammate Bruce Allison," that would be presented to the members of the team in recognition of their Big Ten championship.[67] As football historian Greg Dooley described the charm, it was a "10K gold football with a block 'M' in between the year '1964.' It would read 'Michigan' on top and 'Big Ten Champions' below. The name of the player was to be engraved on the back."[68]

Just as important, every member of the Michigan team, regardless of whether the player made the traveling squad for the Rose Bowl, was to receive a charm as a memento of the championship season. The members of Michigan's Rose Bowl team, 44 players in total, had received gifts of a wristwatch and a transistor radio as mementoes of the Rose Bowl, but more than twenty other players were unable to make the trip to Pasadena. The charms, therefore, stood as valued reminders of their roles in Michigan's memorable season.[69]

When the team returned from California, Elliott informed the players that the athletic department was holding up the money for the charms and planned to use the funds to cover the unanticipated costs of long-distance telephone calls made by the players from California during their Rose Bowl visit. Conley was understandably angry and pressed Elliott to intervene with Crisler to have the funds restored. Instead, Elliott told Conley to make an appointment himself with Athletic Director Fritz Crisler and request that the funds, designated for the production of the charms, be released. So Conley asked for, and received, his appointment with Fritz Crisler.

The meeting was memorable. Conley entered Crisler's office and described the scene. "He's in a swivel chair with his back towards me, staring out the window...." Then, "Fritz spins his chair around and asks, 'Captain Conley, what can I do for you?'" Conley explained the situation in detail, how the funds for the charms were donated to honor the 1964 team, how each player was to receive a charm as a memento of the season, and how, if the funds were not made available, some players would be denied their proper recognition. "In the spirit of the team, I'd like you to release the money," Conley told Crisler. Then, "Fritz spun around in his chair again toward the window. And then he spun back around, looked me in the eye and said, "Captain Conley, [y]ou'll have your souvenir. Is there anything else?" "No sir," Conley responded, looking for a graceful exit from Crisler's office. As he headed out the door, Crisler gave him the parting words: "Congratulations on a great year."[70] The players received their charms as a memento of the 1964 championship season.

In conclusion, the Rose Bowl, as Bill Laskey said, was anticlimactic compared to the thrill of defeating Ohio State and claiming the Big Ten championship for the first time in fourteen years.[71] Upon reflection, it became obvious that the game against Oregon State in the Rose Bowl was one of Michigan's easier games of the season. Like Air Force and Navy, Oregon State was simply another non-conference opponent that was unable to stop the Wolverines' ground game or penetrate the stout Michigan defense. With the exception of Northwestern, shut out by Michigan, 35–0, on October 31, every one of Michigan's Big Ten opponents—Michigan State, Purdue, Minnesota, Illinois, Iowa, and Ohio State—gave the Wolverines a tougher battle than did Oregon State. Michigan won the Rose Bowl by using the same ingredients that it used to win eight games during the regular season: a powerful rushing attack, a virtually impenetrable defense, efficient quarterbacking, and solid play by the special teams. In the process, it set a standard for a margin of victory for a Big Ten team in the Rose Bowl, 27 points, that remains to this day.

The Wolverines savored their Rose Bowl triumph, a fitting and glorious conclusion to a memorable football season, one of the best ever in the annals of Wolverine football. It was a season, as Bill Yearby later described, that "laid the foundation for everything else that happened" in the future.[72] Several sportswriters, such as Bob Pille of the *Detroit Free Press*, Clank Stoppels of the *Grand Rapids Press*, and Sec Taylor of the *Des Moines Register*, echoed the view of Oregon State's coach Tommy Prothro that Michigan was the best team in the country, despite the fact that Alabama finished number one in the national polls at the conclusion of the regular season, thereby becoming the winner of the mythical national championship.[73] Bump Elliott responded philosophically to such an argument. "I'm not saying it wouldn't be nice to be No. 1, because it would," Elliott explained. "That's something already cut and dried. We have our achievements anyway."[74]

So the Rose Bowl victory fit into the category of the Michigan achievements, another milestone for the team, and for individuals like Bump Elliott, who was given the game ball by the team, and for Mel Anthony, the winner of the silver trophy given to the game's outstanding player. When Rick Sygar led the team in singing "The Victors" in the raucous Michigan locker room after the game, the 44 players on the Michigan roster took pride in the knowledge that they had preserved the Wolverines' unbeaten winning streak in the Rose Bowl. Bob Hollway told the Michigan players before the game, "Twenty-five years from now when someone finds out that you played in the Rose Bowl, he will ask you one question: 'Did you win?'"[75] For the next fifty years, the 1964 Wolverines have been able to answer that they had, indeed, won the 1965 Rose Bowl.

Afterword:
Beyond Michigan Stadium

Michigan's championship season in 1964, combined with its victory in the 1965 Rose Bowl, were historic chapters in its football history. Nothing remains unchanged in college football, however, and the passage of time brought inevitable changes to the Michigan football program, both within the ranks of the coaching staff and in the roster of the players. For the most part, these changes were positive, especially for the players, a great number of whom went on to successful careers in professional football or who achieved notable success in other fields, such as business, law, engineering, and education. As Jim Conley observed years later, "those [players] who played for Bump [Elliott] graduated, with character, with a plan for life—and with a sense of humor."[1]

While Bump Elliott and the members of the Michigan coaching staff did not necessarily emphasize the possibility of a future career in professional football as an objective for prospective Michigan players, nor was such a pursuit extensively discussed during the season, the fact remained that an unprecedented number of players on Michigan's 1964 roster entered the professional ranks once they finished their playing careers with the Wolverines. Professional football in the United States expanded rapidly in the early 1960s and provided ever greater opportunities for players coming out of college who wished to pursue a career in one of the two leagues, the National Football League (NFL) or the American Football League (AFL). Since the merger of the NFL and the AFL did not occur until 1967, several Michigan players found themselves drafted by teams in both leagues, and faced a decision as to their choice of team once they turned pro.

As a consequence, the number of Wolverines who embarked upon pro careers in 1965, 1966, and 1967 was startling. In 1965, for example, Bob Timberlake, Mel Anthony, Arnie Simkus, and John Henderson signed contracts to play in the NFL, while Bill Laskey made the roster for the Buffalo Bills of the AFL. In 1966, Tom Mack, Steve Smith, and Charlie Kines signed to play in the NFL, while Bill Yearby and Bill Keating signed contracts with teams in the AFL. In 1967, the number of Wolverines in professional football grew substantially as Jim Detwiler, Rick Volk, Jack Clancy, John Rowser, Carl Ward, Frank Nunley, and Mike Bass all signed contracts with NFL teams. In addition, after the 1965 season, Wally Gabler signed a contract to play with the Toronto Argonauts of the Canadian Football League (CFL). In total, therefore, eighteen members of Michigan's 1964 roster went on to careers in professional football.

The growth of professional football during the 1960s and beyond also provided expanded opportunities for coaches as well as players. The attraction of coaching in the professional ranks opened a path for several members of Bump Elliott's coaching staff, beginning in the late 1960s. Bob Hollway, Jocko Nelson, Tom Cecchini, and Dennis Fitzgerald all coached professionally in the NFL during the 1960s, 1970s, and 1980s after finishing their coaching careers at Michigan.

The Coaches

Bump Elliott remained as Michigan's head football coach through the 1968 season. In his final year as head coach, Michigan posted an 8–2 record and challenged unbeaten Ohio State for the Big Ten championship in Columbus on the final weekend of the season. The Michigan–Ohio State game in 1968 was not a repeat of 1964, however, as the Buckeyes defeated the Wolverines, 50–14, a bitter loss for Michigan made more unpalatable by Ohio State's tasteless attempt at a two-point conversion after fullback Jim Otis's touchdown gave Ohio State its 50th point.[2]

Shortly after the 1968 season, Bump Elliott resigned as Michigan's head coach. In July 1968, Don Canham, Michigan's longtime successful head track coach, succeeded Fritz Crisler as the athletic director, and he and Elliott conferred after the season about Elliott's move into a position as Michigan's first associate athletic director. "There's a misconception that I was moved up to get rid of me," Elliott told sportswriter Jerry Green of the *Detroit News* in 1981. "That's not true. I initiated the move with Don Canham and we both worked to get a replacement [as head football coach], which was Bo Schembechler. The time, the constraints of recruiting, as a coach, you almost have to sacrifice everything to do it. I have no regrets about giving up coaching to go into administration.... I was ready to make a career change. I was looking ahead. I felt the timing was right. We'd just finished and [*sic*] 8-2 season."[3]

So, as Bump Elliott moved into the ranks of athletic administration at Michigan, Bo Schembechler, formerly the head coach at Miami University of Ohio, took over the reins of the Wolverines football program. Under Schembechler's leadership, the Wolverines produced the memorable season of 1969, culminated by their historic victory over Ohio State, 24–12, on November 22. The victory over Ohio State gave Michigan a share of the Big Ten championship and another trip to the Rose Bowl. Observers of college football correctly proclaimed Michigan's victory over Ohio State as the upset of the 1969 season.

In the jubilant Michigan locker room after the game, Bo Schembechler paid tribute to Bump Elliott for leaving him with a team of players capable of contending for the Big Ten championship. As Schembechler later recalled, "[O]nce everyone quieted down, I asked Bump Elliott to come up, and handed the game ball to him. Everyone got choked up, including Bump. Some guys were out and out crying—and I don't remember when I felt better about anything I've done in my entire life."[4]

After eighteen months as Michigan's associate athletic director, Bump Elliott became the athletic director at the University of Iowa on June 11, 1970, and served in that position until he retired in 1991. Elliott's tenure as Iowa's athletic director was resoundingly productive and successful. During that period, Elliott presided over an athletic program that won 27 Big Ten championships and 11 NCAA championships. He undertook the renovation of numerous athletic facilities at Iowa, including the expansion of Kinnick Stadium in 1983 to a capacity of 70,000. He also expanded the football complex to include new locker rooms, weight rooms, new meeting rooms, and a new indoor facility for football. As one sportswriter put it, "The success of Iowa's athletic program is a tribute to Bump."[5]

Not surprisingly, Elliott credited his experience as associate athletic director at Michigan with giving him the tools to succeed as athletic director at Iowa. "It's not that much different [between Michigan and Iowa]," Elliott recalled. "The problems and the objectives are the same, the sources of revenue are the same. The difference is in some of the interest we get. The fact that we don't have competition [from another Big Ten university in the state] helps us to gain more recognition."[6] Elliott's tenure as Iowa's athletic director was the most productive aspect of his professional career.

Don Dufek resigned from the Michigan coaching staff after the 1965 season and entered private business. In 1972, after being encouraged by Don Canham, Dufek accepted the athletic director's position at Grand Valley State College (later Grand Valley State University) in Allendale, Michigan. At the time a small school with fewer than 2500 students, Grand Valley' had an athletic program that was in its infancy. In 1973, Dufek hired Jim Harkema, formerly an outstanding athlete at Kalamazoo College, from Triton Junior College in Illinois as Grand Valley's football coach, and the small college's athletic program showed steady improvement from that point.

In 1976, Dufek left Grand Valley to become athletic director at Kent State University in Ohio. Dufek remained at Kent State until 1980, when he resigned and returned to Ann Arbor to accept a position with the University of Michigan Alumni Association. Now retired, Dufek continues to live in Ann Arbor with his wife Patricia.[7]

Dennis Fitzgerald also remained on the Michigan coaching through the 1968 season. Fitzgerald then began a personal football coaching odyssey, holding positions both at the collegiate and professional levels. After leaving Michigan, he was the defensive coordinator at the University of Kentucky and at Kent State. He was the head coach at Kent State between 1975 and 1977. After leaving Kent State, he coached briefly at Syracuse University before joining the Pittsburgh Steelers in the NFL in 1982. He remained with the Steelers until 1989, coaching the linebackers and the special teams. After leaving the Steelers, Fitzgerald coached in the United States Football League (USFL) and at several small colleges, including at Grand Valley State. Fitzgerald was stricken with lymphoma in 1999 and passed away on January 14, 2001.[8]

Hank Fonde remained on Bump Elliott's staff through the 1968 season. Bo Schembechler retained Fonde as the football program's first academic adviser. Jerry Hanlon, one of Schembechler's assistant coaches, recalled Fonde as "one of the nicest gentlemen I ever met. The players loved him and when he decided to leave Michigan as an academic adviser, I thought it was a big loss."[9] He left the Michigan coaching staff in 1969 and entered private business. He passed away on May 3, 2009.

Bob Hollway resigned from Michigan's coaching staff after the 1965 season and entered private business. In 1967, he returned to coaching and joined Bud Grant's staff as the defensive line coach for the Minnesota Vikings. Then, between 1968 and 1970, Hollway was the defensive coordinator for the Vikings, taking a leading role in the creation of Minnesota's vaunted defensive line, the so-called Purple Eaters, that consisted of defensive ends Carl Eller and Jim Marshall and tackles Alan Page and Gary Larsen.

Between 1971 and 1973, Hollway was the head coach of the St. Louis Cardinals, but was replaced after the 1973 season. He then coached briefly with the Detroit Lions, the San Francisco 49ers, and the Seattle Seahawks before returning once again to the Minnesota Vikings. From 1978 to 1985, he once again served as Bud Grant's defensive coordinator before retiring from coaching. Hollway passed away on March 13, 1999.[10]

Tony Mason's coaching career at Michigan ended after the 1968 season.

In 1969, Mason moved to Purdue University, where he was the defensive line coach through the 1972 season. In 1973, Mason became the head football coach at the University of Cincinnati, inheriting a team that had managed only a 2–9 record in 1972. Mason turned the Cincinnati program in the right direction, however, and led the Bearcats to a 9–2 record in 1976.

In 1977, Mason moved west to the University of Arizona, where he was the head football coach between 1977 and 1979, succeeding Jim Young, one of Bo Schembechler's former assistants, who became the head coach at Purdue. He coached the Wildcats to their first victory in the newly constituted Pacific-10 Conference in 1978 with a victory over Oregon State. In 1979, Arizona finished a successful season with a record of 6–5–1 and received an invitation to play in the Fiesta Bowl. The University of Pittsburgh defeated Arizona in the Fiesta Bowl, 16–10. During his three years as Arizona's head football coach, Mason's team compiled a record of 16–18–1, with obvious improvement showing by 1979.

Unfortunately, Mason's coaching career came to an abrupt conclusion in 1980 when a lengthy investigation of Arizona's football program by the *Arizona Daily Star* uncovered NCAA violations in the handling of travel expenses by the coaching staff. Mason resigned as head coach following the investigation. Knowing of Mason's highly productive coaching years at Michigan, broadcaster Tom Hemingway later wrote, "Hard times would await Tony on his departure from Ann Arbor, which saddened all who played for him."[11]

After leaving coaching, Mason provided broadcast analysis for football games at the University of Pittsburgh, and also continued his motivational speaking schedule. He remained in demand as a motivational speaker for sports teams and major corporations. He passed away suddenly on July 23, 1994, from a massive heart attack suffered in the airport in Cleveland, while he was *en route* to Texas to deliver an address to a convention of high school football coaches.[12]

Jocko Nelson remained on Bump Elliott's coaching staff through the 1965 season. In 1966, he became the head football coach at Gustavus Adolphus College in Minnesota, his *alma mater*. Nelson coached at Gustavus Adolphus from 1966 to 1971, and his teams posted a sterling record of 37–11–4 during that period. In 1967 and 1968, Nelson's teams won their conference title. In 1971, Nelson joined Bud Grant's staff with the Minnesota Vikings as the assistant coach for the linebackers and special teams. Nelson remained with the Vikings throughout the 1970s, and in 1978, he and Bob Hollway were reunited when Hollway rejoined Grant's staff for a second time.

During the 1978 season, Nelson suffered a heart attack early in November while exercising with Hollway and died two weeks later on November 19, 1978.[13]

The Players: The Offense

Bob Timberlake was drafted both by the New York Giants (NFL) and the Buffalo Bills (AFL) in the professional drafts after the 1964 season. He chose to sign with the Giants and played for them in 1965. His pro career came to an end the following year, however, when the Giants released him.

During his senior season at Michigan, Timberlake was outspoken about his Christian beliefs and his eventual desire to attend seminary and prepare for the ministry. "Living as a Christian is more important than playing football," Timberlake said during the season. "I hope to use any football ability I might have to help the cause of Christianity in the United States.... Any success I might achieve [in football] I want to be able to steer people in the direction of Jesus Christ."[14]

After earning his theological degree from Princeton Seminary in 1969, Timberlake served church pastorates in Wisconsin and Michigan before entering the field of hospital administration in Milwaukee. He has also taught a course at Marquette University on the subject of "Decent and Affordable Housing."[15]

Mel Anthony was drafted by the Cleveland Browns (NFL) after the 1964 season, but failed to make the team's final roster. In 1966, he joined the faculty of Washtenaw Community College, where he was employed until 1972. In 1972, he returned to his home town of Cincinnati, where he took a position with Procter and Gamble. In 1975, he joined the States Mutual Insurance Company of Cincinnati.[16]

Carl Ward finished his playing career at Michigan after the 1966 season, earning All-Big Ten honors in his junior season. He was drafted by the Cleveland Browns in 1967 and played in the NFL for three seasons. Ward played for the Browns in 1967 and 1968, and for the New Orleans Saints in 1969. He played primarily as a specialist on kickoff returns and punt returns.[17]

Jim Detwiler also finished his playing career at Michigan in 1966, named All-Big Ten as a senior. The Baltimore Colts drafted him in 1967 and he spent one year with the Colts, but the recurring knee problems that plagued him during his junior and senior years at Michigan prevented him from a successful pursuit of a career in the NFL. While with the Colts, Detwiler enrolled in the dental school of the University of Tennessee in Memphis, at the suggestion of Gary Cuozzo, one of his teammates. Cuozzo had enrolled in the same dental program at the University of Tennessee. After being waived by the Colts in the following season, Detwiler concentrated full-time on his dental studies, using his signing bonus from the Colts to cover his costs of tuition.

After graduating from dental school in 1971, Detwiler joined a dental practice in Perrysburg, Ohio, and after one year, opened his own practice. He retired from the practice of dentistry in 2012.[18]

John Henderson was drafted both by the Philadelphia Eagles (NFL) and Buffalo Bills after the 1964 season. He chose to sign with the Eagles but was moved to the Detroit Lions before the 1965 season. Henderson spent three seasons, 1965, 1966, and 1967, with the Lions. In 1968, he joined the Minnesota Vikings and played with the Vikings through the 1972 season. Henderson's five years with the Vikings were the most productive of his career as he played in the 1970 Super Bowl and made 34 pass receptions in 1969 and 31 receptions in 1970. After his professional playing career ended, Henderson joined the Honeywell Corporation in Minneapolis, where he held positions in human resources and production management.[19]

Steve Smith finished his Michigan football career after the 1965 season. In 1966, he was drafted both by the San Francisco 49ers and the Houston Oilers (AFL). He chose to sign with the 49ers but was moved to the Pittsburgh Steelers before the 1966 season. Drafted as a tight end, Smith nevertheless played tackle on both offense and defense during his eight-year pro career. Smith also played for the Minnesota Vikings between 1968 and 1970 and then with Philadelphia between 1971 and 1974.[20]

Ben Farabee accepted a management position with the Ford Motor Company at its Michigan Truck Plant in Wayne, Michigan, following his graduation from the University of Michigan. In 1967, he was drafted into the United States Army, completing basic training at Fort Knox, Kentucky, and advanced infantry training at Fort Dix, New Jersey. He was sent to Vietnam as a private first class, and was assigned to an ambush battalion west of Saigon and near the border with Cambodia. He spent one year in Vietnam, advancing to the rank of SGT E-5, and returned to the United States in October 1969. He then resumed his management career in labor relations and compensation with the Ford Motor Company. His experience also included a three-year assignment with Ford in Great Britain. He retired from Ford in 2001.[21]

Tom Mack ended his football career at the University of Michigan after the 1965 season, when he earned honors as All-Big Ten and All-America. The Los Angeles Rams selected him in the 1966 draft, and Mack earned a starting position as a rookie with the Rams in 1966. Mack then compiled a distinguished career with the Rams for 13 seasons (1966–1978), playing in 11 Pro Bowls and never missing a game. He was inducted into the Professional Football Hall of Fame in 1999. In the off-seasons, and then after his professional football career, Mack worked with the Bechtel Power Corporation and later for the Jacobs Engineering Corporation.[22]

Charlie Kines finished his playing career at Michigan with the 1965 season. The Chicago Bears drafted him, but Kines did not make the team's final roster. Later, he joined the United States Marines and served in Vietnam from March 12, 1968, to March 30, 1974. He was awarded the Silver Star for conspicuous gallantry and intrepidity in action while involved in combat operations against the enemy on August 12, 1969. Kines died unexpectedly on August 30, 2010, in Ohio.[23]

Brian Patchen attended the University of Michigan Law School after his graduation from Michigan. He earned his J.D. degree in 1969. From 1969 to 1972, he was an assistant trust officer with the Morgan Guaranty Trust Company in New York. Later in 1972, he began the practice of law in Florida with the firm of Kelly, Black, Black, Earle, and Patchen, P.A. In 1983, he became a partner with Earle & Patchen, P.A., which is currently the Law Office of Brian P. Patchen, P.A. In addition to his legal practice, he has been a frequent lecturer at judicial events and conferences, as well as being the author and contributor to several legal publications.[24]

Jack Clancy returned to Michigan's starting lineup in 1965 and 1966 after recovering from the injuries that kept him out of the 1964 season. No longer a running back, however, Clancy excelled as a pass receiver and broke Michigan's career records for touchdown receptions and yards gained receiving. He was the captain of the 1966 Michigan team and also earned All-American honors. In 1967, he was drafted by the St. Louis Cardinals, but began his professional football career with the Miami Dolphins, for whom he played in 1967 and 1969. He finished his playing career in 1970 as a member of the Green Bay Packers.[25]

Wally Gabler finished his playing career at Michigan in the 1965 season. In 1966, he joined the Toronto Argonauts of the Canadian Football League (CFL), earning the position as starting quarterback in his rookie season. Gabler played in the CFL for seven seasons, playing for Toronto for three years, two years with the Hamilton Tiger Cats, and two years with the Winnipeg Blue Bombers.[26]

Dave Fisher was Michigan's starting fullback in 1965 and 1966 and an All-Big Ten selection in 1966. He graduated from Michigan with his undergraduate degree in 1968 and earned his master's degree from Michigan in 1971. After graduation, he pursued business opportunities in management with the Ann Arbor Bank and Trust, as well as in the fields of business consulting, public accounting, and engineering. He also served on the Ann Arbor City Council.[27]

Pete Hollis finished his Michigan football career in 1965 and graduated in 1966. He then earned a master's degree from the University of Tennessee. He taught and coached at a small private school in Tennessee in 1971. In 1971, he entered private business in the management of malls and shopping centers. He retired in 1988 and currently lives in Hawaii.[28]

Peter Mair was a reserve lineman on the 1964 team, although he started on Michigan's teams in 1966 and 1967. Following graduation, he received an offer from the Pittsburgh Steelers but chose to attend law school at Stanford University instead. After graduating from law school in 1975, Mair did prosecutorial work in Washington, D.C., and Seattle, Washington, during the 1970s. In 1979, he entered private practice and has been involved in "innocence work" with Centurion Ministries of Princeton, New Jersey, work that involves the reinvestigation of people involved in murder convictions where strong evidence exists of wrongful convictions.[29]

Tom Parkhill joined General Motors Corporation in 1968 after earning his master's degree from Michigan in 1967. While at General Motors, Parkhill worked in a number of assignments, including at the Chevrolet Willow Run Assembly Plant, the Chevrolet-Muncie plant in Muncie, Indiana, and the Flint Assembly Plant. He retired from General Motors in 2001, but, in retirement, has joined the Detroit Pencil Company, where he markets office supplies.[30]

Gary Schick played for Michigan through the 1965 season. Upon graduation, he began a teaching and coaching career that included assignments at Manchester (Michigan) High School, Kettering High School in Detroit, and then in Vero Beach, Florida. While in Florida, he left teaching and entered the field of sports broadcasting with assignments in Florida and Atlanta. In December 1979, he joined Toyota Motors Sales and was employed in sales for the next 30 years, with assignments in Oregon, Ohio, and California. He retired in 2009 and continues to live in California.[31]

Jim Seiber pursued a career in education following his graduation from Michigan. He was a teacher and junior high principal at Mason Consolidated Schools in Temperance, Michigan.[32]

The Players: The Punter

Stan Kemp was Michigan's punter for the 1965 and 1966 seasons. He led the Big Ten in punting in 1966 with an average of 39.6 yards per punt. Kemp tried out with the Green Bay Packers but failed to make the team, being the last player cut during the 1967 pre-season. He returned to Ann Arbor to assist Bump Elliott, who gave him "complete control" of Michigan's kicking game. Kemp then accepted an assistant coaching position at the University of Wisconsin. After finishing his coaching at the University of Wisconsin, he entered private business while also doing scouting work for the NFL. He also became a successful referee and official, officiating football games in the Mid-American Conference and the Big Ten. Between 1986 and 1992, he officiated football games in the National Football League. He passed away on January 13, 1999, from complications of Lou Gehrig's Disease.[33]

The Players: The Defense

Jim Conley, the captain, graduated from Michigan in 1965 with a degree in business administration. His business career included employment with General Motors, with the Crawford Mazur Company, with the Hoover Ball and Bearing Company, and with the Automotive Products Group of the Ford Motor Company. More recently, he has formed his own business consulting group.[34] He belongs to a select group of Michigan football players, limited to Hugh White (1901), Bruce Hilkene (1947), Allen Wahl (1950), Andy Cannavino and George Lilja (1980), Jon Jansen and Eric Mayes (1997), and Mark Messner and John Vitale (1988), who have been captains of Michigan teams that have defeated Ohio State, won the Big Ten football championship, and won the Rose Bowl.

Bill Yearby finished his playing career at Michigan with the 1965 season, chosen as the Most Valuable Player of that team. As in 1964, he was a consensus All-American and was drafted in 1966 by the New York Jets (AFL). A serious knee injury cut short his playing career in the AFL, however, and he only played in the 1966 season. After his football career ended, Yearby taught at East Catholic High School in Detroit, and also worked as a health specialist for Wayne County. He also volunteered his time to work with African American youth in Detroit. He passed away on December 20, 2010, after an extended illness.[35]

Arnie Simkus was drafted by the Cleveland Browns in 1965. Fulfilling a lifelong ambition, he played professional football for the New York Jets in 1965 and the Minnesota Vikings in 1967.[36]

Bill Keating played his final season for Michigan in 1965. He entered professional football with the Denver Broncos (AFL) in 1966. He played for the Broncos and the Miami Dolphins in 1967. After leaving pro football, Keating attended the College of Law at the University of Denver, graduating with a J.D. degree in 1971. He went into private legal practice as the co-founder of the law firm Keating, Wagner, Polidori, Free in Denver. He continues to practice law in Denver.[37]

John Yanz finished his playing career at Michigan in 1964. After graduating, he returned to Chicago and began a career in the field of industrial sales with MFC Global.[38]

Jerry Mader finished his football career at Michigan in 1964. He graduated in 1965 and spent one year as a graduate assistant coach while working on his master's degree in engineering. He held a number of positions in the engineering field in Michigan before moving to California to accept a position with the Electric Power Research Institute (EPRI) in 1977. He formed a consulting firm, Mader & Associates, in 1992. He returned to the University of

Michigan in 2004 to become the energy research director for the College of Engineering, where he played a major role in the founding of the Transportation Energy Center (TEC) in the Department of Chemical Engineering.[39]

Bill Laskey pursued a career in professional football after graduating from Michigan in 1965. Despite being undrafted, Laskey tried out for a roster spot with the Buffalo Bills in 1965 and made the team. He played for the Bills in 1965, the year that the Bills won the AFL championship, and Laskey was selected to play in the AFL's All-Star game. Then, between 1967 and 1971, Laskey played for the Oakland Raiders as an outside linebacker and participated in Super Bowl II, which the Raiders lost to the Green Bay Packers, 33–14. In 1971, he was traded to the Baltimore Colts, where he played for two years before finishing his professional career with the Denver Broncos in 1973 and 1974. After leaving professional football, he pursued numerous business interests in a variety of industries throughout the United States.[40]

Tom Cecchini was the captain of Michigan's football team in 1965, his senior season. Following graduation, he chose to pursue a career in coaching. He assisted in the Michigan football program, under both Bump Elliott and Bo Schembechler, until 1970. In 1970, he became defensive line coach at Xavier University in Ohio, and then was the head coach in 1972 and 1973. After Xavier discontinued football as a varsity sport in 1973, he accepted a position as the defensive line coach at the University of Iowa, where he spent two seasons. He then became the defensive coordinator at Tulane University for five years. In 1980, he accepted a position as the defensive line coach with the Minnesota Vikings, rejoining his former coach Bob Hollway, and remained until 1984.[41]

Barry Dehlin finished his playing career for Michigan in 1967. Wishing to pursue a career in medicine, he earned a master's degree in biology from Wayne State University and received his medical degree from the Michigan State University College of Osteopathic Medicine. After completing his residency in Lansing and in Chicago, he started his own medical practice, Capital Internal Medicine, which currently has more than 40 physicians at six locations.[42]

Frank Nunley played for Michigan through the 1966 season, after which he was drafted by the San Francisco 49ers. He earned All-Big Ten honors in his senior season. He played with the 49ers for the next ten years, excelling as a linebacker until a knee injury ended his pro career. Nunley chose to remain in the Bay Area and entered private business as a salesman for Michigan-based Whirlpool Corporation. In 1980, he entered the electronics industry.[43]

Rick Volk played for Michigan in 1965 and 1966, and was honored as an All-American in 1966. In 1967, the Baltimore Colts drafted him, and Volk became an instant contributor to the Colts. He played twelve years in the NFL with the Colts (1967–1975), the New York Giants (1976), and the Miami Dolphins (1977–1978). He was selected to play in three NFL Pro Bowls and was named a first team All-Pro in 1971. While playing professional football, he worked as a manufacturing representative for eight industrial corporations in the off-season and remained in that field after he retired from the NFL.[44]

Rick Sygar finished his playing career for Michigan in 1966. He received his bachelor's degree in architecture in 1967. After a brief, unsuccessful tryout with the Detroit Lions, Sygar moved to New York, where he established a successful architectural practice.[45]

Dick Rindfuss tried out with the Washington Redskins after graduating from Michigan in 1965. Injuries continued to hamper his performance, however, and he did not make the final roster with the Redskins. He returned to Ohio and accepted a position with the Packard Electric Company in Warren, Ohio. Once he earned his master's degree, however, he embarked upon a teaching career in secondary-level social studies, teaching first in Milan, Michigan, and then in his home town of Niles, Ohio.[46]

Dick Wells completed his playing career with Michigan in the 1965 season. After graduating from Michigan with a bachelor's degree in business administration in 1966, he enlisted in the United States Air Force, was accepted to officers candidate school, and after graduating, was commissioned as a second lieutenant. During his commitment, he spent eighteen months assigned to several small islands near Okinawa during the period of the Vietnam War. After his honorable discharge, he returned to Orlando, Florida, the site of one of his Air Force assignments. He completed a master's degree in business from Rollins College, and from 1971 to 1977, he held a number of different managerial positions with Burroughs (later Unisys) Corporation. After retiring from Burroughs, he continued to pursue other opportunities in the technology field.[47]

Mike Bass finished his playing career at Michigan in the 1966 season. The Green Bay Packers drafted him in 1967 and then sent Bass to the Detroit Lions, where he was used on special teams for two games in 1967. Bass played on the Lions's "cab" squad in 1968 before signing with the Washington Redskins under Coach Vince Lombardi. According to one account, "Vince Lombardi saw something in Mike Bass that the Detroit Lions just couldn't see."[48] Bass became an immediate starter at cornerback for the Redskins and started every game until he retired in 1976. In the 1973 Super Bowl, Bass returned an interception for a touchdown, Washington's only scoring play in its 14–7 loss to the unbeaten Miami Dolphins. In 2002, upon the occasion of the 70th anniversary of the founding of the Washington Redskins, Bass was honored as one of the 70 Greatest Redskins of All Time by a vote of the fans.[49]

John Rowser finished his playing career at Michigan in 1966, after undergoing an extensive rehabilitation program to strengthen his injured knee. The Green Bay Packers drafted him in 1967, and he played for the Packers between 1967 and 1969. He played on two Super Bowl champion teams. He then played for the Pittsburgh Steelers from 1970 to 1973 and for the Denver Broncos from 1974 to 1976, a total of ten seasons in the NFL. After finishing his professional football career, he joined the Ford Motor Company's dealer development program.[50]

Bob Meilke graduated from Michigan in 1967 with a degree in chemical engineering. After several years of employment with the Union Carbide corporation at various locations throughout the United States, he returned to Illinois, where he became active in the insurance and real estate industries. He is currently a senior vice president with Willis of Illinois.[51]

Michael Gorte graduated from Michigan in 1965 and from the Wayne State University Law School in 1970. After receiving his J.D. degree from Wayne State, he received an offer to join a law practice in Bay City, Michigan, and has continued to practice law in that region since that time. In 2005, he formed his own law firm, Gorte & Day, Attorneys and Counselors at Law.[52]

Pat O'Donnell graduated from Michigan with a degree in education and earned a master's degree from Eastern Michigan. He pursued a career in teaching which spanned more than thirty years and included assignments in the area of Livonia. His teaching specialty was secondary earth science, at the middle school level, but he occasionally taught advanced science courses in high school as well. He also coached football and basketball at various times in his teaching career.[53]

Appendix: The 1964 Michigan Wolverines Roster[1]

No.	Name	Pos.	Ht.	Wt.	Class	Hometown/High School/Coach
36	Allison, Bruce	FB	6-0	195	Jr.	Ypsilanti, Ypsilanti, Bob Moffett
60	Ancona, Perry	G	6-0	215	Jr.	Madeira (OH), Madeira, John Rope
37	*Anthony, Melvin	FB	6-0	201	Sr.	Cincinnati, Roger Bacon, Bron Bacevich
55	Bailey, Donald	G	5-11	190	So.	Greensburg (PA), Greensburg, Bob Wells
15	Bass, Michael	HB	6-0	175	So.	Ypsilanti, Ypsilanti, Bob Moffett
16	Brigstock, Thomas	HB	6-1	188	Jr.	Battle Creek, Lakeview, Richard Colburn
77	Butler, David	G	6-1	215	Sr.	Detroit, Henry Ford, Bob Wyman
99	Buzynski, John	T	6-4	230	So.	East Detroit, Notre Dame, Walt Bazylewicz
79	Cartwright, Henry	T	6-3	238	So.	Detroit, Central, Corky Foster
53	*Cecchini, Thomas	C/LB	6-0	195	Jr.	Detroit, Pershing, Mike Haddad
24	*Clancy, Jack	HB	6-1	198	Jr.	Detroit, Redford St. Mary, Nick Galante
89	Cmejrek, Carl	E	6-2	205	So.	Flint, Southwestern, Dick Leach
82	*Conley, James (Capt.)	E	6-3	198	Sr.	Springdale (PA), Springdale, Jim Hazlett
73	Danhof, Jerome	T	6-3	235	So.	Detroit, Denby, Ed Rutherford
31	*Dehlin, Barry	FB/L3[2]	5-11	204	Sr.	Flushing, Flushing, Al Gratsch
48	Detwiler, James	HB	6-3	209	So.	Toledo, DeVilbiss, Dave Hardy
26	*Evashevski, Forest	QB	6-0	185	Sr.	Iowa City, Iowa City, Frank Bates
80	*Farabee, Ben	E	6-3	205	Sr.	Holland, Holland, Bob Weber
92	Fette, Thomas	E	6-2	185	So.	St. Joseph, St. Joseph, Dick Higgs
33	Fisher, David	FB	5-10	210	So.	Kettering (OH), Fairmount, James Hoover
64	Flanagan, Dennis	G	6-2	205	Jr.	Niles (OH), McKinley, Tony Mason

Appendix

No.	Name	Pos.	Ht.	Wt.	Class	Hometown/High School/Coach
97	Frontczak, Nick	G	5-10	205	Sr.	Detroit, DeLaSalle, Tom Bonino
29	Gabler, Wallace	QB	6-2	180	Jr.	Royal Oak, Kimball, Pin Ryan
10	Gorte, Michael	HB/LB[3]	5-10	195	Sr.[4]	Owosso, Owosso, Bob Dingman
38	Greene, Edward	E	5-11	190	Jr.	Flat Rock, Flat Rock, Marvin Mittelstat
65	*Hahn, Richard	G	6-0	205	Sr.	Norton Village (OH), Norton, Tony Prasher
66	Hardy, William	G	6-1	205	So.	Detroit, Pershing, Mike Haddad
74	Haverstock, Thomas	T	6-3	228	Jr.	Harrisburg (PA), Central Dauphin, Jim Roe
81	*Henderson, John	E	6-3	187	Sr.	Dayton, Roosevelt, Ray Pelfery
22	Hollis, Peter	QB	6-0	190	Jr.	Detroit, Redford, Ed Larimore
88	*Hoyne, Jeffrey	E	6-1	186	Jr.	Chicago, Weber, Joe Sassano
71	Hribal, James	T	6-0	215	So.	Dearborn, Harvey H. Lowery, Ralph Bach
68	Keating, William	G	6-2	226	Jr.	Chicago, St. Patrick, Ralph Dempsey
30	Kemp, Stanley	E/P[5]	6-1	185	So.	Greenville, Greenville, Jack McAvoy
78	Kines, Charles	T	6-0	230	Jr.	Niles, McKinley, Tony Mason
84	*Kirby, Craig	E	6-2	190	Jr.	Royal Oak, Kimball, Pin Ryan
35	Knapp, George	FB	6-1	205	So.	Bay City, Handy, Al Sigman
54	Landsittel, Thomas	G	5-10	193	So.	Delaware (OH), Hayes, Gerald Cornell
83	*Laskey, William	E	6-2	217	Sr.	Milan, Milan, Ti Hassen & Bob Dingman
41	Lee, Louis	HB	6-2	190	So.	Willow Grove (PA), Abington, Charles Weber
96	Mack, Thomas	T	6-3	220	Jr.	Bucyrus (OH), Cleveland Heights, Jim Roberts
94	*Mader, Gerald	T	6-3	220	Sr.	Chicago, Brother Rice, Nick Adducci
57	Mair, Peter	T	6-4	230	So.	Allentown (PA), William Allen, Perry Scott
61	*Marcum, John	G	6-0	210	Sr.	Monroe, Monroe, Roger Chiaverini
46	McLaughlin, David	E	6-0	198	So.	Chelsea, Chelsea, Alan Conkin
63	Mielke, Robert	G	6-1	210	So.	Chicago, Carl Schurz, Fred O'Keefe
58	*Muir, William	C	6-0	200	Sr.	Cuyahoga Falls (OH), Cuyahoga Falls, Dave Martin
59	Nunley, Frank	C/LB[6]	6-2	200	So.	Belleville, Belleville, Harry Hidenfelter
69	O'Donnell, Raymond[7]	G	6-1	200	So.	Milan, Milan, Cliff Hale
14	Ott, Richard	HB	5-11	165	Jr.	Mansfield (OH), Mansfield, Bill Doolittle
93	Parkhill, Thomas	E	6-2	202	Jr.	Ada (OH), Ada, R.H. Watson

The 1964 Michigan Wolverines Roster

No.	Name	Pos.	Ht.	Wt.	Class	Hometown/High School/Coach
51	Patchen, Brian	C	5-11	205	Sr.[8]	Steubenville (OH), Catholic Central, John Baroni
91	Pitlosh, Max	T	6-1	240	So.	Detroit, St. Thomas, Paul Mandziara
32	Ratigan, Timothy	FB	5-11	200	So.	Lansing, St. Mary's, Paul Pozega
12	Reid, Dorie	HB	5-7	160	Jr.	Ferndale, Ferndale, Frank Joranko
17	*Rindfuss, Richard	HB	6-0	192	Sr.	Niles, McKinley, Tony Mason
43	*Rowser, John	HB	6-0	175	Jr.	Detroit, Eastern, Harry Collins
76	*Ruzicka, Charles	T	6-1	235	Jr.	Skokie (IL), Evanston St. George, Max Burnell
39	Schick, Gary	FB	6-2	210	Jr.	Grosse Pointe, St. Paul, Ed Lauer
25	Seiber, James	QB	5-10	180	So.	Niles, McKinley, Tony Mason
70	Simkus, Arnold	T	6-4	230	Sr.	Detroit, Cass Tech, Charles Jenks
86	*Smith, Stephen	E	6-5	230	Jr.	Park Ridge (IL), Maine East, Bud Gates
67	Stagg, Frank	G	6-2	225	Jr.	Hazel Park, Hazel Park, Chuck Skinner
18	Sygar, Richard	HB	5-11	184	So	Niles, McKinley, Tony Mason
50	Tennant, Brian	C	6-0	200	Jr.	Worthington (OH), Worthington, Ralph Sabach
28	*Timberlake, Robert	QB	6-4	210	Sr.	Franklin (OH), Franklin, Alan Parr
95	Van Blaricom, Paul	T	6-3	250	Jr.	Kalamazoo, University, Ray Walters
21[9]	Volk, Richard	QB/HB	6-3	195	So.	Wauseon (OH), Wauseon, Larry Fruth
19	Ward, Carl	HB	5-9	178	So.	Cincinnati, Taft, Joe Corcoran
42	*Wells, Richard	HB	5-9	172	Jr.	Grand Rapids, Ottawa Hills, Rip Collins
85	Wilhite, Clayton	E	6-4	200	So.	Bay City, Handy, Al Sigman
52	Wright, Kenneth	C	6-1	215	So.	Bay City, Central, Elmer Engel
72	*Yanz, John	T	6-3	220	Sr.	Chicago, DeLaSalle, Chet Bulger
75	*Yearby, William	T	6-3	228	Jr.	Detroit, Eastern, Harry Collins

*Indicates Letterman

Chapter Notes

Introduction

1. University of Michigan, Bentley Historical Library, Department of Intercollegiate Athletics. Individual Files, Men's Sports, Box 44, Chalmers (Bump) Elliott, "Michigan All-Americas": "Bump Elliott," 28–30. Hereinafter cited as UM-BHL, Individual Files, box, person, document. The author wishes to acknowledge the assistance of the archival staff of the Bentley Historical Library, including archivists Gregory Kinney, Karen Jania, Malgosia Myc, and Diana Bachman. The Bentley Historical Library is an outstanding research library and the archivists are unparalleled in the support for requests by scholars for documents and records that pertain to Michigan football. I also wish to acknowledge the assistance of Marilyn McNitt, archivist at the Bentley Historical Library, who unfortunately passed away before this study was completed. See also Will Perry, *The Wolverines: A Story of Michigan Football* (Huntsville, AL: Strode, 1974), 278–79.

2. University of Michigan, Bentley Historical Library, Department of Intercollegiate Athletics, Sports Information Office, 1860– (cont.): Football (cont.) Scrapbooks (microfilm), Main Series, 1902–1990 (cont.). Reel 13, Vol. 48, April 17, 1960–November 24, 1963, Mike Block, "Staubach, Casualties, Plague Wolverines, *Michigan Daily*, October 6, 1963; Jerry Green, "QB Dazzles Wolverines," *Detroit News*, October 15, 1963. Hereinafter cited as UM-BHL, SB-48, and article. See also Perry, *The Wolverines*, 308; and Carlton Stowers, *Staubach: Portrait of the Brightest Star* (Chicago: Triumph Books, 2010), 29–30.

3. Robert Hoerner, "UM Game to Attract Big Throng," (Lansing, MI) *The State Journal*, October 9, 1964, A-1, 4.

4. "Pregame and Coaching Legends (Ara, Duffy, Bo, Mo, Bump, Pete)," CD One (#2), *Maximum Meechigan: The Best of Bob Ufer*. Double CD set, Produced and Edited by Dean Erskine, Michael Montpetit, and Art Vuolo.

5. UM-BHL, Individual Files, Chalmers (Bump) Elliott, op cit. The quotation about Elliott's versatility may be found in Ivan Kaye, "The Mad Magicians," *Michigan Today*, October 1987.

6. UM-BHL, Individual Files, Chalmers (Bump) Elliott, op. cit. No author, "CHALMERS (BUMP) ELLIOTT, 45 years old."

7. Perry, *The Wolverines*, 298.

8. University of Michigan, Bentley Historical Library, Department of Intercollegiate Athletics, Sports Information Office, 1860– (cont.), Football, Box 13, "Football Media Guides," 1964 Michigan Gridiron Guide, 8–9. See also "Michigan Gridiron Guide, 1965," 39–44. Hereinafter cited as UM-BHL-SIO, document.

9. UM-BHL-SIO, "Michigan Gridiron Guide, 1965," op. cit.

10. Ibid.

11. Ibid.

12. University of Michigan, Department of Intercollegiate Athletics, Sports Information Office, 1860– (cont.): Football, Scrapbooks (microfilm) Main Series, 1902–1990 (cont.). Reel 13, Vol. 49, November 24, 1963-October 10, 1964, Bill Bullard, "Mason Assumes Offensive Line Duties," *Michigan Daily*, April 2, 1964. Hereinafter cited as UM-BHL, SB-49, article. The players from McKinley High School in Niles, Ohio, who attended Michigan after playing for Tony Mason, were Dick Rind-

fuss, Charlie Kines, Rick Sygar, Dennis Flanagan, and Jim Seiber. See also Jerry Mader, comments on original manuscript, July 2013. See also Corky Simpson, "Mason Never Quite the Same After His Tucson Experience," http://tucsoncitizen.com/morgue2/1994/07/25/10226-mason-never-quit, accessed September 9, 2013.

13. Bump Elliott, interview with the author, Coralville, Iowa, October 22, 2012. Audiotape in author's possession.

14. A variation on the theme of these attributes may be found in Tim Twentyman, "Jim Harbaugh's 49ers have Bo Schembechler influence," *Detroit News*, October 15, 2011; http://detnews.com/article/20111015/SPORTS0101/110150326, accessed October 15, 2011.

15. See UM-BHL-SIO, Box 13, "Media Guide, 1964," for profiles of players on the 1964 team, including their statistics for height and weight.

16. UM-BHL-SIO, Box 4, Press Release, "Michigan Sports News," mailed November 24, 1964. The release contains a table of statistics released by the Big Ten office for individual and team performances of 1964.

17. University of Michigan, Bentley Historical Library, Department of Intercollegiate Athletics, Sports Information Office, 1860 (cont.): Football (cont.) Scrapbooks (microfilm) Main Series, 1902–1990 (cont.). Reel 13, Vol. 50, October 9, 1964–February 28, 1966; Paul Preuss, "Big Ten Passers Couldn't Beat Secondary," *Detroit News*, November 29, 1964. Hereinafter cited as UM-BHL, SB-50, article.

18. Thomas Hemingway, *Life Among the Wolverines: An Inside View of Michigan Sports* (South Bend, IN: Diamond Communications, 1985), 220.

19. UM-BHL-SIO, Box 2, "Preliminary 1964 University of Michigan Football Information, 1964 Football Prospects," 1.

20. UM-BHL, SB-50, Scott Blech, "Mason Sees Desire in Offensive Line," *Michigan Daily*, November 5, 1964. See also UM-BHL, SB-49, Jim LaSovage, "Wolverine Line Play Pleases Mason, *Michigan Daily*, September 24, 1964. Mason's comment about "eliminating all doubt" was supplied by Jerry Mader in his comments on the original manuscript of the study, July 2013.

21. UM-BHL, SB-49, LaSovage, "Wolverine Line Play," *Michigan Daily*, op. cit. See also Jerry Green, *Michigan Football Vault* (Florence, AL: Whitman Publishing, 2008).

22. UM-BHL, Individual Files, Box 20, Mel Anthony, "This I Remember," from program of Michigan-Northwestern game, November 15, 1977, 15, 50. Anthony's article may also be found in Bump Elliott's bound collection, *1964: This I Remember*, a collection of essays compiled by Alice Elliott, Bump Elliott's mother, on loan to the author. Hereinafter cited as Bump Elliott Collection, *1964: This I Remember*, and article.

23. Jim Dent, *Resurrection: The Miracle Season That Saved Notre Dame Football* (New York: Thomas Dunne, 2009), 49–51.

24. UM-BHL, SB-50, Bob Pille, "Timberlake, Friends, Lift U-M to Top," *Detroit Free Press*, November 25, 1964.

25. Bump Elliott, interview with the author.

26. UM-BHL-SIO, Box 4, Press Release, "Michigan Sports News," mailed November 24, 1964.

27. "10 Game Season Totals for 1964," Michigan Athletics Statistics Archive, http://stats.archive.ath.umich.edu/VS-Football/Seasontot.php, accessed October 3, 2013. See also "Jim Detwiler," in Alan Goldenbach, ed., *Where Have You Gone?* (New York: Skyhorse, 2012), 56.

28. Pille, "Timberlake, Friends, Lift U-M to Top," *Detroit Free Press*, op. cit.

29. UM-BHL, Individual Files, Box 108, Bob Timberlake, "This I Remember," from Program for Michigan-Navy game, September 24, 1977, 15, 50. Bump Elliott Collection, *1964: This I Remember*, article by Bob Timberlake. See also, Comments by Bob Timberlake, Transcript of DVD, Bump Elliott Tribute, 40th Anniversary Reception: September 24, 2004, 1964 University of Michigan Rose Bowl Team, Robert H. Lurie Engineering Building, University of Michigan, Transcribed and Edited By E. Bruce Geelhoed and Michael W. Smith, Ball State University, August, 2013, 12. Transcript in author's possession. Hereinafter cited as Transcript, Bump Elliott Tribute, page. The transcript contains brief accounts by various former Michigan players about their experiences with Bump Elliott, including during the 1964 season. The former players were: Jim Conley, Jerry Mader, Brian Patchen, Forest "Frosty" Evashevski, Tom Parkhill, Dave Butler, Bob Timberlake, Rich Hahn, assistant coach Don Dufek, Nick Frontczak, Ben Farabee, Barry Dehlin, Carl Cmejrek, Wally Gabler, Bill Laskey, Frank Nunley, Bill Hardy, Bill Yearby, Rick Volk, John Henderson, and Ron Johnson.

30. Lad Slingerland, " 'M' Star Great Pro

Prospect: Warmath," *Grand Rapids Press*, November 6, 1964; Pille, "Timberlake, Friends, Lift U-M to Top," *Detroit Free Press*, op. cit.

31. UM-BHL-SIO, Box 4, Press release, "Michigan Sports News," mailed October 6, 1964. See also Clank Stoppels, "The View from Here," *Grand Rapids Press*, December 29, 1964.

32. UM-BHL, SB-50, Pille, "Timberlake, Friends, Lift U-M to Top," *Detroit Free Press*, op. cit.

33. UM-BHL, SB-48, Mike Block, "Staubach, Casualties, Plague Wolverines, *Michigan Daily*, op. cit.

34. Bump Elliott, interview; Donald E. Dufek, interview with the author, Ann Arbor, Michigan, July 31, 2012; audiotape in author's possession; John Underwood, "Roses for Wolverines, Blues for Buckeyes," *Sports Illustrated*, November 30, 1964, in *SI Vault*, http://sportsillustrated.cnn.com/vault/article/magazine/MAG1076667 ... accessed June 6, 2013; James P. Conley, interview with the author, Ann Arbor, Michigan, July 23, 2012. Audiotape in author's possession.

35. Letter, C. Michael Gorte to Bruce Geelhoed, September 5, 2013.

36. Hemingway, *Life Among the Wolverines*, 208–09.

37. UM-BHL, SB-49, Roy Damer, "Here's Why This Could Be the Big Michigan Season," *Chicago Tribune*, September 24, 1964.

38. Dan Jenkins, "And Auburn Runs the Most," *Sports Illustrated*, September 21, 1964, *SI Vault*, accessed January 11, 2013.

39. UM-BHL, SB-49, Wayne De Neff, "Elliott Answers Questions," *Ann Arbor News*, September 10, 1964.

40. UM-BHL, SB-50, Frank Finch, "Michigan Mighty, Beavers Bad," *Los Angeles Times*, 1-2-65.

41. "Strikes: Deadlock in Detroit," *Time* 84, No. 10 (September 4, 1964): 72. See also, Hemingway, *Life Among the Wolverines*, 208–09 and (AP), "End of Newspaper Strike," *Michigan Daily*, November 22, 1964. See also comment by Brian Patchen in Transcript, Bump Elliott Tribute, 8.

42. UM-BHL, SB-50, Bud Furillo, "Elliott Pumps Up 'Nameless' Bowl,'" *Los Angeles Herald*, December 21, 1964.

43. UM-BHL, SB-50, Jerry Green, "Player, Coach, or AD, Bump Fits Rose Bowl," *Detroit News*, December 31, 1981.

44. UM-BHL, SB-49, no author, "Two NCAA Telecasts to Feature Wolverines," *Michigan Daily*, September 4, 1964.

45. UM-BHL, SB-50, Wayne De Neff, "Spirited Wolverines Wind Up Drills for OSU," *Ann Arbor News*, November 19, 1964.

46. Ibid.

47. Pille, "Timberlake, Friends, Lift U-M to Top," *Detroit Free Press*, November 25, 1964, op. cit.

48. "Halftime Interviews—Bob Timberlake, Ron Johnson, Tom Harmon," CD One (#5), *Maximum Meechigan: The Best of Bob Ufer*, op. cit.

49. Dent, *Resurrection*, 222–23.

50. "Ara the Beautiful," *Time* 84, No. 1 (November 20, 1964): 85. For mention of Alan Page's importance to the Notre Dame team, see Dent, *Resurrection*, 230.

51. "Ara the Beautiful," *Time*, op. cit.

52. UM-BHL, Individual Files, Box 105, Richard Sygar, "This I Remember," June 4, 1987, 1. See also Sygar, "This I Remember—1964," game program, Michigan vs. Washington State, September 2, 1987, 43–47, 51.

53. Clank Stoppels, "Californians Love Cinderella Story of Elliott," *Grand Rapids Press*, December 27, 1964; Bump Elliott, interview.

Chapter One

1. UM-BHL, SB-50, Joe Hendrickson, "Michigan Sound Team at Finish," newspaper not identified, December 2, 1964. Bump Elliott confirmed Crisler's analysis in an interview with the author, adding that "we wanted to be quick and agile, on both sides of the ball." Bump Elliott, interview.

2. Bump Elliott, interview, op. cit. For a thorough explanation of the recruiting program instituted by Woody Hayes at Ohio State, see Robert Vare, *Buckeye* (New York: Harper's Magazine Press, 1974), 77–101. For a discussion of Duffy Daugherty's recruiting success, see Randy Roberts and Ed Krzemienski, *Rising Tide: Bear Bryant, Joe Namath, & Dixie's Last Quarter* (New York: Grand Central Publishing, 2013), 56–57.

3. Daugherty, quoted in Mervin D. Hyman and Gordon S. White, Jr., *Big Ten Football: Its Life and Times, Great Coaches, Players, and Games* (New York: Macmillan, 1997), 121.

4. Perry, *The Wolverines* 298.

5. UM-BHL, SB-50, no author, "Wolverines Caught in Swirl of Football Honors," *Ann Arbor News*, November 26, 1964.; Donald E. Dufek, interview.

6. Perry, *The Wolverines*, 298; Jerry Mader, comments on original manuscript.

7. See "Jim Detwiler" in Goldenbach, ed., *Where Have You Gone?*, 56, and UM-BHL, Individual Files, Box 57, John Henderson, "This I Remember: The Michigan Experience," 1–2.

8. For Tony Mason, see UM-BHL-SIO, *Michigan Gridiron Guide*, 1965, 44–45.

9. Bump Elliott, interview, op. cit.

10. James Conley, interview with the author, Ann Arbor, Michigan, July 30, 2012, audio tape in author's possession.

11. Ibid.

12. The Archives of the National Collegiate Athletic Association, Indianapolis, Indiana. *The National Collegiate Athletic Association 1964-1965 Yearbook*, "Official Interpretations of NCAA By-Laws," B., Article 6, Section 1. Recruiting–Contracts and Offers, O.I. 120, 47–48. Hereinafter cited as NCAA Archives, document.

13. NCAA Archives. The section on transportation and official campus visits is *NCAA 1964-1965 Yearbook*, Article 6. Recruiting. Section 5a., 40.

14. Ibid. The section on alumni and transportation is *Section 5b*, 40. See also Jerry Mader, comments on original manuscript.

15. Henderson, *This I Remember*, op. cit.

16. UM-BHL, SB-48, Tom Rowland, "Tough Laskey Likes Defense," *Michigan Daily*, November 6, 1963; also, Bump Elliott Collection, *Football Programs—University of Michigan—1964*, game program, Michigan vs. Air Force, September 26, 1964, 6, 31. See also *Bill Laskey's Football Flashbacks: Fifteen Years of Memories*, in author's possession, and Bill Laskey's comments, Transcript, Bump Elliott Tribute, 19; e-mail messages, Dick Wells to Bruce Geelhoed, September 16, 2013; September 17, 2013.

17. "Rick Volk," in Kevin Allen, Nate Brown, and Art Regner," eds., *What It Means to Be a Wolverine* (Chicago: Triumph Books, 2005), 118–19.

18. Ibid., 116. Before the 1964 season, Volk asked Elliott if he could change his assigned number, #21, to #49, the number that Bob Chappuis wore during his playing days at Michigan. Elliott agreed, and Volk wore #49 throughout his career at Michigan. See UM-BHL-SIO, "Michigan Sport News," mailed November 17, 1964.

19. Bump Elliott, interview, op. cit.

20. Donald E. Dufek, interview, op. cit.

21. NCAA Archives, *The National Collegiate Athletic Association 1964-1965 Yearbook*. "Official Interpretations of NCAA By-laws," B. Article 6. Section 2. Recruiting—Use of Funds. O.I. 126.," 48.

22. Bump Elliott, interview, op. cit. We might also add that Michigan's assistant coaches were also frequent speakers at high school athletic banquets, usually held in the spring. The author remembers, for example, Tony Mason being the featured speaker at the annual Varsity Club/Quarterback Club, father-son banquet at Grand Rapids Ottawa Hills High School in May 1965. Mason was a superb after-dinner motivational speaker, much in demand for this type of occasions.

23. See UM-BHL-SIO, Box 13, *Media Guide, 1964*, for profiles of the players on the 1964 roster.

24. UM-BHL, Individual Files, Box 20, Mel Anthony, "This I Remember," from program of Michigan-Northwestern game, November 15, 1977, 15, 50. See also game program from Michigan-Northwestern game, November 5, 1977, in Bump Elliott Collection, *This I Remember: Michigan '64*.

25. UM-BHL, Individual Files, Box 47, Dave Fisher, "This I Remember," no date, 4–5. See also Dave Fisher in "This I Remember," from program of Michigan-Minnesota game, October 28, 1978, in Bump Elliott Collection, *This I Remember: Michigan '64*. Dick Balzizer, mentioned by Fisher, was one of Michigan's most outstanding student athletes. He was a member of the Michigan football teams between 1952 and 1955 and received his bachelor's degree, master's degree, and doctoral degree from Michigan. In 1961, he joined the University of Michigan faculty as a member of the chemical engineering department and became chair of the department in 1971. During the 1960s and 1970s, he also held scientific advisory positions in the administrations of Lyndon B. Johnson and Richard M. Nixon. In 1973, he moved to California to accept a position with the Electric Power Research Institute (EPRI). See "Dick Balzhizer" in Alan Goldenbach, *Where Have You Gone?*, 205. In his memoir, Dave Fisher also mentions that he was recruited by Ben Sproat.

26. "Halftime Interviews—Bob Timberlake, Ron Johnson, Tom Harmon," *Maximum Meechigan*, CD One (#5), op. cit.

27. UM-BHL, SB-50, Lyall Smith, "U-M' 'The Victors' Sing It, Act Part," *Detroit Free Press*, November 25, 1964.

28. Ibid.

29. Jim Conley's comments relative to the singing of "The Victors" were made to the author on July 23, 2012. Rick Sygar confirmed his role in the custom in an e-mail message to the author, June 26, 2013. See also Jerry Green, "U-M Sings In Victory," *Detroit News*, September 21, 1965.

30. NCAA Archives, *The Official National Collegiate Athletic Association Football Guide, Seventy-Fourth Annual Edition, 1964* (New York: National Collegiate Athletic Bureau, 1964), Official NCAA Football Rules, Section 5. Substitutions, 26–27. See also *Yearbook of the 1964-1965 National Collegiate Athletic Association*, Reports of Rules and Tournament Committees: FOOTBALL, 105–07.

31. Hyman and White, *Big Ten Football*, 104–05. See also Francis Fitzgerald, ed., *A Legacy of Champions* (Farmington Hills, MI: CTC Productions and Sports, 1996), 108–09; and Randy Roberts, *A Team for America* (Boston: Houghton-Mifflin, 2011), 156–58.

32. Fitzgerald, ed., *A Tradition of Excellence*, 109.

33. Hyman and White, *Big Ten Football*, 104–05; Fitzgerald, ed., *A Tradition of Excellence*, 109. See also John Kryk, *Natural Enemies: The Notre Dame–Michigan Football Feud* (Kansas City, MO: Andrews and McMeel, 1994), 290, and Douglas S. Looney, "One Is More Like It," *Sports Illustrated* 73, No. 10 (September 3, 1990): 27.

34. Looney, "One Is More Like It," *Sports Illustrated*, op. cit., 36.

35. Hemingway, *Life Among the Wolverines*, 46.

36. Kryk, *Natural Enemies*, 290; Fitzgerald, *A Tradition of Excellence*, 109; Hemingway, *Life Among the Wolverines*, 50; Don B. Canham with Larry Paladinino, *From the Inside: A Half Century of Michigan Athletics* (Ann Arbor, MI: Olympia Sports Press, 1996), 91, 98, 112–13.

37. Brian Patchen's comments, Transcript, Bump Elliott Tribute, 7.

38. The rule was amended, ever so slightly, on an annual basis from the time that it was instituted in 1953. See NCAA Archives, *1964-1965 Yearbook*, FOOTBALL, 106. See also David M. Nelson, *Football, The Rules, and the Men Who Made the Game* (Newark: University of Delaware Press, 1994), 312–14, for an account of the deliberations that occurred to change the rule in 1964. See also UM-BHL, SB-50, Earl Blaik, "Substitution Gains Support," newspaper not identified, October 13,

1964. The author wishes to acknowledge the assistance of Ellen Summers, archivist at the NCAA Archives, for her assistance.

39. UM-BHL, "College Coaches Cheer New Substitution Rule," *Detroit News*, January 13, 1964.

40. Ibid.

41. UM-BHL, SB-49, no author, "NCAA Relaxes Football Substitution Rules," *Michigan Daily*, January 13, 1964.

42. Nelson, *Football, the Rules, and the Men Who Made the Game*, 313.

43. UM-BHL, SB-50, "College Coaches Cheer New Substitution Rule," *Detroit News*, op. cit. See also Roberts and Krzemienski, *Rising Tide*, 329.

44. James Conley, interview, July 30, 2012, op. cit.

45. UM-BHL, SB-49, no author, "Elliott Likes New Rule," newspaper not identified, 1-14-64.

46. Bump Elliott, interview, op. cit.

47. Game program, Michigan vs. Air Force, September 26, 1964, 23. Alice Elliott also compiled a bound volume of game programs, arranged by year. Hereinafter referred to as Bump Elliott Collection, *Football Programs: University of Michigan, 1964*, and date.

48. Bump Elliott, interview, op. cit.

49. UM-BHL, SB-48, no author, "Michigan's Tom Cecchini Is UPI's Best in Midwest," *Michigan Daily*, October 16, 1963.

50. Hemingway, *Life Among the Wolverines*, 218.

51. Green, "U-M Sings in Victory," *Detroit News*, September 21, 1965, op. cit.

52. UM-BHL, SB-49, Wayne De Neff, "M Appears to Have Depth Needed for Two Platoons," *Ann Arbor News*, January 15, 1964

53. For Conley, see UM-BHL, SB-48, Bill Bullard, "Conley Stands Out on 'M' Defense," *Michigan Daily*, November 21, 1963, and Hemingway, *Life Among the Wolverines*, 217. For Laskey, see UM-BHL, Individual Files, Box 73, photo, "Bill Laskey."

54. UM-BHL, SB-48, Wayne De Neff, "No Doubt About It, Wolverines Bigger for '63," *Ann Arbor News*, 8-27-63.

55. Hemingway, *Life Among the Wolverines*, 216.

56. Ibid., 212–13.

57. UM-BHL, SB-49, Jim LaSovage, "Wolverine Line Play Pleases Mason," *Michigan Daily*, September 24, 1964.

58. "Tom Mack," in Allen, Brown, and Regner, eds., *What It Means to Be a Wolverine*,

114. See also Green, *Michigan Football Vault*, 98.
59. UM-BHL, Department of Intercollegiate Athletics, Individual Files, Box 76, Tom Mack, "This I Remember, from Michigan vs. Wisconsin game program, October 15, 1977, 15. See also Bump Elliott Collection, *This I Remember: Michigan '64*.
60. Bump Elliott, interview, op. cit.
61. Hendrickson, "Michigan Sound Team at Finish," op. cit.
62. Bump Elliott, interview, op. cit.
63. UM-BHL, SB-49, De Neff, "M Appears to Have Depth for Two Platoons," *Ann Arbor News*, op. cit.

Chapter Two

1. See UM-BHL, SB-49, see Wayne De Neff, "Wolverine Notes," *Ann Arbor News*, October 5, 1964, for mention of Benny Friedman and Tom Harmon being in attendance at the Michigan–Navy game on October 3. Interestingly, Bennie Friedman also wrote the "This I Remember" feature in the program for the Michigan–Navy game on October 3, 1964. See Bennie Friedman, "This I Remember," in Game Program, Michigan vs. Navy, October 3, 1964, 12–13, 41 in Bump Elliott Collection, *Football Programs, University of Michigan: 1964*.
2. Michigan played Army in 1945, 1946, 1949, 1950, 1954, 1955, 1956, 1961, and 1962. Interestingly, Army won the first five games and Michigan won the next four, something of an indication of how the Army program was beginning to decline by the late 1950s. Michigan played Navy in 1948, 1958, and 1963. Michigan beat Navy in 1948 but Navy won the other two contests. See Christopher Walsh, *Michigan Football: Guide and Record Book* (Chicago: Triumph Books, 2009), 123–39.
3. Bump Elliott, interview, op. cit.
4. UM-BHL, Department of Intercollegiate Athletics, Box 2, Game Rundowns, Summary of Football Game Statistics, September 26, 1964 (Michigan vs. AF), and Summary of Football Game Statistics, October 3, 1964 (Michigan vs. Navy).
5. Lad Slingerland, "Sophomores Help U-M in Fine Football Start," *The (Lansing) State Journal*, October 7, 1964.
6. UM-BHL, SB-48, Bob Pille, "Woody: Michigan The Best Team in Big Ten Over the Final Four Games of the Season," *Detroit Free Press*, December 11, 1963.

7. Harry Molter, "Timberlake Only Part of the Story," *Christian Science Monitor*, December 8, 1964; Hemingway, *Life Among the Wolverines*, 215–16; Brian Patchen, comments on original manuscript, July, 2013.
8. UM-BHL, SB-49, Lloyd Graff, "Gridders Show Promise in Finale," *Michigan Daily*, May 3, 1964.
9. UM-BHL-SIO, "Michigan Sport News," mailed August 4, 1964.
10. UM-BHL-SIO, "Michigan Sport News," mailed September 1, 1964.
11. UM-BHL-SIO, "Michigan Sport News," mailed September 8, 1964.
12. Bump Elliott, interview, op. cit.
13. UM-BHL, SB-50, Wayne De Neff, no title, *Ann Arbor News*, October 7, 1964.
14. Hemingway, *Life Among the Wolverines*, 216–17.
15. Molter, "Timberlake Only Part of the Story," *Christian Science Monitor*, op. cit.
16. UM-BHL, SB-49, "Unheralded Gridder Making His Mark," *Ann Arbor News*, November 27, 1963.
17. UM-BHL-SIO, "Michigan Sport News," mailed September 22, 1964. Dick Rindfuss logged the most minutes of any Michigan player in 1963 but, in 1964, he played virtually the entire season dealing with the effects of an injury that he suffered in an intramural basketball game. See UM-BHL-SIO, "1964 Football Prospects," 1.
18. UM-BHL-SIO," Michigan Sport News," mailed September 22, 1964.
19. Ibid.
20. UM-BHL, Department of Intercollegiate Athletics, Individual Files, Box 113, Rick Volk, "This I Remember," 1. The version cited in the manuscript is taken from Volk's draft, which was edited for eventual inclusion in the Michigan-Michigan State game program, October 4, 1978, 17. See also Bump Elliott Collection, *This I Remember—Michigan, '64*. In his account, Tom Hemingway placed the size of the crowd at 70,000. The official attendance for the game was 69,888, a higher total than Michigan originally estimated. See Hemingway, *Life Among the Wolverines*, 221, and UM-BHL, Box 2, Football Game Rundowns, "Summary of Football Game Statistics, 9/26/64 (Michigan vs. Air Force)."
21. The Air Force players: offense, defense, and two-way are listed in the game program, U.S. Air Force vs. Michigan, September 26, 1964, 27, 29. See Bump Elliott Collection, *Football Programs, University of Michigan, 1964*.

22. UM-BHL, SB-49, LaSovage, "Wolverine Line Play Pleases Michigan," *Michigan Daily*, September 24, 1964, op. cit.
23. The play-by-play account of the game may be in UM-BHL, Game Rundowns, "Summary of Football Game Statistics," September 26, 1964 (Michigan vs. Air Force), op. cit. See also Hemingway, *Life Among the Wolverines* 221–25.
24. Ibid.
25. Hemingway, *Life Among the Wolverines*, 224.
26. Ibid.
27. Green, "U-M Sings to Victory," *Detroit News*, op. cit. See also e-mail message, Richard Sygar to Bruce Geelhoed, June 26, 2013.
28. UM-BHL, SB-49, Wayne De Neff, "Wolverine Notes," *Ann Arbor News*, September 28, 1964.
29. Ibid.
30. UM-BHL, SB-49, Wayne De Neff, "M Shoots Down Air Force, Loads Guns for Navy," *Ann Arbor News*, September 28, 1964.
31. Hemingway, *Life Among the Wolverines*, 225. See also UM-BHL, SB-49, Wayne De Neff, "Wolverines on Charge," *Ann Arbor News*, September 29, 1964.
32. Game Program, "Michigan vs. Navy," October 3, 1964, 5, in Bump Elliott Collection, *Football Programs, University of Michigan: 1964*.
33. UM-BHL, SB-48, "Staubach, Casualties, Plague Wolverines," *Michigan Daily*, October 6, 1963. See also Stowers, *Staubach*, 29–30.
34. Block, "Staubach, Casualties Plague Wolverines," *Michigan Daily*, October 6, 1963, op. cit.
35. UM-BHL, SB-48, "QB Dazzles Wolverines," *Detroit News*, October 6, 1963.
36. Ibid. See also UM-BHL, SB-48, Hal Schram, "'Heavy Seas' Take Toll on Wolverines," *Detroit Free Press*, October 6, 1963.
37. Schram, "'Heavy Seas' Take Toll on Wolverines," *Detroit Free Press*, October 6, 1963, op. cit.
38. Ibid.
39. Block, "Staubach, Casualties, Plague Wolverines," *Michigan Daily*, October 6, 1963, op. cit.
40. Allison Danzig, "Middies Conquer Penn State, 21–8," *New York Times*, September 20, 1964, S 1.
41. Stowers, *Staubach*, 43–44.
42. No author (UPI), "Navy Victor with Late Surge," *New York Times*, September 27, 1964, S 3. See also Stowers, *Staubach*, 43.
43. Stowers, *Staubach*, 43–44.
44. UM-BHL, SB-50, Scott Blech, "Kramer Helps Kirby's Career," *Michigan Daily*, October 9, 1964. One has to wonder if Ron Kramer regularly kept the Michigan coaches informed about Kirby's progress. Given the NCAA policies regarding recruiting then in place, there would have been nothing improper about the assistance that Kramer provided to Kirby.
45. Ibid.
46. Dufek gave his scouting estimate to Clank Stoppels, sports editor of the *Grand Rapids Press*, on the flight to North Carolina where he was scouting the Michigan State–North Carolina game on September 26, 1964. See Stoppels, "The View from Here," *Grand Rapids Press*, September 27, 1964. See also Bump Elliott, interview, op. cit.
47. UM-BHL, UMAD, Individual Files, Box 37, Jim Conley, "This I Remember," from game program, Michigan vs. Texas A&M, October 1, 1977; also Bump Elliott Collection, *Football Programs, University of Michigan, 1964*. Jerry Mader described the 100-yard drill in his comments on the original manuscript. Wally Gabler described his role as Roger Staubach on the demo team in his comments, Transcript, Bump Elliott Tribute, 18. Michael Gorte identified himself as "the unofficial captain of the Red Shirts" in a telephone interview with the author, November 12, 2013. See also Clank Stoppels, "The View from Here," *Grand Rapids Press*, October 4, 1964.
48. Game program, Michigan vs. Navy, October 3, 1964, 26–29, from Bump Elliott Collection, *Football Programs, University of Michigan, 1964*. See also Stowers, *Staubach*, 43–44.
49. UM-BHL, Department of Intercollegiate Athletics, Box 2, Game Rundowns, Summary of Football Game Statistics, October 3, 1964 (Michigan vs. Navy). See also Hemingway, *Life Among the Wolverines*, 225–26.
50. Game program, Michigan vs. Navy, 27, 29, op. cit. See also UM-BHL, SB-50, Wayne De Neff, "Revenge Expected to Spur Elliott's Team," *Ann Arbor News*, October 2, 1964.
51. UM-BHL, Summary of Football Game Statistics, October 3, 1964, Michigan vs. Navy, op. cit.; Hemingway, *Life Among the Wolverines*, 226–27.
52. Ibid.
53. Ibid.
54. Ibid.
55. Ibid.

56. Hemingway, *Life Among the Wolverines*, 227.
57. UM-BHL, Summary of Football Game Statistics, October 3, 1964, Michigan vs. Navy, op. cit.
58. Ibid.
59. Ibid.
60. Ibid.
61. Ibid.
62. Blech, "Kramer Helps Kirby's Career," *Michigan Daily*, October 9, 1964, op. cit.
63. UM-BHL, Summary of Football Game Statistics, October 3, 1964, Michigan vs. Navy, op. cit. See also Hemingway, *Life Among the Wolverines*, 228.
64. Stowers, *Staubach*, 43–44.
65. UM-BHL, Summary of Football Game Statistics, October 3, 1964, Michigan vs. Navy, op. cit.; Hemingway, *Life Among the Wolverines*, 228.
66. UM-BHL, SB-50, Bob Pille, "Nice Guys CAN Finish First," *Detroit Free Press*, December 2, 1964.
67. Clank Stoppels, "Wolverines 'Deep-Freeze' Staubach," *Grand Rapids Press*, October 4, 1964.
68. James Conley, interview, op. cit.
69. Lad Slingerland, "Hitting Pleases Elliott," *(Lansing) State Journal*, October 4, 1964.
70. William N. Wallace, "Michigan Halts Middies by 21–0," *New York Times*, October 4, 1964, S1, 6. See also UM-BHL, SB-49, Jack Hayes, "Michigan Mauls Navy, 21 to 0," *Toledo Blade*, October 4, 1964.
71. Ibid. See also Stowers, *Staubach*, 43–44.
72. Stoppels, "Wolverines 'Deep-Freeze,'" *Grand Rapids Press*, op. cit.; UM-BHL, Individual Files, Box 20, Mel Anthony, "This I Remember," from Game Program, Michigan-Northwestern, November 5, 1977, 15, 50; Brian Patchen, comments on original manuscript. Patchen to this day keeps the ball in his office. See also Bump Elliott Collection, *Michigan: This I Remember, 1964*.
73. UM-BHL, Summary of Football Game Statistics, October 3, 1964, Michigan vs. Navy, op. cit.
74. Hayes, "Michigan Mauls Navy, 21 to 0," *Toledo Blade*, op. cit.
75. Slingerland, "Hitting Pleases Elliott," *(Lansing) State Journal*, October 4, 1964, op. cit.
76. Stoppels, "Wolverines 'Deep-Freeze,'" *Grand Rapids Press*, op. cit.

Chapter Three

1. Bump Elliott, interview, op. cit.
2. Walsh, *Michigan Football: Guide and Record Book*, 279–82.
3. http://www.mgoblue.com/sports/m-footb/spec-re/0'4009aaahtml. Accessed 4/2/2013.
4. Ibid.
5. Although Bump Elliott and Duffy Daugherty competed aggressively in recruiting, and their teams were vigorous competitors against each other on the field, the personal relationship between the two men was cordial and friendly. In fact, during the mid–1960s, Elliott and Daugherty co-hosted a weekly 30-minute television program, *The Bump and Duffy Show*, in which they recounted the highlights of the previous week's games and commented on the upcoming games for both teams. Bump Elliott, interview, op. cit.
6. UM-BHL, SB-48, Joe Falls, "Bump Tries to Look Sad, Can't," *Detroit Free Press*, October 13, 1963; Joe Dowdell, "Tie Is Like a Loss to Daugherty," *Detroit Free Press*, October 13, 1963; Jerry Green, "Punts Foul Strategy, But Bump Praises Wolverines," *Detroit News*, October 13, 1963; Mike Block, "Wolverines, Spartans Fight to 7-7 Standoff," *Michigan Daily*, October 13, 1963.
7. Dowdell, "Tie Is Like a Loss to Daugherty," *Detroit Free Press*, October 13, 1963, op. cit.
8. Green, "Punts Foul Strategy," *Detroit News*, October 13, 1963, op. cit.
9. Game Program, Michigan State vs. Michigan, October 10, 1964, 13. Bump Elliott Collection, *Football Programs: University of Michigan, 1964*.
10. Thomas Krzemienski, telephone interview with the author, March 7, 2013.
11. Game Program, Michigan State vs. Michigan, October 10, 1964, 23. See also Clank Stoppels, "The View from Here," *Grand Rapids Press*, September 27, 1964.
12. Roberts and Krzemienski, *Rising Tide*, 56–57.
13. UM-BHL, SIO, "Michigan Sport News," mailed October 6, 1964.
14. Bob Hoerner, "Munn Praises Win Over USC," *(Lansing) State Journal*, October 9, 1964, E-1.
15. Bob Hoerner, "Michigan Favored To Beat Michigan State," *(Lansing) State Journal*, October 9, 1964, C-1.
16. Bob Hoerner, "State Defense Readied

for Michigan," *(Lansing) State Journal*, October 8, 1964, E-1, 4.

17. Ibid.

18. Robert Hoerner, "U-M Game To Attract Big Throng," *(Lansing) State Journal*, October 9, 1964, A-1, 4. See also UM-BHL, UMAD, Game Rundowns, Summary of Game Statistics, October 10, 1964, Michigan State vs. Michigan.

19. R.W. Apple, Jr., "Michigan Topples Michigan State, 17–10," *New York Times*, October 11, 1964, S-7.

20. Birt Darling, "Day Was Colorful, Chilly, as Spartans Lost to U-M," *(Lansing) State Journal*, October 11, 1964, A-1.

21. UM-BHL, UMAD, Individual Files, Box 113, Rick Volk, "Draft from This I Remember," 5–6; Jim Conley, "This I Remember," op. cit., 45. Rick Volk's memoir of "This I Remember" may be found in the Game Program for Michigan vs. Michigan State, October 14, 1978. That memoir, however, does not contain the information about the episode between Rick Sygar and Pat Gallinagh that was in his original draft. Apparently, that information was edited out of the final copy.

22. Bump Elliott, interview, op. cit.

23. Game Program, Michigan State vs. Michigan, October 10, 1964, 27. Occasionally it was difficult to ascertain who actually started the games for the respective teams, even though the names of the starters were listed in the official program. I have taken the mention of players, and their appearances, from Apple, "Michigan Topples Michigan State," *New York Times*, October 11, 1964, op. cit., as the more authoritative record.

24. Apple, "Michigan Topples Michigan State," *New York Times*, October 11, 1964, op. cit.

25. UM-BHL, Summary of Game Statistics, October 10, 1964, Michigan State vs. Michigan.

26. Ibid.

27. Ibid.

28. Ibid. See also UM-BHL, SB-49, Thomas Weinberg, "Yearby & Co. Halt Spartans," *Michigan Daily*, October 13, 1964.

29. UM-BHL, Summary of Game Statistics, October 10, 1964, Michigan State vs. Michigan. See also Hemingway, *Life Among the Wolverines*, 231.

30. Jim Conley, "This I Remember," op. cit.

31. Ibid.

32. UM-BHL, Summary of Game Statistics, October 10, 1964, Michigan State vs. Michigan.

33. Individual Files, Jim Conley, "This I Remember," op. cit.

34. UM-BHL, Summary of Game Statistics, October 10, 1964, Michigan State vs. Michigan. For the account of Kenney's 49-yard field goal against Southern California, see (no author, AP), "Barefoot Kicker Sets School Mark," *New York Times*, October 4, 1964, S-1.

35. Ibid. See also Hoerner, "Teams Miss Chances After Breaks," *(Lansing) State Journal*, October 11, 1964, E-1.

36. UM-BHL, Summary of Game Statistics, October 10, 1964, Michigan State vs. Michigan.

37. Hemingway, *Life Among the Wolverines*, 234.

38. UM-BHL, Summary of Game Statistics, October 10, 1964, Michigan State vs. Michigan. See also Hemingway, *Life Among the Wolverines*, 234; Apple, "Michigan Topples Michigan State," *New York Times*, October 11, 1964, op. cit.

39. Jerry Mader, comments on original manuscript. Sygar confirmed his elation in a telephone conversation with the author, October 15, 2013.

40. UM-BHL, SB-49, Bill Bullard, "Sygar's Pass Shocks State, Elates Elliott," *Michigan Daily*, October 12, 1964. See also Clank Stoppels, "Wolverines Find New Hero in 17–10 Victory," *Grand Rapids Press*, October 11, 1964; Stoppels, "The View from Here," *Grand Rapids Press*, October 11, 1964.

41. UM-BHL, Summary of Game Statistics, October 10, 1964, Michigan State vs. Michigan.

42. UM-BHL, SB-49, Maurice Shevlin, "Wolverines Win in Fourth Period, 17–10," *Chicago Tribune*, October 11, 1964.

43. UM-BHL, Summary of Game Statistics, October 10, 1964, Michigan State vs. Michigan.

44. UM-BHL, SB-49, Tom Rowland, "Surprise Pass Caps Fourth Quarter Rally," *Michigan Daily*, 10-11-64.

45. James Conley, interview, op. cit.

46. John Henderson, "This I Remember," op. cit., 2. Photographs of the play show Henderson going untouched into the end zone for the touchdown, however. Don Japinga was the closest Spartan defender on the play, and he was unable to catch Henderson.

47. Bullard, "Sygar's Pass Shocks State," *Michigan Daily*, October 12, 1964, op. cit.

48. Henderson, "This I Remember," op. cit.

49. Rowland, "Yearby & Co. Halt Spartans," *Michigan Daily*, October 13 1964, op. cit.

50. Ibid. See also "Brandon's Blog: Remembering Bill Yearby," http://www.mgoblue.com/sprots/brandon/spec-rel/122910aaa.html, accessed September 24, 2013.

51. UM-BHL, SB-49, Ron Tanguay, "Wolverine Notes," *Ann Arbor News*, October 12, 1964.

52. Ibid.

53. Stoppels, "Wolverines Find New Hero," *Grand Rapids Press*, October 11, 1964, op. cit. Jimmy Pace was an All-American running back for Michigan in 1957. He later played in the NFL with the San Francisco 49ers.

54. Rowland, "Yearby & Co. Halt Spartans," *Michigan Daily*, October 13, 1964, op. cit.

55. UM-BHL, UMAD, Individual Files, Box 105, Rick Sygar, photo, Rick Sygar, B-108. Jim Conley praised Sygar's athleticism and versatility. "Rick Sygar was the finest all-around athlete I ever saw," he stated in an interview. James Conley interview, op. cit.

56. UM-BHL, Summary of Game Statistics, October 10, 1964, Michigan State vs. Michigan. See also Apple, "Michigan Topples Spartans," *New York Times*, October 11, 1964, op. cit.

57. Thomas Krzemienski, interview, op. cit.

58. Jim Conley, "This I Remember," op cit. See also Hemingway, *Life Among the Wolverines*, 234.

59. Hemingway, *Life Among the Wolverines*, 235.

60. http://www.sports-reference.com/cfb/years/1964-polls.html.

61. Walsh, *Michigan Football: Guide and Record Book*, 131, 138–39.

62. John Bansch, "Purdue Upsets Big Ten for Michigan," *Indianapolis Star*, October 18, 1964, 1; Tom Schott, "Coaching History, 1956–69: The Golden Years," CS coaching history, 1956, 69. pdf. accessed April 25, 2013.

63. Game Program, Michigan vs. Purdue, October 17, 1964, 15, 48. Bump Elliott Collection, *Football Programs: University of Michigan, 1964*.

64. Randy Minniear, interview with the author, March 19, 2013.

65. Ibid. See also, http://www.purduesports.com/sports/m-footb/spec-rel/cradle-of-que ... accessed April 25, 2013.

66. Game Program, Michigan vs. Purdue, October 17, 1964, 5.

67. Ibid., 29.

68. I am indebted to Rich Ruble, tight end on Purdue's 1964 team, for sending me the scouting report that Purdue coaches prepared for the Michigan game. The document will be referred to as the Ruble Scouting Report, October 17, 1964. Also, Rich Ruble and Randy Minniear, in their interviews with the author, supplied information about the Boilermakers' preparation for Michigan.

69. Hemingway, *Life Among the Wolverines*, 236. See also Maurice Shevlin, "Purdue Stops Wolverines, 21–20," *Chicago Tribune*, October 18, 1964, S1, 5, 6.

70. Ibid.

71. Rich Ruble, telephone interview with the author, March 8, 2013; Randy Minniear, interview, op. cit.

72. Ibid.

73. James Conley, interview.

74. Hemingway, *Life Among the Wolverines*, 238. The phrase "eating drag dust" was recorded by the announcer of the highlights of the game. See *1964 Michigan vs. Purdue*, you tube.com.

75. Ibid. See also Shevlin, "Purdue Tops Michigan," *Chicago Tribune*, October 18, 1964, op. cit.

76. Hemingway, *Life Among the Wolverines*, 238. The phrase, "black jacked in" was used by the announcer of the highlights of the game. See *1964 Michigan vs. Purdue*, youtube.com The phrase obviously related to Coach Mollenkopf's nickname, "Black Jack."

77. UM-BHL, SB-50, Bill Bullard, "Michigan Gains More Yardage, First Downs in Losing Cause," *Michigan Daily*, October 18, 1964.

78. *1964 Michigan vs. Purdue*, youtube.com. See also Mel Anthony, "This I Remember," op. cit.

79. Randy Minniear, interview, op. cit.

80. Hemingway, *Life Among the Wolverines*, 238–40; Shevlin, "Purdue Stops Wolverines, 21–20," *Chicago Tribune*, October 18, 1964, op. cit.; *1964 Michigan vs. Purdue*, youtube.com.

81. Hemingway, *Life Among the Wolverines*, 239.

82. Ibid., 241. See also no author (UPI), "Purdue Conquers Michigan By 21–20," *New York Times*, October 18, 1964, S 9.

83. Elliott's statement about the players' preference is found in UM-BHL, SB-50, Bud Furillo, "Bump Pumps Up 'Nameless' Bowl," *Los Angeles Herald*, December 21, 1964.

84. Bump Elliott, interview, op. cit.

85. Hemingway, *Life Among the Wolverines*, 241; Anthony, "This I Remember," op. cit., 50.

86. Randy Minniear, interview, op. cit.

87. Bullard, "Michigan Gains More Yardage," *Michigan Daily*, October 18, 1964, op. cit.

88. Bansch, "QB in Hospital," *Indianapolis Star*, October 18, 1964, op. cit. Wayne Fuson, "Purdue Future Rosy?" from his column, "Time Out!" in the *Indianapolis News*, October 19, 1964.
89. Randy Minniear, interview, op. cit.
90. Bullard, "Michigan Gains More Yardage," *Michigan Daily*, October 18, 1964, op. cit.
91. Elliott's statement about not singing "The Victors" after the loss to Purdue is found in UM-BHL, SB-50, Lyall Smith, "U-M: The Victors Sing It, Act Part," *Detroit Free Press*, November 25, 1964. For Fisher's reaction after the game, see Hemingway, *Life Among the Wolverines*, 241. Finally, Michigan's assistant coach Tony Mason was a dynamic motivational speaker who often spoke at high school athletic banquets where coaches and athletes were honored for their accomplishments at the end of the school year. Mason was the featured speaker at the author's high school, Ottawa Hills in Grand Rapids, Michigan, in May 1965, when the school held its athletic banquet. In his remarks on the past Michigan season, Mason talked about the effect that the loss to Purdue had on him, as well as the players on the team. "You know what I did after we lost to Purdue?" Mason hollered to the attendees. "I threw up!"
92. Bullard, "Michigan Gains More Yardage," *Michigan Daily*, October 18, 1964, op. cit.
93. Randy Minniear, interview, op. cit.
94. Ibid.
95. Fuson, "Purdue Future Rosy?" *Indianapolis News*, October 19, 1964, op cit.
96. Hemingway, *Life Among the Wolverines*, 241.
97. James Conley, interview, op. cit.
98. Brian Patchen, comments on original manuscript, July, 2013.

Chapter Four

1. UM-BHL, Department of Intercollegiate Athletics, Individual Files, Box 35, Tom Cecchini, "Memory of Michigan–Ohio State game," no date.
2. "Michigan-Minnesota: The Little Brown Jug Series," in http://www.mgoblue.com/sports/m-footbl/spec-rel/061709aaa.html, accessed March 16, 2013.
3. Greg Dooley, "Exploring the Myths," in Brian Cook and Seth Fisher, *Hail to the Victors*, MGoBlog.
4. "Michigan-Minnesota: The Little Brown Jug Series," in mgoblue.com, op. cit.
5. Game program, Minnesota vs. Michigan, October 24, 1964, 5, from Bump Elliott Collection, *Football Programs, University of Michigan: 1964*.
6. Walsh, *Guide and Record Book: Michigan Football*, 137–39.
7. UM-BHL, SB-48, no author (AP), "Mistake Costs 'M' Defense Vital Yardage," *Ann Arbor News*, October 29, 1963.
8. UM-BHL, SB-48, Joe Falls, "Gophers Cling to the Jug, 6–0," *Detroit Free Press*, October 27, 1963.
9. UM-BHL, SIO, "Michigan Sport News," mailed October 20, 1964
10. Ibid. See also UM-BHL, Department of Intercollegiate Athletics, Individual Files, Box 86, Frank Nunley, article by Jack Saylor, "Ex-Wolverine Star Waiting for Lions Visit Sunday," *Detroit Free Press*, December 17, 1971. At the time the article was written, Nunley was a standout linebacker in the NFL for the San Francisco 49ers. Joe Schmidt was the head coach of the Detroit Lions in 1971.
11. UM-BHL, SIO, "Michigan Sport News," mailed October 20, 1964
12. Game program, Michigan vs. Minnesota, October 24, 1964, 27, 29. See also UM-BHL, SB-50, Wayne De Neff, "Michigan Bids Again to Reclaim Little Brown Jug," *Ann Arbor News*, October 24, 1964.
13. Game program, Michigan vs. Minnesota, October 24, 1964, op. cit.
14. UM-BHL, Department of Intercollegiate Athletics, Box 2, Game Rundowns, Summary of Football Game Statistics, October 24, 1964 (Michigan vs. Minnesota). See also Hemingway, *Life Among the Wolverines*, 242–43.
15. Ibid.
16. Ibid.
17. Ibid.
18. UM-BHL, Summary of Football Game Statistics, October 24, 1964 (Michigan vs. Minnesota).
19. Hemingway, *Life Among the Wolverines*, 242–43.
20. UM-BHL, Summary of Football Game Statistics, October 24, 1964 (Michigan vs. Minnesota); Hemingway, *Life Among the Wolverines*, 243.
21. UM-BHL, Summary of Football Game Statistics, October 24, 1964 (Michigan vs. Minnesota).
22. E-mail message, Brian Patchen to Ben Farabee, June 18, 2013, in author's possession.

See also Comments by Bob Timberlake and Dave Butler, Transcript, Bump Elliott Tribute, op. cit., 11, 13–14.

23. Hemingway, *Life Among the Wolverines*, 243.

24. Although there was no evidence of any unnecessary roughness or personal fouls on the part of Minnesota up to this point in the game, Bump Elliott believed that some of Michigan's opponents were targeting Bob Timberlake during the kickoff plays, trying to injure him and knock him out of the game. As a result, Timberlake had clear instructions to stay well back on the coverage, almost in a safety-type position, after he kicked the ball, and another player was assigned to protect Timberlake from any potentially damaging contact. Bump Elliott, interview, op. cit.

25. UM-BHL, Summary of Football Game Statistics, October 24, 1964 (Michigan vs. Minnesota).

26. Ibid. See also Hemingway, *Life Among the Wolverines*, 243–44.

27. Ibid.

28. Wayne De Neff, "Title Road Has Some Toughies for Jug-Winning Michigan," *Ann Arbor News*, October 26, 1964. Also, Brian Patchen, comments on original manuscript, July 2013.

29. James Conley, interview, op. cit.

30. UM-BHL, Summary of Game Statistics, October 24, 1964 (Michigan vs. Minnesota); Hemingway, *Life Among the Wolverines*, 245. See also UM-BHL, SB-50, Bruce Morrison, "Wolves Repulse Gophers Rally, 19–12," *Chicago Sun-Times*, October 25, 1964, and Cooper Rollow, "Gophers' Late Rally Fails, 19–12," *Chicago Tribune*, October 25, 1964.

31. "Pregame and Coaching Legends," *Maximum Meechigan*, CD One, op. cit.; Morrison, "Wolves Repulse Gophers Rally, 19–12," *Chicago Sun-Times*, October 25, 1964.

32. Morrison, "Wolves Repulse Gophers Rally," *Chicago Sun-Times*, October 25, 1964, op. cit.

33. UM-BHL, Summary of Football Game Statistics, October 24, 1964 (Michigan vs. Minnesota).

34. Ibid.

35. Hemingway, *Life Among the Wolverines*, 245.

36. Game program, Michigan vs. Northwestern, October 31, 1964, 17, 48, 52, from Bump Elliott Collection, *Football Programs, University of Michigan: 1964*.

37. Ibid., 26, 23. See also UM-BHL, Department of Intercollegiate Athletics, Football Game Rundowns, Box 2, Summary of Football Game Statistics, October 31, 1964 (Michigan vs. Northwestern).

38. Game program, Michigan vs. Northwestern, October 31, 1964, 27, 29.

39. UM-BHL, Summary of Football Game Statistics, October 24, 1964 (Michigan vs. Northwestern).

40. Ibid. See also Hemingway, *Life Among the Wolverines*, 246.

41. Ibid.

42. UM-BHL, SB-50, Wayne De Neff, "Rampaging Wolverines Look Ahead to Illinois," *Ann Arbor News*, November 1, 64; Thomas Weinberg, "Hollway Lauds Staunch 'M' Defense," *Michigan Daily*, November 6, 1964.

43. UM-BHL, Summary of Football Game Statistics, October 31, 1964 (Michigan vs. Northwestern).

44. Weinberg, "Hollway Lauds Staunch 'M' Defense," *Michigan Daily*, November 6, 1964, op. cit.

45. Ibid.

46. Clank Stoppels, "Californians Love Cinderella Story of Elliott," *Grand Rapids Press*, December 27, 1964.

Chapter Five

1. UM-BHL, SB-50, Charles Bartlett, "Wolverines Retain Title Hopes," *Chicago Tribune*, November 8, 1964.

2. UM-BHL, SB-50, David Condon, "Hail the Victors—Bump and Pete," from Condon's column, "In the Wake of the News," *Chicago Tribune*, July 9, 1980. See also Wayne De Neff, "All-American Family: Elliotts Reunite with Memories of Michigan," *Ann Arbor News*, July 6, 1995.

3. Bump Elliott, interview, op. cit.

4. Richard Goldstein, "Pete Elliott, Football All-American and Coach, Dies at 86," *New York Times*, January 6, 2013. http://www.nytimes.com/2013/01/07/sports/ncaafottbaoll/pete-elliott-f... accessed 5/13/2013.

5. UM-BHL, SB-48, Wayne De Neff, "Mrs. Elliott Plans to Stay at Home," *Ann Arbor News*, November 5, 1963. See also UM-BHL, SB-48, Jerry Green, "Battle of Brothers Has New Interest This Year," *Detroit News*, November 5, 1963, Clank Stoppels, "Oh, Brother: It's Bump vs. Pete Again Saturday," *Grand Rapids Press*, November 6, 1964, and Walsh,

Michigan Football: Guide and Record Book, 130–40.

6. Comments by Rich Hahn, Transcript, Bump Elliott Tribute, 13–14.

7. De Neff, "Mrs. Elliott Plans to Stay at Home," *Ann Arbor News*, November 5, 1963, op. cit.

8. UM-BHL, SB-48, Howard Barry, "Illini Upset," *Chicago Tribune*, November 10, 1963.

9. UM-BHL, SB-48, Dave Good, "Rowser Stars In Upset Win," *Michigan Daily*, November 10, 1963; Bill Bullard, "Rowser Shows Skill as Tough Tackler," *Michigan Daily*, November 14, 1963.

10. Jim Conley, "This I Remember," op cit., 15.

11. UM-BHL, SB-48, Wayne De Neff, "M Men Make Dr. Coxon a Happy Man as Retirement Nears for Physician," *Ann Arbor News*, November 22, 1963.

12. Game Program, Michigan vs. Illinois, November 7, 1964, 5, 48, from Bump Elliott Collection, *Game Programs: University of Michigan, 1964*.

13. James Conley, interview, op. cit.

14. Game Program, Michigan vs. Illinois, November 7, 1964, 23. See also Hemingway, *Life Among the Wolverines*, 248.

15. Game Program, Michigan vs. Illinois, November 7, 1964, 23.

16. Jerry Mader, comments on original manuscript, July, 2013. Bob Hollway and Pete Elliott had known each other for many years, going back to their time as teammates on the Michigan teams between 1946 and 1948.

17. UM-BHL, UMAD, Game Rundowns, Summary of Football Game Statistics, Michigan vs. Illinois, November 7, 1964. See also Hemingway, *Life Among the Wolverines*, 248.

18. Ibid.

19. UM-BHL, SB-50, Charlie Towle, "Michigan Hopes Alive for Title," *Michigan Daily*, November 8, 1964.

20. Ibid.

21. UM-BHL, SB-50, Wayne De Neff, "Wolverine Notes: Michigan Loses John Yanz, Maybe Dick Rindfuss," *Ann Arbor News*, November 9, 1964.

22. UM-BHL, Summary of Game Statistics, Michigan vs. Illinois, November 7, 1964.

23. Ibid.

24. Jerry Mader, comments on original manuscript, July 2013.

25. James Conley, interview, op. cit.

26. Towle, "Michigan Hopes Alive for Title," *Michigan Daily*, November 8, 1964, op. cit.

27. De Neff, "Wolverine Notes: Michigan Loses John Yanz, Maybe Dick Rindfuss," *Ann Arbor News*, November 9, 1964, op. cit.; Hemingway, *Life Among the Wolverines*, 250.

28. Towle, "Michigan Hopes Alive for Title," *Michigan Daily*, November 8, 1964, op. cit.

29. Brian Patchen, comments on original manuscript, July, 2013. Jerry Mader, being a native Illinoisan, was awarded the game ball after the contest against Illinois.

30. De Neff, "Wolverine Notes: Michigan Loses John Yanz, Maybe Dick Rindfuss," *Ann Arbor News*, November 9, 1964, op. cit.

31. Max Stultz, "Spartans Bomb Purdue, Rose Bowl Hopes," *Indianapolis Star*, November 8, 1964, 4–1. See also Bob Collins, "Sports Over Lightly," *Indianapolis Star*, November 8, 1964, 4–2. For a video summary of the game, see *1964: Michigan State vs. Purdue*, youtube.com.

32. Stultz, "Spartans Bomb Purdue," *Indianapolis Star*, November 8, 1964, op. cit.

33. Collins, "Sports Over Lightly," *Indianapolis Star*, November 8, 1964, op. cit.

34. Randy Minniear, interview, op. cit.

35. Ibid.

36. Game Program, Iowa vs. Michigan, November 14, 1964, 4, from Bump Elliott Collection, *Football Programs, University of Michigan*, 1964.

37. Ibid. See also UM-BHL, SB-48, George Puscas, "Anthony Rambles for All 3 Scores, *Detroit Free Press*, November 17, 1963.

38. UM-BHL, SIO, "Michigan Sport News," mailed November 10, 1964. See also UM-BHL, SB-50, Wayne De Neff, "Iowa Termed Very Dangerous," *Ann Arbor News*, November 10, 1964.

39. De Neff, "Iowa Termed Very Dangerous," *Ann Arbor News*, November 10, 1964, op. cit.

40. Ibid. Jerry Burns and the Iowa coaching staff were effective recruiters in landing football talent from the state of Michigan. In addition to Noonan and Kimble, other Hawkeye starters from Michigan included Tony Giacobozzi from Farmington Hills, and Robert Mitchell and Robert Ziolkowski, both from Flint.

41. UM-BHL, UMAD, Game Rundowns, Summary of Football Game Statistics, November 14, 1964, Michigan vs. Iowa.

42. Game Program, Iowa vs. Michigan, November 14, 1964.

43. Ibid.

44. Ibid. See also Summary of Football Game Statistics, November 14, 1964, Michigan vs. Iowa; and Hemingway, *Life Among the Wolverines*, 251.
45. Summary of Game Statistics, November 14, 1964, Michigan vs. Iowa.
46. Ibid.
47. Ibid.
48. Ibid.
49. Ibid.
50. Ibid. See also Brian Patchen, comments on original manuscript, July, 2013.
51. Ibid. See also Hemingway, *Life Among the Wolverines*, 253.
52. Ibid. See also Jerry Mader, comments on original manuscript, July, 2013.
53. UM-BHL, Summary of Game Statistics, November 14, 1964, Michigan vs. Iowa.
54. Ibid.
55. Ibid.
56. Ibid.
57. UM-BHL, Individual Files, Box 35, Tom Cecchini, "Memory of Michigan–Ohio State Game," op. cit., 2.
58. Bump Elliott, interview, op. cit.
59. John Bansch, "Minnesota Aerials Sink Riveters," *Indianapolis Star*, November 15, 1964, 1. For a video summary of the game, see *1964: Purdue vs. Minnesota*, youtube.com.
60. Randy Minniear, interview, op. cit.
61. Bansch, "Minnesota Aerials Sink Riveters," *Indianapolis Star*, November 15, 1964, op. cit.
62. John Bansch, "'Gophers Wanted It More,' Jack Moans," *Indianapolis Star*, November 15, 1964, 4.
63. Randy Minniear, interview, op. cit.
64. UM-BHL, SB-50, Roy Damer, "Errors Help Wolverines Win, 34 to 20," *Chicago Tribune*, November 15, 1964.
65. UM-BHL, Summary of Game Statistics, November 14, 1964, Michigan vs. Iowa.
66. Maury White, "This Wasn't Iowa's Day," *Des Moines Register*, November 15, 1964, 1, 8.
67. UM-BHL, Summary of Game Statistics, November 15, 1964.
68. UM-BHL, SB-50, Wayne De Neff, "Wolverine Notes," *Ann Arbor News*, November 18, 1964.
69. Ibid.
70. Doug Mintline, "'M' Victory Sets Stage for Showdown at OSU," written for the *Flint Journal*, November 15, 1964, and included in the *Grand Rapids Press*, November 15, 1964.
71. White, "This Wasn't Iowa's Day," *Des Moines Register*, November 15, 1964, op. cit.

Chapter Six

1. UM-BHL, SB-50, Lyall Smith, "The Victors Sing it, Act Part," *Detroit Free Press*, November 22, 1964.
2. UM-BHL, Department of Intercollegiate Athletics, Individual Files, Box 105, Richard Sygar, draft, "This I Remember," June 4, 1987, 4.
3. For the best studies of the Michigan–Ohio State games of the 1970s, see Michael Rosenberg, *War as They Knew It: Woody Hayes, Bo Schembechler, and America in a Time of Unrest* (New York: Grand Central Publishing, 2008) and Greg Emmanuel, *The 100-Yard War: Inside the 100-Year-Old Michigan-Ohio State Football Rivalry* (New York: Wiley, 2004).
4. Bump Elliott, interview, op. cit.
5. Ohio State University Archives, Department of Athletics: Media Guides (RG: 9/e–10d), Football Press Guides: 1960, 1961, 1964, 1965, 1969. "1964 Football Information," 8–11. The author wishes to acknowledge the assistance of Kevlin Haire and Michelle Drobik, archivists for the Ohio State University Archives, for their assistance in locating documents and photographs that pertain to the 1964 Ohio State football team.
6. Ibid., 3.
7. Ibid., 4. The information about the individual Ohio State players is taken from the Ohio State University Archives, Department of Athletics: Football Programs (RG: 9/3–10a), "1964." "Michigan–Ohio State," November 21, 1964, 24. A copy of that program may also be found in the Bump Elliott Collection, *Football Programs, University of Michigan, 1964*.
8. Cooper Rollow, "80,736 See Ohio Crush SMU," *Chicago Tribune*, September 27, 1964, Section 2, 2.
9. Harry Warren, "Ohio State Shakes Off Hoosiers, 17 to 9," *Chicago Tribune*, October 4, 1964, Section 2, 1, 4.
10. George Strickler, "Ohio Crush Illini," *Chicago Tribune*, October 11, 1964, Section 2, 1, 3.
11. Robert Markus, "Ohio State Grinds Thru USC," *Chicago Tribune*, October 18, 1964, Section 2, 1, 5.
12. Maurice Shevlin, "Buckeyes Stop 2 Points Play, Win 21–19," *Chicago Tribune*, November 1, 1964, Section 2, 1. Ohio State's 28–3 victory over Wisconsin on October 24, 1964, is covered in George Strickler, "Blocked Kick

Puts Badgers in 28–3 Spin," *Chicago Tribune*, October 25, 1964, Section 2, 1.

13. Joe Paterno, quoted in Hyman and White, *Big Ten Football*, 70.

14. Roy Damer, "Penn State Beats Ohio 27–0," *Chicago Tribune*, November 8, 1964, Section 2, 1, 4.

15. Ibid.

16. No author, "Soundest Trouncing Ever Hayes," *Chicago Tribune*, November 8, 1964, Section 2, 1.

17. Paterno, quoted in Hyman and White, *Big Ten Football*, 70.

18. Dick Otte, " 'Soundest Trouncing' Delivered by 'Great Lion Team,' Says Hayes," *Columbus Dispatch*, November 8, 1964, 34–35B.

19. Richard Dozer, "Wildcats 5th Conference Victim," *Chicago Tribune*, November 15, 1964, Section 2, 1, 5.

20. Dick Otte, "Hayes Pensive in Victory, Too," *Columbus Dispatch*, November 15, 1964, 33B.

21. UM-BHL, SB-50, no author, "Bump Thinks Wolves Ready for Buckeyes," *Columbus Dispatch*, November 17, 1964.

22. UM-BHL, SB-50, Nikki Schwartz and Lynn Metzger, "War of Roses Still Wages On," *Michigan Daily*, November 17, 1964.

23. John Underwood, "Roses for Wolverines, Blues for Buckeyes," *Sports Illustrated*, November 30, 1964, op. cit.; see also Tom Cecchini, draft, "Memory of Michigan–Ohio State Game, 1964," op. cit., 6. See also Cecchini, "This I Remember" from program of Michigan–Ohio State game, November 19, 1977, 15, 54, in Bump Elliott Collection, *This I Remember, Michigan '64*. See also Hemingway, *Life Among the Wolverines*, 256.

24. James Conley, interview.

25. UM-BHL, Cecchini, "Memory of Michigan–Ohio State Game," op. cit., 2–3. One must wonder if Joe Paterno, in preparing for Ohio State, noticed the same tendency with Bo Rein's placement of his hands that Cecchini and the Michigan coaches discovered.

26. Brian Patchen, comments on original manuscript, July 2013.

27. Schwartz and Metzger, "War of Roses," *Michigan Daily*, November 17, 1964, op. cit.; see also Paul Hornung, "Wolves Offense Very Defensive," *Columbus Dispatch*, November 17, 1964, 28A.

28. No author, "This Man Is Dangerous," *Columbus Dispatch*, November 19, 1964, 11A.

29. Paul Hornung, "Offense Key To Ohio Hope," *Columbus Dispatch*, November 16, 1964, 14A. Paul Hornung was a longtime football writer and reporter for the *Columbus Dispatch*. He should not be confused with Paul Hornung, name spelled identically, who was a Heisman Trophy–winning quarterback at Notre Dame and then an All-Pro halfback with the Green Bay Packers during the 1950s and 1960s.

30. No author, "Michigan, Ohio State Can Start 16 Ohio Grads," *Columbus Dispatch*, November 16, 1964, 14A. Actually, the correct number was 17 Ohio grads—8 on the Michigan offense and 9 on the Ohio State offense. In the story, however, the reporter identified all of the players. According to the Ohio State roster, there were no players from Michigan who played for the Buckeyes in 1964. See game program, Michigan–Ohio State, November 21, 1964, 24.

31. UM-BHL, Department of Intercollegiate Athletics, Individual Files, Box 73, Bill Laskey, "This I Remember," from program of Michigan-Michigan State game, October 9, 1976. John Underwood, "Roses for Wolverines, Blues for Buckeyes," *Sports Illustrated*, November 30, 1964; op. cit.

32. Underwood, "Roses for Wolverines, Blues for Buckeyes," *Sports Illustrated*, November 30, 1964, op. cit.; see also UM-BHL, SB-50, Pete Waldmeir, "A Silly Game Helps U-M Ease Tension Before Game," *Detroit News*, November 25, 1964.

33. Underwood, "Roses for Wolverines, Blues for Buckeyes," *Sports Illustrated*, November 30, 1964, op. cit.; Cecchini, "Memory of Michigan–Ohio State Game, 1964," op. cit., 3–4; Hemingway, *Life Among the Wolverines*, 255.

34. UM-BHL, SB-50, no author, "Bump Thinks Wolves Ready," *Columbus Dispatch*, op. cit.

35. Cecchini, "Memory of Michigan–Ohio State Game, 1964," op. cit., 3.

36. Hemingway, *Life Among the Wolverines*, 256; Jerry Mader, comments on original manuscript, July 2013.

37. Hemingway, *Life Among the Wolverines*, 256; Bill Laskey, "Ohio State vs. Michigan," *Bill Laskey's Football Flashbacks*.

38. Cecchini, "Memory of Michigan–Ohio State Game, 1964," op. cit. 4.

39. Ibid., 1.

40. Ibid., 3–4.

41. UM-BHL, Department of Intercollegiate Athletics, Individual Files, Box 86, Frank Nunley, draft, "This I Remember," no date, 3.

See also Hemingway, *Life Among the Wolverines,* 258.
42. Nunley, "This I Remember," op. cit., 3.
43. UM-BHL, SB-50, Thomas Weinberg, "Hollway Lauds Staunch Defense," *Michigan Daily,* November 17, 1964.
44. Hemingway, *Life Among the Wolverines,* 260.
45. *1964: Michigan 10, Ohio State 0,* you tube.com. See also Hemingway, *Life Among the Wolverines,* 260.
46. Stoppels, "Californians Love Cinderella Story," *Grand Rapids Press,* December 27, 1964.
47. Underwood, "Roses for Wolverines, Blues for Buckeyes," *Sports Illustrated,* November 30, 1964, op. cit.; Hemingway, *Life Among the Wolverines,* 261.
48. *1964: Michigan 10, Ohio State 0,* you tube.com. Bump Elliott also referred to the Timberlake-Detwiler touchdown reception as a "throwback," where Timberlake rolled to his right and then "threw back" to his left to Detwiler. Smiling, Elliott also said: "Whatever you want to call it, it worked." Bump Elliott, interview, op. cit. See also e-mail message, James Detwiler to Bruce Geelhoed, June 29, 2013.
49. *1964: Michigan 10, Ohio State 0,* you tube.com. It is entirely possible that these were not Sygar's words on the field during Volk's punt return. Those were the words used by the unidentified television broadcaster in the youtube.com video clip who described the play in that fashion.
50. Ibid.
51. UM-BHL, SB-50, Jim Taylor, "Punts, Fumble, Helped Michigan," *Toledo Blade,* November 22, 1964.
52. Ibid.
53. A record of the play-by-play unfolding of the Michigan-Ohio State game may be found in UM-BHL, Department of Intercollegiate Athletics, Media Relations, Box 2, Game Rundowns, "Summaries of Football Game Statistics, November 21, 1964 (Michigan vs. Ohio State)."
54. Paul Hornung, "Elliott Brothers Do 2 Year Rose Bowl Act," *Columbus Dispatch,* November 22, 1964, 33B.
55. Taylor, "Punts, Fumbles, Helped Michigan," *Toledo Blade,* 11-22-64, op. cit.
56. UM-BHL, SB-50, Thomas Rivera, "Ride 'Trailer' to Rose Bowl," *Chicago Tribune,* November 22, 1964.
57. Taylor, "Punts, Fumbles, Helped Michigan," *Toledo Blade,* op. cit. See also Clank Stoppels, "Michigan Grabs Big Ten Title, Rose Bowl Nod," *Grand Rapids Press,* November 22, 1964.
58. UM-BHL, SB-50, Mike Tressler, "Special Trains Carried Celebrants," *Ann Arbor News,* November 23, 1964. The University of Michigan Alumni Association arranged a train trip for Wolverine supporters who wanted to attend the Ohio State game. In all, more than 1,000 Michigan supporters joined the train trip. Other Michigan fans undoubtedly made it to the game by driving their own cars. See also Hemingway, *Life Among the Wolverines,* 263–64.
59. Hornung, "Elliott Brothers Do 2 Year Rose Bowl Act," *Columbus Dispatch,* op. cit.
60. Ibid.
61. Taylor, "Punts, Fumbles, Helped Michigan," *Toledo Blade,* op. cit.
62. Ibid.
63. Waldmeir, "A Silly Game Helps U-M Ease Tension," *Detroit News,* op. cit.
64. Gary Wyner, "M Earns Rose Bowl Bid," *Michigan Daily,* November 22, 1964, 1, 7.
65. Rivera, "Ride 'Trailer' to Rose Bowl," *Chicago Tribune,* op. cit. See also *Plain Dealer* staff, "Wolverines Prevail, 10–0; End Buckeyes Series Win Streak at 4," *Cleveland Plain Dealer,* November 22, 1964, updated November 20, 2012; http://www.cleveland.com/osu-michigan.2012/03/osu-michigan...196 accessed June 6, 2013.
66. Paul Hornung, "Bucks Rose Fever Cured by Michigan," *Columbus Dispatch,* November 22, 1964, 1–4A.
67. Don Dufek, interview, op. cit.
68. A brief, useful newspaper account of the Michigan–Ohio State game, complete with a helpful chart of game statistics, may be found in Michael Strauss, "Michigan Downs Ohio State by 10–0," *New York Times,* November 22, 1964, Section S, 1, 5.
69. UM-BHL, SB-50, Lloyd Graff, "Victors Land, Fans Take Off," *Michigan Daily,* November 22, 1964.
70. Ibid.
71. Ibid.
72. Ibid.
73. Ibid. See also UM-BHL, SB-50, no author, "Airport Reception Fouled Up By Fears of Safety for Fans," newspaper not identified, November 22, 1964.
74. Bill Laskey, "Ohio State vs. Michigan," *Bill Laskey's Football Flashbacks.*
75. Laskey, "This I Remember," op. cit.

76. Ibid.
77. UM-BHL, SB-50, no author (AP), "Even Fans Find Wolves Elusive," *Columbus Dispatch*, November 22, 1964, 34B; see also Graff, "Victors Land, Fans Take Off," *Michigan Daily*, November 22, 1964, op. cit.
78. Taylor, "Punts, Fumbles, Helped Michigan," *Toledo Blade*, op. cit.
79. Bo Schembechler with Dan Ewald, *Tradition: Bo Schembechler's Michigan Memories* (Ann Arbor: Clock Tower Press, 2003), 210–11. Also, James Conley comments on original manuscript, July 2013.
80. Anthony, "This I Remember," op. cit.
81. UM-BHL, Graff, "Victors Land, Fans Take Off," *Michigan Daily*, op. cit.

Chapter Seven

1. UM-BHL, SIO, "Final Big Ten Football Statistics," mailed November 23, 1964.
2. UM-BHL, SIO, "The National Collegiate Athletic Bureau, Official Football Statistics" (1964), 2, 5.
3. UM-BHL, SB-50, no author (UPI), "M Dominates All Big Ten Team," *Ann Arbor News*, November 27, 1964.
4. The Notre Dame–University of Southern California game on November 28, 1964, has been written about extensively. Two excellent sources are Dent, *Resurrection*, 258–74, and John Underwood, "A Catch—and Crash Goes Notre Dame," *SI Vault*, http://sportsillustratedcnn.com/vault/article/magazine/MAG1076685/htm..., accessed June 19, 2013. See also http://blog.oregonlive.com/behind Beaversbeat/2009/11/post_12.html, accessed June 20, 2013.
5. Underwood, "A Catch—and Crash Goes Notre Dame," *SI Vault*, op. cit.
6. Ibid.
7. Dent, *Resurrection*, 267–69.
8. Ibid.
9. Dent, *Resurrection*, 269; Underwood, "A Catch—and Crash Goes Notre Dame," *SI Vault*, op. cit.
10. Dent, *Resurrection*, 272; Underwood, "A Catch—and Crash Goes Notre Dame," *SI Vault*, op. cit.; George Strickler, "USC Trojans Shatter Irish Dream," *Chicago Tribune*, November 29, 1964.
11. Tom Rants, "Countdown to College Football: A 2002 Column About John McKay," http://tomrants.com/?/p=682, accessed June 20, 2013.
12. Paul Buker, "Oregon's State's Last Appearance in the Rose Bowl Still a Bone of Contention with USC Fans," http://blog.oregon live.old-time.com/behind beaversbeat/2009/11/post.12html, accessed June 20, 2013.
13. No author (UPI), "Trojan Officials Blast 'Rank Injustice of It All,'" *Chicago Tribune*, November 29, 1964.
14. UM-BHL, SB-50 no author (UPI), "Rose Bowl Selection Stirs Storm on West Coast," *Ann Arbor News*, November 30, 1964.
15. Ibid.
16. Ibid.
17. Donald Dufek, telephone interview with the author, August 29, 2013.
18. Tom Rowland, "The Spectator: LA Sports Writers Beat Wolverines to the Punch," *Michigan Daily*, January 7, 1965, Hemingway, *Life Among the Wolverines*, 318; Jerry Mader, comments on original manuscript, February 2014.
19. James Conley, interview; UM-BHL, UMAD, Individual Files, Box 113, Rick Volk, draft of "This I Remember," 4; Bill Laskey, *Bill Laskey's Football Flashbacks*, op. cit., 5. See also e-mail message, Barry Dehlin to Bruce Geelhoed, July 8, 2013.
20. Volk, "This I Remember," op. cit. See also e-mail message, Dehlin to Geelhoed, op. cit., and Peter Waldmeir. "'M' Discipline Is Team Matter," published in the *Grand Rapids Press*, January 2, 1965.
21. Volk, "This I Remember," op. cit.
22. James Conley, interview, op. cit. See also Bump Elliott, interview, and Donald Dufek, interview.
23. Donald Dufek, interview.
24. E-mail message, Brian Patchen to Bruce Geelhoed, February 6, 2014.
25. George Pasero, "Beavers Big Season," from game program, Michigan vs. Oregon State, January 1, 1965, 29 60, from Bump Elliott Collection, *Game Programs, University of Michigan*, 1964.
26. Comment by Barry Dehlin in Transcript, Bump Elliott Tribute, September 29, 2004, 16–17.
27. Game program, Michigan vs. Oregon State, January 1, 1965, Bump Elliott Collection, *Game Programs: University of Michigan, 1964*, op. cit.
28. UM-BHL, UMAD, Box 270, Game Rundowns, Michigan vs. Oregon State, January 1, 1965.
29. Game Program, Michigan vs. Oregon State, January 1, 1965, 50–51, op. cit.

30. UM-BHL, Game Rundowns, Michigan vs. Oregon State, January 1, 1965. See also Sid Ziff, "Michigan By TKO," *Los Angeles Times*, January 2, 1965.
31. UM-BHL, SB-50, no author (UPI), "Bump Elliott Attributes Victory to Two Big Plays," *Ann Arbor News*, January 2, 1965.
32. UM-BHL, SB-50, Floyd Schneiderman, "U-M's Anthony Scoring After Rose Bowl's Longest Run," *Pasadena Independent*, 1-2-65.
33. For a review of Anthony's touchdown, and of the threat that Mel Anthony posed to opposing defenses, see *1965 Rose Bowl: Michigan vs. Oregon State*, youtobe.com; see also Maurice Shevlin, "Wolverines Rout Oregon State, 34–7," *Chicago Tribune*, 1-2-65; Tom Rowland, "Nobody Touched Me," *Michigan Daily*, January 7, 1965; Pete Waldmeir, "3 TDs Put Anthony in Elite Class," *Detroit News*, January 3, 1965; Clank Stoppels, "Pasadena Notebook," *Grand Rapids Press*, January 2, 1965; and Bud Furillo, "Bump Pumps Up Nameless Bowl," *Los Angeles Herald-Examiner*, December 20, 1964, op. cit.
34. Pete Waldmeir, "Michigan Shows Speed and Spirit," published in the *Grand Rapids Press*, January 2, 1965.
35. Game Rundowns, Michigan vs. Oregon State, January 1, 1965.
36. UM-BHL, SB-50, Pete Waldmeir, "Weakness Found in Movies Set Up Big Play for Michigan," *Detroit News*, January 4, 1965.
37. Clank Stoppels, "The View from Here," *Grand Rapids Press*, January 2, 1965.
38. Frank Finch, "Michigan Mighty, Beavers Bad," *Los Angeles Times*, January 2, 1965, op. cit.
39. Pete Waldmeir, "Three TDs Put Anthony in Elite Class," *Detroit News*, January 3, 1965.
40. Paul Preuss, "2-Point Run Called 'Gift,'" *Detroit News*, January 3, 1965.
41. Ibid.
42. No author (UPI), "Oregon State Ridiculed by Coast Fans, Writers," *Washington Post*, January 3, 1965. See also Stoppels, "The View from Here," *Grand Rapids Press*, January 2, 1965.
43. Game Rundowns, Michigan vs. Oregon State, January 1, 1965, op. cit. See also UM-BHL, SB-50, Wayne De Neff, "Rose Bowl Notes," *Ann Arbor News*, January 2, 1965.
44. UM-BHL, Summary of Football Game Statistics, Michigan vs. Oregon State, January 1, 1965; http://statsarchive.ath.umich.edu, op cit.

45. Clank Stoppels, "The View from Here," *Grand Rapids Press*, January 3, 1965.
46. Al Wolf, "The Aftermath: Prothro Wild About Michigan," *Los Angeles Times*, January 3, 1965.
47. Bill Bullard, "Wolverines Cop Roses, Clobber Beavers, 34–7," *Michigan Daily*, January 7, 1965. See also Charlie Park, "Defense Let us Down: Not Our Best Game—Prothro," *Los Angeles Times*, January 2, 1965.
48. Wolf, "The Aftermath," *Los Angeles Times*, January 3, 1965.
49. No author (UPI), "Bump Elliott Attributes Victory to Two Big Plays, *Ann Arbor News*, January 2, 1965.
50. Ibid.
51. Maurice Shevlin, "We Came to Win and We Did," *Chicago Tribune*, January 3, 1965.
52. Rowland, "The Spectator," *Michigan Daily*, January 7, 1965.
53. Sid Ziff, "Michigan by TKO," *Los Angeles Times*, January 2, 1965.
54. Clank Stoppels, "'M' Stakes Claim as Best in Nation After Bowl Rout," *Grand Rapids Press*, January 2, 1965.
55. Rowland, "The Spectator," *Michigan Daily*, January 7, 1965.
56. Ibid.
57. Ibid.
58. No author (UPI), "Oregon State Ridiculed by Coast Fans, Writers," *Washington Post*, January 3, 1965.
59. Stoppels, "The View from Here," *Grand Rapids Press*, January 2, 1965.
60. Maurice Shevlin, "Michigan Routs Oregon State, 34-7," *Chicago Tribune*, January 2, 1965.
61. Park, "Defense Let Us Down," *Los Angeles Times*, January 2, 1965.
62. Ibid.
63. Rowland, "The Spectator," *Michigan Daily*, January 7, 1965.
64. Pete Waldmeir, "Californians Overlook 'M' Victory, Merely Say Oregon State Lost," *Detroit News*, January 5, 1965.
65. Ibid.
66. James Conley, comments to Bruce Geelhoed regarding the original manuscript, July 30, 2013.
67. Greg Dooley, "How Captain Conley Got His Charm Back," http://mvictors.com/?/p=11369, accessed October 3, 2013.
68. Ibid.
69. Ibid.
70. Ibid.

71. Bill Laskey, "This I Remember," op. cit., 4.

72. Bill Yearby, comment at Bump Elliott Tribute, 2004, transcript, Bump Elliott Tribute, 23.

73. Bob Pille, "Michigan's 34-7 Win 'Didn't Just Happen,'" *Detroit Free Press*, January 3, 1965; Clank Stoppels, "'M' Stakes Claim as Best in Nation After Rose Bowl Rout," *Grand Rapids Press*, January 2, 1965; Taylor quoted in Finch, "Michigan Mighty, Beavers Bad," *Los Angeles Times*, January 2, 1965.

74. Pille, "Michigan's 34-7 Win 'Didn't Just Happen,'" *Detroit Free Press*, January 3, 1965, op. cit.

75. Jerry Mader, comments on original manuscript, February 2014.

Afterword

1. James Conley, comments at Bump Elliott Tribute, Transcript, Bump Elliott Tribute, 5.

2. For accounts of Ohio State's two-point conversion attempt in 1968, and the controversy over whether Coach Woody Hayes actually called for the two-point effort, see Dave Hyde, *1968: The Year That Saved Ohio State Football* (Wilmington, OH: Orange Frazer Press, 2008) 207-09, and Rosenberg, *War as They Knew It*, 10-11.

3. UM-BHL, SB-50, Jerry Green, "Player, Coach, AD, Bump Fits Rose Bowl," *Detroit News*, December 13, 1981. Bo Schembechler recounted the interview that led to his hiring as Bump Elliott's successor, as well as his interactions with Elliott and Don Canham during that process, in Bo Schembechler and John U. Bacon, *Bo's Lasting Lessons: The Legendary Coach Teaches the Timeless Fundamentals of Leadership* (New York: Business Plus, 2007) 22-23. For Don Canham's account of his selection of Elliott as Michigan's first associate athletic director, see Canham with Paladino *From the Inside*, 91-96.

4. Schembechler with Bacon, *Bo's Lasting Lessons*, 55.

5. UM-BHL, UMAD, Individual Files Box 44, Chalmers "Bump" Elliott, no author "ATHLETIC DIRECTOR, Chalmers 'Bump' Elliott," 1-2; see also Jim Cnockaert, "Iowa Spotlight Shines on Bump," *Ann Arbor News* October 19, 1990; also, Bump Elliott, interview.

6. Cnockaert, "Iowa Spotlight Shines on Bump," *Ann Arbor News*, October 19, 1990, op. cit.; Bump Elliott, interview.

7. Don Dufek, interview.

8. "Coaching History, Dennis Fitzgerald," http://coachingroots.com/football/coaches/dennis-fitzgerald," accessed June 3, 2013.

9. "Former U-M football player/coach Henry Fonde dies," http://www.mlive.com/wolverines/football/index.ssf/2009/05/former..., accessed June 3, 2013.

10. "Bob Hollway," http://coachingroots.com/football/coaches/bob-hollway, accessed September 20, 2013.

11. Hemingway, *Life Among the Wolverines*, 209.

12. Corky Simpson, "Mason Never Quite the Same After His Tucson Experience," *Tucson Citizen Morgue*, July 25, 1994, op. cit.

13. "Jocko Nelson, '50," https://gustavo.edu/athletes/hall of fame/?id=304, accessed June 7, 2013.

14. UM-BHL, SIO, "Michigan Sport News," mailed November 3, 1964; see also UM-BHL, SIO, Box 13, Football Media Guides, 1931-, *1996 Football Media Guide*, 212, hereinafter cited as *1996 Football Media Guide*, page; see also "Bob Timberlake," in Goldenbach, *Where Have You Gone?*, 198-99.

15. UM-BHL, UMAD, Individual Files, "Bob Timberlake"; also, "Bob Timberlake," in Goldenbach, *Where Have You Gone?*, 198-99.

16. *1996 Football Media Guide*, 212; Anthony, "This I Remember," op. cit., 15.

17. *1996 Football Media Guide*, 212; see also "Carl Ward," http://www.pro-football-reference.com/players/W/Ward/ca-20.htm accessed September 5, 2003.

18. E-mail message, Jim Detwiler to Bruce Geelhoed, June 18, 2013. See also "Jim Detwiler," in Goldenbach, *Where Have You Gone?*, 57-58.

19. *1996 Football Media Guide*, 212; Henderson, "This I Remember," op. cit.; see also "John Henderson," http://www.pro-football-reference.com/players/W/Ward/ca-20.htm, accessed September 5, 2013.

20. *1996 Football Media Guide*, 212-14; see also "Steve Smith," http://www.pro-football-reference.com/players/S/SmitSt20htm, accessed September 5, 2013.

21. E-mail message, Ben Farabee to Bruce Geelhoed, September 19, 2013.

22. *1996 Football Media Guide*, 212-14; Tom Mack, "This I Remember," op. cit.; see also "Tom Mack," profootballhalfof.com/hof/member.aspx?PLAYER ID=137, accessed Sep-

tember 23, 137; also, communication from Tom Mack to Jerry Mader in Transcript, *Bump Elliott Tribute*, 24–25.

23. *1996 Football Media Guide*, 212–14; "Charles G. Kines," obituary notice; *Warren Tribune Chronicle*, September 7, 2010, http://www.tribtoday.com.page/content.detail/id/546633/Charles G..., accessed September 20, 2013; see also "Charles Kines," http://prject.militarytimes.com/citations-medals-wards/recipient.p, accessed September 23, 2013.

24. Brian P. Patchen biography, included in e-mail message, Brian Patchen to Bruce Geelhoed, July 5, 2013.

25. *1996 Football Media Guide*, 212–14; see also "Jack Clancy," http://www.pro-football-references.com/players/C/ClanJ).htm, accessed September 5, 2103.

26. "Wally Gabler," http://cfapedia.com/Players/g/gabler_wally.htm, accessed September 5, 2013.

27. Dave Fisher, "This I Remember," op. cit.

28. E-mail message, Pete Hollis to Bruce Geelhoed, June 18, 2013.

29. E-mail message, Peter K. Mair to Bruce Geelhoed, June 17, 2013.

30. E-mail message, Thomas Parkhill to Bruce Geelhoed, June 17, 2013.

31. E-mail message, Gary Schick to Bruce Geelhoed, September 4, 2013.

32. E-mail message, Jim Seiber to Bruce Geelhoed, August 13, 2013.

33. UM-BHL, UMAD, Individual Files, Box 69, "Stan Kemp." See also http://digicoll.library.wisc.edu/egi,bin/entit..., accessed September 23, 2013.

34. Conley, "This I Remember," op. cit., 15.

35. *1996 Football Media Guide*, 212; Dave Brandon, "Remembering Bill Yearby," in Dave Brandon, "Brandon's Blog," op. cit.

36. *1996 Football Media Guide*, 212; see also "Arnold Simkus," http://pro-football-reference.com/players/s/SimkAr20.htm, accessed September 5, 2013.

37. *1996 Football Media Guide*, 212; see also "Bill Keating," http://www.pro-football-reference.com/players/K/KeatB; 20htm., accessed September 5, 2013; http://www.keatingwagner.com/blog/staff/william-l-keating/, accessed September 24, 2013.

38. E-mail message, John Yanz to Bruce Geelhoed, June 13, 2013.

39. "Jerry Mader," biography, attached to e-mail message, Jerry Mader to Bruce Geelhoed, June 16, 2013.

40. E-mail message, Bill Laskey to Bruce Geelhoed, June 19, 2013. The message contains a personal account by Bill Laskey, entitled "Bill Laskey's Football Flashbacks," that explains his college and professional football career.

41. Cecchini, "This I Remember," op. cit.; see also "Tom Cecchini," http://www.profootballarchives.com/cccc00020coach.html, accessed September 24, 2013.

42. E-mail message, Charles B. Dehlin to Bruce Geelhoed, op. cit.

43. "Frank Nunley: 10 year Club," http://www.49ers.com/news/artilce-1/Frank-Nunley-10-Year-Club-... accessed September 24, 2013.

44. *1996 Football Media Guide*, 212; Rick Volk, "This I Remember," op. cit.; see also "Rick Volk," http://www.pro-football-reference.com/players/V/VolkR.00.htm., accessed September 5, 2–13; see also John Steadman, "Volk Family Tree Branches Out from Foundation of Football Success," *Baltimore Sun*, September 28, 1990.

45. Rick Sygar, "This I Remember—1964," op. cit.; Steadman, "Volk Family Tree," *Baltimore Sun*, September 28, 1990, op. cit.

46. Richard Rindfuss, telephone conversation with Bruce Geelhoed, September 23, 2013.

47. E-mail message, Dick Wells to Bruce Geelhoed, September 16, 2013.

48. *1996 Football Media Guide*, 212; see also "Mike Bass NFL Career Highlights," http://www.mtbass.com/mike-bass-nfl-career-highlights.htm, accessed September 25, 2013.

49. Ibid.

50. *1996 Football Media Guide*; John Rowser, "This I Remember," from game program, Michigan vs. Arizona, October 7, 1978, in Bump Elliott Collection, *This I Remember: Michigan '64;* see also "John Rowser," http://www.database.football.com/players/playerpage.htm?, accessed September 25, 2013.

51. E-mail message and telephone conversation, Robert Mielke to Bruce Geelhoed, January 30, 2014.

52. Letter, C. Michael Gorte to Bruce Geelhoed, September 5, 2013; telephone interview, Michale Gorte with the author.

53. E-mail message, Pat O'Donnell to Bruce Geelhoed, February 1, 2014.

Appendix

1. The source for the format and information contained in the APPENDIX is found in the Bump Elliot Collection, *Game Programs: Michigan '64*, game program, Michigan vs. U.S. Air Force, September 26, 1964, 24. The author

has revised and, in some cases corrected, information in the program that was not accurate. The information in the game program for Michigan's game against Air Force remained the same in subsequent programs for Michigan's games against its other opponents in 1964. The information in the game program for the Rose Bowl, against Oregon State, differed significantly, however, since Michigan only took 44 players to that game.

2. Barry Dehlin is listed in the game program as a fullback but, in 1964, he played almost exclusively on defense as a linebacker.

3. Michael Gorte also played linebacker at Michigan, while being listed in the game program as a halfback.

4. Michael Gorte was a senior in 1964, not a junior, as was listed in the game program. See letter, C. Michael Gorte to Bruce Geelhoed, September 5, 2013.

5. Stan Kemp was listed as an end in the game program, which is accurate. But Kemp's role on the team was as its punter. There was no designation in the game program for the punter, hence the revision herein.

6. Frank Nunley's position in the game program is listed as center, which is accurate. When Nunley entered the starting lineup in Michigan's game against Minnesota, however, replacing the injured Barry Dehlin, he played primarily at the linebacker position, in that game as well as for the rest of the 1964 season.

7. Raymond O'Donnell was better known on the team as Pat O'Donnell.

8. Brian Patchen is listed, erroneously, in the game program as a junior. He was a senior. Unfortunately, Patchen was also listed as a junior, not as a senior, in the game program for the Rose Bowl.

9. Rick Volk wore #49, not #21, throughout the 1964 season. He also played primarily at defensive halfback. In the game program for the Rose Bowl, he is shown correctly as wearing #49.

Bibliography

Manuscript Collections

University of Michigan, Bentley Historical Library, Department of Intercollegiate Athletics-Football.
National Collegiate Athletic Association. Archives, 1964 and 1965 NCAA Football Yearbooks.
The Ohio State University Archives, Department of Athletics.

Unpublished Sources in the Author's Possession

Laskey, Bill. *Bill Laskey's Football Flashbacks: Fifteen Years of Memories.*
Scouting Report, Richard Ruble, "Purdue–Michigan, October 17, 1964."

Newspapers and Periodicals

Ann Arbor News
Chicago Tribune
Christian Science Monitor
Columbus Dispatch
Des Moines Register
Detroit Free Press
Detroit News
Grand Rapids Press
Indianapolis News
Indianapolis Star
[Lansing] State Journal
Los Angeles Times
Michigan Daily
New York Times
Sports Illustrated
Time
Toledo Blade

Published Sources

Allen, Kevin, Nate Brown, and Art Regner, eds. *What It Means to Be a Wolverine*. Chicago: Triumph Books, 2005.
Canham, Donald B., with Larry Paladino. *From the Inside: A Half Century of Michigan Athletics*. Ann Arbor: Olympia Sports Press, 1996.
Dent, Jim. *Resurrection: The Miracle Season That Saved Notre Dame Football*. New York: Thomas Dunne, 2009.
Emmanuel, Greg. *The 100-Yard War: Inside the 100-Year-Old Michigan–Ohio State Football Rivalry*. New York: John Wiley and Sons, 2004.

Fitzgerald, Francis, ed. *A Legacy of Champions.* Farmington Hills, MI: CTC Productions and Sports, 1996.
Frimodig, Lyman L., and Fred W. Stabley. *Spartan Saga: A History of Michigan State Athletics.* East Lansing: Michigan State University, 1971.
Goldenbach, Alan, ed. *Where Have You Gone?* New York: Skyhorse, 2012.
Green, Jerry. *Michigan Football Vault.* Florence, AL: Whitman, 2008.
Hemingway, Thomas C. *Life Among the Wolverines: An Inside View of Michigan Sports.* South Bend, IN: Diamond Communications, 1985.
Hyde, Dave. *1968: The Year That Saved Ohio State Football.* Wilmington, OH: Orange Frazer Press, 2008.
Hyman, Mervin D., and Gordon S. White, Jr. *Big Ten Football: Its Life and Times, Great Coaches, Players, and Games.* New York: Macmillan, 1997.
Kryk, John. *Natural Enemies: The Notre Dame–Michigan Football Feud.* Kansas City, MO: Andrews and McMeel, 1994.
Nelson, David M. *Football, Its Rules, and the Men Who Made the Game.* Newark: University of Delaware Press, 1994.
Perry, Will. *The Wolverines: A Story of Michigan Football.* Huntsville, AL: Strode, 1974.
Roberts, Randy. *A Team for America: The Army–Navy Game That Rallied a Nation.* Boston: Houghton Mifflin Harcourt, 2011.
_____, and Ed Krzemienski. *Rising Tide: Bear Bryant, Joe Namath, & Dixie's Last Quarter.* New York: Grand Central Publishing, 2013.
Rosenberg, Michael. *War as They Knew It: Woody Hayes, Bo Schembechler, and America in a Time of Unrest.* New York: Grand Central Publishing, 2008.
Schembechler, Bo, with John U. Bacon. *Bo's Lasting Lessons: The Legendary Coach Teaches the Timeless Fundamentals of Leadership.* New York: Business Plus, 2007.
_____, with Dan Ewald. *Tradition: Bo Schembechler's Michigan Memories.* Ann Arbor: Clock Tower Press, 2003.
Stowers, Carlton. *Staubach: Portrait of the Brightest Star.* Chicago: Triumph Books, 2010.
Vare, Robert. *Buckeye.* New York: Harper's Magazine Press, 1974.
Walsh, Christopher. *Michigan Football: Guide and Record Book.* Chicago: Triumph Books, 2009.

Oral History

Bump Elliott Tribute, 40th Anniversary Reception: 1964 Rose Bowl Team, September 24, 2004, Robert H. Lurie Engineering Building, University of Michigan. Transcribed and edited by E. Bruce Geelhoed and Michael W. Smith, Ball State University, August, 2013.

Compact Disc Recording

Maximum Meechigan: The Best of Bob Ufer. Double CD set. Ann Arbor, MI: World Class Tapes.

Interviews by the Author

James Conley
Donald Dufek
Chalmers (Bump) Elliott
Michael Gorte
Thomas Krzemienski

Gerald Mader
Robert Mielke
Randy Minniear
Richard Ruble
Richard Sygar

Index

Acks, Ron 121, 122
Agase, Alex 15, 16, 110, 112, 113
Air Force (United States Air Force Academy) 19, 23, 33, 37, 44, 58, 59, 66, 67, 76, 89, 91, 92, 133, 188, 201; 1964 game vs. Michigan 43, 47–55
Allen, Bernie 88
Allison, Bruce 59, 187, 203
Amdor, Steve 50
American Football Coaches Association (AFCA) 35
American Football League (AFL) 190, 191, 195, 196, 199, 200
Ammon, Harry 72, 76, 80, 83
Ancona, Perry 203
Ann Arbor Bank and Trust 197
Ann Arbor City Council 197
Ann Arbor News 20, 39, 42, 118, 119
Annis, Jerry 102
Anthony, Mel 14, 16–18, 21, 32, 40, 45, 47, 50–52, 54, 60–62, 64, 65, 70, 76, 81–83, 90, 95, 96, 104–107, 110–113, 119–124, 129–131, 133–136, 145, 149, 150, 154, 156, 159, 161, 165, 167, 175–181, 183–185, 189, 190, 195, 203
Apple, R.W., Jr. 74
Arizona Daily Star 194
Army (United States Military Academy) 14, 34, 43, 44, 55, 142, 196
Athletic Association of Western Universities (AAWU) 168, 169, 171
Auburn University 36

Bacigalupo, Phil 50
Bacon, John U. 2
Bailey, Donald 18, 203
Baker, Lou 120
Baltimore Colts (NFL) 195, 200
Balzhiser, Dick 33

Banaszek, Casimir 110, 111
Barrington, Tom 140, 143, 145, 149–152, 154
Bartlett, Charles 115
Bass, Mike 12, 18, 31, 40, 45, 48, 64, 130, 132, 191, 201, 203
Bechtel Power Corporation 196
Bellino, Joe 44
Bentley, Rahn 72, 76, 80
Bentley Historical Library, University of Michigan 3, 8, 11, 18, 26, 29, 39, 54, 67, 72, 76, 78, 79–81, 84, 93, 94, 99, 111, 117, 123, 125, 132, 147, 153, 155, 158, 160, 174, 178, 182, 337
Bevan, Bill 103, 105
Bickel, Bruce 57
Bierowicz, Don 72, 76
Big Ten Conference 1–3, 5–7, 12, 14, 15, 17, 19, 21, 23, 24, 25, 38, 39, 41, 42, 44, 45, 48, 56, 58, 66, 68, 69, 71, 72, 74, 85, 87, 88, 89, 97, 98, 100, 102 103, 106, 110, 113–115, 117, 118, 120, 127–129, 133, 135, 136, 138–145, 148, 164–168, 172, 185, 187, 188, 191, 192, 199
"Bird Dogs" 28
Blaik, Earl (Red) 34, 35
Blanchard, Doc 44
Blech, Scott 20
Bobich, Lou 70, 72, 75–78, 83
Boisture, Dan 72
Borchardt, Jack 33
Bossons, Robert 102
Brandstatter, Jim 2
Briggstock, Tom 59, 203
Brown, Aaron 103, 105, 107, 108
Brown, Jim 120
Brueggers, Bob 103
Bruhn, Milt 6, 87
Bryant, Paul "Bear" 73

231

Index

Budzik, Bernard 130
Buffalo Bills (AFL) 191
Bullard, Bill 20
Bullough, Henry (Hank) 72
Burns, Jerry 30, 110, 128, 130, 132
Burns, Jim 110
Burroughs Corporation 201
Butkus, Dick 22, 118, 120–122, 124, 125, 167
Butler, Dave 13, 17, 18, 31, 40, 45, 47, 48, 63, 76, 92, 94, 96, 108, 120, 124, 125, 147, 159, 167, 175, 181, 203
Buzynski, John 203

Callaghan, Rich 121
Callahan, Brian 103
Campbell, Woody 110–112
Canadian Football League (CFL) 191, 197
Canham, Don 2, 191, 192
Cannavino, Andy 199
Capital Internal Medicine 200
Carillot, Vince 72
Carroll, Jim 23
Cartwright, Henry 203
Cecchini, Tom 11, 18, 31, 38, 40, 45, 48, 51, 60–63, 77, 78, 85, 90, 91, 108, 113, 121, 132, 135, 144, 146–149, 152, 155, 167, 176, 180, 191, 200, 203
Centurion Ministries (Princeton, New Jersey) 198
Cerne, Joe 110
Chandler, Bob 70
Chappuis, Bob 30, 31, 86, 184
Charles, John 88, 91, 95, 97
Chicago Sun Times 109
Chicago Tribune Silver Football award 1, 7
Chonko, Arnold 140, 141, 151, 153
Ciampi, Sal 88
Clancy, Jack 16, 31, 40, 56, 113, 191, 197, 203
Clark, Lyal 140
Cleveland Browns (NFL) 195, 199
Cmejrek, Carl 203
College of William and Mary 35, 56, 57, 58
Columbus Dispatch 145, 146, 161
Conley, James F. 86, 87
Conley, Jim 11, 17, 18, 23, 28, 36, 37, 39, 46, 47, 50, 63, 65, 77, 78, 83, 85–87, 90, 97, 108, 113, 119–122, 125, 137, 144, 145, 151, 152, 156, 164, 165, 167, 173–176, 187, 188, 190, 199, 203
Connelly, John 59
Cooke, L.J. 101
Costanza, Willie 103
Cotton, Eddie 72, 76
Cotton Bowl 55
Coxon, Dr. William 119, 120

Crawford, Denver 102
Crawford Mazur Company 199
Crimmins, Bernie 88
Crisler, H.O. "Fritz" 7, 18, 25, 26, 34, 35, 39, 41, 43, 116, 119, 145, 161, 167, 187, 188, 191
Crockett, Bill 103
Crowley, Jim 14
Cuozzo, Gary 195
Curtice, Jack 35
Custardo, Fred 12, 118–120, 122
Czarnota, Dick 50

Damer, Roy 19, 142
Danhof, Jerome 203
Daugherty, Hugh "Duffy" 5, 25, 26, 35, 36, 70–74, 77, 80, 81, 83–87
Davis, Glenn 44
Dawkins, Pete 44
Dawson, Lennie 88
DeFilippo, Lou 88
Dehlin, Barry 11, 17, 18, 31, 40, 41, 48, 56, 77, 81, 83, 91, 96, 102, 113, 173, 175, 183, 200, 203
De Moss, Bob 88, 89
De Neff, Wayne 20, 21, 39, 40, 42, 118, 119
Denver Broncos (NFL) 199, 200, 202
Detroit Free Press 14, 20, 56, 188
Detroit Lions (NFL) 103, 193, 196, 201
Detroit News 20, 56, 161, 186, 191
Detroit Newspaper Strike, July–November, 1964 18, 20–22
Detroit Pencil Company 198
Detwiler, Jim 14–16, 18, 23, 27, 32, 40, 42, 43, 47, 50–54, 60–62, 64, 65, 67, 75, 76, 89, 92, 106–108, 110, 113, 123–125, 129–131, 134, 135, 145, 151–156, 160, 162, 175, 176, 181–183, 191, 195, 203
Deutsch, Phillip 129
Devaney, Bob 35
DiGravio, Ron 88
Donnelly, George 121, 124, 126
Donnelly, Pat 59, 61, 62, 63
Dooley, Greg 101, 187
Dreffer, Steve 140, 149, 154, 155
Dufek, Don 8, 9, 11, 17, 18, 27, 28, 30, 31, 49, 58, 59, 72, 144, 162, 167, 172, 174, 178, 179, 191, 192, 193
Dufek, Patricia 193
Duncan, Lloyd 50, 51, 57
Duniec, Brian 120, 122

Earle & Patchen, P.A. 197
East Catholic High School (Detroit) 199
Eastern Michigan University 9, 202
Eby, Ken 88, 89, 135
Eddy, Nick 23

Eickman, Gary 121, 126
Electric Power Research Institute (EPRI) 199
Eliot, Ray 6
Eller, Carl 193
Elliott, Alice 116, 118
Elliott, Chalmers W. (Bump) 1–3, 5, 7–11, 13–15, 17–28, 30–33, 35–42, 44–48, 52–56, 58, 59, 61, 64, 65, 66, 69–71, 75, 77, 78, 81–83, 85–87, 93, 95–98, 100, 102–104, 106, 109–113, 115–122, 124–126, 128, 129, 131, 134–139, 144, 146–148, 150–152, 154, 156, 157, 159–161, 163, 167, 173–177, 179, 181, 183, 184, 187–194, 198, 200
Elliott, Dr. J. Norman 116
Elliott, Pete 6, 19, 115–117, 119–122, 125, 128
Ellison, Glenn 140
Ellwood, Frank 140
Emmanuel, Greg 2
Engle, Rip 142
Etter, Les 103
Evashevski, Forest "Frosty" 17, 42, 45, 47, 48, 56, 61, 64, 104, 105, 106, 120, 126, 131, 158, 183, 203
Evashevski, Forest, Sr. 5, 7, 116, 128, 167

Falk, Jon 2
Farabee, Ben 13, 15, 18, 31, 39, 64, 103, 104, 106, 110, 124, 129, 131, 149, 151, 152, 154, 175, 177, 179, 196, 203
Farthing, Fred 103, 104, 107, 108
Faust, Paul 103
Fausti, Gary 50
Feola, Tom 57
Ferance, Russell 129
Fesler, Wes 5
Fette, Thomas 203
Fiesta Bowl 194
Filipiak, Steve 127
Fisher, Dave 18, 32, 33, 40, 42, 45, 48, 64, 66, 95–97, 106, 107, 112, 113, 123, 126, 135, 145, 179, 182, 183, 197, 203
Fitzgerald, Dennis 8, 9, 11, 18, 49, 167, 191, 193
Flanagan, Dennis 28, 29
Flanagan, Ed 88
Flint Journal 137
Foley, Terry 136
Fonde, Henry (Hank) 7–9, 11, 14, 18, 27, 28, 152, 167, 177, 193
Ford Motor Company 196, 199, 202
Fort Dix, New Jersey 196
Fort Knox, Kentucky 196
Foss, Don 88
Four Horsemen (Notre Dame) 14
Fouts, Jack 9, 10, 27, 28, 31–33, 162

Frazee, Freeman "Smoky" 20
Freeman, Jim 59
Friedman, Benny 43
Fry, Hayden 140
Funk, Bob 140, 150
Fuson, Wayne 97

Gabler, Wally 45, 59, 64, 191, 197, 204
Gallinagh, Patrick 75, 86
Garcia, Jim 88, 94
Gator Bowl 49
Gehrke, Delbert 129
General Motors Corporation 198, 199
Georgia Tech 65
Giacobazzi, Tony 130
Gillingham, Gale 103
Goovert, Ron 72, 76
Gordon, Dick 72, 85, 127
Gorges, Tom 50
Gorte, Michael 17, 18, 59, 202, 204
Gorte & Day Law firm 202
Graff, Lloyd 20, 162
Grammer, Don 102
Grand Rapids Press 20, 59, 72, 188
Grand Valley State College (later Grand Valley State University) 192, 193
Grant, Bud 193, 194
Greathouse, Boarden 30
Green, Jerry 2, 56, 191
Green Bay Packers 58, 197, 198, 200–202
Greene, Edward 204
Greenlee, Fritz 50
Greth, Jim 50
Griese, Bob 88–93, 96, 97, 127, 136
Gustavus Adolphus College 194

Hadrick, Bob 88–92, 97, 127, 135
Hager, Allen 88
Hahn, Rich 11, 17, 18, 32, 40, 41, 47, 56, 60, 63, 64, 91, 96, 102, 113, 114, 173, 183, 204
Hamilton Tiger Cats (CFL) 197
Hankinson, John 103–105, 107–109, 135
Hanlon, Jerry 193
Hansen, Don 121
Hanseth, George 50
Happel, Bill 128
Hardin, Wayne 55, 56, 64, 65
Hardy, William 204
Harig, Peter 74
Harkema, Jim 192
Harkins, Don 153
Harkleroad, Wendell 50
Harmon, Tom 5, 43, 86, 116, 174
Hart, Jack 120
Hatcher, Dr. Harlan 146, 162, 163
Haverstock, Thomas 204

Hayes, Woody 2, 5, 26, 44, 139–143, 145, 146, 151, 154, 157, 161
Heckert, Don 50
Hemingway, Tom 2, 13, 35, 38, 39, 45, 48, 53, 61, 80, 91, 97, 105, 106, 109, 126, 148, 152, 194
Henderson, John 15, 17, 18, 21, 23, 27, 30, 32, 39, 42, 45, 47, 50–52, 59, 60, 70, 76, 77, 80–86, 90, 105, 110, 111, 119, 120, 123, 124, 130, 131, 133–136, 145, 149, 151, 152, 156, 157, 162, 167, 175–179, 190, 196, 204
Henderson, Neil 59–62
Herndon, Bob 120
Hilkene, Bruce 199
Hindman, Hugh 140
Hitsabeck, Daniel 129
Hoag, Phil 78
Hodoway, Stephen 129
Hoerner, Bob 74
Holaday, Bart 52
Holcomb, Stu 87
Hollis, Pete 45, 197, 204
Hollway, Bob 8–11, 17, 18, 27, 28, 40, 47, 59, 76, 91, 102, 113, 121, 123, 130, 137, 144, 149, 150, 157, 167, 176, 180, 189, 191, 193, 194, 200
Honeywell Corporation 196
Hoover Ball and Bearing Company 199
Hopp, Bob 88
Hornung, Paul (reporter for *Columbus Dispatch*) 145, 161, 162
Houston Oilers (AFL) 196
Howard, Bill 88
Howard, Desmond 2
Hoyne, Jeff 18, 31, 48, 81, 204
Hribal, James 204
Huarte, John 22, 23, 167, 169

I-75 Backfield 47, 50, 51, 54, 60, 61, 63–65, 76, 89, 100, 103, 105, 107, 108–111, 113, 129, 131, 133, 134, 135, 175
Illinois Wesleyan University 116
Indiana University 71, 110, 114, 141, 143, 172
Indianapolis News 97
Ingrahan, Duncan 57, 60
Ingwessen, Burt 120
Iowa Stadium 129, 132, 133

Jackson, Scott 50
Jacobs Engineering Corporation 196
Jaggers, Ken 50
Jansen, Jon 199
Japinga, Don 72, 83
Jardine, John 88
Jardine, Len 88
Jarvis, Jeff 50, 52

Jauch, Ray 128
Jenkins, Dan 19
Johnson, Herm 72, 76
Johnson, Wallace 102
Jones, Clinton 72–74, 76–78, 80
Jordan, Ralph "Shug" 36
Juday, Steve 12, 70, 72, 76, 77, 79, 80, 81, 84, 85

Kadar, Rich 141
Kalamazoo College 193
Kaminski, Larry 88
Karpinski, John 72, 76
Keating, Bill 11, 18, 31, 40, 47, 48, 56, 134, 176, 180, 191, 199, 204
Keating, Tom 41, 120
Keating, Wagner, Polidori, Free Law firm 199
Kee, Dick 121
Kelley, Ike 140, 154
Kelly, Black, Black, Earle, & Patchen P.A. 197; *see also* Earle & Patchen, P.A.
Kemp, Cass 30, 204
Kemp, Stan 12, 13, 18, 30, 31, 49, 52, 55, 60, 66, 77, 79–81, 90, 92, 100, 108, 109, 121, 122, 126, 129, 130, 148–154, 161, 175–177, 180, 198, 204
Kenney, Dick 72, 73, 78, 80
Kenton, Bruce 57, 59, 60, 62
Kettering High School (Detroit) 198
Kimble, Dalton 129, 130, 133
Kines, Charlie 13, 18, 28, 29, 32, 40, 45, 47, 48, 76, 175, 191, 196, 197, 204
King, Charlie 88
Kirby, Craig 31, 39, 58, 60, 62, 64, 66, 107, 110, 182, 204
Knapp, George 204
Kodros, Archie 128
Kornacki, Steve 2
Kramer, Kent 103, 105, 107, 109, 135
Kramer, Ron 58, 64
Krause, Paul 129
Kryk, John 2
Krzemienski, Ed 73
Krzemienski, Tom 72, 73, 76, 86
Kuzniewski, John 88

Lanagan, Mike 50
Landsittel, Thomas 204
Lansing State Journal 74
Larsen, Gary 193
Larson, Dick 102
Laskey, Bill 11, 17, 18, 21, 23, 30, 31, 39, 47, 56, 78, 104, 109, 111, 120, 121, 131, 132, 145, 146, 148, 149, 163, 173, 176, 180, 188, 191, 200, 204

Index

Laskey, Durward 30
Last, Kenny 103, 107–109
Lattimore, Earl 72
Layden, Elmer 14, 181
Leahy, Frank 23
Lee, Louis 18, 48, 64, 183, 204
Leiser, Tom 59
Levy, Marv 35
Lewis, Sherman 70, 72
Lilja, George 199
Lindsey, Leon 143
Little Brown Jug 6, 99–101, 106, 109, 113
Lofquist, Kraig 103, 107–109
Long, Dave 129, 130
Long, Jim 88
Lopes, Roger 70
Los Angeles Rams (NFL) 196
LoSavage, Jim 20
Losh, Dr. Hazel "Doc" 146
Lucas, Harold 72, 127
Lukasik, Larry 72, 80

Mack, Tom 13, 18, 23, 32, 40, 41, 45, 47, 48, 63, 76, 159, 167, 175, 178, 191, 196, 204
Macuga, Ed 72, 76
Mader, Jerry 11, 17, 18, 31, 40, 48, 120, 122, 123, 130, 131, 133, 149, 199, 204
Mader & Associates 199
Mair, Peter 197, 198, 204
Maize and Blue Machine 10, 13, 16, 137
Manchester (Michigan) High School 198
Marchlewski, Frank 103
Marcum, John 13, 17, 18, 31, 40, 47, 76, 92, 120, 124, 125, 160, 175, 181, 204
Marine Corps V-12 Program 116
Markus, Robert 141
Marlin, Fred 59
Marquette University 195
Marshall, Jim 193
Martin, Ben 49, 52, 53
Mason, Tony 9–14, 28, 29, 38–40, 45, 50, 83, 85, 97, 106, 108, 132, 145, 152, 167, 173, 177, 181, 183, 193, 194, 198, 203, 204
Mason Consolidated Schools (Temperance Michigan) 198
Mayes, Eric 199
McCarty, Doug 59, 61, 63
McCormick, Dave 72, 76, 77, 79, 80, 83, 84, 85
McDonald, Andy 128
McDowell, Ivory 129
McKay, John 36, 141, 169–172
McKelvey, Dave 111
McKinley High School (Niles, Ohio) 9, 28, 29, 145, 203–205
McLaughlin, David 204

McVay, John 72
Mellinger, Steve 72
Messner, Mark 199
Metzger, Lynn 144
Meyer Morton Award 13
MFC Global 199
Miami Dolphins 197, 199, 201
Miami University of Ohio 140, 192
Micheloson, John 57
Michigan Daily 20, 56, 144, 162
Michigan Marching Band 146, 154
Michigan Stadium 33, 35, 49, 52, 59, 65, 70, 89, 90, 101, 103, 108, 109, 120, 124, 126, 127, 146, 150, 190
Michigan State University 1, 5, 6, 7, 12, 19, 21–23, 25, 31, 35, 38, 45, 56, 66, 70–72, 88, 91, 93–96, 110, 113–115, 118, 135, 136, 139, 143, 146, 165, 172, 186–188, 203; 1964 game vs. Michigan 69, 73–87; 1964 game vs. Purdue 126–128
Mid-American Conference 87, 198
Mielke, Bob 11, 18, 31, 40, 48, 91, 102, 105, 113, 121, 131, 132, 176, 177, 180, 181, 184, 204
Migyanka, Charlie 72, 76, 82
Miller, Don 14
Miller, Leo 130
Miller, Paul V. 74
Minnesota Vikings (NFL) 193, 194, 196, 199, 200
Minniear, Randy 88–92, 96, 97, 127, 135, 136
Minor, Bill 121
Mintline, Doug 137
Mitchell, Robert 129
Mollenkopf, Jack 87, 88, 91, 97, 127, 136
Morel, Jim 88, 90
Moreland, Daniel 129
Morgan Guaranty Trust Company 197
Morrison, Bruce 109
Moses, Mickey 130, 134
Mueller, Dave 121
Muir, Bill 17, 18, 120, 204
Munn, Clarence "Biggie" 5, 25, 71, 73
Munson, Oscar 101
Murphy, Dr. Bob 158
Murphy, Steve 110
Murphy, Tim 50, 51, 52
Myers, Tommy 12, 110–112

Nash, Butch 102
National Broadcasting Company (NBC) 21
National Collegiate Athletic Association (NCAA) 21, 25, 28–30, 32, 35, 192, 194; Football Rules Committee 3, 33, 34, 36
National Football League (NFL) 190, 191, 193, 195, 196, 198, 200, 201, 202

Navy (United States Naval Academy) 1, 6, 8, 12, 16, 17, 19, 21, 22, 44, 49, 56, 57, 70, 71, 76, 89, 91, 93, 96, 116, 142, 188; 1964 game vs. Michigan 43, 55, 58–69
Nelson, Jack (Jocko) 9, 11, 18, 27, 28, 31, 39, 58, 59, 102, 129, 167, 180, 191, 194
Nemeth, Bill 50
New Orleans Saints (NFL) 195
New York Giants (NFL) 195, 201
New York Jets (AFL) 199
New York Times 74
Newsome, Jerome 103
Neyland, General Bob 34
Niland, John 130
Niles, Ohio 9, 12, 13, 28, 29, 38, 83, 112, 140, 145, 201, 203–205
Niles Special 82–84, 86, 89, 90, 110, 112
Noonan, Karl 129, 130, 132–134
Nord, Fred 103
Northwestern University 12, 15, 71, 87, 103, 118, 138, 143, 145, 150, 172, 188; 1964 game vs. Michigan 98–100, 110–114
Norton, Almond T. 74
Nourse, Craig 129, 130, 131
Nunley, Frank 11, 18, 21, 23, 31, 41, 42, 48, 91, 102–104, 111, 113, 121, 122, 132, 149, 150, 154, 176, 191, 200, 204

Oakland Raiders (AFL) 202
O'Donnell, Joe 119, 120
O'Donnell, Pat 202, 204
O'Gorman, Joe 50
O'Hara, Rich 130, 132, 133
Ohio Stadium 145, 148, 150, 152, 156
The Ohio State University 1, 2, 7, 12, 13, 16, 20–25, 27, 33, 44, 45, 71, 97, 98, 113–115, 118, 120, 128, 129, 132, 135, 137, 138–168, 171, 172, 175, 176, 187, 188, 191, 192, 199; 1964 game vs. Michigan 138–139, 148–162
Ohio University 87
Ohio Wesleyan University 9, 27, 162
Oklahoma National Guard 9
Olson, Rich 110
Oosterbaan, Bennie 7, 9, 116, 119, 167
Oregon State University 12, 20, 116, 166–168, 171–173, 185–188, 194; 1965 Rose Bowl game vs. Michigan 175–184
Orr, Ed (Skip) 59, 60, 61, 63
Otis, Jim 191
Ott, Richard 204
Owens, Buddy 72, 76

Pace, Jimmy 86
Pacific–10 Conference 194
Packard Electric Company 201

Page, Alan 23, 193
Pappas, George 88
Park College 116
Parker, Al 88
Parkhill, Tom 59, 198, 204
Parola, Tony 121
Parseghian, Ara 22, 23, 110, 169, 170
Paskewich, Skip 57, 63
Patchen, Brian 13, 17, 18, 20, 32, 35, 40, 47, 65, 76, 106, 108, 124, 125, 131, 132, 153, 159, 174, 175, 177, 181, 197, 205
Paterno, Joe 142, 143
Paul Bunyan Trophy 70
Paulson, Wayne 121
Pelletier, Jerry 102
Penn State University 23, 56, 57, 114, 128, 142–144
Perry, Will 2
Perrysburg, Ohio 195
Peterson, Larry 103
Philadelphia Eagles (NFL) 196
Philbin, Pat 59, 63
Pille, Bob 14, 15, 188
Piro, "Whitey" 128
Pitlosh, Max 205
Pittsburgh Steelers (NFL) 193, 196, 198, 202
Poretta, Dan 150
Powless, Dave 120
Price, Sam 121, 122, 124
Princeton Theological Seminary 195
Printer's Pressmen Union (Detroit) 20
Procter & Gamble Corporation 195
Prothro, Tommy 1, 172, 175, 176, 179, 184, 185, 186, 188
Pung, Joe 103
Purdue University 1, 2, 11, 19, 23, 38, 41, 66, 71, 87, 88, 98, 100, 102, 105, 106, 113–116, 118, 124, 127–129, 135, 136, 138, 143, 144, 164, 173, 175, 181, 183, 188, 194; 1964 game vs. Michigan 69, 89–97
Purple People Eaters (Minnesota Vikings) 193
Puster, John 50

Ratigan, Timothy 205
Rebitz, Ed 50
Recher, Dave 130
recruiting, importance of 25–33
Rector, Ron 110–112
Reid, Dorie 42, 45, 103, 107, 108, 205
Reid, Mike 103, 107, 108
Rein, Bo 140, 144, 145, 149, 150, 151, 152, 154, 156, 161, 162
Rhome, Jerry 22, 167
Rice, Grantland 14
Rindfuss, Dick 12, 17, 18, 28, 29, 32, 40, 41,

48, 56, 77, 80, 83, 85, 89, 90, 103, 104, 111, 119, 120–122, 124, 130, 150, 176, 201, 205
Rising Tide: Bear Bryant, Joe Namath, & Dixie's Last Stand 73
Rivera, Thomas 159
Roberts, Randy 73
Roberts, Tommy 100, 101
Robinson, Don 110
Robinson, Wayne 128
Rodriguez, Rich 2
Rollins College 201
Romney, George 6, 20, 74
Romney, Lenore 6
Rose Bowl 6–10, 17–21, 25, 36, 41, 68, 69, 71, 88, 102, 115, 117, 127, 128, 139, 143, 146, 148, 150, 159, 160, 164–169, 171–190, 192, 199
Rosen, Don 103
Rosenberg, Michael 2
Ross, Don 72, 76
Rowland, Tom 20
Rowser, John 16, 31, 40, 42, 45, 47, 85, 113, 119, 191, 201, 205
Ruble, Rich 88, 90, 135
Rush, Jerry 72, 76, 80
Russell, Eddie 120, 129
Ruzicka, Charlie 31, 48, 64, 205
Ryan, Jim 60
Ryan, Karlin 129

Sai, Johnny 56
St. Louis Cardinals (NFL) 193, 197
Salem, Joe 102
Samuels, Dale 88
Sander, Willard 140, 145, 149, 150, 156
Sarkkinen, Esko 140, 145
Scarlet and Gray Machine 10, 14
Schembechler, Bo 2, 139, 140, 191, 192, 193, 194, 200
Schick, Gary 59, 198, 205
Schmidt, Joe 103
Schram, Hal 56
Schumacher, Greg 121
Schwager, Mike 110
Schwartz, Nikki 20, 144
Seattle Seahawks (NFL) 193
Seiber, Jim 28, 29, 198, 205
Serr, Gordon 72
Shay, Jerry 88
Shevlin, Maurice 82
Simkus, Arnie 11, 17, 18, 31, 40, 47, 48, 50, 63, 79, 85, 120, 121, 132, 133, 176, 190, 199, 205
Simpson, Gary 129, 130, 132, 134
Singer, Karl 88
Skjei, Stan 103
Smith, Burt 66, 72

Smith, Charles "Bubba" 72, 73, 76
Smith, Dick 110
Smith, Steve 13, 15, 18, 31, 39, 40, 42, 47, 51, 76, 83, 90, 91, 103, 110, 112, 129, 151, 191, 196, 205
Snell, Matt 139
Snitger, Ed 135
Snook, Gary 12, 129, 130–134, 142
Snow, Jack 23, 169
Southern Methodist University (SMU) 140
Sports Illustrated 19
Sproat, Ben 30
Staebler, John 103
Stagg, Frank 205
Stanford University 23, 168, 169, 198
Staten, Randy 103
Staubach, Roger 6, 12, 17, 22, 43, 44, 55–65, 68, 70
Stauber, Gene 120
Stephenson, Curt 2
Stewart, Lynn 121
Stoll, Cal 72
Stoppels, Clark 20, 59, 72, 86, 188
Stowers, Carlton 57
Strobel, Harry 140
Stuhldreher, Harry 14
Summers, Jimmie 72, 73
Sutton, Archie 120
Sygar, Rick 12, 18, 23, 28, 29, 32, 33, 38–40, 42, 45, 47, 48, 52, 53, 61–63, 75, 80–86, 89, 90, 104, 105, 110, 112, 121, 138, 150, 154, 155, 159, 176, 177, 179, 180, 181, 189, 201, 205
Syracuse University 142, 193
Szabo, Steve 60

Taliaferro, Mike 119
Taylor, James 62
Taylor, Kip 7, 116
Taylor, Sec 20, 188
Tellor, Rian 105
Tennant, Brian 205
Teter, Gordon 88, 90, 92, 97, 135
Thornhill, Charlie 72, 73, 127
Timberlake, Bob 1, 14–17, 18, 21–23, 32, 33, 40, 44, 45, 47, 50–56, 59–66, 70, 76, 77, 80–83, 85, 89–96, 100, 103–108, 110–112, 119–126, 130, 131, 133–136, 145, 149–158, 160, 161, 163, 166, 167, 174–177, 179, 181–183, 185, 190, 195, 205
Time magazine 23
Tollstam, Larry 50
Toronto Argonauts (CFL) 191, 197
Toyota Motor Sales 198
Transportation Energy Center (University of Michigan) 200

Triton Junior College 193
Trumpy, Bob 12, 120, 122
Tulane University 200

Ufer, Bob 33, 109, 137
United Press International (UPI) 38, 119, 167
United States Football League (USFL) 193
United States Marines 196
University of Alabama 73, 188
University of Arizona 194
University of California 9, 35, 103, 116–118, 120, 167, 168, 179
University of California–Santa Barbara 35
University of Cincinnati 194
University of Colorado 9
University of Denver Law School 199
University of Illinois 2, 3, 6, 9, 11–13, 19–22, 24, 25, 28, 31, 45, 48, 71, 98, 103, 110, 112, 114, 116–119, 127, 128, 130, 136, 139, 141, 142, 164, 165, 167, 188, 193, 202; 1964 game vs. Michigan 115, 120–126
University of Iowa 5, 7, 12, 20, 23, 30, 71, 98, 114, 116, 117, 135, 138, 142, 145, 148, 166, 167, 188, 192, 200; 1964 game vs. Michigan 115, 128–134, 136–137
University of Kentucky 193
University of Maine 9
University of Maryland 142
University of Michigan Alumni Association 193
University of Michigan Club 55
University of Michigan Law School 197
University of Minnesota 1, 5, 6, 10, 12, 15, 21, 24, 71, 87, 101, 102, 110, 113–115, 118, 129; 1964 game vs. Michigan 98–100, 103–109; 1964 game vs. Purdue 135–136, 138, 139, 143, 165, 188
University of Nebraska 35, 103, 116, 120
University of North Carolina 49, 73, 127
University of Notre Dame 2, 14, 15, 19, 22, 23, 43, 71, 87, 88, 97, 110, 127, 167–172, 181, 203
University of Oklahoma 9, 10, 116
University of Pittsburgh 23, 194
University of Southern California (USC) 21, 23, 73, 141, 168–172, 185, 186
University of Tennessee 34, 195, 197
University of Tennessee–Memphis 195
University of Washington 49, 52, 71–74, 76, 77, 84–86, 102, 120, 168, 171, 172, 175, 176
University of Wisconsin 5, 23, 24, 36, 71, 87, 114, 142, 165, 171, 195, 198
Unverferth, Don 140, 141, 149, 150, 154, 156, 161

Urick, Max 140
Utah State University 9

Van Blaricom, Paul 205
Van De Walker, Bruce 103, 104
Van Raaphorst, Dick 139
"The Victors" (Michigan fight song) 53, 85, 97, 146, 154, 156, 159, 160, 189
Vidmer, Dick 45
Vietnam War 196, 201
Viney, Bob 72, 76
Vitale, John 199
Volk, Rick 12, 18, 21, 23, 30–32, 40, 42, 45, 47–49, 51, 63, 75, 79, 85, 90, 108, 111, 112, 121, 134, 154–156, 159, 161, 162, 167, 176, 191, 200, 205

Wahl, Allen 199
Walsh, John 72
Ward, Carl 14–16, 18, 21, 23, 32, 40, 42, 47, 50–52, 54, 60–65, 76, 78, 83, 89, 90, 95, 104–107, 110, 111, 113, 122–125, 130, 131, 134, 135, 145, 154, 159, 163, 167, 175–179, 181, 183, 185, 191, 195, 205
Warfield, Paul 139
Wargo, Paul 50, 51
Warmath, Murray 5, 15, 87, 102, 108, 109
Warren, Jim 119
Washington, Ed 120
Washington, Gene 72–74, 76, 77, 84–86
Washington Redskins (NFL) 201
Wauseon, Ohio 12, 30, 112, 159, 205
Wayne State University 200, 202
Webster, George 72, 73, 76
Weinberg, Thomas 20
Wells, Dick 12, 18, 30, 21, 40, 42, 45, 48, 56, 88, 130, 131, 133, 183, 201
Wells, Harold 88, 92, 95, 97
Wells, Robert 30
West Virginia University 142
Western Athletic Conference 101
Wheatland, Al 119
Whirlpool Corporation 200
White, Hugh 199
Wilder, Cliff 129
Wilhite, Clayton 18, 42, 66, 107, 205
Wilkinson, Bud 9, 116
Williams, G. Mennen 70
Williams, Tom 62, 63
Willow Run Airport 137, 147, 162, 163, 165, 198
Winnipeg Blue Bombers (CFL) 197
Wolski, Bill 23, 169
Wright, Kenneth 205
Wyner, Gary 20

Xavier University (Ohio) 200

Yanz, John 11, 17, 18, 31, 40, 45, 47, 59, 62–64, 83, 85, 108, 111, 113, 120–123, 130, 199, 205
Yearby, Bill 1, 11, 17, 18, 21, 31, 40, 42, 45, 47, 48, 56, 59, 61–64, 77, 85, 108, 113, 121, 151, 156, 157, 167, 176, 185, 188, 191, 199, 205
Yost, Fielding H. 35, 100, 101, 167
Young, Jim 194

Ziolkowski, Robert 130
Zwahlen, Ernie 88

www.ingramcontent.com/pod-product-compliance
Ingram Content Group UK Ltd.
Pitfield, Milton Keynes, MK11 3LW, UK
UKHW041940140426
5217IPUK00014B/588